ADVANCE PRAISE FOR

Nineteenth-Century Black Women's Literary Emergence

"*Nineteenth-Century Black Women's Literary Emergence* invites scholars of the humanities to wake up and smell the Darwinian aroma wafting off of some of their most intellectually challenging themes. In this work SallyAnn H. Ferguson presents a provocative thesis. Women of African descent were subjected to slavery, rape, and ideological derision throughout American history, in part due to deeply ingrained biological imperatives within European American men. While this notion is not unfamiliar to students of evolutionary biology and human behavior, it is surprising to see this perspective arising *de novo* within the spiritual writings of African American women. Dr. Ferguson demonstrates the startling parallels between the claims of these spiritual writings and ideas central to social subordination theory. This conclusion cannot help but spawn important new examinations of the literary history of African American women as well as more general studies into the social biology of oppression."

> *Joseph L. Graves, Jr., Dean, University Studies, and Professor of Biological Sciences, North Carolina A&T State University; Fellow, American Association for the Advancement of Science*

"SallyAnn H. Ferguson's *Nineteenth-Century Black Women's Literary Emergence* collects some of the most important writings by African American women in the nineteenth and early twentieth centuries. By framing these texts within a discourse of Afrocentric evolutionary theories, she provides readers with a provocative new lens through which to analyze the African American woman writer's resistance to the ethnocentric colonizing of her mind and body for 'scientific' purposes. This collection is sure to stimulate debate among scholars and challenge all of us to reread these texts with a new consideration for their ability to challenge conventional ideas about evolutionary theories."

> *Sharon M. Harris, Professor of English, University of Connecticut, Storrs*

Nineteenth-Century Black Women's Literary Emergence

AFRICAN AMERICAN LITERATURE AND CULTURE

Expanding and Exploding the Boundaries

Carlyle V. Thompson
General Editor

Vol. 17

PETER LANG
New York • Washington, D.C./Baltimore • Bern
Frankfurt am Main • Berlin • Brussels • Vienna • Oxford

Nineteenth-Century Black Women's Literary Emergence

Evolutionary Spirituality, Sexuality, and Identity

AN ANTHOLOGY

SallyAnn H. Ferguson, EDITOR

PETER LANG
New York • Washington, D.C./Baltimore • Bern
Frankfurt am Main • Berlin • Brussels • Vienna • Oxford

Library of Congress Cataloging-in-Publication Data

Nineteenth-century Black women's literary emergence: evolutionary spirituality,
sexuality, and identity; an anthology / edited by SallyAnn H. Ferguson.
p. cm. — (African American literature and culture:
expanding and exploding the boundaries; v. 17)
Includes bibliographical references.
1. American literature—African American authors.
2. African American women—Literary collections. 3. American literature—
Women authors. 4. African American women—Intellectual life.
5. African American women in literature. 6. Race in literature.
7. Identity (Philosophical concept) in literature 8. Sex role in literature.
I. Ferguson, SallyAnn H.
PS508.N3N565   810.9'896073—dc22   2007032716
ISBN 978-1-4331-0158-8 (hardcover)
ISBN 978-1-4331-0157-1 (paperback)
ISSN 1528-3887

Bibliographic information published by **Die Deutsche Bibliothek**.
Die Deutsche Bibliothek lists this publication in the "Deutsche
Nationalbibliografie"; detailed bibliographic data is available
on the Internet at http://dnb.ddb.de/.

Cover image, *Guiding Spirit*, courtesy of Frank Woods

© 2008 Peter Lang Publishing, Inc., New York
29 Broadway, 18th floor, New York, NY 10006
www.peterlang.com

To my sisters—Charlotte, Lorraine, and Charlene—and the memory of Shaindy Rudoff

---

Acknowledgments

I wish to thank evolutionary biologists Dr. Joseph L. Graves, Jr., of North Carolina Agricultural & Technical State University and Dr. Vincent Henrich of the University of North Carolina at Greensboro, who generously shared their expertise and good wishes.

Table of Contents

Note on the Text

All of the texts reprinted in *Nineteenth-Century Black Women's Literary Emergence: Evolutionary Spirituality, Sexuality, and Identity* are based on the original first editions with only minor corrections of obvious printers' errors. There have been no attempts to standardize spelling, capitalization, paragraphing, and such.

Evolutionary Sexuality, Spirituality, and Identity

19th-Century Black Women's Literary Emergence

In *The Origin of Species by Means of Natural Selection or the Preservation of Favored Races in the Struggle for Life* (1859), naturalist Charles Darwin (1809–1882) outlines the evolutionary process, stating that over time, "Owing to this struggle [for life], variations, however slight and from whatever cause proceeding, if they be in any degree profitable to the individuals of a species, in their infinitely complex relations to other organic beings and to their physical conditions of life, will tend to the preservation of such individuals, and will generally be inherited by the offspring."[1] By praising contemporary Herbert Spencer's essay addressing "the necessary acquirement of each mental power and capacity for gradation," Darwin also emphasizes the importance of a favorable psychological environment in his scientific theorizing (14). Since her forced migration to this country, the African American woman has both instinctively and consciously developed a literary tradition based on these fundamental evolutionary principles of mind and body that prefigures contemporary studies of evolutionary biology. More significantly, she has consistently resisted attempts by patriarchs and matriarchs alike to romanticize and redefine that biologically based literary heritage. This volume of ten classic texts by nineteenth-century African American females documents for teachers and general readers how this self-portrait gradually crystallized over some three centuries of legalized psychological and physical rape brutally imposed by white men and their surrogates, who then branded her an immoral whore. This anthology also explores how its features were further defined during the ensuing postbellum eras of Reconstruction, Jim Crow segregation, and civil rights abuses. Readers cannot adequately understand this woman's unique story without asking exactly what and, more importantly, why mental and physical atrocities so gruesome that most people cringe to think of them were inflicted upon her black female self in this land.

Although scholars as diverse as Paula Giddings, Barbara Smith, Barbara Christian, and Jennifer Fleischner rightly observe that this oppression for too long silenced her voice, their greater emphasis on its social, economic, and political effects rather than the genetic causes of her victimization—the fact that Nature created her black and female, which this collection emphasizes—may itself inadvertently prolong her relegation to virtual second-class citizenship.[2] Indeed, this critical reticence, especially from those in the humanities whose scientific ignorance often leads them to confuse the social fiction and biology reality of words like "race," serves to minimize and obscure the complex genetic motives of Founding Fathers like first Supreme Court chief justice John Jay and presidents George Washington and Thomas Jefferson—all celebrated and privileged exemplars of a hypocritical American Enlightenment culture and themselves her unabashed slaveholding torturers. An evolutionary theoretical approach to the writings of the African American women included in this volume invites readers to consider how and why these white men sought to establish myths of global Eurocentric genetic supremacy and numerical majority that would correct what they deemed a mistake at Creation. In the final analysis, this critical perspective exposes how and why these racist and sexist men of reason ultimately used Nature's chosen black mother and her progeny to help mold their American citizenry into perpetual chasers of an impossible dream to be first in an antediluvian, once-only human Genesis.

Ethnocentric and consumed by an instinctual sense of jealousy and parental rejection, the earliest Europeans had already drifted far enough away from their African roots to presume that Nature was flawed because neither white women nor men of any color were models for the human race but—as numerous evolutionary biologists including L. Luca Cavalli-Sforza, Paola Menozzi, and Alberto Piazza now verify—the genetic and environmental offspring of black African mothers.[3] In a dismayed understanding of Nature's selectivity regarding racial groups, Founding Father Benjamin Franklin decried in *Observations Concerning the Increase of Mankind* (1751) that "the number of 'purely white people' in the world was proportionately very small [approximately ten percent]. All Africa was black or tawny, Asia chiefly tawny, and 'America (exclusive of the new comers [European colonizers]) wholly so.'"[4] Rather than accept Nature's designations, the Euro-Americans, like their European forebears, dismissed any concept of human origin not based entirely on their majority and maleness and set about to revise genetic history, realistically conceding its African female prototype as they used merciless psychological and physical rape in a vain effort to reduce this unwilling woman to mere progenitor of slave chattel fathered by them.

If, like Sophocles's King Oedipus seeking to overturn Apollo's mandate to commit patricide and marry his mother, they too became the father of their mother's children and ruled everything in the material world, these self-proclaimed gods reasoned, then who could deny their sovereignty at Creation. In *Notes on the State of Virginia*, Thomas Jefferson particularly prefigures Darwinian evolutionary theory by railing against the fact that black skin color was forever "fixed in nature." Therefore, with little more than an illogical "suspicion only," this Enlightenment leader emotionally demonized African Americans as "inferior[s] to the whites in the endowments of both body and mind,"[5] while simultaneously raping, impregnating, and subsequently siphoning off the nearly depleted black bloodline—the symbol of African Creation—of light-skinned teenage slave Sally Hemings. After over three centuries of this savagery, these white Americans transformed their short-circuited biological logic into institutionalized myth, and "The nineteenth century would spawn new pseudoscientific theories related to race and human biological diversity, among these social Darwinism and eugenics, the study of human 'improvement' by genetic control. Anthropology in the nineteenth century was almost wholly devoted to the research paradigm of Anglo-Saxon, Teutonic superiority."[6] Cavalli-Sforza, Menozzi, and Piazza reiterate that: "Racism has existed from time immemorial but only in the nineteenth century were there attempts to justify it on the basis of scientific arguments."[7] Generations of Caucasians continued to resent so virulently the chronological primacy of the black African woman in human history that they assembled vicious social, political, economic, and military systems which enabled them to disseminate already institutionalized racist and sexist myths designed to deny their secondary evolution and, by extension, direct kinship to her African-based humankind. They sought to dissociate all Eurocentric peoples from that "ancient and biological factor" and redefine themselves as a separate, "nonracial" "nationstate"—"a modern conception and product, the result of certain peculiar social and economic circumstances. The [human] family has been produced by Nature, the nation by [Eurocentric] Man himself."[8] Paradoxically, in order to comply with Darwin's Nature-based evolutionary doctrine dictating survival of the fittest as well as erect their republican "civilization," uncolored Americans could only overtly reject while covertly embracing human longevity that requires genetic diversity. With a sustained quest for white supremacy co-existent in a democracy buttressed by arsenals of mass destruction and terrorism, these clearly insecure Euro-Americans promoted globally their various racist and sexual mythologies and appeared for all time to have reconstructed humanity's genetic tree, placing themselves at its roots.

Although the nineteenth-century African American female writer shows little formal study of Darwinian science, she nonetheless developed within this savage color- and gender-struck environment and remained its greatest foe because she too harbored the power of self-definition and freedom found at Creation, namely the biology of "Natural Selection or Survival of the Fittest," which Darwin defines in *The Origin of Species* as "The preservation [over time] of favourable individual [mental and physical] differences and variations, and the destruction of those which are injurious . . ." (108). Because Nature equipped *all* humans with the ability to choose "variations" compatible with their instinctual needs for survival, this woman's texts portray her as caught in the crossfire among uncolored and colored males and white females who hated, envied, and lusted after her the degree to which their personal insecurities generated enough racism and sexism to override her unique biological and psychological prerogatives. Her greatest challenge was to control both body and spirit under such ominous circumstances and thus maintain her humanity. In the present collection, a novel evolutionary theoretical approach to works by representative African American women of the nineteenth century invites readers to discover how these authors both instinctively and consciously coped with this challenge and—lacking precise literary models expressive of their unique experiences—concomitantly developed a distinctive eclectic writing style incorporating a variety of genres. They were unlike the near-mythic feminist and activist Sojourner Truth (1797–1883), who supposedly stood over six feet tall, saw herself equalizing if not exceeding the physical and mental prowess of others, and may have once declared:

> "I have ploughed, and planted, and gathered into barns, and no man could head me!' And a'n't I a woman? I could work as much and eat as much as a man . . . and bear the lash as well. . . . I have borne thirteen chilern, and seen 'em mos' all sold off to slavery, and when I cried out with my mother's grief, none but Jesus heard me!"[9]

Instead, most African American women writers of the time conceded the greater political, economic, and physical strength of their captors. But as this prey devised bold and ingenious ways to retain a black female identity savaged by the perverse genetic ambitions of the majority of nineteenth-century white folks, these authors simultaneously developed a literary tradition that puts to rest continuing debates about its very existence.

The first sixty-three years of the nineteenth century were also the waning years of Euro-America's terrifying slavery regime, their principal stratagem for achieving the goal of economic and importantly biological conquest. An appalling concession to white America's profound sense of color minority, inferiority, and desperation, the slavocracy was the country's longest and most comprehensive noncompete program ever, designed to supply Caucasians only with every possible opportunity to accumulate material power and self-importance by legally stealing the wealth, labor, and genes of black-skinned people. It was a vampirish American feasting that specifically sought to counter a Darwinian black mind seeking its own continued existence by feeding it the blood-sacrifice theology explicit in ancestral European Christianity, which promised an eternal heavenly life if converts endured earthly torment from bloodsucking whites—a moral legacy that resounds today as people worldwide still presume that, once they reach American shores, a light skin color confers instant privilege.[10] Though born free, educated in northern states, and less subject to physical attack, several early–nineteenth-century black women authors—represented in this volume by spiritual narrators Maria Stewart (1803–1879) and Jarena Lee (1783-?)—found themselves confronting this peculiar psychological deceit disguised as a route to divine salvation. In order to defeat its soul-stultifying design to make them suffering servants participatory in their own dehumanization, these women authors came to view their experiences only in terms of what ex-slave Frederick Douglass would eventually call a benevolent "Christianity proper," which inspired them and fellow colored people to build strong identities and self-esteem.[11] Their texts are replete with conversion stories and exhortations that may seem self-indulgent but are actually mediations between the paradoxical earthly evil and heavenly good whites constantly preached. Like their black brothers, who also lacked defensive war arsenals, these women writers signify on and eventually shape Euro-American religious hypocrisy into formidable self-defenses that empower them to outthink exploiters. Through this kind of indirect, trickster-like combat, African American women writers, as scholar Hazel Carby asserts, eventually built a literary tradition that reconstructed a white- and male-defined black womanhood based on psychological control, made it both their greatest strength, and—only when taken to an extreme—an unfortunate weakness.[12]

Specifically, in her twelve-page pamphlet entitled *Religion and the Pure Principles of Morality, the Sure Foundation on Which We Must Build*, published in 1831, Maria Stewart, America's first female political writer of any hue,[13] willfully wrests thinking and group organizing from the exclusive domain of "The Americans [who] have practiced nothing but head-work these 200 years . . . [while] we have done their drudgery." She pointedly asks: ". . . is it not high time for us to . . . practice head-work too, and keep what we have got, and get what we can?" Stewart's subtitle, the *Sure Foundation on Which We Must Build*, sets the practical tone and purpose of the pamphlet as she urges blacks to discover their divine selves through Christianity's ethical paradox and recalls: "From the moment I experienced the change [Christian conversion], I felt a strong desire . . . to devote the remainder of my days to piety and virtue, and now possess the spirit of independence, that, were I called upon, I would willingly sacrifice my life for the cause of God and my brethren." She soon reinforces the material promise of this religious decision by rejecting biblical passages that urge absolute obedience to even cruel masters and emphasizing spirit-liberating possibilities that inspire black self-determination, love, and morality. As her narrative voice periodically reaches a level of evangelical ecstasy—the very antithesis of Enlightenment rationalism—she evokes the morality and spirituality of human Genesis and advises African Americans to embrace it even though "the Americans"—like Aesop foxes that brand sour the coveted grapes always beyond their reach—"think, because your skins are tinged with a sable hue, that you are an inferior race of beings; but God does not consider you such. *He* [my emphasis] has formed and fashioned you in his own glorious image. . . ." In this way, Stewart not only situates the black church as a powerful spiritual, political, and economic force within its community—a major theme of black female writing—but also subjugates the culture-based Christian faith to a mere conduit through which she reaffirms the universal scientific primacy of African Creation and humanity.

Toward the end of her essay, however, the distinction between an interminable God's will and Stewart's own contemporary, earthbound one blurs to the point that they appear entwined, suggesting that her decision to become an itinerant minister and proclaim God's message was as much her own as her advocacy of such Pauline pronouncements as: "There is neither Jew nor Greek, there is neither bond nor free, there is neither male nor female: for ye are all one in Christ Jesus" (Galatians iii). Indeed, she makes herself seem virtually divine through her association with Jesus, just as Christian slaveowners themselves did through their advocacy of blood sacrifice.[14] Clearly sensing the ambiguous nature of her role as spiritual liaison between God and her readers, the author somewhat defensively declares that "God alone"—and not she—"has inspired my heart to feel for Afric's woes." Stewart ends the pamphlet without relinquishing her position as religious power-broker, however, protesting defiantly that "I have never taken one step, my friends, with a design to raise myself in your esteem, or to gain applause." She thereby evokes the complex motif of destructive self-righteousness that marks the literary tradition of African American females who—aware of the problems caused by saintly sinners—often portray oppressed but pious black female characters who become destructive when they mask their own private agendas as God's will.[15]

The Life and Religious Experience of Jarena Lee, A Coloured Lady, Giving an Account of Her Call to Preach the Gospel (1836)—the first spiritual autobiography by an African American female[16]—also includes familiar Christian images of conviction, sanctification, and conversion, but for strikingly different reasons. Unlike the more sophisticated Maria Stewart, whose firm purpose amounts to consciously "tricking" whitefolks' Christianity into curing a myriad of black psychological ills rooted in social, political, and economic oppression, Lee portrays herself as an emotionally fragile naïf first exposed to religious hypocrisy at the age of seven when her poor, freeborn parents were forced to put their young daughter into domestic service with whites. She repeatedly characterizes herself as "extremely ignorant," an easy prey for mental abuse disguised as Christian piety and clearly ill-equipped to resist a Calvinist Methodism designed to convince her that black genes mandated her to suffer for whites. Many silences throughout her narrative suggest that, after Lee encountered elements of Frederick Douglass's "slaveholding religion," she felt extreme guilt for petty offenses such as lying to an employer about completing a task or harboring "roots of bitterness" "against one particular individual, who had strove deeply to injure me." Not surprisingly, after she read a passage about "Original Sin" from the Psalms, her innate spirit was made "to feel . . . the weight of my sins" to such an extent that she contemplated suicide.[17] Nonetheless, her *Account* eventually charts an emotionally mature adult's path to New Testament benevolence capable of redeeming both her own soul and those of fellow Americans of all colors. It outlines how, like Maria Stewart, Lee struck a balance between evangelical emotionalism and Enlightenment reason. Through mystical visions of absolution and superstitious dreams, loud praying that once woke an entire household, and even being spiritually driven to leave her sick son in order to pursue God's grace, Lee built up a will strong enough to guide her through the Christian moral labyrinth.

When Jarena Lee makes her oppressor's culturally based religion the basis for a literary pursuit of salvation, she initially appears willing to surrender her innate Creation spirit and participate in her own dehumanization. As critic Frances Smith Foster observes, her text does "conform to the basic patterns of spiritual autobiography as derived from the New Testament example of Saul of Tarsus."[18] Indeed, as Lee herself admits, her *Account* could be dismissed as "fiction" and "the mere ravings of a disordered mind" had her personal suffering not also spawned an enduring itinerant ministry that eventually emboldened her to challenge the sexism of the African Methodist Episcopal Church, then led by the legendary black bishop Richard Allen. Overcoming psychic pain promoted by Christian gender bigotry, Jerena Lee specifically defied prohibitions that made the pulpit the exclusive domain of men—including black males—just as Maria Stewart denied that self-preservation was the absolute province of whites. In so doing, Lee heroically fought to advance black feminist issues in the nineteenth-century American church, a struggle that continues to this day. If she sometimes seems arrogant, it is probably because she held such a high opinion of her own exhortation performance, calling it "so effectual . . . that I have seen them fall to the floor crying aloud for mercy."

Northerner Harriet E. Wilson's *Our Nig or Sketches from the Life of a Free Black* (1859), the first novel written by an African American woman, and Southerner Harriet A. Jacobs's fugitive slave narrative *Incidents in the Life of a Slave Girl* (1861) testify to the fact that, failing to gain genetic dominance by controlling the African

American female mind, predatory whites aggressively targeted her black body. Wilson and Jacobs graphically detail how they fought off brutal physical assaults when, first as children and then as young adults, they found themselves trapped among sadistic whites. Although religion might seem their most obvious balm, these outspoken mid-century women writers—more like Frederick Douglass than Stewart and Lee—openly question its value in the face of combined mental and physical cruelty. Additionally, both self-published their works and highlight the black female author's recurring problem finding, within mainstream America's limited literary tradition, genres licensing her more-candid discussion of themes such as child and sexual violence that plagued her American existence. Discovering no one form equal to the task, these women followed a growing trend and eclectically combined various canonical types, both fictional and nonfictional. As a result, Wilson and Jacobs's texts tend to mirror each other stylistically, with *Our Nig* emerging as autobiographical fiction and *Incidents* resembling a fictional fugitive slave narrative.[19]

Wilson's young protagonist Frado, the daughter of a white mother and black father, accepts that Christianity at once embraces her biologically diverse self and the gentle white friend James but rejects its embrace of Mrs. Bellmont, James's monstrous mother and Mary, his vicious sister who at one point "commenced beating her [Frado] inhumanly; then propping her mouth open with a piece of wood, shut her up in a dark room without any supper." Thus, even before her liberation at eighteen from a horrific indentured servitude distinguished by the female Bellmonts' Christian savagery, Frado had instinctively decided to survive the moment and "give over all thought of the future world [after death], and . . . put her anxiety far from her." Moreover, the silence of liberal whites—those "good" members of the northern Bellmont household and community who disingenuously claimed to care about Frado but never enough to stop the mean Bellmont women—also influenced her developing humanism.[20] As historian Lerone Bennett, Jr., notes in his study of white liberalism: "For reasons no psychologist can really explain, oppressed people have always preferred a declared enemy to a false or, at least, an uncertain friend."[21] In her incisive analysis of the religious sadism of white women and their protectors, Harriet Wilson more decisively than any authors mentioned so far intuitively declares her freedom from white Christian mind-control to choose spiritual humanism as the black woman's primary emotional and physical healer, as she initiates the African American female novelistic tradition.

Harriet Jacobs's *Incidents in the Life of a Slave Girl* (1861), an unflinching examination of rape and unwanted racial amalgamation with global implications, is by far the most compelling black female narrative of the nineteenth century. Masquerading as mainstream sentimental fiction, *Incidents* unrelentingly attacks the romance of slaveholding, not only depicting how and why white people worldwide moralized as they terrorized blacks, but also laying bare the American white male's failure to make the slavery regime the setting for achieving both economic and, more importantly, genetic superiority by reducing black females to mere human mules with vaginas and wombs. Jacobs labels America's slavocracy an aggressive culture of rape and without evidence that she formally studied Darwinian evolution, nonetheless, eloquently analyzes laws and policies that desperate white men systematically enacted to undermine natural psychological and sexual adaptations slave women, in turn, would use to deny these men access to their black genes. Throughout her narrative, she deliberately exposes key elements of their scheme, after emphatically asserting in the opening line of the preface: "Reader, be assured this narrative is *no fiction* [my emphasis]." Like Harriet E. Wilson's Frado, Linda Brent, Jacobs's narrative persona, also overtly rejects Christian moral deceit, sarcastically labeling the religion of her beloved and admired grandmother Aunt Marthy (Molly Horniblow) "a beautiful faith, coming from a mother who could not call her children her own. But I, and Benjamin [Joseph], her youngest boy, condemned it." Instead, to protect her genes, Harriet Jacobs opposes her Genesis-based "determined will" against the "power and law" of her slaveholding Episcopalian sexual harasser Dr. Flint (Dr. James Norcom) and concludes: "There is might in each."

In their thought-provoking study, *A Natural History of Rape: Biological Bases of Sexual Coercion,* evolutionary biologists Randy Thornhill and Craig T. Palmer provide a dynamic genetic context for interpreting Jacobs's mid–nineteenth-century literary account of her sexual battles. They argue:

> The ultimate causes of human rape are clearly to be found in the distinctive evolution of male and female sexuality. The evidence demonstrates that rape has evolved as a response to the evolved psychological mechanisms regulating female sexuality, which enabled a woman to discriminate among potential sexual partners. If human females had been selected to be willing to mate with any male under any circumstance [as American slavery demanded], rape would not occur. On the other hand, if human males had been selected to be sexually attracted to only certain females under certain limited circumstances, rape would be far less frequent. Indeed, if human males had been selected to desire sexual intercourse only with females who showed unmistakable willingness to copulate with them, rape would be an impossibility. Human rape exists because selection did not favor these types of adaptations, and the proximate causes of human rape lie in the different adaptations of male and female sexuality that were formed by selection in human evolutionary history.[22]

Although many scholars and Jacobs herself document how slavery helped white Americans build an economic dynasty,[23] her narrative shrewdly provides a virtual textbook case of white males who tried to destroy the sexual choice geneticists like Thornhill and Palmer assert occurs naturally in all women. In its portrayal of fifteen-year-old protagonist Linda Brent's uncompromising choice of a colored male as mate and her ceaseless resistance to the unrelenting sexual pursuit of villainous uncolored Dr. Flint, who is also three times her age, Jacobs's text puts the lie to white stereotypes about consenting black slave whores and, instead, catches the "good" doctor—without regard to morality—satiating across racial lines a biological imperative to fertilize youthful colored victims because of their favorable reproductive potential (Thornhill, Palmer 70–73). Predisposed by evolution to choose a mate based on her own perception of biological quality, Linda Brent repeatedly asserts her humanity by exercising her genetic prerogative, defiantly asking Flint: "Don't you suppose, sir, that a slave can have some *preference* [my emphasis] about marrying? Do you suppose that all men are alike to *her* [my emphasis]?" Jacobs then repeatedly lists and criticizes behaviors Flint's slaveholding culture criminalized in order to circumvent Brent's natural selection ability: "She [the slave woman] is not allowed to have any pride of character. It is deemed a *crime* [my emphasis] in her to wish to be virtuous." Jacobs also recounts how Flint suddenly sold a slave "wife" and her family because "She had forgotten that it was a *crime* [my emphasis] for a slave to tell who was the [white] father of her child." Additionally, when white liberal Mr. Sands (Samuel Tredwell Sawyer) "was not unwilling" to have their son "bear his name," Brent refuses his offer precisely because ". . . my master would have regarded it a new *crime* [my emphasis]. . . ." Moreover, as Jacobs observes, the "*laws* [my emphasis] gave no sanction to the marriage" between Brent and a freeborn black carpenter, the only man she actually chooses throughout her narrative despite the fact that "the husband of a slave has no power to protect her."

Brent's instinctive preference for the black carpenter even though he cannot protect her like any white man is instructive, because it points to biological and cultural whiteness as the key factor that leads Brent to reject Flint and his white genes. Because he is a cruel old man without sperm that can produce melanin—a "good," color-making adaptation to blacks—Flint evokes both the moral condition of brutal racial and sexual discrimination and the genetic disease of albinism, neither of which would serve to promote the mental or physical survival of African American progeny either in the short or long term.[24] Indeed, Linda Brent intuits basic biology well enough not to bear willingly a child who resembles even a mild oppressor and, after being manipulated into giving birth to Sands's whiter-skinned daughter who would likely inherit her mother's biological and social fate, laments: "Slavery is terrible for men; but it is far more terrible for women," who have "mortifications peculiarly their own." While some critics dismissed psychologist Frances Cress Welsing's genetic arguments as specious when first published, recent biological study lends credence to *The Cress Theory of Color: Confrontation and Racism (White Supremacy)* and further reinforces both the depth of despair underlying the whites' feelings of racial inferiority and its ensuing racism, and Brent's resistance to miscegenation during and after slavery. Cress Welsing writes:

. . . the white or color-deficient Europeans responded psychologically with a profound sense of numerical inadequacy and color inferiority upon their confrontations with the massive majority of the world's people all of whom possessed varying degrees of color producing capacity. This psychological response, be it described as conscious or unconscious, was one of deeply sensed inadequacy which struck a blow at the most obvious and fundamental part of their being, their external appearance. As might be anticipated in terms of modern psychological theories, an uncontrollable sense of hostility and aggression developed defensively . . . [and] has continued to manifest itself throughout the entire historical epoch of the mass confrontations of the whites with peoples of color. That the initial hostility and aggression came only from the whites is recorded in innumerable diaries, journals, and books written by whites. It is a matter of record, also, that only after long periods of great abuse have the "non-whites" responded defensively. . . . [25]

In this view, Jacobs and her sexual pursuers are essentially reacting differently to the same biological fact: that, while violence made white skin the rule in America, it is as Benjamin Franklin understood in eighteenth-century America, the exception in Nature and thus a recessive genetic marker universally antagonistic to the survival of colored peoples. While Brent instinctively fights to protect her descendants from Flint's biological inheritance, he and (to a lesser degree) Sands struggle to promote their myth of genetic supremacy and sexual potency within the confines of a recently conquered and colonized America. Although some antebellum and postbellum African Americans adhered to Darwinian evolutionary principles and envisioned advantageous material "variations" from even forced racial amalgamation, Jacobs sees little benefit in her progeny's having either "good" hair or looking whiter and fiercely combats the insecurity and concomitant violence white minority and self-hatred breed. In fact, at one point her heroine effectively counters Flint's ploy to demonize the black carpenter and thus separate her from his biology by asserting: ". . . *we are both of the negro race*. It is right and honorable for *us* [my emphases] to love each other." In other words, Jacobs unambiguously makes "a grand show of choice"[26] of the black male, thereby forcing Flint to concede the debate and defend his genetic shortcomings to black women the way his slaveholding kind knows best: "He sprang upon me [Linda] like a tiger, and gave me a stunning blow. It was the first time he had struck me; and fear did not enable me to control my anger." Refusing to play masochist to this sadistic suitor, Brent contemptuously watches as evolutionary principles of natural selection force Flint to conform to historic type and stoop to violently begging a lowly black slave to fortify the gene pool of his descendants. He continues this behavior until Brent's Northern employer eventually purchases her freedom and removes his pretext for unrelenting and shameless stalking, exposing as well a general United States scheme to make concubinage the black slave woman's primary job description.

Indeed, further debunking the widespread Eurocentric fantasy about colored peoples aggressively pursuing whites for sex rather than the other way around, an evolutionary reading of *Incidents* reinforces Harriet Jacobs's distinction between love for and sex with the "liberal" Mr. Sands, submission to whose advances persona Brent actually regards as just one among her many Maria Stewart–like "deliberate calculation[s]"—along with sassing and avoiding Flint, appealing her case to his wife, hiding for nearly seven years in her grandmother's attic, and fleeing to the North and to England—designed to give her "something akin to freedom" over both her biological soul and reproductive system. As Brent makes clear in her signifying pleas for moral understanding from a white and privileged female Victorian reading audience, her copulation with Sands was in no way a love match but merely a calculated ploy to make sexually repugnant Dr. Flint jealous enough to sell her, and the best she could manage under a slavery regime that forced her to settle for Sands's limited affection and their two whiter-skinned children.[27] She unequivocally preferred the mutual, heartfelt love of the African American carpenter that would have in time surely increased the already global nonwhite majority. The fact that the slaveholder legally denied marriage to the black slave woman and then forced either himself or his surrogates onto her body evokes a theme of sterility and romantic deprivation that numerous modern African American authors continue to sound. Jacobs satirizes such sexual perversion during this time by having Brent deliberately flaunt before a jealous Flint her children by Sands—who himself later exploits their vulnerable young daughter by trying to make the child a relative's concubine. When none of her various evasive techniques cools Flint's evolutionary lust, Brent flees first to her grandmother's attic for nearly seven years and eventually out of the South altogether.

Thirty-one years later in *Southern Horrors: Lynch Law in All Its Phases* (1892), Ida B. Wells-Barnett (1862–1931), this country's first black female journalist, complements Jacob's narrative by exploring the issue of white sexual coercion and black manhood. Understanding the complex relationship between lynching—including the one on March 9, 1892, that took the lives of her friends Thomas Moss, Calvin McDowell, and Henry Stewart in Memphis, Tennessee—and the white need to counter primal genetic insecurity with rituals of moral and sexual prowess,[28] Wells-Barnett also does not invoke the Christian signifying of Maria Stewart and Jarena Lee but the cultural humanism of Harriet Wilson and Harriet Jacobs to address directly American sexual mythologizing at the black man's expense. She argues in *Southern Horrors* that the usually false rape charges against him were merely an ironic attention-getting tactic used jointly by Caucasian men and women to bully reluctant African American males into recognizing white female sexuality just when these women were exercising greater reproductive choice in a postbellum age. Not unlike the black-whore myth that ultimately manipulated Jacobs's Linda Brent to appear to *choose* Mr. Sands, the myth of the black male criminally lusting after the virtuous white woman who rebuffs him, also feeds the illusion that he *chooses* her and, thereby, redeems the sexual pride of white women and men biologically undermined by an inability to generate enough color to attract blacks sexually. Accordingly, while *Incidents in the Life of a Slave Girl* argues that antebellum white men twisted America into a society where female slave rape appeared consensual, *Southern Horrors* posits that white females and males tacitly agreed after slavery to use rape charges, castration, and lynching to give white men an image of virility when, like Harriet Jacobs, white women also more openly chose the genetically diverse—albeit physically vulnerable—African American male. Decisive evidence of white female and male complicity appears when, unlike typical rape families shamefacedly seeking anonymity, these whites proudly advertise their women's being sexually *chosen* by black men during ritualized lynching events and require the "victims'" husbands to strike the first blow against alleged attackers. The ultimate advantage in all this violent duplicity is direct access to diversifying, melanin-containing black genes, which the white man self-righteously cut off, when he caught *his* white woman—the only female with whom he has the greatest certainty of reproducing his white biological self—coveting color across racial lines.[29]

Consequently, Wells-Barnett's narrative technique—which historian August Meier calls a "deliberately used" collage of "southern whites, speaking for themselves" and providing "the damning truth about lynch law and mob violence"—openly mocks the idea that blacks naturally find whites sexually attractive and that whites do not lust after black genes.[30] Linking the African-American male's sexual behavior to his basic evolutionary quest for biological and cultural longevity, Wells-Barnett refers to an idea voiced earlier by Frederick Douglass, whose supportive letter prefaces her volume: ". . . the crime of rape was unknown during the four years of civil war, when the white women of the South were at the mercy of the race which is all at once charged with being a bestial one."[31] She also cites journalists such as J. C. Duke of Montgomery, Alabama, who was run out of town when he asked in the *Herald*: "Why is it that white women attract negro [sic] men now more than in former days? There was a time when such a thing was unheard of. There's a secret to this thing, and we greatly suspect it is the growing appreciation of white Juliets for colored Romeos." Thus, by documenting the black man's historical sexual reserve toward the white woman and suggesting that changing political, social, and economic times have apparently unleashed her historically suppressed evolutionary lust for him, Wells-Barnett highlights how white biological insecurity posed as great a postbellum threat to African American men as it had to black women during slavery.[32]

Wells-Barnett fills her text with many reliable published accounts of both white lying and truth-telling that repeatedly scorn the myth of Southern white female virginity and insinuate that "the white man's woman" found him so sexually wanting that she actively sought out black lovers, cried rape only after getting caught at it, and soothed his wounded ego with opportunities to play hero in castration and lynching rituals.[33] Wells-Barnett quotes the testimony of white Mrs. J. S. Underwood from Elyria, Ohio, a rueful minister's wife who, after causing black and married William Offett to be wrongly sentenced to a long jail sentence, recanted her rape accusation and acknowledged their consensual sex, admitting that "He had a strange fascination for me and I invited him to call on me." In the May 21, 1892, issue of the *Free Speech* reprinted in *Southern Horrors*, Wells-Barnett bluntly debunks white sexual mythmaking and editorializes: "Nobody in this section of the country believes the old thread bare lie that Negro men rape white women. If Southern men are not careful, they will over-reach themselves and public sentiment will have a reaction . . . which will be very damaging to the moral reputation of their women." Wells-Barnett additionally refuses to equate economic success with sexual prowess and portrays the former as just another face-saving, consolation prize from white women to their cuckolded men, another collaborative ruse designed "to get rid of Negroes who were acquiring wealth and property" (*Autobiography* 64) in postbellum America. While she concedes that black men also defined their manhood through materialism—her three lynched friends were upwardly mobile community leaders who recently opened a store that greatly reduced the profit margin of a white competitor—Wells-Barnett emphasizes that after the murders, these white men sought manhood vicariously through looting black male enterprise: "This mob took possession of the People's Grocery Company, helping themselves to food and drink, and destroyed what they could not steal" (*Autobiography* 51). In the final analysis, Wells-Barnett chronicles the superficiality of the black/white sisterhood that several current scholars tout as a mutually profitable alliance of female antebellum abolitionism and depicts a more-liberated, post–Civil War white female sexual predator who mimics her man and "love[s] the Afro-American's company even as there are white men notorious for their *preference* [my emphasis] for Afro-American women." In her view, most whites of both sexes pretend to reject color even as they are driven by Nature to brutally seek it from blacks—a theme that black writers like Ralph Ellison continue to address in their works.[34]

Orator, abolitionist, teacher, and feminist Frances E. Watkins Harper (1824–1911) was perhaps the most prolific and accomplished African American female creative writer of the nineteenth century, whose literary productions include short stories, essays, and poetry. Indeed, she may have been the first to transform the cultural critiques of earlier black female authors into aesthetically and philosophically appealing fiction.[35] The first freeborn Southerner among the writers discussed in this collection, Harper uses themes and characters that also signal economic, social, and educational changes in the status of women nationwide. All of the previous African American women authors under discussion, whether born slave or free, primarily emphasized the perils of racism and sexism within American culture. But just four years before Emancipation, Harper prophetically echoes in "The Two Offers" (1859), the first short story written by a black woman, Harriet Jacobs's images of spiritual and physical sterility and imagines a world in which two middle-class heroines, apparently unencumbered by either racism or male sexual predators like Dr. Flint and sexual scavengers like Mr. Sands, risk an "intense wretchedness" if they fail to act judiciously on the genetic principle of natural selection. In order to warn that poor sexual choices by free women of any hue have potentially dire consequences for evolutionary survival, Harper deliberately de-emphasizes sexual orientation and the "racial dimension to the characters," as biographer Melba Joyce Boyd puts it.[36]

Through contrasting protagonists, Harper celebrates a woman's greater ability to live with wisdom and freedom gained from both natural endowment and personal achievement, even if that experience includes a deceptive religion. In fact, when the omniscient narrator alludes to Christianity in "The Two Offers," the language fuses biology and theology, stressing a woman's need to exercise "her Heaven-endowed and God-given faculties."[37] But when a pampered Laura Lagrange foolishly squanders her genetic inheritance on a vain and superficial man who "bowed at her shrine" but could not see their marriage "as a divine sacrament for the soul's development and human progression," she and their child die. In contrast, Laura's more complex cousin, Janette Alston, has "known the mystic and solemn strength of an all-absorbing love" with a sexually ambiguous "object of her heart's worship" and uses their doomed love affair to define an "inner life [that] had grown beautiful, and . . . was constantly developing the outer." Despite this success, Harper nonetheless strongly implies that Janette also chooses unwisely because she wastes half of her sexual endowment in a possible lesbian affair that fortifies her spirit at the expense of her reproductive ability. More simply, Harper warns that women should make sexual choices that comport more with evolutionary longevity than human extinction.

Harper's refusal to identify her female characters racially and her allusion to homosexuality—literary devices not usually employed by early African American female authors—suggest her growing concern about the impact some mainstream sexual practices would have on an increasing need for racial uplift, especially for black women. Her staunch interracial activism in the uplift, temperance, and feminist movements is well documented, but Harper's message of sexual prudence in "The Two Offers" implies that this experience led her to perceive the coming emancipation as a potential rival to Christian mind control and violence in its ability to offer women a third sexual choice that threatens to compromise the African American female's soul and body.[38] Indeed, with both Laura's hollow marriage and death and

Janette's spiritual self-absorption and chosen sterility, "The Two Offers" implies that efforts to improve racial relations is not occasion for an African American writer to neglect portraying a community that tends to associate sex with genetic reproduction.[39] Although she herself was probably the prototype for Janette Alston, whose genius won her "a position in the literary world," Harper eventually married Fenton Harper and gave birth to a daughter. Interestingly, in *Loving Her* (1974) by Ann Allen Shockley, the first lesbian novel written by an African American female, and the gay-themed *The Color Purple* (1982) by Alice Walker, both authors add other dimensions to the literary tradition pioneered by Harper and only depict married black women who, after fleeing abusive heterosexual relationships, choose same-sex unions that result in spiritual peace rooted in lesbian materialism. In order to promote an interracial affair of this sort, Shockley even kills off a black child, making "The Two Offers" a provocative introduction of this theme in early African American female writing.

"Life on the Sea Islands," an essay by Charlotte L. Forten Grimké (1837–1919) published by the *Atlantic Monthly*,[40] shows a shifting mindset between earlier authors like Harper, and some mid– to late–nineteenth-century, upwardly mobile black female writers who envisage beneficial Darwinian "variations" in duplicitous white American materialism. Social historian Paula Giddings suggests why they might have been tempted by it: "At a time when their White peers were riding the wave of moral superiority that sanctioned their [social] activism, Black women were seen as moral scourges. Despite their achievements . . . the idea of a moral Black woman was [considered] incredible."[41] Unlike Maria Stewart and Jarena Lee, who instinctively fortified their black female identities by successfully negotiating Christianity's ethical morass in antebellum America, these postbellum women writers became so acculturated by privileges associated with white skin color and economic success that they prematurely minimized and even discarded invaluable qualities of earlier black female spiritual survival. Writing when the country was simultaneously exorcizing and fostering Harriet Jacobs's culture of rape, preaching uplift while still using the black whore myth to splash slavery's filth all over newly emancipated African American female bodies, these later African American women authors clearly considered American class and status more soul sustaining and nurturing than earlier evolutionary concerns.[42] Through a tone of isolation from and shame for her black folk roots in "Life on the Sea Islands," Charlotte Forten Grimké—the upper-class Northern granddaughter of wealthy abolitionist James Forten[43]—exhibits a divided black female self that mirrors the racism still disparaging postbellum African American life.

Despite often being the only black student in classes at elite but racist Philadelphia and Boston schools and encountering discrimination during the latter days of the Civil War, Charlotte Forten Grimké consciously capitalizes on her light skin and social standing when she seeks mainstream acceptance and joins an otherwise all-white group of liberal Northern teachers in the dangerous business of helping to educate newly freed slaves in a South Carolina battle zone. But the crusading tone of this experience in "Life" is undermined by Forten Grimké's alienation from the Sea Islanders, who share her racial heritage but not her exclusive class, an estrangement reflected stylistically in the frequent "our"/"their" and "them"/"us" pronoun distinctions that she draws throughout the piece. While sincerely celebrating the Sea Islanders' educational achievement, courage, politeness, and freedom, Forten Grimké—like her presumptuous white colleagues—does not hesitate to give these same fellow blacks "some directions for cleaning the house" and cooking, with no more reference to payment than was the practice during slavery. Sounding like a Eurocentric raconteur of travel narratives, Forten Grimké casts a condescending gaze on "people [who] had much better taste in selecting materials for dresses than *we* [my emphasis] had supposed"; mocks their dances; and is genuinely shocked by their actual biological blackness. Forten Grimké has apparently been lured by her erudition, bourgeoisie Northern upbringing, and genetic and cultural assimilation into what historian Carter G. Woodson would later call a "mis-education" dead end of racial self-hatred, the inevitable result of uncritically accepting the American one-drop rule that effectively taints all black bloodlines and ethnicities.[44] Thus, the author echoes Harriet Wilson's ignorant white liberals intrigued by Frado's racial difference and sees "strange" Sea Islanders such as the driver Harry, who "amused *us* [my emphasis] much." Indeed, like her restless and bored white female elites, Forten Grimké is occasionally titillated and energized by her mission of mercy because of its proximity to and danger from the Civil War for black freedom, seemingly on a sightseeing adventure during which she imagines, in an "excited jubilant state of mind," that "a band of guerrillas, had they chanced that way[,] . . . [might] seize and hang *us* [my emphasis]."

Nevertheless, her text is noteworthy for the inadvertent testimony it provides of now-venerable African American traditions such as the rudimentary "dignity . . . [black women found in wearing to church] straw hats with gay feathers," a custom that Michael Cunningham and Craig Marberry proudly document in its contemporary form. The nearly extinct Gullah language that Forten Grimké found "so broken that to *our* [my emphasis] unaccustomed ears it was quite unintelligible," we now know outlines the basic call and response patterns of African American poetry and music such as the blues. Reflecting upon the Sea Islanders' music, the author could not distinguish between Euro-American hymns and their African American spirituals in which ". . . the words seem to have but little meaning; but the tones,—a whole lifetime of despairing sadness is concentrated in them." She just does not recognize that, when ". . . the succeeding lines are sung in the most touching, mournful tones; and then the chorus . . . swells triumphantly, in glad contrast," these blacks are lining out the historic African American survival strategy of contrasting pain and joy in order to create a cultural aesthetic that heals physical and psychic wounds. Critic William L. Andrews perceptively observes that Forten Grimké's essay offers "white middle-class readers a positive assessment of the potential of the former slaves while testifying to the success of interracial cooperation in social reform and missionary work."[45] Clearly, if unwittingly, Forten Grimké also illustrates the fact that racist acculturation subtly debilitates the nascent black female soul, a dominant motif in the African American woman's texts. Like many white-looking, upper-class blacks, essayist Forten Grimké fully expects that the "almost indescribable" shouts of the Islanders and their "barbarous expression" will "pass away under the influence of Christian teaching," a hypocritical role model still justifying the nation's savage trafficking in human flesh.

Behind the Scenes, Or, Thirty Years a Slave, and Four Years in the White House (1868) by Elizabeth Keckley (1818?-1907) also serves as a cautionary tale about the spiritual challenges light-skinned, upwardly mobile black females encounter while becoming amalgamated socially and economically into a still racist and sexist postbellum America. Riveting and empowering, Keckley's survival narrative includes an unvarnished account of the four years of legalized rape she endured in Hillsborough, North Carolina, as the slave concubine of white persecutor Alexander Kirkland. Like Harriet Jacobs, she also testifies to the power of slavery law to disrupt the process of natural selection and sexual choice in black females and, at one point, candidly states: "If my poor boy [George W. D. Kirkland] ever suffered any humiliating pangs on account of his birth, he could not blame his mother, for God knows that she did not wish to give him life; he must blame that society which deemed it *no crime* [my emphasis] to undermine the virtue of girls in my position." Further signaling her repulsion of Kirkland's genes, Keckley makes scant reference to their son of rape in comparison to several paragraphs devoted to Abraham Lincoln's children. Significantly, like Harriet Jacobs, the only man Keckley actually chooses throughout her volume is also black, though not so faithful.

But more important for this narrative is that, long before business-oriented racial accommodationist Booker T. Washington delivered his famous Atlanta Exposition Speech in 1895 and urged black ex-slaves to "cast down your buckets" and make the economic best of their new-found freedom in post–Civil War America, Keckley—herself the offspring of slave rapist Colonel Armistead Burwell—was carving a path of African American female industry and entrepreneurship. Before Emancipation, she proudly bought her and son George's freedom, and used sewing skills acquired during her years of bondage to help transform powerful white people—whether slaveholding or not—into her clients and "friends." Unlike Maria Stewart and Jarena Lee, she does not signify around American religion and although, like Harriet Wilson, a white mistress brutally whipped her as a child and a white female slaveholder arranged even more vicious beatings later when Keckley was a young adult, she does not dwell exclusively on such cruelties. Rather, when Keckley sat down with amanuensis James Redpath to tell her story, she, like earlier nineteenth-century black women writers, eclectically combined slave narrative, autobiography, memoir, and even biographical information about First Lady Mary Todd Lincoln to speak open truths and "myriad subtleties" about the private and public lives she encountered while becoming a self-made woman.

Her only publication concentrates on the entrepreneurial spirit and personal energy that enabled Keckley to turn the biological atrocities of her enslavement into postbellum material advantages that empowered her to write from firsthand experience about Abraham Lincoln, Jefferson Davis, and other prominent mid-nineteenth-century luminaries—an ex-slave chronicler whose life encompassed both antebellum and postbellum American political and literary history. In *They Knew Lincoln* (1942), her biographer John E. Washington calls Keckley's book the single greatest source of information about Mary Todd Lincoln's White House years.[46] Like stenographer and writer Charles W. Chesnutt later in the century, Elizabeth Keckley was among the first postbellum African Americans to master the art of doing business with white Americans because she, for the most part, expertly walked the thin line between employee and "friend." But when Keckley began to ignore this crucial distinction and claimed to have written *Behind the Scenes* to redeem the reputation of spendthrift Mary Todd Lincoln, racism and sexism began to rear their ugly heads in earnest. Her volume drew condemnation from large segments of the public and so outraged Mr. D. Ottolengual of "New York literary circles" that he blatantly attacked her biologically in his parody *Behind the Seams, a Nigger Woman Who Took in Work from Mrs. Lincoln and Mrs. [Varina] Davis* (1868) by "Betsey Kickley." Keckley eventually lost both employment and white "friends" and was ultimately forced to support herself on a Civil War army pension that she received from the death of her rape-conceived son, George Kirkland, who was killed on August 10, 1861, at the Battle of Wilson's Creek in Missouri.

As the lead essay in a collection entitled *A Voice from the South by a Black Woman of the South* (1892)[47] by Dr. Anna Julia Haywood Cooper (1858–1964), "Womanhood a Vital Element in the Regeneration and Progress of a Race" also exemplifies a persistent survival tendency among the black educated elite to identify with the beneficiaries of slave-holding powerbrokers who nonetheless set contemporary standards of morality. Although Cooper bitterly expressed personal effects from slavery—such as "Presumably my father was her [mother Hannah Stanley Haywood's] master, if so I owe him not a sou—she was always too modest & shamefaced ever to mention him"[48]—Cooper nevertheless embraced aspects of her father's culture inimical to the advancement of black women. Born a slave in

Raleigh, North Carolina, just seven years before the Civil War ended, Cooper became a dedicated feminist and educational advocate for African American students. Biographer Louise Daniel Hutchinson documents her subject's gallant but losing battle with the District of Columbia that sought to limit black instruction to industrial training. Older friend and confidant Charlotte Forten Grimké placed so much trust in Cooper's scholarly expertise that she directed her husband Francis, upon her death, to deliver to the younger woman her diaries and journals for editing.[49] Presented in 1886 before the convocation of black clergymen of the Protestant Episcopal Church in Washington, D.C., Cooper's essay resounds with the following widely quoted, soul-inspiring expression of racial and gender solidarity:

> Only the Black Woman can say "when and where I enter, in the quiet, undisputed dignity of my womanhood, without violence and without suing or special patronage, then and there the whole *Negro race enters with me.*"

But the direct quotation marks in this passage signal its lack of origin with Cooper and an ambivalent narrative voice undermines her attempts to span racial and sexual divides. Despite a supposedly broad understanding of "race" and gender, the learned ex-slave mimics the behavior of her friend Charlotte Forten Grimké and internalizes Euro-American sexism and Christian hypocrisy rejected earlier by Maria Stewart and Jarena Lee.[50] For instance, Cooper valiantly proposes in the "Our Raison d' Être" section of her volume to tell "the other side" of "the one mute and voiceless note" of the Southern black woman but then abdicates this responsibility to a black male, Bishop Alexander Crummell. In a paper entitled "The Black Woman of the South" read in 1883 before The Freedman's Aid Society, Crummell observed that despite Emancipation: " . . . coarse food, coarse clothes, coarse living, coarse manners, coarse companions, coarse surroundings, coarse neighbors, both black and white, yea, every thing coarse, down to the coarse, ignorant, senseless religion, which excites her sensibilities and starts her passions, go to make up the life of the masses of black women . . . of the rural South."[51] Cooper gives the bishop this last word on her subject, amazingly conceding that "It is not for us to dwell on the needs, the neglects, and the ways of the succor, pertaining to the black woman of the South." When she eventually "beg[s] . . . the Doctor's permission, to add my plea for the *Colored Girls* of the South," Cooper insinuates her primary concern to correct Crummell's characterization of light-skinned women like herself who, "often without a stronger brother to espouse their cause and defend their honor with his lifeblood; in the midst of pitfalls and snares," [are most likely] "waylaid by the lower classes of white men."[52] In other words, "Womanhood a Vital Element" essentially leaves mute the views of the darker-skinned female masses—as literary critic Mary Helen Washington notes—and instead elaborately documents that Anna Julia Cooper, escaping the fate of Crummell's black female, is now erudite enough to discuss broader issues concerning cultures and thinkers from Mahomet to Ralph Waldo Emerson who address universal racism and sexism.[53] Indeed, Cooper devotes so much space to a "survey of the[ir] failures and achievements of the past" that she must periodically remind herself to return to "the subject assigned"—namely that: " . . . there can be no issue more vital and momentous than this of the womanhood of the race."

Perhaps biographer Paul Cooke reveals more about Cooper's level of commitment to telling the black woman's story than does Washington's speculation that Cooper sought to avoid the limelight. According to Cooke, "Cooper was continually the scholar. She was in the library when Mary Church Terrell was picketing the drugstores and cafeterias in downtown Washington, D.C."[54] The author's performance in "Womanhood a Vital" suggests that Cooper was mainly interested in impressing her cultural achievements upon her immediate black male audience and, eventually, the larger white public. Although one must admire the courage that led this ex-slave to gain an education—even earning a doctorate degree from the Sorbonne in her sixties—Cooper's text stands as another example of Carter G. Woodson's "mis-education" argument, especially when she, like her mentor Charlotte Forten Grimké, unquestioningly touts Christianity as the panacea for suffering black folks, declaring "We look forward with hope and trust that the same God whose guiding hand led our fathers through and out of the gall and bitterness of oppression, will still lead and direct their children, to the honor of His name, and for their ultimate salvation." On balance, then, Anna Julia Cooper's contribution to African American female uplift is substantial, but her "Womanhood a Vital Element" essay also shows an inability to question fully the evolutionary impact of conquest. Cooper's unreflective social uplift ultimately compromises her commitment to black women, thereby complicating a problem of identity and survival scholars have only begun to fathom.[55]

Charlotte Forten Grimké's niece by marriage, poet and dramatist Angelina Weld Grimké (1880–1958), the only child of white-looking lawyer Archibald Henry Grimké, was embraced by her father's white Southern abolitionist aunts Sarah M. Grimké and namesake Angelina Grimké Weld and thus inherited a biology culturally linked to mainstream American values most likely to foster black upper class racial and sexual ambivalence. Abandoned at an early age by her white mother Sarah E. Stanley Grimké, Angelina Weld Grimké developed an unusually close attachment to her father, which poetry critic Gloria T. Hull characterizes as "almost incestuous," as well as showed lesbian tendencies, particularly toward teacher/playwright Mamie (Mary) Burrill."[56] This complicated biography, marked by episodes of racism from which her privileged class status did not entirely insulate her, apparently cultivated an especially pernicious strain of self-hatred exhibited in the drama *Rachel: A Play in Three Acts* (1920). First produced in Washington,

D.C., during March 1916 under the auspices of the recently founded and integrated National Association for the Advancement of Colored People (NAACP), *Rachel* is generally regarded by critics as "the first twentieth century full-length play written, performed, and produced by blacks."[57] Critic Will Harris notes that *Rachel* also "brought into focus the themes of social inequality, hiring discrimination, the black frustration and familial erosion which resulted from economic strictures, and the pervasive, blighting effects of racism—in the process setting the pace for 'race' drama to come." As critic Robert J. Fehrenbach also correctly observes, "The Afro-American clearly had cause to defend the race from white friends and foes alike, to tell the black side of the story, and to present the race more realistically in literature and drama, the very instruments by which it had so long been demeaned."[58]

Accordingly, Grimké's play reflects the aesthetic values of NAACP Drama Committee organizer W. E. B. DuBois, who deemed all art propaganda.[59] Like the playwright herself, Rachel, Grimké's lower middle class heroine, vows to remain unmarried in order to avoid producing colored children who would otherwise risk exposure to a relentlessly racist world that lynches blacks. Throughout the play, Grimké portrays various African American victims such as dark-skinned Mrs. Lane, who unquestioningly accepts Thomas Jefferson's infamous "black equals ugly" racial slur, warns Rachel: "Don't marry," and bitterly asserts: "If I had another [child]—I'd kill it. It's kinder."[60] Compromised by the racial mythmaking that equates biological blackness with inferiority, the drama unsurprisingly also promotes various symbols of Eurocentric consumption, including an African American home decorated with such paintings as Milet's "The Reapers," Burne-Jones's "Golden Stairs," and Raphael's "Sistine Madonna." More significantly, *Rachel* is so blatant in its campaign to stop whites from lynching blacks, a prominent theme in Grimké's writing generally, that some of her contemporary theater professionals regarded the work as too propagandistic to merit serious artistic consideration.[61]

When accused of using her play to advocate black genocide, the antithesis of evolutionary survival—a theme subtly implied earlier in Harper's "The Two Offers" and Keckley's emotional distance from her son George in *Behind the Scenes*—Angelina Grimké wrote in the essay "*Rachel:* The Play of the Month": " . . . I would emphasize that that was not my intention. To the contrary, the appeal is not primarily to the colored people, but to the whites."[62] Grimké adds that she thought the subject of motherhood would, particularly, lure white females—"about the worst enemies with which the black race has to contend" (414)—away from their racial prejudice. Apparently, this artistic approach inspired her friend and fellow dramatist Georgia Douglas Johnson to write *Safe* (c. 1929), a play that portrays a young African American mother who, after witnessing a lynching, kills her newborn son. Much later and with greater skill, Toni Morrison revisited this theme in her prize-winning novel *Beloved* (1987) where, moved by the dire tale of ex-slave Margaret

Garner, who killed her daughter in order to prevent her re-enslavement, the author probes the philosophical and moral dilemmas arising out of black infanticide. Nonetheless, at the turn of the twentieth century, upper middle-class, "bi-racial," and sexually ambiguous Angelina Grimké herself embodies a biological and spiritual amalgam of the major advantages and threats to postbellum African-American female identity, of which nineteenth-century writers and Frances Watkins Harper, in particular, forewarned.

An evolutionary approach to the texts in this volume challenges readers to consider that nineteenth-century Darwinian biological discoveries put Euro-Americans under increased pressure to give up the fantasy to be first in Nature and accept the fact that human genesis occurred just once millennia ago. They were there, but only in the gene pool of their African ancestors. But emboldened by historic material success achieved through numerical and political majorities gained violently on the North American continent, they arrogantly pursued their dreams of a new world order dominated by Benjamin Franklin's "lovely white." Indeed, evolutionary literary theory exposes how the Euro-Americans continued to use Christian moral and spiritual duplicity as a weapon that centuries earlier had allowed their European ancestors to defy reality in the extreme and anoint a white male god who created a first white male named "Adam" who, in turn, facilitated the biological impossibility of giving birth to a first white female named "Eve." But the essays of Maria Stewart and Jarena Lee document that without direct study of Darwinian science, they clearly recognized and fought such grand delusions and turned religious hypocrisy into a methodology for defining and coping with their own genetic-based realities. That is they combated a white male who vehemently declared that this country would empower him to reproduce his whitest self with the "pure" white woman only, while instinctively conceding that her genetic makeup largely duplicated his own and fostered inbreeding that hinders racial longevity and leads to racial extinction. Thus, following dictates of Darwinian Natural Selection—as geneticists Thornhill and Palmer affirmed—these men used their slavocracy to rape with impunity the more genetically diverse black slave woman, then castrated and lynched her supportive black male protector when postbellum white women also seeking genetic diversity made the black male his competition. In other words, these black women's texts show that America's Founding Fathers like George Washington eventually became slaves to their own moral paradoxes, with hypocritical Thomas Jefferson conceding Nature's "immoveable veil of black" while defiantly mythmaking about a white superiority that required—as Harriet Jacobs declared—"violating the most sacred commandments of nature."

Attacked by the oppressor's combined psychological and physical arsenals, Harriet E. Wilson, Harriet A. Jacobs, and Ida B. Wells-Barnett particularly embraced a humanism that generally reaffirmed black female identity. Wilson specifically condemned duplicitous white Christian liberalism, while Jacobs and Wells-Barnett exposed the white man and woman's obsessive sexual pursuit of black-skinned people. While Frances Watkins Harper's "The Two Offers" recalled this latter theme and forewarned that greater freedom offered a third, homosexual option destined to curtail African American sexual reproduction, the writings of white-looking Charlotte Forten Grimké and "bi-racials" Elizabeth Keckley and Anna Julia Cooper testify to a dangerous self-hatred that results from bourgeois sexual and racial accommodation. Angelina Weld Grimké's *Rachel* depicts the extremes of this problem when, under the sentimental guise of saving black children, she would eliminate African American bloodlines.

Despite their various strengths and weaknesses, all the women authors in this collection leave a literary legacy defined by degrees of resistance to mainstream America's attempts to hide recessive genes at their expense, a practice which continues still to plague black female life. In an interview with critic Claudia Tate, poet-autobiographer Maya Angelou emphatically recalls the United States's historic designation of blacks as chattel slaves and resolves not to be redefined outside the human race, declaring "I'm a human being. I refuse to indulge any man-made differences between myself and another human being. I will not do it. . . . Never happen! Not me!"[63] Toni Morrison's *The Bluest Eye* (1970) ridicules the genetic engineering of pervert Soaphead Church and his black ancestors who deliberately married "'up'" until they had "lighten[ed] . . . the family complexion and thinn[ed] . . . out the family features [and moral gene pool]." Morrison further satirizes a presumptive Eurocentric "nationstate," candidly mocking French theorist Arthur Comte de Gobineau's rant to replace Nature's will with his own: "' . . . all civilizations derive from the white race, that none can exist without its help, and that a society is great and brilliant only so far as it preserves the blood of the noble group that created it'."[64]

Most directly, Alice Walker's *The Color Purple* (1982) literarily evokes Afro-centric evolutionary theory that suggests Eurocentric peoples essentially repeat the racist behavior of African progenitors, linking African, EuroAmerican, and African American settings and themes and having protagonist Celie sardonically tell her husband Mister: " . . . folks in Africa . . . believe white people is black peoples [sic] children" killed because " . . . they [Africans] don't like nothing around them that look or act different."[65] Walker's Olinka tribesmen, indeed, assert that Christianity's Adam was neither the universal first man nor even the first white man but "the first [white] one the [African] people didn't kill" (280). More significantly, Walker insinuates in *The Color Purple* the negative impact of this ancient African rejection by having strong-willed "Mammy" Sophia answer her unwanted EuroAmerican surrogate daughter Eleanor Jane, who asks: "Don't you just love him [Eleanor Jane's son]?" with "I do not love Reynolds Stanley Earl. . . . And now you know" (271).

Walker further underscores the continuing negative consequences of white people abruptly cut off from ancient African parental love by having Sophia then add: "I got my own troubles, and when Reynolds Stanley grows up, he's gon be one of them" (273), suggesting that even contemporary surrogate parents who deny their children create unforgetting, vengeful victims determined to pursue ancestry through time immemorial. Toni Morrison reiterates Walker's grim prediction about the human failure to love all children in the novel *Beloved* (1987), when slave mother Sethe echoes Angelina Grimké's maternalism and kills her biological daughter in order to save the child, a saintly pride Morrison mitigates by having Beloved's evolutionary psychological needs prompt a return that haunts her murderous mother unmercifully. In *1996* (2005), a bizarre tale about the National Security Association's use of technology to invade the black woman's home and self-image, novelist Gloria Naylor again returns readers to mainstream America's desperate need to be recognized by and interact with the black female. Harassing laser beams and other scientific gadgets now replace earlier societal restraints such as slavery, Christian duplicity, and Jim Crow. As these later devices empower white males to have two-way conversations against her will, they once again penetrate her peace and leave Naylor's financially and spiritually independent protagonist rest-broken and psychologically raped.

Notes

1. 1859 Rpt. (New York: Random House, 1993), p. 88. All future references are to this edition and will be cited parenthetically in the text.
2. *When and Where I Enter: The Impact of Black Women on Race and Sex in America* (New York: William Morrow and Company, Inc., 1984), Giddings's excellent narrative history of the African American woman's battles with the combined forces of racism and sexism, nonetheless, ignores the biological aspect of this discrimination—the likelihood that the white male targets her precisely because of his and her respective genetic traits. Although Smith discusses the idea of "the blood" connection in *Home Girls: A Black Feminist Anthology* (New Brunswick, NJ: Rutgers University Press, 2000), her study, too, is more sociological and political than genetic, as is the case with Christian's *Black Feminist Criticism: Perspectives on Black Women Writers* (New York: Pergamon Press, 1985), which adds a literary dimension to the discussion. Fleischner's *Mrs. Lincoln and Mrs. Keckley: The Remarkable Story of the Friendship between a First Lady and a Former Slave* (New York: Broadway Books, 2003), a recent biography of Elizabeth Keckley, does emphasize familial history but with the implicit purpose of portraying the slavewoman/slaveowner relationship sentimentally. Fleischner even resurrects the slave name of Keckley's mother, calling her "Abby Mammy" rather than "Mrs. Agnes Hobbs," the appellation used by Keckley, who repeatedly attempts to erase the stigma of slavery in a postbellum narrative that documents her pursuits of the American dream of material success (*Behind the Scenes, Or, Thirty Years a Slave, and Four Years in the*

White House (New York: G. W. Carleton & Co., 1868). All future references are to this edition and will be cited parenthetically in the text.

3. In their groundbreaking study *The History and Geography of Human Genes* (Princeton, NJ: Princeton University Press, 1994), Cavalli-Sforza, P. Menozzi, and A. Piazza document humankind's "unilinear" inheritance, in which " . . . the mt[mitochondrial]DNA of all children is identical to that of the mother, barring mutation, and receives no contribution from the father"—that is, in which " . . . mitochondria originate from only one parent [the mother] . . ." (86). They also indicate that " . . . all mtDNA present today can be traced to a single common [female] ancestor" and that " . . . the separation date of African and non-African populations must be later than the date of origin of the mtDNA types common to all human groups" (87), thus confirming earlier scientific projections that human genetic history was based not in Europe but Africa. In other words, mtDNA establishes that "Eve" was a black African woman and that males of every hue as well as white females are all her offspring. Even popular American magazines now extol this new genetic literacy. In "In Our Blood," *Newsweek* columnist Claudia Kalb recently notes: "Scientists say that by using Y and mitochondrial DNA, they can date the earliest female to 150,000 to 250,000 years ago and the earliest male to 60,000 to 100,000 years ago. Until DNA testing, scientists debated whether humans originated in Africa or in a number of different places around the globe. These recent findings support the theory that humans descended from a small group of people who lived in Africa tens of thousands of years ago" (Vol. CXLVII [February 6, 2006]): 54.

4. Quoted by Ronald T. TakaKi in *Iron Cages: Race and Culture in 19th-Century America*. (New York: Oxford University Press, 1990), p. 14. All future references are to this edition and will be cited parenthetically in the text.

5. "Query XIV: Laws." 1785 Rpt. Frank Shuffelton, Ed. (New York: Penguin, 1999), p. 145, 150. All future references are to this edition and will be cited parenthetically in the text.

6. Joseph L. Graves, Jr. *The Emperor's New Clothes: Biological Theories of Race at the Millennium*. (New Brunswick, NJ: Rutgers University Press, 2001), p. 4.

7. Cavalli-Sforza, Menozzi, and Piazza base their arguments largely on scientific history and recent discoveries about human DNA, citing such corroborative evidence as Charles Darwin's pioneering treatise *The Origin of Species* that "concluded . . . the [human] species is likely to be one because all races 'graduate into each other'" . . . (17). To counter claims that, over time, humans mutated into multiple "races" among which the white is superior, they assert: " . . . there is no doubt that there is only one human species" (19). Thus the current popularity of biologically impossible terms such as "multi-racial," "bi-racial," and "races" among humans is testimony to the power of mythology to obscure scientific fact. In *The Race Myth: Why We Pretend Race Exists in America* (New York: Dutton, 2004), Joseph Graves, Jr., bluntly states "The traditional concept of race is a myth." Although "Most Americans still believe in the concept of race the way they believe in the law of gravity—they believe in it without even knowing what it is they believe in" (ix).

8. Julian Huxley. *Race in Europe*. (London: Oxford University Press, 1939), p. 3.

9. "Sojourner Truth." Frances D. Gage. *New York Independent* 15 (April 23, 1863), p. 1. See also Nell Irvin Painter's discussion of the circumstances surrounding Gage's account of Truth's speech—which was originally delivered at a women's convention held in Akron, Ohio, May 28–29, 1851—in *Sojourner Truth: A Life, a Symbol* (New York: W. W. Norton & Company, 1996). Painter's portrait of an illiterate, Dutch-speaking Truth, who was transformed into

a mythic symbol of feminism by mostly white women authors, is especially compelling.

10. See a recent discussion of the casual acceptance of this presumption in Peggy McIntosh's *White Privilege and Male Privilege: A Personal Account of Coming to See Correspondences through Work in Women's Studies* (Wellesley, MA: Wellesley College Center for Research on Women, 1988).

11. In *Narrative of the Life of Frederick Douglass, An American Slave, Written by Himself.* (1845 Rpt. New York: New American Library, 1968), the narrator declares: "What I have said respecting and against religion, I mean strictly to apply to the *slaveholding religion* . . . and with no possible reference to Christianity proper; for between the Christianity of this land, and the Christianity of Christ, I recognize the widest possible difference—so wide, that to receive the one as good, pure, and holy [the Christianity of Christ] is of necessity to reject the other as bad, corrupt, and wicked [the slaveholding religion]" (120).

12. *Reconstructing Womanhood: The Emergence of the Afro-American Woman Novelist* (New York: Oxford University Press, 1987). See also critical studies such as *Saints, Sinners, Saviors: Strong Black Women in African American Literature* by Trudier Harris (New York: Palgrave, 2001) that explore the problem of African American women having so much personal strength that it prevents them from fully loving and being loved.

13. See Marilyn Richardson, Ed. *Maria W. Stewart: America's First Black Woman Political Writer, Essays and Speeches* (Bloomington, IN: Indiana University Press, 1987).

14. See my essay "Christian Violence and the Slave Narrative" (*American Literature* 68 [June 1996]: 297–320).

15. For example, in the Pulitzer Prize–winning drama *A Raisin in the Sun*, playwright Lorraine Hansberry portrays Lena "Mama" Younger as a saintly matriarch who keeps her daughter Beneatha *beneath her* in the family hierarchy, which the older woman establishes and controls. Hansberry's depiction of a similar power relationship between Mama and her son Walter Lee is no less intriguing. Trudier Harris devotes a chapter to *Raisin* and Mama Younger, whom she calls an "Acceptable Tyrant" (21). See also Sue E. Houchins's "Introduction" in *Spiritual Narratives* (New York: Oxford University Press, 1988), pp. xxix–xliv, which addresses, among other things, the controversial issue of the black female spiritual autobiographer's quest for perfection.

16. *Revised and Corrected from the Original Manuscript, written by herself* [sic]. Philadelphia, PA: Printed and Published for the Author, 1836.

17. Her narrative documents white America's early psychological strategies on another suicidal occasion, when Lee found herself tempted by "a vessel of water—into this I was strongly impressed to plunge my head, so as to extinguish the life God had given me." White males in Gloria Naylor's novel *1996* (2005) continue the same mind-altering practice but use technological rather than religious contrivances against a more spiritually liberated black female protagonist.

18. *Written by Herself: Literary Productions by African American Women, 1746–1982* (Bloomington, IN: Indiana University Press, 1993), p. 63. See also discussions of Jarena Lee in the "Introduction" to *Spiritual Narratives* by Sue E. Houchins.

19. See further discussion of literary form and African American texts in Henry Louis Gates, Jr.'s introduction to *Our Nig* (1859 Rpt. New York: Random House, 1983), pp. xi–lv and Thomas Doherty's "Harriet Jacobs' Narrative Strategies: *Incidents in the Life of a Slave Girl.*" *Southern Literary Journal* 19 (1986): 79–91.

20. For an enlightening account of the Bellmont family and other influences on *Our Nig*, see Barbara A. White's "'Our Nig' and the She-Devil: New Information about Harriet Wilson and the 'Bellmont' Family." *American Literature* 65 (March 1993): 19–52, as well as David Ames Curtis and Henry Louis Gates Jr.'s "Establishing the Identity of the Author of *Our Nig*" in *Wild Women in the Whirlwind: Afra-American Culture and the Contemporary Literary Renaissance*. Joanne M. Braxton and Andrée Nicola McLaughlin, Eds. (Rutgers University Press, 1990), pp. 48–69.

21. *The Black Mood and Other Essays.* (New York: Barnes & Noble, Inc., 1964), p. 76.

22. Cambridge, MA: The MIT Press, 2000, 84. Also see critiques of Thornhill and Palmer's evolutionary views in editor Cheryl Brown Travis's *Evolution , Gender, and Rape* (Cambridge, MA: MIT Press, 2003) and Alan Wertheimer's *Consent to Sexual Relations* (New York: Cambridge University Press, 2003).

23. See, for example, Kenneth M. Stamp's *The Peculiar Institution: Slavery in the Ante-Bellum South* (New York: Alfred A. Knopf, 1956) and Eugene D. Geneovese's *Roll Jordan Roll: The World the Slaves Made* (New York: Pantheon, 1974).

24. Thornhill and Palmer state that: "We evolutionists use the term *reproductive success* to . . . mean not the mere production of offspring but the production of offspring that survive to produce offspring. . . . A trait that increases this ability is 'good' in terms of natural selection even though one might consider it undesirable in moral terms. There is no connection here between what is biologically or naturally selected and what is morally right or wrong" (5–6). In *Adaptation and Natural Selection: A Critique of Some Current Evolutionary Thought* (Princeton, NJ: Princeton University Press, 1966), George C. Williams also notes that " . . . an individual who maximizes his friendships and minimizes his antagonisms will have an evolutionary advantage" (94), an idea Jacobs illustrates in Brent's settling for sex with Mr. Sands precisely because not having "to submit [directly] to compulsion" made him the lesser of two slaveholding evils.

25. Washington, D.C.: C-R Publishers, 1970, p. 6. The author reprinted this pamphlet in the broader study entitled *The Isis (Yssis) Papers: The Keys to the Colors.* Chicago: Third World Press, 1991. See also "The Body Politic: Black Female Sexuality and the Nineteenth-Century Imagination" by Beverly Guy-Sheftall and "'Some Could Suckle over Their Shoulder': Male Travelers, Female Bodies, and the Gendering of Racial Ideology, 1500–1770" by Jennifer L. Morgan in *Skin Deep, Spirit Strong: The Black Female Body and American Culture.* Kimberly Wallace-Sanders, Ed. (Ann Arbor, MI: University of Michigan Press), pp. 13–65. Guy-Sheftall and Morgan examine several of these early interactions between black females and Europeans to provide a historical context for white male attitudes described by Harriet Jacobs and many other African American women. Other relevant essays about the white European's ambivalent sexual responses to the African and African American female body also appear in this volume.

26. "Green-eyed Monsters of the Slavocracy: Jealous Mistresses in Two Slave Narratives" by Minrose C. Gwin in *Conjuring: Black Women, Fiction, and Literary Tradition.* Marjorie Pryse and Hortense Spillers, Eds. (Bloomington, IN: Indiana University Press, 1985), p. 44.

27. In *Harriet Jacobs: A Life* (New York: Basic Civatas, 2004), biographer Jean Fagan Yellin reiterates: "It is, however, clear that at fifteen, she did not have the option of choosing virginity, nor did she have the option of choosing marriage with a young [black] man she loved" (27).

28. See Wells-Barnett's discussion of this event in her posthumously published *Crusade for Justice: The Autobiography of Ida B. Wells*. Alfreda Duster, Ed. (Chicago: University of Chicago Press, 1970), pp. 47–52. All future references are to this edition and will be cited parenthetically in the text. See also Trudier Harris's *Exorcising Blackness: Historical and Literary Lynching and Burning Rituals* (Bloomington: Indiana University Press, 1984), a full-length critical study of white folks' ritualistic behavior and psycho-sexual motivations for lynching.

29. Whites today are perhaps less violent because they tend to satisfy their need for color with tanning lotions and salons that have become billion-dollar businesses.

30. Ida B. Wells-Barnett. "Introduction." *On Lynchings: Southern Horrors, A Red Record, Mob Rule in New Orleans* (New York: Arno Press, 1969). All future references are to this Press edition and will be cited parenthetically in the text.

31. See "Why Is the Negro Lynched" in *The Life and Writings of Frederick Douglass*, IV. Philip S. Foner, Ed. New York: International Publishers, 1955. In his autobiography *Up from Slavery*, ex-slave Booker T. Washington also notes: "The slave who was selected to sleep in the 'big house' during the absence of the males was considered to have the place of honour. Any one attempting to harm 'young Mistress' or 'old Mistress' during the night would have had to cross the dead body of the slave to do so" (Rpt. 1901. New York: The Sun Dial Press, 1937, p. 13.)

32. White female novelist Harper Lee further develops this theme in her novel *To Kill a Mockingbird* (1960), which explores the impact of a homely Southern white woman's vindictively accusing a black man of rape after he, too, rejects her sexually.

33. See Trudier Harris's provocative discussion of castration in *Exorcising Blackness*, especially her observation that by lynching, the white male literally "eliminates the mythic phallic symbol [of black male sexual supremacy], which he himself has created, from competition with himself; for there is the realistic possibility that if black men are so favorably endowed, white women may prefer them as sexual partners" (20). Also see Martha Hodes's *White Women, Black Men: Illicit Sex in the 19th-Century South* (New Haven, CT: Yale University Press, 1997), especially the chapter entitled "Murder: Black Men, White Women, and Lynching."

34. In *Invisible Man* (1952), Ellison's unnamed protagonist declares that he would have chosen death had that been the price of looking at a certain naked white woman who allowed white men to use her sexuality to arouse and then reject black boys. To emphasize further the woman's complicity in her own objectification, Ellison describes her impassive face and buttocks tattooed with the United States flag—all the exclusive province of white males.

35. See Mary Emma Graham's edition of *The Complete Poems of Frances E. W. Harper* (New York: Oxford University Press, 1988) and also the three following volumes edited by Frances Smith Foster: *A Brighter Coming Day: A Frances Ellen Watkins Harper Reader* (New York: Feminist Press, 1990); *Minnie's Sacrifice, Sowing and Reaping, Trial and Triumph: The Rediscovered Novels of Frances E. W. Harper* (Boston: Beacon Press, 1994); and *Iola Leroy or Shadows Uplifted* (1892 Rpt. New York: Oxford University Press, 1988).

36. *Discarded Legacy: Politics and Poetics in the Life of Frances E. W. Harper* (Detroit: Wayne State University Press, 1994), p. 117.

37. See a more-extensive discussion of "The Two Offers" and other Harper texts in Frances Smith Foster's *Written by Herself: Literary Production by African American Women, 1746–1892* (Bloomington, IN: Indiana University Press, 1993), pp. 88–94.

38. In *Black Women in Nineteenth-Century American Life: Their Words Their Thoughts Their Feelings* (University Park, PA: Pennsylvania State University Press, 1976), editors Bert James Loewenberg and Ruth Bogin provide this introduction to Harper: "Beyond the struggle for the rights of blacks she was sensitive to other forms of human deprivation. An awareness of moral and spiritual impoverishment among the wealthy and the privileged stirred her ..." (243). Barbara Christian calls Harper "an abolitionist elder," observes in *Black Women Novelists: The Development of a Tradition, 1892–1976* (Westport, CT: Greenwood Press, 1980) that Harper sets her novel *Iola Leroy* (1892) during slavery to counter the romanticism of the plantation literary tradition, and further notes that the author "had participated ... also in the struggle for Negro suffrage and the passage of the Fifteenth Amendment" (pp. 24–25). See also contemporary Anna Julia Cooper's reference to Harper as a pioneer, "who could sing with prophetic exaltation in the darkest days," in *A Voice from the South: By a Black Woman of the South* (Xenia, Ohio: The Aldine Printing House, 1892), p. 140.

39. In *Living by the Word: Selected Writings, 1973–1987* (San Diego, CA: Harcourt Brace Jovanovich, 1988), writer/activist Alice Walker summarizes the traditional experience of Southern black women as follows: "I have no memory ... of ever seeing, hearing about or even being able to imagine homosexuality" (p. 163).

40. 13 (May and June, 1864): pp. 587–596.

41. *When and Where I Enter*, p. 82.

42. In *Black Women in White America: A Documentary History* (New York: Vintage Books, 1973), pp. 172–193, editor Gerda Lerner reprints congressional testimonies and newspaper accounts of lustful and riotous white males ravaging African American women in their communities during this period.

43. Julie Winch notes that Robert Bridges Forten, Charlotte Forten-Grimké's father, was very smitten with her mother, Mary Virginia Wood who, along with her sister, Annie Wood, had arrived in Philadelphia in the early 1830s from the small town of Hertford, off the Ablemarle Sound, in Perquimans County, North Carolina. Winch insinuates Mary's white roots by adding that "There were no black Woods in Hertford, but various white men by the name of Wood ...," mentioning also that the background of the two sisters "is not easy to trace" but that "They had wealthy friends. Money had been spent on Mary's education." Additionally, Winch mentions the possibility that rumors may have arisen because a large gap in the ages of teenage Mary and toddler Annie made them appear to be mother and daughter rather than sisters (*A Gentleman of Color: The Life of James Forten* [New York: Oxford, University Press, 2002]), p. 279.

44. Woodson writes in the first chapter of *The Mis-Education of the Negro* (Washington, D.C.: Associated Publishers, 1933) that "the 'educated Negroes' have the attitude of contempt toward their own people because in their own as well as in their mixed schools Negroes are taught to admire the Hebrew, the Greek, the Latin and the Teuton and to despise the African" (1). According to Woodson biographer Jacqueline Goggin, he also combined the educational theories of both Booker T. Washington and W. E. B. DuBois and concluded that " ... members of the black bourgeoisie were unable to provide leadership for the race because they had become estranged from the masses; they had been 'emasculated' by their education...." See *Carter G. Woodson: A Life in Black History* (Baton Rouge, LA: Louisiana University Press, 1993), p. 158. In his groundbreaking study *Black Bourgeoisie: The Rise of a New Middle Class in the United States*, sociologist E. Franklin Frazier notes that free blacks

"had made the greatest progress in acquiring European culture" (Rpt. 1957, New York: Collier Books, 1962), p. 19.

45. *Crowns: Portraits of Black Women in Church Hats.* New York: Doubleday, 2000. *Classic African American Women's Narratives* New York: Oxford University Press, 2003, p. 363.

46. "Elizabeth Keckley: Companion and Confidante of Mrs. Lincoln." (New York: E. P. Dutton & Co., 1942), pp. 205–244, 249–252.

47. Xenia, Ohio: The Aldine Printing House, 1892.

48. *Anna J. Cooper: Voice of the South.* Louise Daniel Hutchinson, Ed. (Washington, D.C.: Smithsonian Institution Press, 1981), pp. 3–4.

49. Unable to complete the task, Cooper loaned "both the original manuscript diaries and the typewritten copy of them that she had laboriously made, together with other biographical data collected over the years," to Ray Allen Billington, who edited and published excerpts as *The Journal of Charlotte L. Forten* (London: Collier Books, 1953), p. 40. *The Journals of Charlotte Forten Grimké*, a complete collection edited with an introduction by Brenda Stevenson, appeared in 1988 as part of The Schomburg Library Nineteenth-Century Black Women Writers Series (New York: Oxford University Press). Editor William L. Andrews also considers Forten-Grimké's journals "The most substantial volume of life writing produced by an African-American woman of the nineteenth century" (363).

50. In *The Mis-Education of the Negro*, Carter G. Woodson explains that in their quest for conformity, "educated people" like Cooper "hope to . . . remove the pretext for the barriers between the races" but end up creating "a larger number of persons doing what others have been doing" and trading away "The unusual gifts of the race [that] have not thereby been developed . . ." (p. 7).

51. *Africa and America: Addresses and Discourses.* 1891 Rpt. Miami, FL: Mnemosyne Publishing Inc., 1969, p. 68.

52. Cooper apparently responds to what she considers a false distinction Crummell drew in his essay between the "negro [sic] *population*," of which his black Southern woman was a part, and the "*colored people*," whom he describes as recipients of such advantages as the "kindness and generosity of their white kindred—white fathers and relatives" (*Africa and America*, p. 62).

53. For an excellent summary of the racial and gender environment that Cooper inhabited, see Mary Helen Washington's introduction to *A Voice from the South* (New York: Oxford University Press, 1988). Washington perceptively notes that while Cooper clearly "sees herself as the *voice* for these women, . . . nothing in her essays suggests that they existed in her imagination as audience or as peer" (p. xxx).

54. Quoted in Washington, p. xxvii.

55. Frances Watkins Harper anticipates this class conflict in *Minnie's Sacrifice*, which was serialized in the *Christian Recorder* in 1869 and, more recently, has been edited by Frances Smith Foster and reprinted by Beacon Press (see footnote 35). But Harper refuses to have her mulatto protagonist either stereotypically pass for white or die tragically for the sin of being a white-looking black. Instead, the novella's narrator concludes that "The lesson of Minnie's sacrifice is this, that it is braver to suffer with one's own branch of the human race . . . than to attempt to creep out of all identity with them in their feebleness, for the sake of mere personal advantages . . ." (91). Years later, when E. Franklin Frazier echoed Harper's concerns in *The Black Bourgeoisie*, he created a virtual firestorm of controversy by observing that

XLIV | NINETEENTH-CENTURY BLACK WOMEN'S LITERARY EMERGENCE

light-skinned, upwardly mobile blacks often lacked an unqualified commitment to African American identity.

56. *Color, Sex, and Poetry: Three Women Writers of the Harlem Renaissance* (Bloomington, IN: Indiana University Press, 1987), pp. 139–140, 149. In the introduction to *Selected Works of Angelina Grimké* (New York: Oxford University Press, 1991), editor Carolivia Herron also discusses Grimké's sexual preference and suggests that " . . . he [Archibald Grimké] seems to have been the source of some restriction and oppression in her own sexual self-consciousness as a lesbian" (6–7).

57. "Introduction." *Black Female Playwrights: An Anthology of Plays before 1950*. Kathy A. Perkins, Ed. (Bloomington, IN: Indiana University Press, 1989), p. 8. See also William Storm's "Reactions of a 'Highly-Strung Girl': Psychology and Dramatic Representation in Angelina W. Grimké's *Rachel*. *African American Review* 27 (Fall 1993): 461–471.

58. "Early Black Women Playwrights and the Dual Liberation Motif." *African American Review* 28 (Summer 1994): 206 and "An Early Twentieth-Century Problem Play of Life in Black America: Angelina Grimké's *Rachel* in *Wild Women in the Whirlwind*. Braxton and McLaughlin, Eds. pp. 89–106. In the latter essay, using archival material from the Angelina Weld Grimké collection at Howard University among other sources, Fehrenbach also gives a detailed literary evolution of *Rachel*, from its original title "Blessed Are the Barren" to its performance and publication history.

59. See DuBois's essay "Criteria of Negro Art." *Crisis* 32 (October 1926): 290–297 in which he rejects the idea of art for art's sake and argues that blacks should start creating their own racially conscious versions of artistic propaganda.

60. *Rachel: A Play in Three Acts*. (1920 Rpt. College Park, MD: McGrath Publishing Company, 1969), p. 58.

61. See, for example, Perkins, pp. 8–9 and Storm, pp. 461–462.

62. Reprinted from the *Competitor* 1 (January 1920): 51–52 in *Selected Works of Angelina Weld Grimké*, p. 413.

63. *Black Women Writers at Work* (New York: Continuum, 1984), p. 7.

64. New York: Pocket Books, 1970, p. 133. Also, see J. Saunders Redding's similar depiction of de Gobineau in the novel *Stranger and Alone* (1950).

65. New York: Pocket Books, 1985, pp. 179–280. All future references are to this edition and cited parenthetically in the text.

Religion and the Pure Principles of Morality, the Sure Foundation on Which We Must Build

1831 | SHORT ESSAY

Introduction

Feeling a deep solemnity of soul, in view of our wretched and degraded situation, and sensible of the gross ignorance that prevails among us, I have thought proper thus publicly to express my sentiments before you. I hope my friends will not scrutinize these pages with too severe an eye, as I have not calculated to display either elegance or taste in their composition, but have merely written the meditations of my heart as far as my imagination led; and have presented them before you, in order to arouse you to exertion, and to enforce upon your minds the great necessity of turning your attention to knowledge and improvement.

I was born in Hartford, Connecticut, in 1803; was left an orphan at five years of age; was bound out in a clergyman's family; had the seeds of piety and virtue early sown in my mind; but was deprived of the advantages of education, though my soul thirsted for knowledge. Left them at 15 years of age; attended Sabbath Schools until I was 20; in 1826, was married to James W. Steward; was left a widow in 1829; was, as I humbly hope and trust, brought to the knowledge of the truth, as it is in Jesus, in 1830; in 1831, made a public profession of my faith in Christ.

From the moment I experienced the change, I felt a strong desire, with the help and assistance of God, to devote the remainder of my days to piety and virtue, and now possess that spirit of independence, that, were I called upon, I would willingly sacrifice my life for the cause of God and my brethren.

All the nations of the earth are crying out for Liberty and Equality. Away, away with tyranny and oppression! And shall Afric's sons be silent any longer? Far be it from me to recommend to you, either to kill, burn, or destroy. But I would strongly recommend to you, to improve your talents; let not one lie buried in the earth. Show forth your powers of mind. Prove to the world, that

> Though black your skins as shades of night,
> Your hearts are pure, your souls are white.

This is the land of freedom. The press is at liberty. Every man has a right to express his opinion. Many think, because your skins are tinged with a sable hue, that you are an inferior race of beings; but God does not consider you as such. He hath formed and fashioned you in his own glorious image, and hath bestowed upon you reason and strong powers of intellect. He hath made you to have dominion over the beasts of the field, the fowls of the air, and the fish of the sea. He hath crowned you with glory and honor; hath made you but a little lower than the angels; and, according to the Constitution of these United States, he hath made all men free and equal. Then why should one worm say to another, "Keep you down there, while I sit up yonder; for I am better than thou?" It is not the color of the skin that makes the man, but it is the principles formed within the soul.

Many will suffer for pleading the cause of oppressed Africa, and I shall glory in being one of her martyrs; for I am firmly persuaded, that the God in whom I trust is able to protect me from the rage and malice of mine enemies, and from them that will rise up against me; and if there is no other way for me to escape, he is able to take me to himself, as he did the most noble, fearless, and undaunted David Walker.

NEVER WILL VIRTUE, KNOWLEDGE, AND TRUE POLITENESS BEGIN TO FLOW, TILL THE PURE PRINCIPLES OF RELIGION AND MORALITY ARE PUT INTO FORCE.

My Respected Friends,

I feel almost unable to address you; almost incompetent to perform the task; and, at times, I have felt ready to exclaim, O that my head were waters, and mine eyes a fountain of tears, that I might weep day and night, for the transgressions of the daughters of my people. Truly, my heart's desire and prayer is, that Ethiopia might stretch forth her hands unto God. But we have a great work to do. Never, no, never will the chains of slavery and ignorance burst, till we become united as one, and cultivate among ourselves the pure principles of piety, morality and virtue. I am sensible of my ignorance; but such knowledge as God has given to me, I impart to you. I am sensible of former prejudices; but it is high time for prejudice and animosities to cease from among us. I am sensible of exposing myself to calumny and reproach; but shall I, for fear of feeble man who shall die, hold my peace? shall I for fear of scoffs and frowns, refrain my tongue? Ah, no! I speak as one that must give an account at the awful bar of God; I speak as a dying mortal, to dying mortals. O, ye daughters of Africa, awake! awake! arise! no longer sleep nor slumber, but distinguish yourselves. Show forth to the world that ye are endowed with noble and exalted faculties. O, ye daughters of Africa! what have ye done to immortalize your names beyond the grave? What examples have ye set before the rising generation? What foundation have ye laid for generations yet unborn? where are our union and love? and where is our sympathy, that weeps at another's wo, and hides the faults we see? And our daughters, where are they? blushing in innocence and virtue? And our sons, do they bid fair to become crowns of glory to our hoary heads? Where is the parent who is conscious of having faithfully discharged his duty, and at the last awful day of account, shall be able to say, here, Lord, is thy poor, unworthy servant, and the children thou hast given me? And where are the children that will arise, and call them blessed? Alas, O God! forgive me if I speak amiss; the minds of our tender babes are tainted as soon as they are born; they go astray, as it were, from the womb. Where is the maiden who will blush at vulgarity and where is the youth who has written upon his manly brow a thirst for knowledge; whose ambitious mind soars above trifles, and longs for the time to come, when he shall redress the wrongs of his father, and plead the cause of his brethren? Did the daughters of our land possess a delicacy of manners, combined with gentleness and dignity; did their pure minds hold vice in abhorrence and contempt, did they frown when their ears were polluted with its vile accents, would not their influence become powerful? Would not our brethren fall in love with their virtues? Their souls would become fired with a holy zeal for freedom's cause. They would become ambitious to distinguish themselves. They would become proud to display their talents. Able advocates would arise in our defence. Knowledge would begin to flow, and the chains of slavery and ignorance would melt like wax before the flames. I am but a feeble instrument. I am but as one particle of the small dust of the earth. You may frown or smile. After I am dead, perhaps before, God will surely raise up those who will more powerfully and eloquently plead the cause of virtue and the pure principles of morality than I am able to do. O virtue! how sacred is thy name! How pure are thy principles! Who can find a virtuous woman? for her price is far above rubies. Blessed is the man who shall call her his wife; yea, happy is the child who shall call her mother. O, woman, woman, would thou only strive to excel in merit and virtue; would thou only store thy mind with useful knowledge, great would be thine influence. Do you say, you are too far advanced in life now to begin? You are not too far advanced to instill these principles into the minds of your tender infants. Let them by no means be neglected. Discharge your duty faithfully, in every point of view: leave the event with God. So shall your skirts become clear of their blood.

When I consider how little improvement has been made the last eight years; the apparent cold and indifferent state of the children of God; how few have been hopefully brought to the knowledge of the truth as it is in Jesus; that our young men and maidens are fainting and drooping, as it were, by the way-side, for the want of knowledge; when I see how few care to distinguish themselves either in religious or moral improvement, and when I see the greater part of our community following the vain bubbles of life with so much eagerness, which will only prove to them like the serpent's sting upon the bed of death, I really think we are in as wretched and miserable a state as was the house of Israel in the days of Jeremiah.

I suppose many of my friends will say, "Religion is all your theme," I hope my conduct will ever prove me to be what I profess, a true follower of Christ; and it is the religion of Jesus alone, that will constitute your happiness here, and support you in a dying hour. O, then, do not trifle with God and your own souls any longer. Do not presume to offer him the very dregs of your lives; but now, whilst you are blooming in health and vigor, consecrate the remnant of your days to him. Do you wish to become useful in your day and generation? Do you wish to promote the welfare and happiness of your friends, as far as your circle extends? Have you one desire to become truly great? O, then, become truly pious, and God will endow you with wisdom and knowledge from on high.

> Come, turn to God, Who did thee make,
> And at his presence fear and quake;
> Remember him now in thy youth,
> And let thy soul take told of truth.
>
> The devil and his ways defy,
> Believe him not, he doth but lie;
> His ways seem sweet: but youth, beware!
> He for thy soul hath laid a snare.

Religion is pure; it is ever new; it is beautiful; it is all that is worth living for; it is worth dying for. O, could I but see the church built up in the most holy faith; could I but see men spiritually minded, walking in the fear of God, nor given to filthy lucre, not holding religion in one hand and the world in the other, but diligent in business, fervent in spirit, serving the Lord, standing upon the walls of Zion, crying to passers by, "He, every one that thirsteth, come ye to the waters, and he that hath no money; yea, come and buy wine and milk without money and without price; Turn ye, turn ye, for why will ye die?" Could I but see mothers in Israel, chaste, keepers at home, not busy bodies, meddlers in other men's matters, whose adorning is of the inward man, possessing a meek and quiet spirit, whose sons were like olive-plants, and whose daughters were as polished corner-stones; could I but see young men and maidens turning their feet from impious ways, rather choosing to suffer affliction with the people of God than to enjoy the pleasures of sin for a season; could I but see the rising youth blushing in artless innocence, then could I say, now, Lord, let thine unworthy handmaiden depart in peace, for I have seen the desire of mine eyes, and am satisfied.

Prayer

O, Lord God, the watchmen of Zion have cried peace, when there was no peace; they have been, as it were, blind leaders of the blind. Wherefore hast thou so long withheld from us the divine influences of thy Holy Spirit? Wherefore hast thou hardened our hearts and blinded our eyes? It is because we have honored thee with our lips, when our hearts were far from thee. We have regarded iniquity in our hearts, therefore thou will not hear. Return again unto us. O Lord God, we beseech thee, and pardon this the iniquity of thy servants. Cause thy face to shine upon us, and we shall be saved. O visit us with thy salvation. Raise up sons and daughters unto Abraham, and grant that there might come a mighty shaking of dry bones among us, and a great in gathering of souls. Quicken thy professing children. Grant that the young may be constrained to believe that there is a reality in religion and a beauty in the fear of the Lord. Have mercy on the blighted sons and daughters of Africa. Grant that we may soon become so distinguished for our moral and religious improvements, that the nations of the earth may take knowledge of us; and grant that our cries may come up before thy throne like holy incense. Grant that every daughter of Africa may consecrate her sons to thee from the birth. And do thou, Lord, bestow upon them wise and understanding hearts. Clothe us with humility of souls, and give us a becoming dignity of manners: may we imitate the character of the meek and lowly Jesus; and do thou grant that Ethiopia may soon stretch forth her hands unto thee. And now, Lord, be pleased to grant that Satan's kingdom may be destroyed; that the kingdom of our Lord Jesus Christ may be built up; that all nations, and hundreds, and tongues, and people might be brought to the knowledge of the truth, as it is in Jesus, and we at last meet around thy throne, and join in celebrating thy praises.

I have been taking a survey of the American people in my own mind, and I see them thriving in arts, and sciences, and in polite literature. Their highest aim is to excel in political, moral and religious improvement. They early consecrate their children to God, and their youth indeed are blushing in artless innocence; they wipe the tears from the orphan's eyes, and they cause the widow's heart to sing for joy! and their poorest ones, who have the least wish to excel, they promote! And those that have but one talent, they encourage. But how very few are there among them that bestow one thought upon the benighted sons and daughters of Africa, who have enriched the soils of America with their tears and blood: few to promote their cause, none to encourage their talents. Under these circumstances, do not let our hearts be any longer discouraged; it is no use to murmur nor to repine; but let us promote ourselves and improve our own talents. And I am rejoiced to reflect that there are many able and talented ones among us, whose names might be recorded on the bright annals of fame. But, "I can't," is a great barrier in the way, I hope it will soon be removed, and "I will" resume its place.

Righteousness exalteth a nation, but sin is a reproach to any people. Why is it, my friends, that our minds have been blinded by ignorance, to the present moment? 'Tis on account of sin. Why is it that our church is involved in so much difficulty? It is on account of sin. Why is it that God has cut down, upon our right hand and upon our left, the most learned and intelligent of our men? O, shall I say, is it on account of sin! Why is it that thick darkness is mantled upon every brow, and we, as it were, look sadly upon one another? It is on account of sin. O, then, let us bow before the Lord our God, with all our hearts, and humble our very souls in the dust before him; sprinkling, as it were, ashes upon our heads, and awake to righteousness and sin not. The arm of the Lord is not shortened, that it cannot save; neither is his ear heavy, that it cannot hear; but it is your iniquities that have separated you from me, saith the Lord. Return, O ye backsliding children, and I will return unto you, and ye shall be my people, and I will be your God.

O, ye mothers, what a responsibility rests on you! You have souls committed to your charge, and God will require a strict account of you. It is you that must create in the minds of your little girls and boys a thirst for knowledge, the love of virtue, the abhorrence of vice, and the cultivation of a pure heart. The seeds thus sown will grow with their growing years; and the love of virtue thus early formed in the soul will protect their inexperienced feet from many dangers. O, do not say, you cannot make any thing of your children; but say, with the help and assistance of God, we will try. Do not indulge them in their little stubborn ways; for a child left to himself, bringeth his mother to shame. Spare not, for their crying; thou shalt beat them with a rod, and they shall not die; and thou shalt save their souls from hell. When you correct them, do it in the fear of God, and for their own good. They will not thank you for your false and foolish indulgence; they will rise up, as it were, and curse you in this world, and, in the world to come, condemn you. It is no use to say, you can't do this, or, you can't do that; you will not tell your Maker so, when you meet him at the great day of account. And you must be careful that you set an example worthy of following, for you they will imitate. There are many instances, even among us now, where parents have discharged their duty faithfully, and their children now reflect honor upon their gray hairs.

Perhaps you will say, that many parents have set pure examples at home, and they have not followed them. True, our expectations are often blasted; but let not this dishearten you. If they have faithfully discharged their duty; even after they are dead, their works may live; their prodigal children may then return to God, and become heirs of salvation; if not, their children cannot rise and condemn them at the awful bar of God.

Perhaps you will say, that you cannot send them to high schools and academies. You can have them taught in the first rudiments of useful knowledge, and then you can have private teachers, who will instruct them in the higher branches; and their intelligence will become greater than ours, and their children will attain to higher advantages and their children still higher; and then though we are dead, our works shall live: though we are mouldering, our names shall not be forgotten.

Finally, my heart's desire and prayer to God is, that there might come a thorough reformation among us. Our minds have too long grovelled in ignorance and sin. Come, let us incline our ears to wisdom, and apply our hearts to understanding; promote her, and she shall exalt thee; she shall bring thee to honor when thou dost embrace her. An ornament of grace shall she be thy head, and a crown of glory shall she delivers to thee. Take fast hold of instruction; let her not go; keep her, for she is thy life. Come, let us turn unto the Lord our God, with all our heart and soul, and put away every unclean and unholy thing from among us, and walk before the Lord our God, with a perfect heart, all the days of our lives; then we shall be a people with whom God shall delight to dwell; yea, we shall be that happy people whose God is the Lord.

I am of a strong opinion, that the day on which we unite, heart and soul, and turn our attention to knowledge and improvement, that day the hissing and reproach among the nations of the earth against us will cease. And even those who now point at us with the finger of scorn, will aid and befriend us. It is of no use for us to sit with our hands folded, hanging our heads like bulrushes, lamenting our wretched condition; but let us make a mighty effort, and arise; and if no one will promote or respect us, let us promote and respect ourselves.

The American ladies have the honor conferred on them, that by prudence and economy in their domestic concerns, and their unwearied attention in forming the minds and manners of their children, they laid the foundation of their becoming what they now are. The good women of Wethersfield, Conn. toiled in the blazing sun, year after year, weeding onions, then sold the seed and procured money enough to erect them a house of worship; and shall we not imitate their examples, as far as they are worthy of imitation? Why cannot we do something to distinguish ourselves, and contribute some of our hard earnings that would reflect honor upon our memories, and cause our children to arise and call us blessed? Shall it any longer be said of the daughters of Africa, they have no ambition, they have no force? By no means. Let every female heart become united, and let us raise a fund ourselves; and at the end of one year and a half, we might be able to lay the corner-stone for the building of a High School, that the higher branches of knowledge might be enjoyed by us; and God would raise us up, and enough to aid us in our laudable designs. Let each one strive to excel in good housewifery, knowing that prudence and economy are the road to wealth. Let us not say, we know this, or we know that, and practise nothing; but let us practise what we do know.

How long shall the fair daughters of Africa be compelled to bury their minds and talents beneath a load of iron pots and kettles? Until union, knowledge and love begin to flow among us. How long shall a mean set of men flatter us with their smiles, and enrich themselves with our hard earnings; their wives' fingers sparkling with rings, and they themselves laughing at our folly? Until we begin to promote and patronize each other. Shall we be a by-word among the nations any longer? Shall they laugh us to scorn forever? Do you ask, what can we do? Unite and build a store of your own, if you cannot procure a license. Fill one side with dry goods, and other with groceries. Do you ask, where is the money? We have spent more than enough for nonsense, to do what building we should want. We have never had an opportunity of displaying our talents; therefore the world thinks we know nothing. And we have been possessed of by far too mean and cowardly a disposition, though I highly disapprove of an insolent or impertinent one. Do you ask the disposition I would have you possess? Possess the spirit of independence. The Americans do, and why should not you? Possess the spirit of men, bold and enterprising, fearless and undaunted. Sue for your rights and privileges. Know the reason that you can attain them. Weary them with your importunities. You can but die, if you make the attempt; and we shall certainly die if you do not. The Americans have practiced nothing but head-work these 200 years, and we have done their drudgery. And is it not high time for us to imitate their examples, and practise head-work too, and keep what we have got, and get what we can? We need never to think that any body is going to feel interested for us, if we do not feel interested for ourselves. That day we, as a people, hearken unto the voice of the Lord our God, and walk in his ways and ordinances, and become distinguished for our ease, elegance and grace, combined with other virtues, that day the Lord will raise us up, and enough to aid and befriend us, and we shall begin to flourish.

Did every gentleman in America realize, as one, that they had got to become bondmen, and their wives, their sons, and their daughters, servants forever, to Great Britain, their very joints would become loosened, and tremblingly would smite one against another; their countenance would be filled with horror, every nerve and muscle would be forced into action, their souls would recoil at the very thought, their hearts would die within them, and death would be far more preferable. Then why have not Africa's sons a right to feel the same? Are not their wives, their sons, and their daughters, as dear to them as those of the white man's? Certainly, God has not deprived them of the divine influences of his Holy Spirit, which is the greatest of all blessings, if they ask him. Then why should man any longer deprive his fellow-man of equal rights and privileges? Oh, America, America, foul and indelible is thy stain! Dark and dismal is the cloud that hangs over thee, for thy cruel wrongs and injuries to the fallen sons of Africa. The blood of her murdered ones cries to heaven for vengeance against thee. Thou art almost become drunken with the blood of her slain; thou hast enriched thyself through her toils and labors; and now thou refuseth to make even a small return. And thou hast caused the daughters of Africa to commit whordoms and fornications; but upon thee be their curse.

O, ye great and mighty men of America, you much and powerful ones, many of you will call for the rocks and mountains to fall upon you, and to hide you from the wrath of the Lamb, and from him that sitteth upon the throne; whilst many of the sable-skinned Africans you now despise, will shine in the kingdom of heaven as the stars forever and ever. Charity begins at home, and those that provide not for their own, are worse than infidels. We know that you are raising contributions to aid the gallant Poles; we know that you have befriended Greece and Ireland; and you have rejoiced with France, for her heroic deeds of valor. You have acknowledged all the nations of the earth, except Hayti; and you may publish, as far as the East is from the West, that you have two millions of negroes, who aspire no higher than to bow at your feet, and to court your smiles. You may kill, tyrannize, and oppress as much as you choose, until our cry shall come up before the throne of God; for I am firmly persuaded, that he will not suffer you to quell the proud, fearless and undaunted spirits of the African forever; for in his own time, he is able to plead our cause against you, and to pour out upon you the ten plagues of Egypt. We will not come out against you with swords and staves, as against a thief; but we will tell you that our souls are fired with the same love of liberty and independence with which your souls are fired. We will tell you that too much of your blood flows in our veins, and too much of your color in our skins, for us not to possess your spirits. We will tell you that it is our gold that clothes you in fine linen and purple, and causes you to fare sumptuously every day; and it is the blood of our fathers, and the tears of our brethren that have enriched your soils. AND WE CLAIM OUR RIGHTS. We will tell you, that we are not afraid of them that kill the body, and after that can do no more; but we will tell you whom we do fear. We fear Him who is able, after he hath killed, to destroy both souls and body in hell forever. Then, my brethren, sheath your swords, and calm your angry passions. Stand still, and know that the Lord he is God. Vengeance is his, and he will repay. It is a long lane that has no turn. America has risen to her meridian. When you begin to thrive, she will begin to fall. God hath raised you up a Walker and a Garrison. Though Walker sleeps, yet he lives, and his name shall be had in everlasting remembrance. I, even I, who am but a child, inexperienced to many of you, am a living witness to testify unto you this day, that I have seen the wicked in great power, spreading himself like a green bay tree, and lo, he passed away; yea, I diligently sought him, but he could not be found; and it is God alone that has inspired my heart to feel for Afric's woes. Then fret not yourselves because of evil doers. Fret not yourselves because of evil who bring wicked devices to pass; for they shall be cut down as the grass, and wither as the green herb. Trust in the Lord, and do good; so shalt thou dwell in the land, and verily thou shalt be fed. Encourage the noble-hearted Garrison. Prove to the world that you are neither ourang-outangs, nor a species of mere animals, but that you possess the same powers of intellect as those of the proud-boasting American.

I am sensible, my brethren and friends, that many of you have been deprived of advantages, kept in utter ignorance, and that your minds are now darkened; and if any of you have attempted to aspire after high and noble enterprises, you have met with so much opposition that your souls have become discouraged. For this very cause, a few of us have ventured to expose our lives in your behalf, to plead your cause against the great; and it will be of no use, unless you feel for yourselves and your little ones, and exhibit the spirits of men. Oh, then, turn your attention to knowledge and improvement; for knowledge is power. And God is able to fill you with wisdom and understanding, and to dispel your fears. Arm yourselves with the weapons of prayer. Put your trust in the living God. Persevere strictly in the paths of virtue. Let nothing be lacking on your part; and, in God's own time, and his time is certainly the best, he will surely deliver you with a mighty hand and with an outstretched arm.

I have never taken one step, my friends, with a design to raise myself in your esteem, or to gain applause. But what I have done, has been done with an eye single to the glory of God, and to promote the good of souls. I have neither kindred nor friends. I stand alone in your midst, exposed to the fiery darts of the devil, and to the assaults of wicked men. But though all the powers of earth and hell were to combine against me, though all nature should sink into decay, still would I trust in the Lord, and joy in the God of my salvation. For I am fully persuaded, that he will bring me off conqueror, yea, more than conqueror, through him who hath loved me and given himself for me.

Boston, October, 1831.

Further Reading

Peterson, Carla L. *"Doers of the Word": African American Women Speakers in the North (1830–1880)*. New York: Oxford University Press, 1995.

The Life and Religious Experience of Jarena Lee, A Coloured Lady, Giving an Account of Her Call To Preach the Gospel.

Revised and Corrected from the Original Manuscript, Written by Herself.

1836 | SHORT SPIRITUAL NARRATIVE

" And it shall come to pass. . . . . . . that I will pour out my Spirit upon all flesh; and your sons, and your daughters shall prophecy."
                                                                    JOEL II. 28.

I was born February 11th, 1783, at Cape May, state of New Jersey. At the age of seven years I was parted from my parents, and went to live as a servant maid, with a Mr. Sharp, at the distance of about sixty miles from the place of my birth.

My parents being wholly ignorant of the knowledge of God, had not therefore instructed me in any degree in this great matter. Not long after the commencement of my attendance on this lady, she had bid me do something respecting my work, which in a little while after, she asked me if I had done, when I replied, Yes— but this was not true.

At this awful point, in my early history, the spirit of God moved in power through my conscience, and told me I was a wretched sinner. On this account so great was the impression, and so strong were the feelings of guilt, that I promised in my heart that I would not tell another lie.

But notwithstanding this promise my heart grew harder, after a while, yet the spirit of the Lord never entirely forsook me, but continued mercifully striving with me, until his gracious power converted my soul.

The manner of this great accomplishment, was as follows: In the year 1804, it so happened that I went with others to hear a missionary of the Presbyterian order preach. It was an afternoon meeting, but few were there, the place was a school room; but the preacher was solemn, and in his countenance the earnestness of his master's business appeared equally strong, as though he were about to speak to a multitude.

At the reading of the Psalms, a ray of renewed conviction darted into my soul. These were the words, composing the first verse of the Psalms for the service:

"Lord, I am vile, conceived in sin,
Born unholy and unclean.
Sprung from man, whose guilty fall
Corrupts the race, and taints us all."

This description of my condition struck me to the heart, and made me to feel in some measure, the weight of my sins, and sinful nature. But not knowing how to run immediately to the Lord for help, I was driven of Satan in the course of a few days, and tempted to destroy myself.

There was a brook about a quarter of a mile from the house, in which there was a deep hole, where the water whirled about among the rocks; to this place it was suggested, I must go and drown myself.

At the time I had a book in my hand; it was on a Sabbath morning, about ten o'clock; to this place I resorted, where on coming to the water I sat down on the bank, and on my looking into it; it was suggested, that drowning would be an easy death. It seemed as if some one was speaking to me, saying put your head under, it will not distress you. But by some means, of which I can give no account, my thoughts were taken entirely from this purpose, when I went from the place to the house again. It was the unseen arm of God which saved me from self murder.

But notwithstanding this escape from death, my mind was not at rest—but so great was the labour of my spirit and the fearful oppressions of a judgment to come, that I was reduced as one extremely ill. On which account a physician was called to attend me, from which illness I recovered in about three months.

But as yet I had not found him of whom Moses and the prophets did write, being extremely ignorant: there being no one to instruct me in the way of life and salvation as yet. After my recovery, I left the lady, who during my sickness, was exceedingly kind, and went to Philadelphia. From this place I soon went a few miles into the country, where I resided in the family of a Roman Catholic. But my anxiety still continued respecting my poor soul, on which account I used to watch my opportunity to read in the Bible; and this lady observing this, took the Bible from me and hid it, giving me a novel in its stead—which when I perceived, I refused to read.

Soon after this I again went to the city of Philadelphia; and commenced going to the English Church, the pastor of which was an Englishman, by the name of Pilmore, one of the number who at first preached Methodism in America, in the city of New York.

But while sitting under the ministration of this man, which was about three months, and at the last time, it appeared that there was a wall between me and a communion with that people, which was higher than I could possibly see over, and seemed to make this impression upon my mind, *this is not the people for you.*

But on returning home at noon I inquired of the head cook of the house respecting the rules of the Methodists, as I knew she belonged to that society, who told me what they were; on which account I replied, that I should not be able to abide by such strict rules not even one year; however, I told her that I would go with her and hear what they had to say.

The man who was to speak in the afternoon of that day, was the Rev. Richard Allen, since bishop of the African Episcopal Methodists in America. During the labors of this man that afternoon, I had come to the conclusion, that this is the people to which my heart unites, and it so happened, that as soon as the service closed he invited such as felt a desire to flee the wrath to come, to unite on trial with them—I embraced the opportunity. Three weeks from that day, my soul was gloriously converted to God, under preaching, at the very outset of the sermon. The text was barely pronounced, which was: " I perceive thy heart is not right in the sight of God," when there appeared to *my* view, in the centre of the heart one sin; and this was *malice*, against one particular individual, who had strove deeply to injure me, which I resented. At this discovery I said, *Lord* I forgive every creature. That instant, it appeared to me, as if a garment, which had entirely enveloped my whole person, even to my fingers ends, split at the crown of my head, and was stripped away from me, passing like a shadow, from my sight—when the glory of God seemed to cover me in its stead.

That moment, though hundreds were present, I did leap to my feet, and declare that God, for Christ's sake, had pardoned the sins of my soul. Great was the ecstasy of my mind, for I felt that not only the sin of *malice* was pardoned, but all other sins were swept away together. That day was the first when my heart had believed, and my tongue had made confession unto salvation—the first words uttered, a part of that song, which shall fill eternity with its sound, was *glory to God*. For a few moments I had power to exhort sinners, and to tell of the wonders and of the goodness of him who had clothed me with his salvation. During this, the minister was silent, until my soul felt its duty had been performed, when he declared another witness of the power of Christ to forgive sins on earth, was manifest in my conversion.

From the day on which I first went to the Methodist church, until the hour of my deliverance, I was strangely buffeted by that enemy of all righteousness—the devil.

I was naturally of a lively turn of disposition; and during the space of time from my first awakening until I knew my peace was made with God, I rejoiced in the vanities of this life, and then again sunk back into sorrow.

For four years I had continued in this way, frequently labouring under the awful apprehension, that I could never be happy in this life. This persuasion was greatly strengthened, during the three weeks, which was the last of Satan's power over me, in this peculiar manner: on which account, I had come to the conclusion that I had better be dead than alive. Here I was again tempted to destroy my life by drowning; but suddenly this mode was changed—and while in the dusk of the evening, as I was walking to and fro in the yard of the house, I was beset to hang myself, with a cord suspended from the wall enclosing the secluded spot.

But no sooner was the intention resolved on in my mind, than an awful dread came over me, when I ran into the house; still the tempter pursued me. There was standing a vessel of water—into this I was strongly impressed to plunge my head, so as to extinguish the life which God had given me. Had I have done this, I have been always of the opinion that I should have been unable to have released myself; although the vessel was scarcely large enough to hold a gallon of water. Of me may it not be said, as written by Isaiah, (chap. 65. verses 1, 2.) "I am sought of them that asked not for me; I am found of them that sought me not." Glory be to God for his redeeming power, which saved me from the violence of my own hands, from the malice of Satan, and from eternal death; for had I have killed myself, a great ransom could not have delivered me; for it is written—"No murderer hath eternal life abiding in him." How appropriately can I sing—

> "Jesus sought me, when a stranger.
>   Wandering from the fold of God;
> He to rescue me from danger,
>   Interposed his precious blood."

But notwithstanding the terror which seized upon me, when about to end my life, I had no view of the precipice on the edge of which I was tottering, until it was over, and my eyes were opened. Then the awful gulf of hell seemed to be open beneath me, covered only, as it were, by a spider's web, on which I stood. I seemed to hear the howling of the damned, to see the smoke of the bottomless pit, and to hear the rattling of those chains, which hold the impenitent under clouds of darkness to the judgment of the great day.

I trembled like Belshazzar, and cried out in the horror of my spirit, "God be merciful to me a sinner." That night I formed a resolution to pray; which, when resolved upon, there appeared, sitting in one corner of the room, Satan, in the form of a monstrous dog, and in a rage, as if in pursuit, his tongue protruding from his mouth to a great length, and his eyes looked like two balls of fire; it soon, however, vanished out of my sight. From this state of terror and dismay, I was happily delivered under the preaching of the Gospel as before related.

This view, which I was permitted to have of Satan, in the form of a dog, is evidence, which corroborates in my estimation, the Bible account of a hell of fire, which burneth with brimstone, called in Scripture the bottomless pit; the place where all liars, who repent not, shall have their portion; as also the Sabbath breaker, the adulterer, the fornicator, with the fearful, the abominable, and the unbelieving, this shall be the portion of their cup.

This language is too strong and expressive to be applied to any state of suffering in *time*. Were it to be thus applied, the reality could no where be found in human life; the consequence would be, that *this* scripture would be found a false testimony. But when made to apply to an endless state of perdition, in eternity, beyond the bounds of human life, then this language is found not to exceed our views of a state of eternal damnation.

During the latter part of my state of conviction, I can now apply to my case, as it then was, the beautiful words of the poet:

"The more I strove against its power,
I felt its weight and guilt the more;
"Till late I hear'd my Saviour say,
Come hither soul, I am the way."

This I found to be true, to the joy of my disconsolate and despairing heart, in the hour of my conversion to God.

During this state of mind, while sitting near the fire one evening, after I had heard Rev. Richard Allen, as before related, a view of my distressed condition so affected my heart, that I could not refrain from weeping and crying aloud; which caused the lady with whom I then lived, to inquire, with surprise, what ailed me; to which I answered, that I knew not what ailed me. She replied that I ought to pray. I arose from where I was sitting, being in an agony, and weeping convulsively, requested her to pray for me; but at the very moment when she would have done so, some person wrapped heavily at the door for admittance; it was but a person of the house, but this occurrence was sufficient to interrupt us in our intentions; and I believe to this day, I should then have found salvation to my soul. This interruption was, doubtless, also the work of Satan.

Although at this time, when my conviction was so great, yet I knew not that Jesus Christ was the Son of God, the second person in the adorable trinity. I knew him not in the pardon of my sins, yet I felt a consciousness that if I died without pardon, that my lot must inevitably be damnation. If I would pray—I knew not how. I could form no connexion of ideas into words; but I knew the Lord's prayer; this

I uttered with a loud voice, and with all my might and strength. I was the most igno-rant creature in the world; I did not even know that Christ had died for the sins of the world, and to save sinners. Every circumstance, however, was so directed as still to continue and increase the sorrows of my heart, which I now know to have been a godly sorrow which wrought repentance, which is not to be repented of. Even the falling of the dead leaves from the forests, and the dried spires of the mown grass, showed me that I too must die, in like manner. But my case was awfully different from that of the grass of the field, or the wide spread decay of a thousand forests, as I felt within me a living principle, an immortal spirit, which cannot die, and must forever either enjoy the smiles of its Creator, or feel the pangs of ceaseless damnation.

But the Lord led me on; being gracious, he took pity on my ignorance; he heard my wailings, which had entered into the ear of the Lord of Sabbath. Circumstances so transpired that I soon came to a knowledge of the being and character of the Son of God, of whom I knew nothing.

My strength had left me. I had become feverish and sickly through the violence of my feelings on which account I left my place of service to spend a week with a coloured physician, who was a member of the Methodist society, and also to spend this week in going to places where prayer and supplication was statedly made for such as me.

Through this means I had learned much, so as to be able in some degree to com-prehend the spiritual meaning of the text, which the minister took on the Sabbath morning, as before related, which was, "I perceive thy heart is not right in the sight of God." Acts, chap. 8, verse 21.

This text, as already related, became the power of God unto salvation to me, because I believed. I was baptized according to the direction of our Lord, who said, as he was about to ascend from the mount, to his disciples, "Go ye into all the world and preach my gospel to every creature, he that believeth and is baptized shall be saved."

I have now passed through the account of my conviction, and also of my con-version to God; and shall next speak of the blessing of sanctification.

A time after I had received forgiveness flowed sweetly on; day and night my joy was full, no temptation was permitted to molest me. I could say continually with the psalmist, that "God had separated my sin from me, as far as the east is from the west." I was ready continually to cry,

> "Come all the world, come sinner thou,
> All things in Christ are ready now."

I continued in this happy state of mind for almost three months, when a cer-tain coloured man, by name William Scott, came to pay me a religious visit. He had been for many years a faithful follower of the Lamb; and he had also taken much time in visiting the sick and distressed of our colour, and understood well the great things belonging to a man of full stature in Christ Jesus.

In the course of our conversation, he inquired if the Lord had justified my soul. I answered, yes. He then asked me if he had sanctified me. I answered, no; and that I did not know what that was. He then undertook to instruct me further in the knowledge of the Lord respecting this blessing.

He told me the progress of the soul from a state of darkness, or of nature, was three-fold; or consisted in three degrees, as follows:—First, conviction for sin. Second, justification from sin. Third, the entire sanctification of the soul to God. I thought this description was beautiful, and immediately believed in it. He then inquired if I would promise to pray for this in my secret devotions. I told him, yes. Very soon I began to call upon the Lord to show me all that was in my heart, which was not according to his will. Now there appeared to be a new struggle commencing in my soul, not accompanied with fear, guilt, and bitter distress, as while under my first conviction for sin; but a labouring of the mind to know more of the right way of the Lord. I began now to feel that my heart was not clean in his sight; that there yet remained the roots of bitterness, which if not destroyed, would ere long sprout up from these roots, and overwhelm me in a new growth of the brambles and brushwood of sin.

By the increasing light of the Spirit, I had found there yet remained the root of pride, anger, self-will, with many evils, the result of fallen nature. I now became alarmed at this discovery, and began to fear that I had been deceived in my experience. I was now greatly alarmed, lest I should fall away from what I knew I had enjoyed; and to guard against this I prayed almost incessantly, without acting faith on the power and promises of God to keep me from falling. I had not yet learned how to war against temptation of this kind. Satan well knew that if he could succeed in making me disbelieve my conversion, that he would catch me either on the ground of complete despair, or on the ground of infidelity. For if all I had passed through was to go for nothing, and was but a fiction, the mere ravings of a disordered mind, that I would naturally be led to believe that there is nothing in religion at all.

From this snare I was mercifully preserved, and led to believe that there was yet a greater work than that of pardon to be wrought in me. I retired to a secret place, (after having sought this blessing, as well as I could, for nearly three months, from the time brother Scott had instructed me respecting it,) for prayer, about four o'clock in the afternoon. I had struggled long and hard, but found not the desire of my heart. When I rose from my knees, there seemed a voice speaking to me, as I yet stood in a leaning posture—"Ask for sanctification." When to my surprise, I recollected that I had not even thought of it in my whole prayer. It would seem Satan had hidden the very object from my mind, for which I had purposely kneeled to pray.

But when this voice whispered in my heart, saying, "Pray for sanctification," I again bowed in the same place, at the same time, and said, "Lord *sanctify* my soul for Christ's sake?" That very instant, as if lightning had darted through me, I sprang to my feet, and cried, "The Lord has sanctified my soul!" There was none to hear this but the angels who stood around to witness my joy—and Satan, whose malice raged the more. That Satan was there, I knew for no sooner had I cried out "The Lord has sanctified my soul," than there seemed another voice behind me, saying, "No, it is too great a work to be done." But another spirit said, "Bow down for the witness—I received it—*thou art sanctified!*" The first I knew of myself after that, I was standing in the yard with my hands spread out, and looking with my face toward heaven.

I now ran into the house and told them what had happened to me, when, as it were, a new rush of the same ecstasy came upon me, and caused me to feel as if I were in an ocean of light and bliss.

During this, I stood perfectly still, the tears rolling in a flood from my eyes. So great was the joy, that it is past description. There is no language that can describe it, except that which was heard by St. Paul, when he was caught up to the third heaven, and heard words which it was not lawful to utter.

My Call To Preach The Gospel.

Between four and five years after my sanctification, on a certain time, an impressive silence fell upon me, and I stood as if some one was about to speak to me, yet I had no such thought in my heart. But to my utter surprise there seemed to sound a voice which I thought I distinctly heard, and most certainly understood, which said to me, "Go preach the Gospel!" I immediately replied aloud, "No one will believe me." Again I listened, and again the same voice seemed to say—"Preach the Gospel; I will put words in your mouth, and will turn your enemies to become your friends."

At first I supposed that Satan had spoken to me, for I had read that he could transform himself into an angel of light, for the purpose of deception. Immediately I went into a secret place, and called upon the Lord to know if he had called me to preach, and whether I was deceived or not; when there appeared to my view the form and figure of a pulpit, with a Bible lying thereon; the back of which was presented to me as plainly as if it had been a literal fact.

In consequence of this, my mind became so exercised, that during the night following, I took a text, and preached in my sleep. I thought there stood before me a great multitude, while I expounded to them the things of religion. So violent were my exertions, and so loud were my exclamations, that I awoke from the sound of my own voice, which also awoke the family of the house where I resided. Two days after, I went to see the preacher in charge of the African Society, who was the Rev. Richard Allen, the same before named in these pages, to tell him that I felt it my duty to preach the gospel. But as I drew near the street in which his house was, which was in the city of Philadelphia, my courage began to fail me; so terrible did the cross appear, it seemed that I should not be able to bear it. Previous to my setting out to go to see him, so agitated was my mind, that my appetite for my daily food failed me entirely. Several times on my way there, I turned back again; but as often I felt my strength again renewed, and I soon found that the nearer I approached to the house of the minister, the less was my fear. Accordingly, as soon as I came to the door, my fears subsided, the cross was removed, all things appeared pleasant–I was tranquil.

I now told him, that the Lord had revealed it to me, that I must preach the gospel. He replied, by asking, in what sphere I wished to move in? I said, among the Methodists. He then replied, that a Mrs. Cook, a Methodist lady, had also some time before requested the same privilege; who it was believed, had done much good in the way of exhortation, and holding prayer meetings; and who had been permitted to do so by the verbal license of the preacher in charge at the time. But as to women preaching, he said that our Discipline knew nothing at all about it—that it did not call for women preachers. This I was glad to hear, because it removed the fear of the cross—but not no sooner did this feeling cross my mind, than I found that a love of souls had in a measure departed from me; that holy energy which burned within me, as a fire, began to be smothered. This I soon perceived.

O how careful ought we to be, lest through our by-laws of church government and discipline, we bring into disrepute even the word of life. For as unseemly as it may appear now-a-days for a woman to preach, it should be remembered that nothing is impossible with God. And why should it be thought impossible, heterodox, or improper for a woman to preach? seeing the Saviour died for the woman as well as the man.

If the man may preach, because the Saviour died for him, why not the woman? seeing he died for her also. Is he not a whole Saviour, instead of a half one? as those who hold it wrong for a woman to preach, would seem to make it appear.

Did not Mary *first* preach the risen Saviour, and is not the doctrine of the resurrection the very climax of Christianity—hangs not all our hope on this, as argued by St. Paul? Then did not Mary, a woman, preach the gospel? for she preached the resurrection of the crucified Son of God.

But some will say, that Mary did not expound the Scripture, therefore, she did not preach, in the proper sense of the term. To this I reply, it may be that the term *preach*, in those primitive times, did not mean exactly what it is now *made* to mean; perhaps it was a great deal more simple then, than it is now:—if it were not, the unlearned fishermen could not have preached the gospel at all, as they had no learning.

To this it may be replied, by those who are determined not to believe that it is right for a woman to preach, that the disciples, though they were fishermen, and ignorant of letters too, were inspired so to do. To which I would reply, that though they were inspired, yet that inspiration did not save them from showing their ignorance of letters, and of man's wisdom; this the multitude soon found out, by listening to the remarks of the envious Jewish priests. If then, to preach the gospel by the gift of heaven, comes by inspiration solely, is God straitened; must he take the man exclusively? May he not, did he not, and can he not inspire a female to preach the simple story of the birth, life, death, and resurrection of our Lord, and accompany it too, with power to the sinner's heart. As for me, I am fully persuaded that the Lord called me to labour according to what I have received, in his vineyard. If he has not, how could he consistently bear testimony in favour of my poor labours, in awakening and converting sinners?

In my wanderings up and down among men, preaching according to my ability, I have frequently found families who told me that they had not for several years been to a meeting, and yet, while listening to hear what God would say by his poor coloured female instrument, have believed with trembling—tears rolling down their cheeks, the signs of contrition and repentance towards God. I firmly believe that I have sown seed, in the name of the Lord, which shall appear with its increase at the great day of accounts, when Christ shall come to make up his jewels.

At a certain time, I was beset with the idea, that soon or late I should fall from grace, and lose my soul at last. I was frequently called to the throne of grace about this matter, but found no relief; the temptation pursued me still. Being more and more afflicted with it, till at a certain time when the spirit strongly impressed it on my mind to enter into my closet, and carry my case once more to the Lord; the Lord enabled me to draw nigh to him, and to his mercy seat, at this time, in an extraordinary manner; for while I wrestled with him for the victory over this disposition to doubt whether I should persevere, there appeared a form of fire, about the size of a man's hand, as I was on my knees; at the same moment, there appeared to the eye of faith a man robed in a white garment, from the shoulders down to the feet; from him a voice proceeded, saying: "Thou shalt never return from the cross." Since that time I have never doubted, but believe that God will keep me until the day of redemption. Now I could adopt the very language of St. Paul, and say that nothing could have separated my soul from the love of God, which is in Christ Jesus. From that time, 1807, until the present, 1833, I have not yet doubted the power and goodness of God to keep me from falling, through sanctification of the spirit and belief of the truth.

My Marriage

In the year 1811, I changed my situation in life, having married Mr. Joseph Lee, Pastor of a Coloured Society at Snow Hill, about six miles from the city of Philadelphia. It became necessary therefore for me to remove. This was a great trial at first, as I knew no person at Snow Hill, except my husband; and to leave my associates in the society, and especially those who composed the *band* of which I was one. Not but those who have been in sweet fellowship with such as really love God, and have together drank bliss and happiness from the same fountain, can tell how dear such company is, and how hard it is to part from them.

At Snow Hill, as was feared, I never found that agreement and closeness in communion and fellowship, that I had in Philadelphia, among my young companions, nor ought I to have expected it. The manners and customs at this place were somewhat different, on which account I became discontented in the course of a year, and began to importune my husband to remove to the city. But this plan did not suit him, as he was the Pastor of the Society, he could not bring his mind to leave them. This afflicted me a little. But the Lord soon showed me in a dream what his will was concerning this matter.

I dreamed that as I was walking on the summit of a beautiful hill, that I saw near me a flock of sheep, fair and white, as if but newly washed; when there came walking toward me, a man of a grave and dignified countenance, dressed entirely in white, as it were in a robe, and looking at me, said emphatically, "Joseph Lee must take care of these sheep, or the wolf will come and devour them." When I awoke, I was convinced of my error, and immediately, with a glad heart, yielded to the right way of the Lord. This also greatly strengthened my husband in his care over them, for fear the wolf should by some means take any of them away. The following verse was beautifully suited to our condition, as well as to all the little flocks of God scattered up and down this land:

"Us into Thy protection take,
And gather with Thine arm;
Unless the fold we first forsake,
The wolf can never harm."

After this, I fell into a state of general debility, and in an ill state of health, so much so, that I could not sit up; but a desire to warn sinners to flee the wrath to come, burned vehemently in my heart, when the Lord would send sinners into the house to see me. Such opportunities I embraced to press home on their consciences the things of eternity, and so effectual was the word of exhortation made through the Spirit, that I have seen them fall to the floor crying aloud for mercy.

From this sickness I did not expect to recover, and there was but one thing which bound me to earth, and this was, that I had not yet preached the gospel to the fallen sons and daughters of Adam's race, to the satisfaction of my mind. I wished to go from one end of the earth to the other, crying, Behold, behold the Lamb! To this end I earnestly prayed the Lord to raise me up, if consistent with his will. He condescended to hear my prayer, and give me a token in a dream, that in due time I should recover my health. The dream was as follows: I thought I saw the sun rise in the morning, and ascend to an altitude of about half an hour high, and then become obscured by a dense black cloud, which continued to hide its rays for about one third part of the day, and then it burst forth again with renewed splendour.

This dream I interpreted to signify my early life, my conversion to God, and this sickness, which was a great affliction, as it hindered me, and I feared would forever hinder me from preaching the gospel, was signified by the cloud; and the bursting forth of the sun, again, was the recovery of my health, and being permitted to preach.

I went to the throne of grace on this subject, where the Lord made this impressive reply in my heart, while on my knees: "You shall be restored to thy health again, and worship God in full purpose of heart."

This manifestation was so impressive, that I could but hide my face, as if some one was gazing upon me, to think of the great goodness of the Almighty God to my poor soul and body. From that very time I began to gain strength of body and mind, glory to God in the highest, until my health was fully recovered.

For six years from this time I continued to receive from above, such baptisms of the Spirit as mortality could scarcely bear. About that time I was called to suffer in my family, by death—five, in the course of about six years, fell by his hand; my husband being one of the number, which was the greatest affliction of all.

I was now left alone in the world, with two infant children, one of the age of about two years, the other six months, with no other dependance than the promise of Him who hath said—I will be the widow's God, and a father to the fatherless. Accordingly, he raised me up friends, whose liberality comforted and solaced me in my state of widowhood and sorrows. I could sing with the greatest propriety the words of the poet;

"He helps the stranger in distress,
The widow and the fatherless, And grants the prisoner sweet release."

I can say even now, with the Psalmist, "Once I was young, but now I am old, yet I have never seen the righteous forsaken, nor his seed begging bread." I have ever been fed by his bounty, clothed by his mercy, comforted and healed when sick, succoured when tempted, and every where upheld by his hand.

The Subject of My Call to Preach Renewed.

It was now eight years since I had made application to be permitted to preach the gospel, during which time I had only been allowed to exhort, and even this privilege but seldom. This subject now was renewed afresh in my mind; it was as a fire shut up in my bones. About thirteen months passed on, while under this renewed impression. During this time, I had solicited of the Rev. Bishop Richard Allen, who at this time had become Bishop of the African Episcopal Methodists in America, to be permitted the liberty of holding prayer meetings in my own hired house, and of exhorting as I found liberty, which was granted me. By this means, my mind was relieved, as the house was soon filled when the hour appointed for prayer had arrived.

I cannot but relate in this place, before I proceed further with the above subject, the singular conversion of a very wicked young man. He was a coloured man, who had generally attended our meetings, but not for any good purpose; but rather to disturb and to ridicule our denomination. He openly and uniformly declared that he neither believed in religion, nor wanted any thing to do with it. He was of a Gallio disposition, and took the lead among the young people of colour. But after a while he fell sick, and lay about three months in a state of ill health. His disease was a consumption. Toward the close of his days, his sister who was a member of the society, came and desired me to go and see her brother, as she had no hopes of his recovery, perhaps the Lord might break into his mind. I went alone, and found him very low. I soon commenced to inquire respecting his state of feeling, and how he found his mind. His answer was, "O tolerable well," with an air of great indifference. I asked him if I should pray for him. He answered in a sluggish and careless manner, "O yes, if you have time." I then sung a hymn, kneeled down and prayed for him, and then went my way.

Three days after this, I went again to visit the young man. At this time there went with me two of the sisters in Christ. We found the Rev. Mr. Cornish, of our denomination, labouring with him. But he said he received but little satisfaction from him. Pretty soon, however, brother Cornish took his leave; when myself, with the other two sisters, one of which was an elderly woman named Jane Hutt, the other was younger, both coloured, commenced conversing with him, respecting his eternal interest, and of his hopes of a happy eternity, if any be had. He said but little; we then kneeled down together and besought the Lord in his behalf, praying that if mercy were not clear gone forever, to shed a ray of softening grace upon the hardness of his heart. He appeared now to be somewhat more tender, and we thought we could perceive some tokens of conviction, as he wished us to visit him again, in a tone of voice not quite as indifferent as he had hitherto manifested.

But two days had elapsed after this visit, when his sister came to me in haste, saying, that she believed her brother was then dying, and that he had sent for me. I immediately called on Jane Hutt, who was still among us as a mother in Israel, to go with me. When we arrived there, we found him sitting up in his bed, very restless and uneasy, but he soon laid down again. He now wished me to come to him, by the side of his bed. I asked him how he was. He said, Very ill; and added, "Pray for me, quick?" We now perceived his time in this world to be short. I took up the hymn-book, and opened to a hymn suitable to his case, and commenced to sing. But there seemed to be a *horror* in the room—a darkness of a mental kind, which was felt by us all; there being five persons, except the sick young man and his nurse. We had sung but one verse, when they all gave over singing, on account of this unearthly sensation, but myself. I continued to sing on alone, but in a dull and heavy manner, though looking up to God all the while for help. Suddenly, I felt a spring of energy awake in my heart, when darkness gave way in some degree. It was but a glimmer from above. When the hymn was finished, we all kneeled down to pray for him. While calling on the name of the Lord, to have mercy on his soul, and to grant him repentance unto life, it came suddenly into my mind never to rise from my knees until God should hear prayer in his behalf, until be should convert and save his soul.

Now, while I thus continued importuning heaven, as I felt I was led, a ray of light, more abundant, broke forth among us. There appeared to my view, though my eyes were closed, the Saviour in full stature, nailed to the cross, just over the head of the young man, against the ceiling of the room. I cried out, brother look up, the Saviour is come, he will pardon you, your sins he will forgive. My sorrow for the soul of the young man was gone; I could no longer pray—joy and rapture made it impossible. We rose up from our knees, when lo, his eyes were gazing with ecstasy upward; over his face there was an expression of joy; his lips were clothed in a sweet and holy smile; but no sound came from his tongue; it was heard in its stillness of bliss; full of hope and immortality. Thus, as I held him by the hand, his happy and purified soul soared away, without a sigh or a groan, to its eternal rest.

I now closed his eyes, straightened out his limbs, and left him to be dressed for the grave. But as for me, I was filled with the power of the Holy Ghost—the very room seemed filled with glory. His sister and all that were in the room rejoiced, nothing doubting but he had entered into Paradise; and I believe I shall see him at the last and great day, safe on the shores of salvation.

But to return to the subject of my call to preach. Soon after this, as above related, the Rev. Richard Williams was to preach at Bethel Church, where I with others were assembled. He entered the pulpit, gave out the hymn, which was sung, and than addressed the throne of grace; took his text, passed through the exordium, and commenced to expound it. The text he took is in Jonah 2d chap. 9th verse,—

"Salvation is of the Lord." But as he proceeded, to explain, he seemed to have, lost the spirit; when in the same instant, I sprang, as by an altogether supernatural impulse, to my feet, when I was aided from above to give an exhortation on the very text which my brother Williams had taken.

I told them that I was like Jonah; for it had been then nearly eight years since the Lord had called me to preach his gospel to the fallen sons and daughters of Adam's race, but that I had lingered like him, and delayed to go at the bidding of the Lord, and warn those who are as deeply guilty as were the people of Ninevah.

During the exhortation, God made manifest his power in a manner sufficient to show the world that I was called to labour according to my ability, and the grace given unto me, in the vineyard of the good husbandman.

I now sat down, scarcely knowing what I had done, being frightened. I imagined, that for this indecorum, as I feared it might be called; I should be expelled from the church. But instead of this, the Bishop rose up in the assembly, and related that I had called upon him eight years before, asking to be permitted to preach, and that he had put me off; but that he now as much believed that I was called to that work, as any of the preachers present. These remarks greatly strengthened me, so that my fears of having given an offense, and made myself liable as an offender, subsided, giving place to a sweet serenity, a holy joy of a peculiar kind, untasted in my bosom until then.

The next Sabbath day, while sitting under the word of the gospel, I felt moved to attempt to speak to the people in a public manner, but I could not bring my mind to attempt it in the church. I said, Lord, anywhere but here. Accordingly, there was a house not far off which was pointed out to me, to this I went. It was the house of a sister belonging to the same society with myself. Her name was Anderson. I told her I had come to hold a meeting in her house, if she would call in her neighbours. With this request she immediately complied. My congregation consisted of but five persons. I commenced by reading and singing a hymn, when I dropped to my knees by the side of a table to pray. When I arose I found my hand resting on the Bible, which I had not noticed till that moment. It now occurred to me to take a text. I opened the Scripture, as it happened, at 141st Psalm, fixing my eye on the 3d verse, which reads: "Set a watch, O Lord, before my mouth, keep the door of my lips." My sermon, such as it was, I applied wholly to myself, and added an exhortation. Two of my congregation wept much, as the fruit of my labour this time. In closing, I said to the few, that if any one would open a door, I would hold a meeting the next sixth-day evening; when one answered that her house was at my service. Accordingly I went, and God made manifest his power among the people. Some wept, while others shouted for joy. One whole seat of females, by the power of God, as the rushing of a wind, were all bowed to the floor at once, and screamed out. Also a sick man and woman in one house, the Lord convicted them both; one lived, and the other

died. God wrought a judgment—some were well at night, and died in the morning. At this place I continued to hold meetings about six months. During that time
I kept house with my little son, who was very sickly. About this time I had a call to
preach at a place about thirty miles distant, among the Methodists, with whom I
remained one week, and during the whole time, not a thought of my little son came
into my mind; it was hid from me, lest I should have been diverted from the work
I had to do, to look after my son. Here by the instrumentality of a poor coloured
woman, the Lord poured forth his spirit among the people. Though, as I was told,
there were lawyers, doctors, and magistrates present, to hear me speak, yet there was
mourning and crying among sinners, for the Lord scattered fire among them of his
own kindling. The Lord gave his hand maiden power to speak for his great name,
for he arrested the hearts of the people, and caused a shaking amongst the multitude, for God was in the midst.

I now returned home, found all well; no harm had come to my child, although
I left it very sick. Friends had taken care of it which was of the Lord. I now began
to think seriously of breaking up housekeeping, and forsaking all to preach the everlasting Gospel. I felt a strong define to return to the place of my nativity, at Cape
May, after an absence of about fourteen years. To this place, where the heaviest cross
was to be met with, the Lord sent me, as Saul of Tarsus was sent to Jerusalem, to
preach the same gospel which he had neglected and despised before his conversion.
I went by water, and on my passage was much distressed by sea sickness, so much
so that I expected to have died, but such was not the will of the Lord respecting me.
After I had disembarked, I proceeded on as opportunities offered, toward where my
mother lived. When within ten miles of that place, I appointed an evening meeting. There were a goodly number came out to hear. The Lord was pleased to give
me light and liberty among the people. After meeting, there came an elderly lady
to me and said, she believed the Lord had sent me among them; she then appointed me another meeting there two weeks from that night. The next day I hastened
forward to the place of my mother, who was happy to see me, and the happiness
was mutual between us. With her I left my poor sickly boy, while I departed to do
my Master's will. In this neighborhood I had an uncle, who was a Methodist, and
who gladly threw open his door for meetings to be held there. At the first meeting
which I held at my uncle's house, there was with others who had come from curiosity to hear the coloured woman preacher, an old man, who was a deist, and who said
he did not believe the coloured people had any souls—he was sure they had none.
He took a seat very near where I was standing, and boldly tried to look me out of
countenance. But as I laboured on in the best manner I was able, looking to God
all the while, though it seemed to me I had but little liberty, yet there went an arrow
from the bent bow of the gospel, and fastened in his [s]till then obdurate heart. After
I had done speaking, he went out, and called the people around him, said that my

preaching might seem a small thing, yet he believed I had the worth of souls at heart. This language was different from what it was a little time before, as he now seemed to admit that coloured people had souls, as it was to these I was chiefly speaking; and unless they had souls, whose good I had in view, his remark must have been without meaning. He now came into the house, and in the most friendly manner shook hands with me, saying, he hoped God had spared him to some good purpose. This man was a great slave holder, and had been very cruel, thinking nothing of knocking down a slave with a fence stake, or whatever might come to hand. From this time it was said of him that he became greatly altered in his ways for the better. At that time he was about seventy years old, his head as white as snow; but whether he became a converted man or not, I never heard.

The week following, I had an invitation to hold a meeting at the Court House of the County, when I spoke from the 53d chap. of Isaiah, 3d verse. It was a solemn time, and the Lord attended the word; I had life and liberty, though there were people there of various denominations. Here again I saw the aged slaveholder, who notwithstanding his age, walked about three miles to hear me. This day I spoke twice, and walked six miles to the place appointed. There was a magistrate present, who showed his friendship, by saying in a friendly manner, that he had heard of me: he handed me a hymnbook, pointing to a hymn which he had selected. When the meeting was over, he invited me to preach in a schoolhouse in his neighbourhood, about three miles distant from where I then was. During this meeting one back-slider was reclaimed. This day I walked six miles, and preached twice to large congregations, both in the morning and evening. The Lord was with me, glory be to his holy name. I next went six miles and held a meeting in a coloured friend's house, at eleven o'clock in the morning, and preached to a well behaved congregation of both coloured and white. After service I again walked back, which was in all twelve miles in the same day. This was on Sabbath, or as I sometimes call it, seventh-day; for after my conversion I preferred the plain language of the quakers. On fourth day, after this, in compliance with an invitation received by note, from the same magistrate who had heard me at the above place, I preached to a large congregation, where we had a precious time: much weeping was heard among the people. The same gentleman, now at the close of the meeting, gave out another appointment at the same place, that day week. Here again I had liberty, there was a move among the people. Ten years from that time, in the neighbourhood of Cape May, I held a prayer meeting in a school house, which was then the regular place of preaching for the Episcopal Methodists; after service, there came a white lady of the first distinction, a member of the Methodist Society, and told me that at the same schoolhouse, ten years before, under my preaching the Lord first awakened her. She rejoiced much to see me, and invited me home with her, where I staid till the next day. This was bread cast on the waters, seen after many days.

From this place I next went to Dennis Creek meeting house, where at the invitation of an elder, I spoke to a large congregation of various and conflicting sentiments, when a wonderful shock of God's power was felt, shown everywhere by groans, by sighs, and loud and happy amens. I felt as if aided from above. My tongue was cut loose, the stammerer spoke freely; the love of God, and of his service, burned with a vehement flame within me—his name was glorified among the people.

But here I felt myself constrained to give over, as from the smallness of this pamphlet I cannot go through with the whole of my journal, as it would probably make a volume of two hundred pages; which, if the Lord be willing, may at some future day be published. But for the satisfaction of such as may follow after me, when I am no more, I have recorded how the Lord called me to his work, and how he has kept me from falling from grace, as I feared I should. In all things he has proved himself a God of truth to me; and in his service I am now as much determined to spend and be spent, as at the very first. My ardour for the progress of his cause abates not a whit, so far as I am able to judge, though I am now something more than fifty years of age.

As to the nature of uncommon impressions, which the reader cannot but have noticed, and possibly sneered at in the course of these pages, they may be accounted for in this way: It is known that the blind have the sense of hearing in a manner much more acute than those who can see: also their sense of feeling is exceedingly fine, and is found to detect any roughness on the smoothest surface, where those who can see find none. So it may be with such as I am, who has never had more than three months schooling; and wishing to know much of the way and law of God, have therefore watched the more closely, the operations of the Spirit, and have in consequence been led thereby. But let it be remarked that I have never found that Spirit to lead me contrary to the Scriptures of truth, as I understand them. "For as many as are led by the Spirit of God are the sons of God."—Rom. Viii.14.

I have now only to say, May the blessing of the Father, and of the Son, and of the Holy Ghost, accompany the reading of this poor effort to speak well of his name, wherever it may be read. Amen.

FINIS

Further Reading

Braxton, Joanne M. *Black Women Writing Autobiography: A Tradition within a Tradition.* Philadelphia, PA: Temple University Press, 1989, pp. 54–60.

From: *Our Nig;*
or, *Sketches from the Life*
of a Free Black, in a Two-Story
White House, North, Showing That
Slavery's Shadows Fall even There.

By "Our Nig."

1859 | SHORT NOVEL

"I know That care has iron crowns for many brows;
That Calvaries are everywhere, whereon
Virtue is crucified, and nails and spears
Draw guiltless blood; that sorrow sits and drinks
At sweetest hearts, till all their life is dry;
That gentle spirits on the rack of pain
Grow faint or fierce, and pray and curse by turns;
That hell's temptations, clad in heavenly guise
And armed with might, lie evermore in wait
Along life's path, giving assault to all."

HOLLAND.

BOSTON: PRINTED BY GEO. C. RAND & AVERY. 1859.

Chapter I. Mag Smith, My Mother.

Oh, Grief beyond all other griefs, when fate
First leaves the young heart lone and desolate
In the wide world, without that only tie
For which it loved to live or feared to die;
Lorn as the hung-up lute, that ne'er hath spoken
Since the sad day its master-chord was broken!

MOORE.

LONELY MAG SMITH! See her as she walks with downcast eyes and heavy heart. It was not always thus. She *had* a loving, trusting heart. Early deprived of parental guardianship, far removed from relatives, she was left to guide her tiny boat over life's surges alone and inexperienced. As she merged into womanhood, unprotected, uncherished, uncared for, there fell on her ear the music of love, awakening an intensity of emotion long dormant. It whispered of an elevation before unaspired to; of ease and plenty her simple heart had never dreamed of as hers. She knew the voice of her charmer, so ravishing, sounded far above her. It seemed like an angel's, alluring her upward and onward. She thought she could ascend to him and become an equal. She surrendered to him a priceless gem, which he proudly garnered as a trophy, with those of other victims, and left her to her fate. The world seemed full of hateful deceivers and crushing arrogance. Conscious that the great bond of union to her former companions was severed, that the disdain of others would be insupportable, she determined to leave the few friends she possessed, and seek an asylum among strangers. Her offspring came unwelcomed, and before its nativity numbered weeks, it passed from earth, ascending to a purer and better life.

"God be thanked," ejaculated Mag, as she saw its breathing cease; "no one can taunt *her* with my ruin."

Blessed release! may we all respond. How many pure, innocent children not only inherit a wicked heart of their own, claiming life-long scrutiny and restraint, but are heirs also of parental disgrace and calumny, from which only long years of patient endurance in paths of rectitude can disencumber them.

Mag's new home was soon contaminated by the publicity of her fall; she had a feeling of degradation oppressing her; but she resolved to be circumspect, and try regain in a measure what she had lost. Then some foul tongue would jest of her shame, and averted looks and cold greetings disheartened her. She saw she could not bury in forgetfulness her misdeed, so she resolved to leave her home and seek another in the place she at first fled from.

Alas, how fearful are we to be first in extending a helping hand to those who stagger in the mires of infamy; to speak the first words of hope and warning to those emerging into the sunlight of morality! Who can tell what numbers, advancing just far enough to hear a cold welcome and join in the reserved converse of professed reformers, disappointed, disheartened, have chosen to dwell in unclean places, rather than encounter these "holier-than-thou" of the great brotherhood of man!

Such was Mag's experience; and disdaining to ask favor or friendship from a sneering world, she resolved to shut herself up in a hovel she had often passed in better days, and which she knew to be untenanted. She vowed to ask no favors of familiar faces; to die neglected and forgotten before she would be dependent on any. Removed from the village, she was seldom seen except as upon your introduction, gentle reader, with downcast visage, returning her work to her employer, and thus providing herself with the means of subsistence. In two years many hands craved the same avocation; foreigners who cheapened toil and clamored for a livelihood, competed with her, and she could not thus sustain herself. She was now above no drudgery. Occasionally old acquaintances called to be favored with help of some kind, which she was glad to bestow for the sake of the money it would bring her; but the association with them was such a painful reminder of by-gones, she returned to her hut morose and revengeful, refusing all offers of a better home than she possessed. Thus she lived for years, hugging her wrongs, but making no effort to escape. She had never known plenty, scarcely competency; but the present was beyond comparison with those innocent years when the coronet of virtue was hers.

Every year her melancholy increased, her means diminished. At last no one seemed to notice her, save a kind-hearted African, who often called to inquire after her health and to see if she needed any fuel, he having the responsibility of furnishing that article, and she in return mending or making garments.

"How much you earn dis week, Mag?" asked he one Saturday evening.

"Little enough, Jim. Two or three days without any dinner. I washed for the Reeds, and did a small job for Mrs. Bellmont; that's all. I shall starve soon, unless I can get more to do. Folks seem as afraid to come here as if they expected to get some awful disease. I do n't believe there is a person in the world but would be glad to have me dead and out of the way."

"No, no, Mag! do n't talk so. You shan't starve so long as I have barrels to hoop. Peter Greene boards me cheap. I'll help you, if nobody else will."

A tear stood in Mag's faded eye. "I'm glad," she said, with a softer tone than before, "if there is *one* who isn't glad to see me suffer. I b'lieve all Singleton wants to see me punished, and feel as if they could tell when I've been punished long enough. It's a long day ahead they'll set it, I reckon."

After the usual supply of fuel was prepared, Jim returned home. Full of pity for Mag, he set about devising measures for her relief. "By golly!" said he to himself one day—for he had become so absorbed in Mag's interest that he had fallen into a habit of musing aloud—"By golly! I wish she'd *marry* me."

"Who?" shouted Pete Greene, suddenly starting from an unobserved corner of the rude shop.

"Where you come from, you sly nigger!" exclaimed Jim.

"Come, tell me, who is't?" said Pete; "Mag Smith, you want to marry?"

"Git out, Pete! and when you come in dis shop again, let a nigger know it. Don't steal in like a thief."

Pity and love know little severance. One attends the other. Jim acknowledged the presence of the former, and his efforts in Mag's behalf told also of a finer principle.

This sudden expedient which he had unintentionally disclosed, roused his thinking and inventive powers to study upon the best method of introducing the subject to Mag.

He belted his barrels, with many a scheme revolving in his mind, none of which quite satisfied him, or seemed, on the whole, expedient. He thought of the pleasing contrast between her fair face and his own dark skin; the smooth, straight hair, which he had once, in expression of pity, kindly stroked on her now wrinkled but once fair brow. There was a tempest gathering in his heart, and at last, to ease his pent-up passion, he exclaimed aloud, "By golly!" Recollecting his former exposure, he glanced around to see if Pete was in hearing again. Satisfied on this point, he continued: "She'd be as much of a prize to me as she'd fall short of coming up to the mark with white folks. I don't care for past things. I've done things 'fore now I's 'shamed of. She's good enough for me, any how."

One more glance about the premises to be sure Pete was away.

The next Saturday night brought Jim to the hovel again. The cold was fast coming to tarry its apportioned time. Mag was nearly despairing of meeting its rigor.

"How's the wood, Mag?" asked Jim.

"All gone; and no more to cut, any how," was the reply.

"Too bad!" Jim said. His truthful reply would have been, I'm glad.

"Anything to eat in the house?" continued he.

"No," replied Mag.

"Too bad!" again, orally, with the same *inward* gratulation as before.

"Well, Mag," said Jim, after a short pause, "you's down low enough. I don't see but I've got to take care of ye. 'Sposin' we marry!"

Mag raised her eyes, full of amazement, and uttered a sonorous "What?"

Jim felt abashed for a moment. He knew well what were her objections.

"You's had trial of white folks any how. They run off and left ye, and now none of 'em come near ye to see if you's dead or alive. I's black outside, I know, but I's got a white heart inside. Which you rather have, a black heart in a white skin, or a white heart in a black one?"

"Oh, dear!" sighed Mag; "Nobody on earth cares for *me*—"

"I do," interrupted Jim.

"I can do but two things," said she, "beg my living, or get it from you."

"Take me, Mag. I can give you a better home than this, and not let you suffer so."

He prevailed; they married. You can philosophize, gentle reader, upon the impropriety of such unions, and preach dozens of sermons on the evils of amalgamation. Want is a more powerful philosopher and preacher. Poor Mag. She has sundered another bond which held her to her fellows. She has descended another step down the ladder of infamy.

Chapter II. My Father's Death.

> Misery! we have known each other,
> Like a sister and a brother,
> Living in the same lone home
> Many years—we must live some
> Hours or ages yet to come.
>
> SHELLEY

JIM, proud of his treasure,—a white wife,—tried hard to fulfil his promises; and furnished her with a more comfortable dwelling, diet, and apparel. It was comparatively a comfortable winter she passed after her marriage. When Jim could work, all went on well. Industrious, and fond of Mag, he was determined she should not regret her union to him. Time levied an additional charge upon him, in the form of two pretty mulattos, whose infantile pranks amply repaid the additional toil. A few years, and a severe cough and pain in his side compelled him to be an idler for weeks together, and Mag had thus a reminder of by-gones. She cared for him only as a means to subserve her own comfort; yet she nursed him faithfully and true to marriage vows till death released her. He became the victim of consumption. He loved Mag to the last. So long as life continued, he stifled his sensibility to pain, and toiled for her sustenance long after he was able to do so.

A few expressive wishes for her welfare; a hope of better days for her; an anxiety lest they should not all go to the "good place;" brief advice about their children; a hope expressed that Mag would not be neglected as she used to be; the manifestation of Christian patience; these were *all* the legacy of miserable Mag. A feeling of cold desolation came over her, as she turned from the grave of one who had been truly faithful to her.

She was now expelled from companionship with white people; this last step— her union with a black—was the climax of repulsion.

Seth Shipley, a partner in Jim's business, wished her to remain in her present home; but she declined, and returned to her hovel again, with obstacles threefold more insurmountable than before. Seth accompanied her, giving her a weekly allowance which furnished most of the food necessary for the four inmates. After a time, work failed; their means were reduced.

How Mag toiled and suffered, yielding to fits of desperation, bursts of anger, and uttering curses too fearful to repeat. When both were supplied with work, they prospered; if idle, they were hungry together. In this way their interests became united; they planned for the future together. Mag had lived an outcast for years. She had ceased to feel the gushings of penitence; she had crushed the sharp agonies of an awakened conscience. She had no longings for a purer heart, a better life. Far easier to descend lower. She entered the darkness of perpetual infamy. She asked not the rite of civilization or Christianity. Her will made her the wife of Seth. Soon followed scenes familiar and trying.

"It's no use," said Seth one day; "we must give the children away, and try to get work in some other place."

"Who'll take the black devils?" snarled Mag.

"They're none of mine," said Seth; "what you growling about?"

"Nobody will want any thing of mine, or yours either," she replied. "We'll make 'em, p'r'aps," he said. "There's Frado's six years old, and pretty, if she is yours, and white folks'll say so. She'd be a prize somewhere," he continued, tipping his chair back against the wall, and placing his feet upon the rounds, as if he had much more to say when in the right position.

Frado, as they called one of Mag's children, was a beautiful mulatto, with long, curly black hair, and handsome, roguish eyes, sparkling with an exuberance of spirit almost beyond restraint.

Hearing her name mentioned, she looked up from her play, to see what Seth had to say of her.

"Wouldn't the Bellmonts take her?" asked Seth.

"Bellmonts?" shouted Mag. "His wife is a right she-devil! and if—"

"Hadn't they better be all together?" interrupted Seth, reminding her of a like epithet used in reference to her little ones.

Without seeming to notice him, she continued, "She can't keep a girl in the house over a week; and Mr. Bellmont wants to hire a boy to work for him, but he can't find one that will live in the house with her; she's so ugly, they can't."

"Well, we've got to make a move soon," answered Seth; "if you go with me, we shall go right off. Had you rather spare the other one?" asked Seth, after a short pause.

"One's as bad as t'other," replied Mag. "Frado is such a wild, frolicky thing, and means to do jest as she's a mind to; she won't go if she don't want to. I don't want to tell her she is to be given away."

"I will," said Seth. "Come here, Frado?"

The child seemed to have some dim foreshadowing of evil, and declined.

"Come here," he continued; "I want to tell you something."

She came reluctantly. He took her hand and said: "We're going to move, by-'-m-bye; will you go?"

"No!" screamed she; and giving a sudden jerk which destroyed Seth's equilibrium, left him sprawling on the floor, while she escaped through the open door.

"She's a hard one," said Seth, brushing his patched coat sleeve. "I'd risk her at Bellmonts."

They discussed the expediency of a speedy departure. Seth would first seek employment, and then return for Mag. They would take with them what they could carry, and leave the rest with Pete Greene, and come for them when they were wanted. They were long in arranging affairs satisfactorily, and were not a little startled at the close of their conference to find Frado missing. They thought approaching night would bring her. Twilight passed into darkness, and she did not come. They thought she had understood their plans, and had, perhaps, permanently withdrawn. They could not rest without making some effort to ascertain her retreat. Seth went in pursuit, and returned without her. They rallied others when they discovered that another little colored girl was missing, a favorite playmate of Frado's. All effort proved unavailing. Mag felt sure her fears were realized, and that she might never see her again. Before her anxieties became realities, both were safely returned, and from them and their attendant they learned that they went to walk, and not minding the direction soon found themselves lost. They had climbed fences and walls, passed through thickets and marshes, and when night approached selected a thick cluster of shrubbery as a covert for the night. They were discovered by the person who now restored them, chatting of their prospects, Frado attempting to banish the childish fears of her companion. As they were some miles from home, they were kindly cared for until morning. Mag was relieved to know her child was not driven to desperation by their intentions to relieve themselves of her, and she was inclined to think severe restraint would be healthful.

The removal was all arranged; the few days necessary for such migrations passed quickly, and one bright summer morning they bade farewell to their Singleton hovel, and with budgets and bundles commenced their weary march. As they neared the village, they heard the merry shouts of children gathered around the schoolroom, awaiting the coming of their teacher.

"Halloo!" screamed one, "Black, white and yeller!" "Black, white and yeller," echoed a dozen voices.

It did not grate so harshly on poor Mag as once it would. She did not even turn her head to look at them. She had passed into an insensibility no childish taunt could penetrate, else she would have reproached herself as she passed familiar scenes, for extending the separation once so easily annihilated by steadfast integrity. Two miles beyond lived the Bellmonts, in a large, old fashioned, two-story white house, environed by fruitful acres, and embellished by shrubbery and shade trees. Years ago a youthful couple consecrated it as home; and after many little feet had worn paths to favorite fruit trees, and over its green hills, and mingled at last with brother man in the race which belongs neither to the swift or strong, the sire became grey-haired and decrepit, and went to his last repose. His aged consort soon followed him. The old homestead thus passed into the hands of a son, to whose wife Mag had applied the epithet "she-devil," as may be remembered. John, the son, had not in his family arrangements departed from the example of the father. The pastimes of his boyhood were ever freshly revived by witnessing the games of his own sons as they rallied about the same goal his youthful feet had often won; as well as by the amusements of his daughters in their imitations of maternal duties.

At the time we introduce them, however, John is wearing the badge of age. Most of his children were from home; some seeking employment; some were already settled in homes of their own. A maiden sister shared with him the estate on which he resided, and occupied a portion of the house.

Within sight of the house, Seth seated himself with his bundles and the child he had been leading, while Mag walked onward to the house leading Frado. A knock at the door brought Mrs. Bellmont, and Mag asked if she would be willing to let that child stop there while she went to the Reed's house to wash, and when she came back she would call and get her. It seemed a novel request, but she consented.

Why the impetuous child entered the house, we cannot tell; the door closed, and Mag hastily departed. Frado waited for the close of day, which was to bring back her mother. Alas! it never came. It was the last time she ever saw or heard of her mother.

Chapter III. A New Home For Me

Oh! did we but know of the shadows so nigh,
The world would indeed be a prison of gloom;
All light would be quenched in youth's eloquent eye,
And the prayer-lisping infant would ask for the tomb.

For if Hope be a star that may lead us astray,
And "deceiveth the heart," as the aged ones preach;
Yet 'twas Mercy that gave it, to beacon our way,
Though its halo illumes where it never can reach.

ELIZA COOK.

AS the day closed and Mag did not appear, surmises were expressed by the family that she never intended to return. Mr. Bellmont was a kind, humane man, who would not grudge hospitality to the poorest wanderer, nor fail to sympathize with any sufferer, however humble. The child's desertion by her mother appealed to his symathy [sic], and he felt inclined to succor her. To do this in opposition to Mrs. Bellmont's wishes, would be like encountering a whirlwind charged with fire, daggers and spikes. She was not as susceptible of fine emotions as her spouse. Mag's opinion of her was not without foundation. She was self-willed, haughty, undisciplined, arbitrary and severe. In common parlance, she was a *scold*, a thorough one. Mr. B. remained silent during the consultation which follows, engaged in by mother, Mary and John, or Jack, as he was familiarly called.

"Send her to the County House," said Mary, in reply to the query what should be done with her, in a tone which indicated self-importance in the speaker. She was indeed the idol of her mother, and more nearly resembled her in disposition and manners than the others.

Jane, an invalid daughter, the eldest of those at home, was reclining on a sofa apparently uninterested.

"Keep her," said Jack. "She's real handsome and bright, and not very black, either."

"Yes," rejoined Mary; "that's just like you, Jack. She'll be of no use at all these three years, right under foot all the time."

"Poh! Miss Mary; if she should stay, it would n't be two days before you would be telling the girls about *our nig, our nig!*" retorted Jack.

"I don't want a nigger 'round *me*, do you, mother?" asked Mary.

"I do n't mind the nigger in the child. I should like a dozen better than one," replied her mother. "If I could make her do my work in a few years, I would keep her. I have so much trouble with girls I hire, I am almost persuaded if I have one to train up in my way from a child, I shall be able to keep them awhile. I am tired of changing every few months."

"Where could she sleep?" asked Mary. "I do n't want her near me."

"In the L chamber," answered the mother.

"How'll she get there?" asked Jack. "She'll be afraid to go through that dark passage, and she can't climb the ladder safely."

"She'll have to go there; it's good enough for a nigger," was the reply.

Jack was sent on horseback to ascertain if Mag was at her home. He returned with the testimony of Pete Greene that they were fairly departed, and that the child was intentionally thrust upon their family.

The imposition was not at all relished by Mrs. B., or the pert, haughty Mary, who had just glided into her teens.

"Show the child to bed, Jack," said his mother. "You seem most pleased with the little nigger, so you may introduce her to her room."

He went to the kitchen, and, taking Frado gently by the hand, told her he would put her in bed now; perhaps her mother would come the next night after her.

It was not yet quite dark, so they ascended the stairs without any light, passing through nicely furnished rooms, which were a source of great amazement to the child. He opened the door which connected with her room by a dark, unfinished passage-way. "Don't bump your head," said Jack, and stepped before to open the door leading into her apartment,—an unfinished chamber over the kitchen, the roof slanting nearly to the floor, so that the bed could stand only in the middle of the room. A small half window furnished light and air. Jack returned to the sitting room with the remark that the child would soon outgrow those quarters.

"When she *does*, she'll outgrow the house," remarked the mother.

"What can she do to help you?" asked Mary. "She came just in the right time, didn't she? Just the very day after Bridget left," continued she.

"I'll see what she can do in the morning," was the answer.

While this conversation was passing below, Frado lay, revolving in her little mind whether she would remain or not until her mother's return. She was of willful, determined nature, a stranger to fear, and would not hesitate to wander away should she decide to. She remembered the conversation of her mother with Seth, the words "given away" which she heard used in reference to herself; and though she did not know their full import, she thought she should, by remaining, be in some relation to white people she was never favored with before. So she resolved to tarry, with the hope that mother would come and get her some time. The hot sun had penetrated her room, and it was long before a cooling breeze reduced the temperature so that she could sleep.

Frado was called early in the morning by her new mistress. Her first work was to feed the hens. She was shown how it was *always* to be done, and in no other way; any departure from this rule to be punished by a whipping. She was then accompanied by Jack to drive the cows to pasture, so she might learn the way. Upon her return she was allowed to eat her breakfast, consisting of a bowl of skimmed milk, with brown bread crusts, which she was told to eat, standing, by the kitchen table, and must not be over ten minutes about it. Meanwhile the family were taking their morning meal in the dining-room. This over, she was placed on a cricket to wash the common dishes; she was to be in waiting always to bring wood and chips, to run hither and thither from room to room.

A large amount of dish-washing for small hands followed dinner. Then the same after tea and going after the cows finished her first day's work. It was a new discipline to the child. She found some attractions about the place, and she retired to rest at night more willing to remain. The same routine followed day after day, with slight variation; adding a little more work, and spicing the toil with "words that burn," and frequent blows on her head. These were great annoyances to Frado, and had she known where her mother was, she would have gone at once to her. She was often greatly wearied, and silently wept over her sad fate. At first she wept aloud, which Mrs. Bellmont noticed by applying a rawhide, always at hand in the kitchen. It was a symptom of discontent and complaining which must be "nipped in the bud," she said.

Thus passed a year. No intelligence of Mag. It was now certain Frado was to become a permanent member of the family. Her labors were multiplied; she was quite indispensable, although but seven years old. She had never learned to read, never heard of a school until her residence in the family.

Mrs. Bellmont was in doubt about the utility of attempting to educate people of color, who were incapable of elevation. This subject occasioned a lengthy discussion in the family. Mr. Bellmont, Jane and Jack arguing for Frado's education; Mary and her mother objecting. At last Mr. Bellmont declared decisively that she *should* go to school. He was a man who seldom decided controversies at home. The word once spoken admitted of no appeal; so, notwithstanding Mary's objection that she would have to attend the same school she did, the word became law.

It was to be a new scene to Frado, and Jack had many queries and conjectures to answer. He was himself too far advanced to attend the summer school, which Frado regretted, having had too many opportunities of witnessing Miss Mary's temper to feel safe in her company alone.

The opening day of school came. Frado sauntered on far in the rear of Mary, who was ashamed to be seen "walking with a nigger." As soon as she appeared, with scanty clothing and bared feet, the children assembled, noisily published her approach: "See that nigger," shouted one. "Look! look!" cried another. "I won't play with her," said one little girl. "Nor I neither," replied another.

Mary evidently relished these sharp attacks, and saw a fair prospect of lowering Nig where, according to her views, she belonged. Poor Frado, chagrined and grieved, felt that her anticipations of pleasure at such a place were far from being realized. She was just deciding to return home, and never come there again, when the teacher appeared, and observing the downcast looks of the child, took her by the hand, and led her into the school-room. All followed, and, after the bustle of securing seats was over, Miss Marsh inquired if the children knew "any cause for the sorrow of that little girl?" pointing to Frado. It was soon all told. She then reminded them of their duties to the poor and friendless; their cowardice in attacking a young innocent child; referred them to one who looks not on outward appearances, but on the heart. "She looks like a good girl; I think *I* shall love her, so lay aside all prejudice, and vie with each other in shewing kindness and good-will to one who seems different from you," were the closing remarks of the kind lady. Those kind words! The most agreeable sound which ever meets the ear of sorrowing, grieving childhood.

Example rendered her words efficacious. Day by day there was a manifest change of deportment towards "Nig." Her speeches often drew merriment from the children; no one could do more to enliven their favorite pastimes than Frado. Mary could not endure to see her thus noticed, yet knew not how to prevent it. She could not influence her schoolmates as she wished. She had not gained their affections by winning ways and yielding points of controversy. On the contrary, she was self-willed, domineering; every day reported "mad" by some of her companions. She availed herself of the only alternative, abuse and taunts, as they returned from school. This was not satisfactory; she wanted to use physical force "to subdue her," to "keep her down."

There was, on their way home, a field intersected by a stream over which a single plank was placed for a crossing. It occurred to Mary that it would be a punishment to Nig to compel her to cross over; so she dragged her to the edge, and told her authoritatively to go over. Nig hesitated, resisted. Mary placed herself behind the child, and, in the struggle to force her over, lost her footing and plunged into the stream. Some of the larger scholars being in sight, ran, and thus prevented Mary from drowning and Frado from falling. Nig scampered home fast as possible, and Mary went to the nearest house, dripping, to procure a change of garments. She came loitering home, half crying, exclaiming, "Nig pushed me into the stream!" She then related the particulars. Nig was called from the kitchen. Mary stood with anger flashing in her eyes. Mr. Bellmont sat quietly reading his paper. He had witnessed too many of Miss Mary's outbreaks to be startled. Mrs. Bellmont interrogated Nig.

"I did n't do it! I did n't do it!" answered Nig, passionately, and then related the occurrence truthfully.

The discrepancy greatly enraged Mrs. Bellmont. With loud accusations and angry gestures she approached the child. Turning to her husband, she asked,

"Will you sit still, there, and hear that black nigger call Mary a liar?"

"How do we know but she has told the truth? I shall not punish her," he replied, and left the house, as he usually did when a tempest threatened to envelop him. No sooner was he out of sight than Mrs. B. and Mary commenced beating her inhumanly; then propping her mouth open with a piece of wood, shut her up in a dark room, without any supper. For employment, while the tempest raged within, Mr. Bellmont went for the cows, a task belonging to Frado, and thus unintentionally prolonged her pain. At dark Jack came in, and seeing Mary, accosted her with, "So you thought you'd vent your spite on Nig, did you? Why can't you let her alone? It was good enough for you to get a ducking, only you did not stay in half long enough."

"Stop!" said his mother. "You shall never talk so before me. You would have that little nigger trample on Mary, would you? She came home with a lie; it made Mary's story false."

"What was Mary's story?" asked Jack.

It was related.

"Now," said Jack, sallying into a chair, "the school-children happened to see it all, and they tell the same story Nig does. Which is most likely to be true, what a dozen agree they saw, or the contrary?"

"It is very strange you will believe what others say against your sister," retorted his mother, with flashing eye. "I think it is time your father subdued you."

"Father is a sensible man," argued Jack. "He would not wrong a dog. Where *is* Frado?" he continued.

"Mother gave her a good whipping and shut her up," replied Mary.

Just then Mr. Bellmont entered, and asked if Frado was "shut up yet."

The knowledge of her innocence, the perfidy of his sister, worked fearfully on Jack. He bounded from his chair, searched every room till he found the child; her mouth wedged apart, her face swollen, and full of pain.

How Jack pitied her! He relieved her jaws, brought her some supper, took her to her room, comforted her as well as he knew how, sat by her till she fell asleep, and then left for the sitting room. As he passed his mother, he remarked, "If that was the way Frado was to be treated, he hoped she would never wake again!" He then imparted her situation to his father, who seemed untouched, till a glance at Jack exposed a tearful eye. Jack went early to her next morning. She awoke sad, but refreshed. After breakfast Jack took her with him to the field, and kept her through the day. But it could not be so generally. She must return to school, to her household duties. He resolved to do what he could to protect her from Mary and his mother. He bought her a dog, which became a great favorite with both. The invalid, Jane, would gladly befriend her; but she had not the strength to brave the iron will of her mother. Kind words and affectionate glances were the only expressions of sympathy she could safely indulge in. The men employed on the farm were always glad to hear her prattle; she was a great favorite with them. Mrs. Bellmont allowed them the privilege of talking with her in the kitchen. She did not fear but she should have ample opportunity of subduing her when they were away. Three months of schooling, summer and winter, she enjoyed for three years. Her winter over-dress was a cast-off overcoat, once worn by Jack, and a sun-bonnet. It was a source of great merriment to the scholars, but Nig's retorts were so mirthful, and their satisfaction so evident in attributing the selection to "Old Granny Bellmont," that it was not painful to Nig or pleasurable to Mary. Her jollity was not to be quenched by whipping or scolding. In Mrs. Bellmont's presence she was under restraint; but in the kitchen, and among her schoolmates, the pent up fires burst forth. She was ever at some sly prank when unseen by her teacher, in school hours; not unfrequently some outburst of merriment, of which she was the original, was charged upon some innocent mate, and punishment inflicted which she merited. They enjoyed her antics so fully that any of them would suffer wrongfully to keep open the avenues of mirth. She would venture far beyond propriety, thus shielded and countenanced.

The teacher's desk was supplied with drawers, in which were stored his books and other *et ceteras* of the profession. The children observed Nig very busy there one morning before school, as they flitted in occasionally from their play outside. The master came; called the children to order; opened a drawer to take the book the occasion required; when out poured a volume of smoke. "Fire! fire!" screamed he, at the top of his voice. By this time he had become sufficiently acquainted with the peculiar odor, to know he was imposed upon. The scholars shouted with laughter to see the terror of the dupe, who, feeling abashed at the needless fright, made no very strict investigation, and Nig once more escaped punishment. She had provided herself with cigars, and puffing, puffing away at the crack of the drawer, had filled it with smoke, and then closed it tightly to deceive the teacher, and amuse the scholars. The interim of terms was filled up with a variety of duties new and peculiar. At home, no matter how powerful the heat when sent to rake hay or guard the grazing herd, she was never permitted to shield her skin from the sun. She was not many shades darker than Mary now; what a calamity it would be ever to hear the contrast spoken of. Mrs. Bellmont was determined the sun should have full power to darken the shade which nature had first bestowed upon her as best befitting.

Chapter VII. Spiritual Condition Of Nig.

"What are our joys but dreams? and what our hopes But goodly shadows in the summer cloud?"

H. K. W.

JAMES did not improve as was hoped. Month after month passed away, and brought no prospect of returning health. He could not walk far from the house for want of strength; but he loved to sit with Aunt Abby in her quiet room, talking of unseen glories, and heart-experiences, while planning for the spiritual benefit of those around them. In these confidential interviews, Frado was never omitted. They would discuss the prevalent opinion of the public, that people of color are really inferior; incapable of cultivation and refinement. They would glance at the qualities of Nig, which promised so much if rightly directed. "I wish you would take her, James, when you are well, home with *you*," said Aunt Abby, in one of these seasons.

"Just what I am longing to do, Aunt Abby. Susan is just of my mind, and we intend to take her; I have been wishing to do so for years."

"She seems much affected by what she hears at the evening meetings, and asks me many questions on serious things; seems to love to read the Bible; I feel hopes of her."

"I hope she *is* thoughtful; no one has a kinder heart, one capable of loving more devotedly. But to think how prejudiced the world are towards her people; that she must be reared in such ignorance as to drown all the finer feelings. When I think of what she might be, of what she will be, I feel like grasping time till opinions change, and thousands like her rise into a noble freedom. I have seen Frado's grief, because she is black, amount to agony. It makes me sick to recall these scenes. Mother pretends to think she don't know enough to sorrow for anything; but if she could see her as I have, when she supposed herself entirely alone, except her little dog Fido, lamenting her loneliness and complexion, I think, if she is not past feeling, she would retract. In the summer I was walking near the barn, and as I stood I heard sobs. 'Oh! oh!' I heard, 'why was I made? why can't I die? Oh, what have I to live for? No one cares for me only to get my work. And I feel sick; who cares for that? Work as long as I can stand, and then fall down and lay there till I can get up. No mother, father, brother or sister to care for me, and then it is, You lazy nigger, lazy nigger—all because I am black! Oh, if I could die!'

"I stepped into the barn, where I could see her. She was crouched down by the hay with her faithful friend Fido, and as she ceased speaking, buried her face in her hands, and cried bitterly; then, patting Fido, she kissed him, saying, 'You love me, Fido, don't you? but we must go work in the field.' She started on her mission; I called her to me, and told her she need not go, the hay was doing well.

"She has such confidence in me that she will do just as I tell her; so we found a seat under a shady tree, and there I took the opportunity to combat the notions she seemed to entertain respecting the loneliness of her condition and want of sympathizing friends. I assured her that mother's views were by no means general; that in our part of the country there were thousands upon thousands who favored the elevation of her race, disapproving of oppression in all its forms; that she was not unpitied, friendless, and utterly despised; that she might hope for better things in the future. Having spoken these words of comfort, I rose with the resolution that if I recovered my health I would take her home with me, whether mother was willing or not."

"I do n't know what your mother would do without her; still, I wish she was away."

Susan now came for her long absent husband, and they returned home to their room.

The month of November was one of great anxiety on James's account. He was rapidly wasting away.

A celebrated physician was called, and performed a surgical operation, as a last means. Should this fail, there was no hope. Of course he was confined wholly to his room, mostly to his bed. With all his bodily suffering, all his anxiety for his family, whom he might not live to protect, he did not forget Frado. He shielded her from many beatings, and every day imparted religious instructions. No one, but his wife, could move him so easily as Frado; so that in addition to her daily toil she was often deprived of her rest at night.

Yet she insisted on being called; she wished to show her love for one who had been such a friend to her. Her anxiety and grief increased as the probabilities of his recovery became doubtful.

Mrs. Bellmont found her weeping on his account, shut her up, and whipped her with the raw-hide, adding an injunction never to be seen snivelling again because she had a little work to do. She was very careful never to shed tears on his account, in her presence, afterwards.

Chapter VIII. Visitor And Departure.

—"Other cares engross me, and my tired soul with emulative haste, Looks to its God."

THE brother associated with James in business, in Baltimore, was sent for to confer with one who might never be able to see him there.

James began to speak of life as closing; of heaven, as of a place in immediate prospect; of aspirations, which waited for fruition in glory. His brother, Lewis by name, was an especial favorite of sister Mary; more like her, in disposition and preferences than James or Jack.

He arrived as soon as possible after the request, and saw with regret the sure indications of fatality in his sick brother, and listened to his admonitions—admonitions to a Christian life—with tears, and uttered some promises of attention to the subject so dear to the heart of James.

How gladly he would have extended healing aid. But, alas! it was not in his power; so, after listening to his wishes and arrangements for his family and business, he decided to return home.

Anxious for company home, he persuaded his father and mother to permit Mary to attend him. She was not at all needed in the sick room; she did not choose to be useful in the kitchen, and then she was fully determined to go.

So all the trunks were assembled and crammed with the best selections from the wardrobe of herself and mother, where the last-mentioned articles could be appropriated.

"Nig was never so helpful before," Mary remarked, and wondered what had induced such a change in place of former sullenness.

Nig was looking further than the present, and congratulating herself upon some days of peace, for Mary never lost opportunity of informing her mother of Nig's delinquencies, were she otherwise ignorant.

Was it strange if she were officious, with such relief in prospect?

The parting from the sick brother was tearful and sad. James prayed in their presence for their renewal in holiness; and urged their immediate attention to eternal realities, and gained a promise that Susan and Charlie should share their kindest regards.

No sooner were they on their way, than Nig slyly crept round to Aunt Abby's room, and tip-toeing and twisting herself into all shapes, she exclaimed,—

"She's gone, Aunt Abby, she's gone, fairly gone;" and jumped up and down, till Aunt Abby feared she would attract the notice of her mistress by such demonstrations.

"Well, she's gone, gone, Aunt Abby. I hope she'll never come back again."

"No! no! Frado, that's wrong! you would be wishing her dead; that won't do."

"Well, I'll bet she'll never come back again; somehow, I feel as though she would n't."

"She is James's sister," remonstrated Aunt Abby.

"So is our cross sheep just as much, that I ducked in the river; I'd like to try my hand at curing *her* too."

"But you forget what our good minister told us last week, about doing good to those that hate us."

"Did n't I do good, Aunt Abby, when I washed and ironed and packed her old duds to get rid of her, and helped her pack her trunks, and run here and there for her?"

"Well, well, Frado; you must go finish your work, or your mistress will be after you, and remind you severely of Miss Mary, and some others beside."

Nig went as she was told, and her clear voice was heard as she went, singing in joyous notes the relief she felt at the removal of one of her tormentors.

Day by day the quiet of the sick man's room was increased. He was helpless and nervous; and often wished change of position, thereby hoping to gain momentary relief. The calls upon Frado were consequently more frequent, her nights less tranquil. Her health was impaired by lifting the sick man, and by drudgery in the kitchen. Her ill health she endeavored to conceal from James, fearing he might have less repose if there should be a change of attendants; and Mrs. Bellmont, she well knew, would have no sympathy for her. She was at last so much reduced as to be unable to stand erect for any great length of time. She would *sit* at the table to wash her dishes; if she heard the well-known step of her mistress, she would rise till she returned to her room, and then sink down for further rest. Of course she was longer than usual in completing the services assigned her. This was a subject of complaint to Mrs. Bellmont; and Frado endeavored to throw off all appearance of sickness in her presence.

But it was increasing upon her, and she could no longer hide her indisposition. Her mistress entered one day, and finding her seated, commanded her to go to work. "I am sick," replied Frado, rising and walking slowly to her unfinished task, "and cannot stand long, I feel so bad."

Angry that she should venture a reply to her command, she suddenly inflicted a blow which lay the tottering girl prostrate on the floor. Excited by so much indulgence of a dangerous passion, she seemed left to unrestrained malice; and snatching a towel, stuffed the mouth of the sufferer, and beat her cruelly.

Frado hoped she would end her misery by whipping her to death. She bore it with the hope of a martyr, that her misery would soon close. Though her mouth was muffled, and the sounds much stifled, there was a sensible commotion, which James' quick ear detected.

"Call Frado to come here," he said faintly, "I have not seen her to-day."

Susan retired with the request to the kitchen, where it was evident some brutal scene had just been enacted.

Mrs. Bellmont replied that she had "some work to do just now; when that was done, she might come."

Susan's appearance confirmed her husband's fears, and he requested his father, who sat by the bedside, to go for her. This was a messenger, as James well knew, who could not be denied; and the girl entered the room, sobbing and faint with anguish.

James called her to him, and inquired the cause of her sorrow. She was afraid to expose the cruel author of her misery, lest she should provoke new attacks. But after much entreaty, she told him all, much which had escaped his watchful ear. Poor James shut his eyes in silence, as if pained to forgetfulness by the recital. Then turning to Susan, he asked her to take Charlie, and walk out; "she needed the fresh air," he said. "And say to mother I wish Frado to sit by me till you return. I think you are fading, from staying so long in this sick room." Mr. B. also left, and Frado was thus left alone with her friend. Aunt Abby came in to make her daily visit, and seeing the sick countenance of the attendant, took her home with her to administer some cordial. She soon returned, however, and James kept her with him the rest of the day; and a comfortable night's repose following, she was enabled to continue, as usual, her labors. James insisted on her attending religious meetings in the vicinity with Aunt Abby.

Frado, under the instructions of Aunt Abby and the minister, became a believer in a future existence—one of happiness or misery. Her doubt was, *is* there a heaven for the black? She knew there was one for James, and Aunt Abby, and all good white people; but was there any for blacks? She had listened attentively to all the minister said, and all Aunt Abby had told her; but then it was all for white people.

As James approached that blessed world, she felt a strong desire to follow, and be with one who was such a dear, kind friend to her.

While she was exercised with these desires and aspirations, she attended an evening meeting with Aunt Abby, and the good man urged all, young or old, to accept the offers of mercy, to receive a compassionate Jesus as their Saviour. "Come to Christ," he urged, "all, young or old, white or black, bond or free, come all to Christ for pardon; repent, believe."

This was the message she longed to hear; it seemed to be spoken for her. But he had told them to repent; "what was that?" she asked. She knew she was unfit for any heaven, made for whites or blacks. She would gladly repent, or do anything which would admit her to share the abode of James.

Her anxiety increased; her countenance bore marks of solicitude unseen before; and though she said nothing of her inward contest, they all observed a change.

James and Aunt Abby hoped it was the springing of good seed sown by the Spirit of God. Her tearful attention at the last meeting encouraged his aunt to hope that her mind was awakened, her conscience aroused. Aunt Abby noticed that she was particularly engaged in reading the Bible; and this strengthened her conviction that a heavenly Messenger was striving with her. The neighbors dropped in to inquire after the sick, and also if Frado was "*serious?*" They noticed she seemed very thoughtful and tearful at the meetings. Mrs. Reed was very inquisitive; but Mrs. Bellmont saw no appearance of change for the better. She did not feel responsible for her spiritual culture, and hardly believed she had a soul.

Nig was in truth suffering much; her feelings were very intense on any subject, when once aroused. She read her Bible carefully, and as often as an opportunity presented, which was when entirely secluded in her own apartment, or by Aunt Abby's side, who kindly directed her to Christ, and instructed her in the way of salvation.

Mrs. Bellmont found her one day quietly reading her Bible. Amazed and half crediting the reports of officious neighbors, she felt it was time to interfere. Here she was, reading and shedding tears over the Bible. She ordered her to put up the book, and go to work, and not be snivelling about the house, or stop to read again.

But there was one little spot seldom penetrated by her mistress' watchful eye: this was her room, uninviting and comfortless; but to herself a safe retreat. Here she would listen to the pleadings of a Saviour, and try to penetrate the veil of doubt and sin which clouded her soul, and long to cast off the fetters of sin, and rise to the communion of saints.

Mrs. Bellmont, as we before said, did not trouble herself about the future destiny of her servant. If she did what she desired for *her* benefit, it was all the responsibility she acknowledged. But she seemed to have great aversion to the notice Nig would attract should she become pious. How could she meet this case? She resolved to make her complaint to John. Strange, when she was always foiled in this direction, she should resort to him. It was time something was done; she had begun to read the Bible openly.

The night of this discovery, as they were retiring, Mrs. Bellmont introduced the conversation, by saying:

"I want your attention to what I am going to say. I have let Nig go out to evening meetings a few times, and, if you will believe it, I found her reading the Bible to-day, just as though she expected to turn pious nigger, and preach to white folks. So now you see what good comes of sending her to school. If she should get converted she would have to go to meeting: at least, as long as James lives. I wish he had not such queer notions about her. It seems to trouble him to know he must die and

leave her. He says if he should get well he would take her home with him, or educate her here. Oh, how awful! What can the child mean? So careful, too, of her! He
says we shall ruin her health making her work so hard, and sleep in such a place.
O, John! do you think he is in his right mind?"

"Yes, yes; she is slender."

"Yes, *yes!*" she repeated sarcastically, "you know these niggers are just like black
snakes; you *can't* kill them. If she wasn't tough she would have been killed long ago.
There was never one of my girls could do half the work."

"Did they ever try?" interposed her husband. "I think she can do more than all
of them together."

"What a man!" said she, peevishly. "But I want to know what is going to be done
with her about getting pious?"

"Let her do just as she has a mind to. If it is a comfort to her, let her enjoy the
privilege of being good. I see no objection."

"I should think *you* were crazy, sure. Don't you know that every night she will
want to go toting off to meeting? and Sundays, too? and you know we have a great
deal of company Sundays, and she can't be spared."

"I thought you Christians held to going to church," remarked Mr. B.

"Yes, but who ever thought of having a nigger go, except to drive others there?
Why, according to you and James, we should very soon have her in the parlor, as
smart as our own girls. It's of no use talking to you or James. If you should go on
as you would like, it would not be six months before she would be leaving me; and
that won't do. Just think how much profit she was to us last summer. We had no
work hired out; she did the work of two girls—"

"And got the whippings for two with it!" remarked Mr. Bellmont.

"I'll beat the money out of her, if I ca n't get her worth any other way," retorted Mrs. B. sharply. While this scene was passing, Frado was trying to utter the prayer
of the publican, "God be merciful to me a sinner."

Chapter X. Perplexities.—Another Death.

> Neath the billows of the ocean,
> Hidden treasures wait the hand,
> That again to light shall raise them
> With the diver's magic wand.
>
> G. W. Cook.

THE family, gathered by James' decease, returned to their homes. Susan and
Charles returned to Baltimore. Letters were received from the absent, expressing
their sympathy and grief. The father bowed like a "bruised reed," under the loss of

his beloved son. He felt desirous to die the death of the righteous; also, conscious that he was unprepared, he resolved to start on the narrow way, and some time solicit entrance through the gate which leads to the celestial city. He acknowledged his too ready acquiescence with Mrs. B., in permitting Frado to be deprived of her only religious privileges for weeks together. He accordingly asked his sister to take her to meeting once more, which she was ready at once to do.

The first opportunity they once more attended meeting together. The minister conversed faithfully with every person present. He was surprised to find the little colored girl so solicitous, and kindly directed her to the flowing fountain where she might wash and be clean. He inquired of the origin of her anxiety, of her progress up to this time, and endeavored to make Christ, instead of James, the attraction of Heaven. He invited her to come to his house, to speak freely her mind to him, to pray much, to read her Bible often.

The neighbors, who were at meeting,—among them Mrs. Reed,—discussed the opinions Mrs. Bellmont would express on the subject. Mrs. Reed called and informed Mrs. B. that her colored girl "related her experience the other night at the meeting."

"What experience?" asked she, quickly, as if she expected to hear the number of times she had whipped Frado, and the number of lashes set forth in plain Arabic numbers.

"Why, you know she is serious, don't you? She told the minister about it."

Mrs. B. made no reply, but changed the subject adroitly. Next morning she told Frado she "should not go out of the house for one while, except on errands; and if she did not stop trying to be religious, she would whip her to death."

Frado pondered; her mistress was a professor of religion; was *she* going to heaven? then she did not wish to go. If she should be near James, even, she could not be happy with those fiery eyes watching her ascending path. She resolved to give over all thought of the future world, and strove daily to put her anxiety far from her.

Mr. Bellmont found himself unable to do what James or Jack could accomplish for her. He talked with her seriously, told her he had seen her many times punished undeservedly; he did not wish to have her saucy or disrespectful, but when she was *sure* she did not deserve a whipping, to avoid it if she could. "You are looking sick," he added, "you cannot endure beating as you once could."

It was not long before an opportunity offered of profiting by his advice. She was sent for wood, and not returning as soon as Mrs. B. calculated, she followed her, and, snatching from the pile a stick, raised it over her.

"Stop!" shouted Frado, "strike me, and I'll never work a mite more for you;" and throwing down what she had gathered, stood like one who feels the stirring of free and independent thoughts.

By this unexpected demonstration, her mistress, in amazement, dropped her weapon, desisting from her purpose of chastisement. Frado walked towards the house, her mistress following with the wood she herself was sent after. She did not know, before, that she had a power to ward off assaults. Her triumph in seeing her enter the door with *her* burden, repaid her for much of her former suffering.

It was characteristic of Mrs. B. never to rise in her majesty, unless she was sure she should be victorious.

This affair never met with an "after clap," like many others.

Thus passed a year. The usual amount of scolding, but fewer whippings. Mrs. B. longed once more for Mary's return, who had been absent over a year; and she wrote imperatively for her to come quickly to her. A letter came in reply, announcing that she would comply as soon as she was sufficiently recovered from an illness which detained her.

No serious apprehensions were cherished by either parent, who constantly looked for notice of her arrival, by mail. Another letter brought tidings that Mary was seriously ill; her mother's presence was solicited.

She started without delay. Before she reached her destination, a letter came to the parents announcing her death.

No sooner was the astounding news received, than Frado rushed into Aunt Abby's, exclaiming:—

"She's dead, Aunt Abby!"

"Who?" she asked, terrified by the unprefaced announcement.

"Mary; they've just had a letter."

As Mrs. B. was away, the brother and sister could freely sympathize, and she sought him in this fresh sorrow, to communicate such solace as she could, and to learn particulars of Mary's untimely death, and assist him in his journey thither.

It seemed a thanksgiving to Frado. Every hour or two she would pop in into Aunt Abby's room with some strange query:

"She got into the *river* again, Aunt Abby, didn't she; the Jordan is a big one to tumble into, any how. S'posen she goes to hell, she'll be as black as I am. Would n't mistress be mad to see her a nigger!" and others of a similar stamp, not at all acceptable to the pious, sympathetic dame; but she could not evade them.

The family returned from their sorrowful journey, leaving the dead behind. Nig looked for a change in her tyrant; what could subdue her, if the loss of her idol could not?

Never was Mrs. B. known to shed tears so profusely, as when she reiterated to one and another the sad particulars of her darling's sickness and death. There was, indeed, a season of quiet grief; it was the lull of the fiery elements. A few weeks revived the former tempests, and so at variance did they seem with chastisement sanctified, that Frado felt them to be unbearable. She determined to flee. But where? Who would take her? Mrs. B. had always represented her ugly. Perhaps every one thought her so. Then no one would take her. She was black, no one would love her. She might have to return, and then she would be more in her mistress' power than ever.

She remembered her victory at the wood-pile. She decided to remain to do as well as she could; to assert her rights when they were trampled on; to return once more to her meeting in the evening, which had been prohibited. She had learned how to conquer; she would not abuse the power while Mr. Bellmont was at home.

But had she not better run away? Where? She had never been from the place far enough to decide what course to take. She resolved to speak to Aunt Abby. *She* mapped the dangers of her course, her liability to fail in finding so good friends as John and herself. Frado's mind was busy for days and nights. She contemplated administering poison to her mistress, to rid herself and the house of so detestable a plague.

But she was restrained by an overruling Providence; and finally decided to stay contentedly through her period of service, which would expire when she was eighteen years of age.

In a few months Jane returned home with her family, to relieve her parents, upon whom years and affliction had left the marks of age. The years intervening since she had left her home, had, in some degree, softened the opposition to her unsanctioned marriage with George. The more Mrs. B. had about her, the more energetic seemed her directing capabilities, and her fault-finding propensities. Her own, she had full power over; and Jane after vain endeavors, became disgusted, weary, and perplexed, and decided that, though her mother might suffer, she could not endure her home. They followed Jack to the West. Thus vanished all hopes of sympathy or relief from this source to Frado. There seemed no one capable of enduring the oppressions of the house but her. She turned to the darkness of the future with the determination previously formed, to remain until she should be eighteen. Jane begged her to follow her so soon as she should be released; but so wearied out was she by her mistress, she felt disposed to flee from any and every one having her similitude of name or feature. . . .

Further Readings

Davis, Cynthia J. "Speaking the Body's Pain: Harriet Wilson's *Our Nig.*" *African American Review* 27 (Fall 1993):391–404.

Gates, Henry Louis, Jr. "Harriet E. Adams Wilson." Harris, Trudier and Davis, Thadious, eds. *Dictionary of Literary Biography: Afro-American Writers before the Harlem Renaissance*. Detroit, MI: Gale, 1986.

Leveen, Lois. "Dwelling in the House of Oppression: The Spatial, Racial, and Textual Dynamics of Harriet Wilson's *Our Nig.*" *African American Review* 35 (Winter 2001):561–580.

Stern, Julia. "Excavating Genre in *Our Nig.*" *American Literature* 67 (1995): 439–464.

West, Elizabeth J. "Reworking the Conversion Narrative: Race and Christianity in *Our Nig.* *MELUS* 24 (Summer 1999):3–27.

Wilson, Harriet E. Ed. Henry Louis Gates, Jr., *Our Nig; or Sketches from the Life of a Free Black.* New York: Vintage Books, 1983.

From: *Incidents in the Life of a Slave Girl, Written by Herself*

1861 | FUGITIVE SLAVE NARRATIVE

"Northerners know nothing at all about Slavery. They think it is per-petual bondage only. They have no conception of the depth of *degradation* involved in that word, SLAVERY; if they had, they would never cease their efforts until so horrible a system was over-thrown."

A WOMAN OF NORTH CAROLINA.

"Rise up, ye women that are at ease! Hear my voice, ye careless daughters! Give ear unto my speech."

ISAIAH XXXII. 9.

Edited By L. Maria Child. Boston: Published For The Author, 1861.

Entered, according to Act of Congress, in the year 1860, by L. MARIA CHILD. In the Clerk's Office of the District Court of the District of Massachusetts.

Preface By The Author.

READER, be assured this narrative is no fiction. I am aware that some of my adventures may seem incredible; but they are, nevertheless, strictly true. I have not exaggerated the wrongs inflicted by Slavery; on the contrary, my descriptions fall far short of the facts. I have concealed the names of places, and given persons fictitious names. I had no motive for secrecy on my own account, but I deemed it kind and considerate towards others to pursue this course.

I wish I were more competent to the task I have undertaken. But I trust my readers will excuse deficiencies in consideration of circumstances. I was born and reared in Slavery; and I remained in a Slave State twenty-seven years. Since I have been at the North, it has been necessary for me to work diligently for my own support, and the education of my children. This has not left me much leisure to make up for the loss of early opportunities to improve myself; and it has compelled me to write these pages at irregular intervals, whenever I could snatch an hour from household duties.

When I first arrived in Philadelphia, Bishop Paine advised me to publish a sketch of my life, but I told him I was altogether incompetent to such an undertaking. Though I have improved my mind somewhat since that time, I still remain of the same opinion; but I trust my motives will excuse what might otherwise seem presumptuous. I have not written my experiences in order to attract attention to myself; on the contrary, it would have been more pleasant to me to have been silent about my own history. Neither do I care to excite sympathy for my own sufferings. But I do earnestly desire to arouse the women of the North to a realizing sense of the condition of two millions of women at the South, still in bondage, suffering what I suffered, and most of them far worse. I want to add my testimony to that of abler pens to convince the people of the Free States what Slavery really is. Only by experience can any one realize how deep, and dark, and foul is that pit of abominations. May the blessing of God rest on this imperfect effort in behalf of my persecuted people!

LINDA BRENT.

Introduction By The Editor.

THE author of the following autobiography is personally known to me, and her conversation and manners inspire me with confidence. During the last seventeen years, she has lived the greater part of the time with a distinguished family in New York, and has so deported herself as to be highly esteemed by them. This fact is sufficient, without further credentials of her character. I believe those who know her will not be disposed to doubt her veracity, though some incidents in her story are more romantic than fiction.

At her request, I have revised her manuscript; but such changes as I have made have been mainly for purposes of condensation and orderly arrangement. I have not added any thing to the incidents, or changed the import of her very pertinent remarks. With trifling exceptions, both the ideas and the language are her own. I pruned excrescences a little, but otherwise I had no reason for changing her lively and dramatic way of telling her own story. The names of both persons and places are known to me; but for good reasons I suppress them.

It will naturally excite surprise that a woman reared in Slavery should be able to write so well. But circumstances will explain this. In the first place, nature endowed her with quick perceptions. Secondly, the mistress, with whom she lived till she was twelve years old, was a kind, considerate friend, who taught her to read and spell. Thirdly, she was placed in favorable circumstances after she came to the North; having frequent intercourse with intelligent persons, who felt a friendly interest in her welfare, and were disposed to give her opportunities for self-improvement.

I am well aware that many will accuse me of indecorum for presenting these pages to the public; for the experiences of this intelligent and much-injured woman belong to a class which some call delicate subjects, and others indelicate. This peculiar phase of Slavery has generally been kept veiled; but the public ought to be made acquainted with its monstrous features, and I willingly take the responsibility of presenting them with the veil withdrawn. I do this for the sake of my sisters in bondage, who are suffering wrongs so foul, that our ears are too delicate to listen to them. I do it with the hope of arousing conscientious and reflecting women at the North to a sense of their duty in the exertion of moral influence on the question of Slavery, on all possible occasions. I do it with the hope that every man who reads this narrative will swear solemnly before God that, so far as he has power to prevent it, no fugitive from Slavery shall ever be sent back to suffer in that loathsome den of corruption and cruelty.

L. MARIA CHILD.

I. Childhood.

I WAS born a slave; but I never knew it till six years of happy childhood had passed away. My father was a carpenter, and considered so intelligent and skilful in his trade, that, when buildings out of the common line were to be erected, he was sent for from long distances, to be head workman. On condition of paying his mistress two hundred dollars a year, and supporting himself, he was allowed to work at his trade, and manage his own affairs. His strongest wish was to purchase his children; but, though he several times offered his hard earnings for that purpose, he never succeeded. In complexion my parents were a light shade of brownish yellow, and were termed mulattoes. They lived together in a comfortable home; and, though we were all slaves, I was so fondly shielded that I never dreamed I was a piece of merchandise, trusted to them for safe keeping, and liable to be demanded of them at any moment. I had one brother, William, who was two years younger than myself—a bright, affectionate child. I had also a great treasure in my maternal grandmother, who was a remarkable woman in many respects. She was the daughter of a planter in South Carolina, who, at his death, left her mother and his three children free, with money to go to St. Augustine, where they had relatives. It was during the Revolutionary War; and they were captured on their passage, carried back, and sold to different purchasers. Such was the story my grandmother used to tell me; but I do not remember all the particulars. She was a little girl when she was captured and sold to the keeper of a large hotel. I have often heard her tell how hard she fared during childhood. But as she grew older she evinced so much intelligence, and was so faithful, that her master and mistress could not help seeing it was for their interest to take care of such a valuable piece of property. She became an indispensable personage in the household, officiating in all capacities, from cook and wet nurse to seamstress. She was much praised for her cooking; and her nice crackers became so famous in the neighborhood that many people were desirous of obtaining them. In consequence of numerous requests of this kind, she asked permission of her mistress to bake crackers at night, after all the household work was done; and she obtained leave to do it, provided she would clothe herself and her children from the profits. Upon these terms, after working hard all day for her mistress, she began her midnight bakings, assisted by her two oldest children. The business proved profitable; and each year she laid by a little, which was saved for a fund to purchase her children. Her master died, and the property was divided among his heirs. The widow had her dower in the hotel, which she continued to keep open. My grandmother remained in her service as a slave; but her children were divided among her master's children. As she had five, Benjamin, the youngest one, was sold, in order that each heir might have an equal portion of dollars and cents. There was so little difference in our ages that he seemed more like my brother than my uncle. He was a bright, handsome lad, nearly white; for he inherited the complexion my grandmother had derived from Anglo-Saxon ancestors. Though only ten years old, seven hundred and twenty dollars were paid for him. His sale was a terrible blow to my grandmother; but she was naturally hopeful, and she went to work with renewed energy, trusting in time to be able to purchase some of her children. She had laid up three hundred dollars, which her mistress one day begged as a loan, promising to pay her soon. The reader probably knows that no promise or writing given to a slave is legally binding; for, according to Southern laws, a slave, *being* property, can *hold* no property. When my grandmother lent her hard earnings to her mistress, she trusted solely to her honor. The honor of a slaveholder to a slave!

To this good grandmother I was indebted for many comforts. My brother Willie and I often received portions of the crackers, cakes, and preserves, she made to sell; and after we ceased to be children we were indebted to her for many more important services.

Such were the unusually fortunate circumstances of my early childhood. When I was six years old, my mother died; and then, for the first time, I learned, by the talk around me, that I was a slave. My mother's mistress was the daughter of my grandmother's mistress. She was the foster sister of my mother; they were both nourished at my grandmother's breast. In fact, my mother had been weaned at three months old, that the babe of the mistress might obtain sufficient food. They played together as children; and, when they became women, my mother was a most faithful servant to her whiter foster sister. On her death-bed her mistress promised that her children should never suffer for any thing; and during her lifetime she kept her word. They all spoke kindly of my dead mother, who had been a slave merely in name, but in nature was noble and womanly. I grieved for her, and my young mind was troubled with the thought who would now take care of me and my little brother. I was told that my home was now to be with her mistress; and I found it a happy one. No toilsome or disagreeable duties were imposed upon me. My mistress was so kind to me that I was always glad to do her bidding, and proud to labor for her as much as my young years would permit. I would sit by her side for hours, sewing diligently, with a heart as free from care as that of any free-born white child. When she thought I was tired, she would send me out to run and jump; and away I bounded, to gather berries or flowers to decorate her room. Those were happy days—too happy to last. The slave child had no thought for the morrow; but there came that blight, which too surely waits on every human being born to be a chattel.

When I was nearly twelve years old, my kind mistress sickened and died. As I saw the cheek grow paler, and the eye more glassy, how earnestly I prayed in my heart that she might live! I loved her; for she had been almost like a mother to me. My prayers were not answered. She died, and they buried her in the little churchyard, where, day after day, my tears fell upon her grave.

I was sent to spend a week with my grandmother. I was now old enough to begin to think of the future; and again and again I asked myself what they would do with me. I felt sure I should never find another mistress so kind as the one who was gone. She had promised my dying mother that her children should never suffer for any thing; and when I remembered that, and recalled her many proofs of attachment to me, I could not help having some hopes that she had left me free.

My friends were almost certain it would be so. They thought she would be sure to do it, on account of my mother's love and faithful service. But, alas! we all know that the memory of a faithful slave does not avail much to save her children from the auction block.

After a brief period of suspense, the will of my mistress was read, and we learned that she had bequeathed me to her sister's daughter, a child of five years old. So vanished our hopes. My mistress had taught me the precepts of God's Word: "Thou shalt love thy neighbor as thyself." "Whatsoever ye would that men should do unto you, do ye even so unto them." But I was her slave, and I suppose she did not recognize me as her neighbor. I would give much to blot out from my memory that one great wrong. As a child, I loved my mistress; and, looking back on the happy days I spent with her, I try to think with less bitterness of this act of injustice. While I was with her, she taught me to read and spell; and for this privilege, which so rarely falls to the lot of a slave, I bless her memory.

She possessed but few slaves; and at her death those were all distributed among her relatives. Five of them were my grandmother's children, and had shared the same milk that nourished her mother's children. Notwithstanding my grandmother's long and faithful service to her owners, not one of her children escaped the auction block. These God-breathing machines are no more, in the sight of their masters, than the cotton they plant, or the horses they tend.

II. The New Master And Mistress.

DR. FLINT, a physician in the neighborhood, had married the sister of my mistress, and I was now the property of their little daughter. It was not without murmuring that I prepared for my new home; and what added to my unhappiness, was the fact that my brother William was purchased by the same family. My father, by his nature, as well as by the habit of transacting business as a skilful mechanic, had more of the feelings of a freeman than is common among slaves. My brother was a spirited boy; and being brought up under such influences, he early detested the name of master and mistress. One day, when his father and his mistress both happened to call him at the same time, he hesitated between the two; being perplexed to know which had the strongest claim upon his obedience. He finally concluded to go to his mistress. When my father reproved him for it, he said, "You both called me, and I didn't know which I ought to go to first."

"You are *my* child," replied our father, "and when I call you, you should come immediately, if you have to pass through fire and water."

Poor Willie! He was now to learn his first lesson of obedience to a master. Grandmother tried to cheer us with hopeful words, and they found an echo in the credulous hearts of youth.

When we entered our new home we encountered cold looks, cold words, and cold treatment. We were glad when the night came. On my narrow bed I moaned and wept, I felt so desolate and alone.

I had been there nearly a year, when a dear little friend of mine was buried. I heard her mother sob, as the clods fell on the coffin of her only child, and I turned away from the grave, feeling thankful that I still had something left to love. I met my grandmother, who said, "Come with me, Linda;" and from her tone I knew that something sad had happened. She led me apart from the people, and then said, "My child, your father is dead." Dead! How could I believe it? He had died so suddenly I had not even heard that he was sick. I went home with my grandmother. My heart rebelled against God, who had taken from me mother, father, mistress, and friend. The good grandmother tried to comfort me. "Who knows the ways of God?" said she. "Perhaps they have been kindly taken from the evil days to come." Years afterwards I often thought of this. She promised to be a mother to her grandchildren, so far as she might be permitted to do so; and strengthened by her love, I returned to my master's. I thought I should be allowed to go to my father's house the next morning; but I was ordered to go for flowers, that my mistress's house might be decorated for an evening party. I spent the day gathering flowers and weaving them into festoons, while the dead body of my father was lying within a mile of me. What cared my owners for that? he was merely a piece of property. Moreover, they thought he had spoiled his children, by teaching them to feel that they were human beings. This was blasphemous doctrine for a slave to teach; presumptuous in him, and dangerous to the masters.

The next day I followed his remains to a humble grave beside that of my dear mother. There were those who knew my father's worth, and respected his memory.

My home now seemed more dreary than ever. The laugh of the little slave-children sounded harsh and cruel. It was selfish to feel so about the joy of others. My brother moved about with a very grave face. I tried to comfort him, by saying, "Take courage, Willie; brighter days will come by and by."

"You don't know any thing about it, Linda," he replied. "We shall have to stay here all our days; we shall never be free."

I argued that we were growing older and stronger, and that perhaps we might, before long, be allowed to hire our own time, and then we could earn money to buy our freedom. William declared this was much easier to say than to do; moreover, he did not intend to *buy* his freedom. We held daily controversies upon this subject.

Little attention was paid to the slaves' meals in Dr. Flint's house. If they could catch a bit of food while it was going, well and good. I gave myself no trouble on that score, for on my various errands I passed my grandmother's house, where there was always something to spare for me. I was frequently threatened with punishment if I stopped there; and my grandmother, to avoid detaining me, often stood at the gate with something for my breakfast or dinner. I was indebted to *her* for all my comforts, spiritual or temporal.

It was *her* labor that supplied my scanty wardrobe. I have a vivid recollection of the linsey-woolsey dress given me every winter by Mrs. Flint. How I hated it! It was one of the badges of slavery.

While my grandmother was thus helping to support me from her hard earnings, the three hundred dollars she had lent her mistress were never repaid. When her mistress died, her son-in-law, Dr. Flint, was appointed executor. When grandmother applied to him for payment, he said the estate was insolvent, and the law prohibited payment. It did not, however, prohibit him from retaining the silver candelabra, which had been purchased with that money. I presume they will be handed down in the family, from generation to generation.

My grandmother's mistress had always promised her that, at her death, she should be free; and it was said that in her will she made good the promise. But when the estate was settled, Dr. Flint told the faithful old servant that, under existing circumstances, it was necessary she should be sold.

On the appointed day, the customary advertisement was posted up, proclaiming that there would be "a public sale of negroes, horses, &c." Dr. Flint called to tell my grandmother that he was unwilling to wound her feelings by putting her up at auction, and that he would prefer to dispose of her at private sale. My grandmother saw through his hypocrisy; she understood very well that he was ashamed of the job. She was a very spirited woman, and if he was base enough to sell her, when her mistress intended she should be free, she was determined the public should know it. She had for a long time supplied many families with crackers and preserves; consequently, "Aunt Marthy," as she was called, was generally known, and every body who knew her respected her intelligence and good character. Her long and faithful service in the family was also well known, and the intention of her mistress to leave her free. When the day of sale came, she took her place among the chattels, and at the first call she sprang upon the auction-block. Many voices called out, "Shame! Shame! Who is going to sell *you*, aunt Marthy? Don't stand there! That is no place for *you*." Without saying a word, she quietly awaited her fate. No one bid for her. At last, a feeble voice said, "Fifty dollars." It came from a maiden lady, seventy years old, the sister of my grandmother's deceased mistress. She had lived forty years under the same roof with my grandmother; she knew how faithfully she had served her owners, and how cruelly she had been defrauded of her rights; and she resolved to protect her. The auctioneer waited for a higher bid; but her wishes were respected; no one bid above her. She could neither read nor write; and when the bill of sale was made out, she signed it with a cross. But what consequence was that, when she had a big heart overflowing with human kindness? She gave the old servant her freedom.

At that time, my grandmother was just fifty years old. Laborious years had passed since then; and now my brother and I were slaves to the man who had defrauded her of her money, and tried to defraud her of her freedom. One of my mother's sisters, called Aunt Nancy, was also a slave in his family. She was a kind, good aunt to me; and supplied the place of both housekeeper and waiting maid to her mistress. She was, in fact, at the beginning and end of every thing.

Mrs. Flint, like many southern women, was totally deficient in energy. She had not strength to superintend her household affairs; but her nerves were so strong, that she could sit in her easy chair and see a woman whipped, till the blood trickled from every stroke of the lash. She was a member of the church; but partaking of the Lord's supper did not seem to put her in a Christian frame of mind. If dinner was not served at the exact time on that particular Sunday, she would station herself in the kitchen, and wait till it was dished, and then spit in all the kettles and pans that had been used for cooking. She did this to prevent the cook and her children from eking out their meagre fare with the remains of the gravy and other scrapings. The slaves could get nothing to eat except what she chose to give them. Provisions were weighed out by the pound and ounce, three times a day. I can assure you she gave them no chance to eat wheat bread from her flour barrel. She knew how many biscuits a quart of flour would make, and exactly what size they ought to be.

Dr. Flint was an epicure. The cook never sent a dinner to his table without fear and trembling; for if there happened to be a dish not to his liking, he would either order her to be whipped, or compel her to eat every mouthful of it in his presence. The poor, hungry creature might not have objected to eating it; but she did object to having her master cram it down her throat till she choked.

They had a pet dog, that was a nuisance in the house. The cook was ordered to make some Indian mush for him. He refused to eat, and when his head was held over it, the froth flowed from his mouth into the basin. He died a few minutes after. When Dr. Flint came in, he said the mush had not been well cooked, and that was the reason the animal would not eat it. He sent for the cook, and compelled her to eat it. He thought that the woman's stomach was stronger than the dog's; but her sufferings afterwards proved that he was mistaken. This poor woman endured many cruelties from her master and mistress; sometimes she was locked up, away from her nursing baby, for a whole day and night.

When I had been in the family a few weeks, one of the plantation slaves was brought to town, by order of his master. It was near night when he arrived, and Dr. Flint ordered him to be taken to the work house, and tied up to the joist, so that his feet would just escape the ground. In that situation he was to wait till the doctor had taken his tea. I shall never forget that night. Never before, in my life, had I heard hundreds of blows fall, in succession, on a human being. His piteous groans, and his "O, pray don't, massa," rang in my ear for months afterwards. There were many conjectures as to the cause of this terrible punishment. Some said master accused him of stealing corn; others said the slave had quarrelled with his wife, in presence of the overseer, and had accused his master of being the father of her child. They were both black, and the child was very fair.

I went into the work house next morning, and saw the cowhide still wet with blood, and the boards all covered with gore. The poor man lived, and continued to quarrel with his wife. A few months afterwards Dr. Flint handed them both over to a slave-trader. The guilty man put their value into his pocket, and had the satisfaction of knowing that they were out of sight and hearing. When the mother was delivered into the trader's hands, she said, "You *promised* to treat me well." To which he replied, "You have let your tongue run too far; damn you!" She had forgotten that it was a crime for a slave to tell who was the father of her child.

From others than the master persecution also comes in such cases. I once saw a young slave girl dying soon after the birth of a child nearly white. In her agony she cried out, "O Lord, come and take me!" Her mistress stood by, and mocked at her like an incarnate fiend. "You suffer, do you?" she exclaimed. "I am glad of it. You deserve it all, and more too."

The girl's mother said, "The baby is dead, thank God; and I hope my poor child will soon be in heaven, too."

"Heaven!" retorted the mistress. "There is no such place for the like of her and her bastard."

The poor mother turned away, sobbing. Her dying daughter called her, feebly, and as she bent over her, I heard her say, "Don't grieve so, mother; God knows all about it; and HE will have mercy upon me."

Her sufferings, afterwards, became so intense, that her mistress felt unable to stay; but when she left the room, the scornful smile was still on her lips. Seven children called her mother. The poor black woman had but the one child, whose eyes she saw closing in death, while she thanked God for taking her away from the greater bitterness of life.

IV. The Slave Who Dared To Feel Like A Man.

TWO years had passed since I entered Dr. Flint's family, and those years had brought much of the knowledge that comes from experience, though they had afforded little opportunity for any other kinds of knowledge.

My grandmother had, as much as possible, been a mother to her orphan grandchildren. By perseverance and unwearied industry, she was now mistress of a snug little home, surrounded with the necessaries of life. She would have been happy could her children have shared them with her. There remained but three children and two grandchildren, all slaves. Most earnestly did she strive to make us feel that it was the will of God: that He had seen fit to place us under such circumstances; and though it seemed hard, we ought to pray for contentment.

It was a beautiful faith, coming from a mother who could not call her children her own. But I, and Benjamin, her youngest boy, condemned it. We reasoned that it was much more the will of God that we should be situated as she was. We longed for a home like hers. There we always found sweet balsam for our troubles. She was so loving, so sympathizing! She always met us with a smile, and listened with patience to all our sorrows. She spoke so hopefully, that unconsciously the clouds gave place to sunshine. There was a grand big oven there, too, that baked bread and nice things for the town, and we knew there was always a choice bit in store for us.

But, alas! even the charms of the old oven failed to reconcile us to our hard lot. Benjamin was now a tall, handsome lad, strongly and gracefully made, and with a spirit too bold and daring for a slave. My brother William, now twelve years old, had the same aversion to the word master that he had when he was an urchin of seven years. I was his confidant. He came to me with all his troubles. I remember one instance in particular. It was on a lovely spring morning, and when I marked the sunlight dancing here and there, its beauty seemed to mock my sadness. For my master, whose restless, craving, vicious nature roved about day and night, seeking whom to devour, had just left me, with stinging, scorching words; words that scathed ear and brain like fire. O, how I despised him! I thought how glad I should be, if some day when he walked the earth, it would open and swallow him up, and disencumber the world of a plague.

When he told me that I was made for his use, made to obey his command in *every* thing; that I was nothing but a slave, whose will must and should surrender to his, never before had my puny arm felt half so strong.

So deeply was I absorbed in painful reflections afterwards, that I neither saw nor heard the entrance of any one, till the voice of William sounded close beside me. "Linda," said he, "what makes you look so sad? I love you. O, Linda, isn't this a bad world? Every body seems so cross and unhappy. I wish I had died when poor father did."

I told him that every body was *not* cross, or unhappy; that those who had pleasant homes, and kind friends, and who were not afraid to love them, were happy. But we, who were slave-children, without father or mother, could not expect to be happy. We must be good; perhaps that would bring us contentment.

"Yes," he said, "I try to be good; but what's the use? They are all the time troubling me." Then he proceeded to relate his afternoon's difficulty with young master Nicholas. It seemed that the brother of master Nicholas had pleased himself with making up stories about William. Master Nicholas said he should be flogged, and he would do it. Whereupon he went to work; but William fought bravely, and the young master, finding he was getting the better of him, undertook to tie his hands behind him. He failed in that likewise. By dint of kicking and fisting, William came out of the skirmish none the worse for a few scratches.

He continued to discourse on his young master's *meanness*; how he whipped the *little* boys, but was a perfect coward when a tussle ensued between him and white boys of his own size. On such occasions he always took to his legs. William had other charges to make against him. One was his rubbing up pennies with quicksilver, and passing them off for quarters of a dollar on an old man who kept a fruit stall. William was often sent to buy fruit, and he earnestly inquired of me what he ought to do under such circumstances. I told him it was certainly wrong to deceive the old man, and that it was his duty to tell him of the impositions practised by his young master. I assured him the old man would not be slow to comprehend the whole, and there the matter would end. William thought it might with the old man, but not with *him*. He said he did not mind the smart of the whip, but he did not like the *idea* of being whipped.

While I advised him to be good and forgiving I was not unconscious of the beam in my own eye. It was the very knowledge of my own shortcomings that urged me to retain, if possible, some sparks of my brother's God-given nature. I had not lived fourteen years in slavery for nothing. I had felt, seen, and heard enough, to read the characters, and question the motives, of those around me. The war of my life had begun; and though one of God's most powerless creatures, I resolved never to be conquered. Alas, for me!

If there was one pure, sunny spot for me, I believed it to be in Benjamin's heart, and in another's, whom I loved with all the ardor of a girl's first love. My owner knew of it, and sought in every way to render me miserable. He did not resort to corporal punishment, but to all the petty, tyrannical ways that human ingenuity could devise. . . . .

V. The Trials Of Girlhood.

DURING the first years of my service in Dr. Flint's family, I was accustomed to share some indulgences with the children of my mistress. Though this seemed to me no more than right, I was grateful for it, and tried to merit the kindness by the faithful discharge of my duties. But I now entered on my fifteenth year—a sad epoch in the life of a slave girl. My master began to whisper foul words in my ear. Young as I was, I could not remain ignorant of their import. I tried to treat them with indifference or contempt. The master's age, my extreme youth, and the fear that his conduct would be reported to my grandmother, made him bear this treatment for many months. He was a crafty man, and resorted to many means to accomplish his purposes. Sometimes he had stormy, terrific ways, that made his victims tremble; sometimes he assumed a gentleness that he thought must surely subdue. Of the two, I preferred his stormy moods, although they left me trembling. He tried his utmost to corrupt the pure principles my grandmother had instilled. He peopled my young mind with unclean images, such as only a vile monster could think of. I turned from him with disgust and hatred. But he was my master. I was compelled to live under the same roof with him—where I saw a man forty years my senior daily violating the most sacred commandments of nature. He told me I was his property; that I must be subject to his will in all things. My soul revolted against the mean tyranny. But where could I turn for protection? No matter whether the slave girl be as black as ebony or as fair as her mistress. In either case, there is no shadow of law to protect her from insult, from violence, or even from death; all these are inflicted by fiends who bear the shape of men. The mistress, who ought to protect the helpless victim, has no other feelings towards her but those of jealousy and rage. The degradation, the wrongs, the vices, that grow out of slavery, are more than I can describe. They are greater than you would willingly believe. Surely, if you credited one half the truths that are told you concerning the helpless millions suffering in this cruel bondage, you at the north would not help to tighten the yoke. You surely would refuse to do for the master, on your own soil, the mean and cruel work which trained bloodhounds and the lowest class of whites do for him at the south.

Every where the years bring to all enough of sin and sorrow; but in slavery the very dawn of life is darkened by these shadows. Even the little child, who is accustomed to wait on her mistress and her children, will learn, before she is twelve years old, why it is that her mistress hates such and such a one among the slaves. Perhaps the child's own mother is among those hated ones. She listens to violent outbreaks of jealous passion, and cannot help understanding what is the cause. She will become prematurely knowing in evil things. Soon she will learn to tremble when she hears her master's footfall. She will be compelled to realize that she is no longer a child. If God has bestowed beauty upon her, it will prove her greatest curse. That which commands admiration in the white woman only hastens the degradation of the female slave. I know that some are too much brutalized by slavery to feel the humiliation of their position; but many slaves feel it most acutely, and shrink from the memory of it. I cannot tell how much I suffered in the presence of these wrongs, nor how I am still pained by the retrospect. My master met me at every turn, reminding me that I belonged to him, and swearing by heaven and earth that he would compel me to submit to him. If I went out for a breath of fresh air, after a day of unwearied toil, his footsteps dogged me. If I knelt by my mother's grave, his dark shadow fell on me even there. The light heart which nature had given me became heavy with sad forebodings. The other slaves in my master's house noticed the change. Many of them pitied me; but none dared to ask the cause. They had no need to inquire. They knew too well the guilty practices under that roof; and they were aware that to speak of them was an offence that never went unpunished.

I longed for some one to confide in. I would have given the world to have laid my head on my grandmother's faithful bosom, and told her all my troubles. But Dr. Flint swore he would kill me, if I was not as silent as the grave. Then, although my grandmother was all in all to me, I feared her as well as loved her. I had been accustomed to look up to her with a respect bordering upon awe. I was very young, and felt shamefaced about telling her such impure things, especially as I knew her to be very strict on such subjects. Moreover, she was a woman of a high spirit. She was usually very quiet in her demeanor; but if her indignation was once roused, it was not very easily quelled. I had been told that she once chased a white gentleman with a loaded pistol, because he insulted one of her daughters. I dreaded the consequences of a violent outbreak; and both pride and fear kept me silent. But though I did not confide in my grandmother, and even evaded her vigilant watchfulness and inquiry, her presence in the neighborhood was some protection to me. Though she had been a slave, Dr. Flint was afraid of her. He dreaded her scorching rebukes. Moreover, she was known and patronized by many people; and he did not wish to have his villany made public. It was lucky for me that I did not live on a distant plantation, but in a town not so large that the inhabitants were ignorant of each other's affairs. Bad as are the laws and customs in a slaveholding community, the doctor, as a professional man, deemed it prudent to keep up some outward show of decency.

O, what days and nights of fear and sorrow that man caused me! Reader, it is not to awaken sympathy for myself that I am telling you truthfully what I suffered in slavery. I do it to kindle a flame of compassion in your hearts for my sisters who are still in bondage, suffering as I once suffered.

I once saw two beautiful children playing together. One was a fair white child; the other was her slave, and also her sister. When I saw them embracing each other, and heard their joyous laughter, I turned sadly away from the lovely sight. I foresaw the inevitable blight that would fall on the little slave's heart. I knew how soon her laughter would be changed to sighs. The fair child grew up to be a still fairer woman. From childhood to womanhood her pathway was blooming with flowers, and overarched by a sunny sky. Scarcely one day of her life had been clouded when the sun rose on her happy bridal morning.

How had those years dealt with her slave sister, the little playmate of her childhood? She, also, was very beautiful; but the flowers and sunshine of love were not for her. She drank the cup of sin, and shame, and misery, whereof her persecuted race are compelled to drink.

In view of these things, why are ye silent, ye free men and women of the north? Why do your tongues falter in maintenance of the right? Would that I had more ability! But my heart is so full, and my pen is so weak! There are noble men and women who plead for us, striving to help those who cannot help themselves. God bless them! God give them strength and courage to go on! God bless those, every where, who are laboring to advance the cause of humanity!

VI. The Jealous Mistress.

I WOULD ten thousand times rather that my children should be the half-starved paupers of Ireland than to be the most pampered among the slaves of America. I would rather drudge out my life on a cotton plantation, till the grave opened to give me rest, than to live with an unprincipled master and a jealous mistress. The felon's home in a penitentiary is preferable. He may repent, and turn from the error of his ways, and so find peace; but it is not so with a favorite slave. She is not allowed to have any pride of character. It is deemed a crime in her to wish to be virtuous.

Mrs. Flint possessed the key to her husband's character before I was born. She might have used this knowledge to counsel and to screen the young and the inno-cent among her slaves; but for them she had no sympathy. They were the objects of her constant suspicion and malevolence. She watched her husband with unceas-ing vigilance; but he was well practiced in means to evade it. What he could not find opportunity to say in words he manifested in signs. He invented more than were ever thought of in a deaf and dumb asylum. I let them pass, as if I did not under-stand what he meant; and many were the curses and threats bestowed on me for my stupidity. One day he caught me teaching myself to write. He frowned, as if he was not well pleased, but I suppose he came to the conclusion that such an accomplish-ment might help to advance his favorite scheme. Before long, notes were often slipped into my hand. I would return them, saying, "I can't read them, sir." "Can't you?" he replied; "then I must read them to you." He always finished the reading by asking, "Do you understand?" Sometimes he would complain of the heat of the tea room, and order his supper to be placed on a small table in the piazza. He would seat himself there with a well-satisfied smile, and tell me to stand by and brush away the flies. He would eat very slowly, pausing between the mouthfuls. These intervals were employed in describing the happiness I was so foolishly throwing away, and in threatening me with the penalty that finally awaited my stubborn disobedience. He boasted much of the forbearance he had exercised towards me, and reminded me that there was a limit to his patience. When I succeeded in avoiding opportu-nities for him to talk to me at home, I was ordered to come to his office, to do some errand. When there, I was obliged to stand and listen to such language as he saw fit to address to me. Sometimes I so openly expressed my contempt for him that he would become violently enraged, and I wondered why he did not strike me. Circumstanced as he was, he probably thought it was better policy to be forbearing. But the state of things grew worse and worse daily. In desperation I told him that I must and would apply to my grandmother for protection. He threatened me with death, and worse than death, if I made any complaint to her. Strange to say, I did not despair. I was naturally of a buoyant disposition, and always I had hope of somehow getting out of his clutches. Like many a poor, simple slave before me, I trusted that some threads of joy would yet be woven into my dark destiny.

I had entered my sixteenth year, and every day it became more apparent that my presence was intolerable to Mrs. Flint. Angry words frequently passed between her and her husband. He had never punished me himself, and he would not allow any body else to punish me. In that respect, she was never satisfied; but, in her angry moods, no terms were too vile for her to bestow upon me. Yet I, whom she detested so bitterly, had far more pity for her than he had, whose duty it was to make her life happy. I never wronged her, or wished to wrong her; and one word of kindness from her would have brought me to her feet.

After repeated quarrels between the doctor and his wife, he announced his intention to take his youngest daughter, then four years old, to sleep in his apartment. It was necessary that a servant should sleep in the same room, to be on hand if the child stirred. I was selected for that office, and informed for what purpose that arrangement had been made. By managing to keep within sight of people, as much as possible during the day time, I had hitherto succeeded in eluding my master, though a razor was often held to my throat to force me to change this line of policy. At night I slept by the side of my great aunt, where I felt safe. He was too prudent to come into her room. She was an old woman, and had been in the family many years. Moreover, as a married man, and a professional man, he deemed it necessary to save appearances in some degree. But he resolved to remove the obstacle in the way of his scheme; and he thought he had planned it so that he should evade suspicion. He was well aware how much I prized my refuge by the side of my old aunt, and he determined to dispossess me of it. The first night the doctor had the little child in his room alone. The next morning, I was ordered to take my station as nurse the following night. A kind Providence interposed in my favor. During the day Mrs. Flint heard of this new arrangement, and a storm followed. I rejoiced to hear it rage.

After a while my mistress sent for me to come to her room. Her first question was, "Did you know you were to sleep in the doctor's room?"

"Yes, ma'am."

"Who told you?"

"My master."

"Will you answer truly all the questions I ask?"

"Yes, ma'am."

"Tell me, then, as you hope to be forgiven, are you innocent of what I have accused you?"

"I am."

She handed me a Bible, and said, "Lay your hand on your heart, kiss this holy book, and swear before God that you tell me the truth."

I took the oath she required, and I did it with a clear conscience.

"You have taken God's holy word to testify your innocence," said she. "If you have deceived me, beware! Now take this stool, sit down, look me directly in the face, and tell me all that has passed between your master and you."

I did as she ordered. As I went on with my account her color changed frequently, she wept, and sometimes groaned. She spoke in tones so sad, that I was touched by her grief. The tears came to my eyes; but I was soon convinced that her emotions arose from anger and wounded pride. She felt that her marriage vows were desecrated, her dignity insulted, but she had no compassion for the poor victim of her husband's perfidy. She pitied herself as a martyr; but she was incapable of feeling for the condition of shame and misery in which her unfortunate, helpless slave was placed.

Yet perhaps she had some touch of feeling for me; for when the conference was ended, she spoke kindly, and promised to protect me. I should have been much comforted by this assurance if I could have had confidence in it; but my experiences in slavery had filled me with distrust. She was not a very refined woman, and had not much control over her passions. I was an object of her jealousy, and, consequently, of her hatred; and I knew I could not expect kindness or confidence from her under the circumstances in which I was placed. I could not blame her. Slaveholders' wives feel as other women would under similar circumstances. The fire of her temper kindled from small sparks, and now the flame became so intense that the doctor was obliged to give up his intended arrangement.

I knew I had ignited the torch, and I expected to suffer for it afterwards; but I felt too thankful to my mistress for the timely aid she rendered me to care much about that. She now took me to sleep in a room adjoining her own. There I was an object of her especial care, though not of her especial comfort, for she spent many a sleepless night to watch over me. Sometimes I woke up, and found her bending over me. At other times she whispered in my ear, as though it was her husband who was speaking to me, and listened to hear what I would answer. If she startled me, on such occasions, she would glide stealthily away; and the next morning she would tell me I had been talking in my sleep, and ask who I was talking to. At last, I began to be fearful for my life. It had been often threatened; and you can imagine, better than I can describe, what an unpleasant sensation it must produce to wake up in the dead of night and find a jealous woman bending over you. Terrible as this experience was, I had fears that it would give place to one more terrible.

My mistress grew weary of her vigils; they did not prove satisfactory. She changed her tactics. She now tried the trick of accusing my master of crime, in my presence, and gave my name as the author of the accusation. To my utter astonishment, he replied, "I don't believe it; but if she did acknowledge it, you tortured her into exposing me." Tortured into exposing him! Truly, Satan had no difficulty in distinguishing the color of his soul! I understood his object in making this false representation. It was to show me that I gained nothing by seeking the protection of my mistress; that the power was still all in his own hands. I pitied Mrs. Flint. She was a second wife, many years the junior of her husband; and the hoary-headed miscreant was enough to try the patience of a wiser and better woman. She was completely foiled, and knew not how to proceed. She would gladly have had me flogged for my supposed false oath; but, as I have already stated, the doctor never allowed any one to whip me. The old sinner was politic. The application of the lash might have led to remarks that would have exposed him in the eyes of his children and grandchildren. How often did I rejoice that I lived in a town where all the inhabitants knew each other! If I had been on a remote plantation, or lost among the multitude of a crowded city, I should not be a living woman at this day.

The secrets of slavery are concealed like those of the Inquisition. My master was, to my knowledge, the father of eleven slaves. But did the mothers dare to tell who was the father of their children? Did the other slaves dare to allude to it, except in whispers among themselves? No, indeed! They knew too well the terrible consequences.

My grandmother could not avoid seeing things which excited her suspicions. She was uneasy about me, and tried various ways to buy me; but the never-changing answer was always repeated: "Linda does not belong to *me*. She is my daughter's property, and I have no legal right to sell her." The conscientious man! He was too scrupulous to *sell* me; but he had no scruples whatever about committing a much greater wrong against the helpless young girl placed under his guardianship, as his daughter's property. Sometimes my persecutor would ask me whether I would like to be sold. I told him I would rather be sold to any body than to lead such a life as I did. On such occasions he would assume the air of a very injured individual, and reproach me for my ingratitude. "Did I not take you into the house, and make you the companion of my own children?" he would say. "Have I ever treated you like a negro? I have never allowed you to be punished, not even to please your mistress. And this is the recompense I get, you ungrateful girl!" I answered that he had reasons of his own for screening me from punishment, and that the course he pursued made my mistress hate me and persecute me. If I wept, he would say, "Poor child! Don't cry! don't cry! I will make peace for you with your mistress. Only let me arrange matters in my own way. Poor, foolish girl! you don't know what is for your own good. I would cherish you. I would make a lady of you. Now go, and think of all I have promised you."

I did think of it.

Reader, I draw no imaginary pictures of southern homes. I am telling you the plain truth. Yet when victims make their escape from this wild beast of Slavery, northerners consent to act the part of bloodhounds, and hunt the poor fugitive back into his den, "full of dead men's bones, and all uncleanness." Nay, more, they are not only willing, but proud, to give their daughters in marriage to slaveholders. The poor girls have romantic notions of a sunny clime, and of the flowering vines that all the year round shade a happy home. To what disappointments are they destined! The young wife soon learns that the husband in whose hands she has placed her happiness pays no regard to his marriage vows. Children of every shade of complexion play with her own fair babies, and too well she knows that they are born unto him of his own household. Jealousy and hatred enter the flowery home, and it is ravaged of its loveliness.

Southern women often marry a man knowing that he is the father of many little slaves. They do not trouble themselves about it. They regard such children as property, as marketable as the pigs on the plantation; and it is seldom that they do not make them aware of this by passing them into the slavetrader's hands as soon as possible, and thus getting them out of their sight. I am glad to say there are some honorable exceptions.

I have myself known two southern wives who exhorted their husbands to free those slaves towards whom they stood in a "parental relation;" and their request was granted. These husbands blushed before the superior nobleness of their wives' natures. Though they had only counselled them to do that which it was their duty to do, it commanded their respect, and rendered their conduct more exemplary. Concealment was at an end, and confidence took the place of distrust.

Though this bad institution deadens the moral sense, even in white women, to a fearful extent, it is not altogether extinct. I have heard southern ladies say of Mr. Such a one, "He not only thinks it no disgrace to be the father of those little niggers, but he is not ashamed to call himself their master. I declare, such things ought not to be tolerated in any decent society!"

VII. The Lover.

WHY does the slave ever love? Why allow the tendrils of the heart to twine around objects which may at any moment be wrenched away by the hand of violence? When separations come by the hand of death, the pious soul can bow in resignation, and say, "Not my will, but thine be done, O Lord!" But when the ruthless hand of man strikes the blow, regardless of the misery he causes, it is hard to be submissive. I did not reason thus when I was a young girl. Youth will be youth. I loved, and I indulged the hope that the dark clouds around me would turn out a bright lining. I forgot that in the land of my birth the shadows are too dense for light to penetrate. A land

"Where laughter is not mirth; nor thought the mind;
Nor words a language; nor e'en men mankind.
Where cries reply to curses, shrieks to blows,
And each is tortured in his separate hell."

There was in the neighborhood a young colored carpenter; a free born man. We had been well acquainted in childhood, and frequently met together afterwards. We became mutually attached, and he proposed to marry me. I loved him with all the ardor of a young girl's first love. But when I reflected that I was a slave, and that the laws gave no sanction to the marriage of such, my heart sank within me. My lover wanted to buy me; but I knew that Dr. Flint was too wilful and arbitrary a man to consent to that arrangement. From him, I was sure of experiencing all sorts of opposition, and I had nothing to hope from my mistress. She would have been delighted to have got rid of me, but not in that way. It would have relieved her mind of a burden if she could have seen me sold to some distant state, but if I was married near home I should be just as much in her husband's power as I had previously been,—for the husband of a slave has no power to protect her. Moreover, my mistress, like many others, seemed to think that slaves had no right to any family ties of their own; that they were created merely to wait upon the family of the mistress. I once heard her abuse a young slave girl, who told her that a colored man wanted to make her his wife. "I will have you peeled and pickled, my lady," said she, "if I ever hear you mention that subject again. Do you suppose that I will have you tending *my* children with the children of that nigger?" The girl to whom she said this had a mulatto child, of course not acknowledged by its father. The poor black man who loved her would have been proud to acknowledge his helpless offspring.

Many and anxious were the thoughts I revolved in my mind. I was at a loss what to do. Above all things, I was desirous to spare my lover the insults that had cut so deeply into my own soul. I talked with my grandmother about it, and partly told her my fears. I did not dare to tell her the worst. She had long suspected all was not right, and if I confirmed her suspicions I knew a storm would rise that would prove the overthrow of all my hopes.

This love-dream had been my support through many trials; and I could not bear to run the risk of having it suddenly dissipated. There was a lady in the neighborhood, a particular friend of Dr. Flint's, who often visited the house. I had a great respect for her, and she had always manifested a friendly interest in me. Grandmother thought she would have great influence with the doctor. I went to this lady, and told her my story. I told her I was aware that my lover's being a free-born man would prove a great objection; but he wanted to buy me; and if Dr. Flint would consent to that arrangement, I felt sure he would be willing to pay any reasonable price. She knew that Mrs. Flint disliked me; therefore, I ventured to suggest that perhaps my mistress would approve of my being sold, as that would rid her of me. The lady listened with kindly sympathy, and promised to do her utmost to promote my wishes. She had an interview with the doctor, and I believe she pleaded my cause earnestly; but it was all to no purpose.

How I dreaded my master now! Every minute I expected to be summoned to his presence; but the day passed, and I heard nothing from him. The next morning, a message was brought to me: "Master wants you in his study." I found the door ajar, and I stood a moment gazing at the hateful man who claimed a right to rule me, body and soul. I entered, and tried to appear calm. I did not want him to know how my heart was bleeding. He looked fixedly at me, with an expression which seemed to say, "I have half a mind to kill you on the spot." At last he broke the silence, and that was a relief to both of us.

"So you want to be married, do you?" said he, "and to a free nigger."

"Yes, sir."

"Well, I'll soon convince you whether I am your master, or the nigger fellow you honor so highly. If you *must* have a husband, you may take up with one of my slaves."

What a situation I should be in, as the wife of one of *his* slaves, even if my heart had been interested!

I replied, "Don't you suppose, sir, that a slave can have some preference about marrying? Do you suppose that all men are alike to her?"

"Do you love this nigger?" said he, abruptly.

"Yes, sir."

"How dare you tell me so!" he exclaimed, in great wrath. After a slight pause, he added, "I supposed you thought more of yourself; that you felt above the insults of such puppies."

I replied, "If he is a puppy I am a puppy, for we are both of the negro race. It is right and honorable for us to love each other. The man you call a puppy never insulted me, sir; and he would not love me if he did not believe me to be a virtuous woman."

He sprang upon me like a tiger, and gave me a stunning blow. It was the first time he had ever struck me; and fear did not enable me to control my anger. When I had recovered a little from the effects, I exclaimed, "You have struck me for answering you honestly. How I despise you!"

There was silence for some minutes. Perhaps he was deciding what should be my punishment; or, perhaps, he wanted to give me time to reflect on what I had said, and to whom I had said it. Finally, he asked, "Do you know what you have said?"

"Yes, sir; but your treatment drove me to it."

"Do you know that I have a right to do as I like with you,—that I can kill you, if I please?"

"You have tried to kill me, and I wish you had; but you have no right to do as you like with me."

"Silence!" he exclaimed, in a thundering voice. "By heavens, girl, you forget yourself too far! Are you mad? If you are, I will soon bring you to your senses. Do you think any other master would bear what I have borne from you this morning? Many masters would have killed you on the spot. How would you like to be sent to jail for your insolence?"

"I know I have been disrespectful, sir," I replied; "but you drove me to it; I couldn't help it. As for the jail, there would be more peace for me there than there is here."

"You deserve to go there," said he, "and to be under such treatment, that you would forget the meaning of the word *peace*. It would do you good. It would take some of your high notions out of you. But I am not ready to send you there yet, notwithstanding your ingratitude for all my kindness and forbearance. You have been the plague of my life. I have wanted to make you happy, and I have been repaid with the basest ingratitude; but though you have proved yourself incapable of appreciating my kindness, I will be lenient towards you, Linda. I will give you one more chance to redeem your character. If you behave yourself and do as I require, I will forgive you and treat you as I always have done; but if you disobey me, I will punish you as I would the meanest slave on my plantation. Never let me hear that fellow's name mentioned again. If I ever know of your speaking to him, I will cowhide you both; and if I catch him lurking about my premises, I will shoot him as soon as I would a dog. Do you hear what I say? I'll teach you a lesson about marriage and free niggers! Now go, and let this be the last time I have occasion to speak to you on this subject."

Reader, did you ever hate? I hope not. I never did but once; and I trust I never shall again. Somebody has called it "the atmosphere of hell;" and I believe it is so.

For a fortnight the doctor did not speak to me. He thought to mortify me; to make me feel that I had disgraced myself by receiving the honorable addresses of a respectable colored man, in preference to the base proposals of a white man. But though his lips disdained to address me, his eyes were very loquacious. No animal ever watched its prey more narrowly than he watched me. He knew that I could write, though he had failed to make me read his letters; and he was now troubled lest I should exchange letters with another man. After a while he became weary of silence; and I was sorry for it. One morning, as he passed through the hall, to leave the house, he contrived to thrust a note into my hand. I thought I had better read it, and spare myself the vexation of having him read it to me. It expressed regret for the blow he had given me, and reminded me that I myself was wholly to blame for it. He hoped I had become convinced of the injury I was doing myself by incurring his displeasure. He wrote that he had made up his mind to go to Louisiana; that he should take several slaves with him, and intended I should be one of the number. My mistress would remain where she was; therefore I should have nothing to fear from that quarter. If I merited kindness from him, he assured me that it would be lavishly bestowed. He begged me to think over the matter, and answer the following day.

The next morning I was called to carry a pair of scissors to his room. I laid them on the table, with the letter beside them. He thought it was my answer, and did not call me back. I went as usual to attend my young mistress to and from school. He met me in the street, and ordered me to stop at his office on my way back. When I entered, he showed me his letter, and asked me why I had not answered it. I replied, "I am your daughter's property, and it is in your power to send me, or take me, wherever you please." He said he was very glad to find me so willing to go, and that we should start early in the autumn. He had a large practice in the town, and I rather thought he had made up the story merely to frighten me. However that might be, I was determined that I would never go to Louisiana with him.

Summer passed away, and early in the autumn Dr. Flint's eldest son was sent to Louisiana to examine the country, with a view to emigrating. That news did not disturb me. I knew very well that I should not be sent with *him*. That I had not been taken to the plantation before this time, was owing to the fact that his son was there. He was jealous of his son; and jealousy of the overseer had kept him from punishing me by sending me into the fields to work. Is it strange that I was not proud of these protectors? As for the overseer, he was a man for whom I had less respect than I had for a bloodhound.

Young Mr. Flint did not bring back a favorable report of Louisiana, and I heard no more of that scheme. Soon after this, my lover met me at the corner of the street, and I stopped to speak to him. Looking up, I saw my master watching us from his window. I hurried home, trembling with fear. I was sent for, immediately, to go to his room. He met me with a blow. "When is mistress to be married?" said he, in a sneering tone. A shower of oaths and imprecations followed. How thankful I was that my lover was a free man! that my tyrant had no power to flog him for speaking to me in the street!

Again and again I revolved in my mind how all this would end. There was no hope that the doctor would consent to sell me on any terms. He had an iron will, and was determined to keep me, and to conquer me. My lover was an intelligent and religious man. Even if he could have obtained permission to marry me while I was a slave, the marriage would give him no power to protect me from my master.

It would have made him miserable to witness the insults I should have been subjected to. And then, if we had children, I knew they must "follow the condition of the mother." What a terrible blight that would be on the heart of a free, intelligent father! For *his* sake, I felt that I ought not to link his fate with my own unhappy destiny. He was going to Savannah to see about a little property left him by an uncle; and hard as it was to bring my feelings to it, I earnestly entreated him not to come back. I advised him to go to the Free States, where his tongue would not be tied, and where his intelligence would be of more avail to him. He left me, still hoping the day would come when I could be bought. With me the lamp of hope had gone out. The dream of my girlhood was over. I felt lonely and desolate.

Still I was not stripped of all. I still had my good grandmother, and my affectionate brother. When he put his arms round my neck, and looked into my eyes, as if to read there the troubles I dared not tell, I felt that I still had something to love. But even that pleasant emotion was chilled by the reflection that he might be torn from me at any moment, by some sudden freak of my master. If he had known how we loved each other, I think he would have exulted in separating us. We often planned together how we could get to the north. But, as William remarked, such things are easier said than done. My movements were very closely watched, and we had no means of getting any money to defray our expenses. As for grandmother, she was strongly opposed to her children's undertaking any such project. She had not forgotten poor Benjamin's sufferings, and she was afraid that if another child tried to escape, he would have a similar or a worse fate. To me, nothing seemed more dreadful than my present life. I said to myself, "William *must* be free. He shall go to the north, and I will follow him." Many a slave sister has formed the same plans.

X. A Perilous Passage In The Slave Girl's Life.

AFTER my lover went away, Dr. Flint contrived a new plan. He seemed to have an idea that my fear of my mistress was his greatest obstacle. In the blandest tones, he told me that he was going to build a small house for me, in a secluded place, four miles away from the town. I shuddered; but I was constrained to listen, while he talked of his intention to give me a home of my own, and to make a lady of me. Hitherto, I had escaped my dreaded fate, by being in the midst of people. My grandmother had already had high words with my master about me. She had told him pretty plainly what she thought of his character, and there was considerable gossip in the neighborhood about our affairs, to which the open-mouthed jealousy of Mrs. Flint contributed not a little. When my master said he was going to build a house for me, and that he could do it with little trouble and expense, I was in hopes something would happen to frustrate his scheme; but I soon heard that the house was actually begun. I vowed before my Maker that I would never enter it. I had rather toil on the plantation from dawn till dark; I had rather live and die in jail, than drag on, from day to day, through such a living death. I was determined that the master, whom I so hated and loathed, who had blighted the prospects of my youth, and made my life a desert, should not, after my long struggle with him, succeed at last in trampling his victim under his feet. I would do any thing, every thing, for the sake of defeating him. What *could* I do? I thought and thought, till I became desperate, and made a plunge into the abyss.

And now, reader, I come to a period in my unhappy life, which I would gladly forget if I could. The remembrance fills me with sorrow and shame. It pains me to tell you of it; but I have promised to tell you the truth, and I will do it honestly, let it cost me what it may. I will not try to screen myself behind the plea of compulsion from a master; for it was not so. Neither can I plead ignorance or thoughtlessness. For years, my master had done his utmost to pollute my mind with foul images, and to destroy the pure principles inculcated by my grandmother, and the good mistress of my childhood. The influences of slavery had had the same effect on me that they had on other young girls; they had made me prematurely knowing, concerning the evil ways of the world. I knew what I did, and I did it with deliberate calculation.

But, O, ye happy women, whose purity has been sheltered from childhood, who have been free to choose the objects of your affection, whose homes are protected by law, do not judge the poor desolate slave girl too severely! If slavery had been abolished, I, also, could have married the man of my choice; I could have had a home shielded by the laws; and I should have been spared the painful task of confessing what I am now about to relate; but all my prospects had been blighted by slavery. I wanted to keep myself pure; and, under the most adverse circumstances, I tried hard to preserve my self-respect; but I was struggling alone in the powerful grasp of the demon Slavery; and the monster proved too strong for me. I felt as if I was forsaken by God and man; as if all my efforts must be frustrated; and I became reckless in my despair.

I have told you that Dr. Flint's persecutions and his wife's jealousy had given rise to some gossip in the neighborhood. Among others, it chanced that a white unmarried gentleman had obtained some knowledge of the circumstances in which I was placed. He knew my grandmother, and often spoke to me in the street. He became interested for me, and asked questions about my master, which I answered in part. He expressed a great deal of sympathy, and a wish to aid me. He constantly sought opportunities to see me, and wrote to me frequently. I was a poor slave girl, only fifteen years old.

So much attention from a superior person was, of course, flattering; for human nature is the same in all. I also felt grateful for his sympathy, and encouraged by his kind words. It seemed to me a great thing to have such a friend. By degrees, a more tender feeling crept into my heart. He was an educated and eloquent gentleman; too eloquent, alas, for the poor slave girl who trusted in him. Of course I saw whither all this was tending. I knew the impassable gulf between us; but to be an object of interest to a man who is not married, and who is not her master, is agreeable to the pride and feelings of a slave, if her miserable situation has left her any pride or sentiment. It seems less degrading to give one's self, than to submit to compulsion. There is something akin to freedom in having a lover who has no control over you, except that which he gains by kindness and attachment. A master may treat you as rudely as he pleases, and you dare not speak; moreover, the wrong does not seem so great with an unmarried man, as with one who has a wife to be made unhappy. There may be sophistry in all this; but the condition of a slave confuses all principles of morality, and, in fact, renders the practice of them impossible.

When I found that my master had actually begun to build the lonely cottage, other feelings mixed with those I have described. Revenge, and calculations of interest, were added to flattered vanity and sincere gratitude for kindness. I knew nothing would enrage Dr. Flint so much as to know that I favored another; and it was something to triumph over my tyrant even in that small way. I thought he would revenge himself by selling me, and I was sure my friend, Mr. Sands, would buy me. He was a man of more generosity and feeling than my master, and I thought my freedom could be easily obtained from him. The crisis of my fate now came so near that I was desperate. I shuddered to think of being the mother of children that should be owned by my old tyrant. I knew that as soon as a new fancy took him, his victims were sold far off to get rid of them; especially if they had children. I had seen several women sold, with his babies at the breast. He never allowed his offspring by slaves to remain long in sight of himself and his wife. Of a man who was not my master I could ask to have my children well supported; and in this case, I felt confident I should obtain the boon. I also felt quite sure that they would be made free. With all these thoughts revolving in my mind, and seeing no other way of escaping the doom I so much dreaded, I made a headlong plunge. Pity me, and pardon me, O virtuous reader! You never knew what it is to be a slave; to be entirely unprotected by law or custom; to have the laws reduce you to the condition of a chattel, entirely subject to the will of another. You never exhausted your ingenuity in avoiding the snares, and eluding the power of a hated tyrant; you never shuddered at the sound of his footsteps, and trembled within hearing of his voice. I know I did wrong. No one can feel it more sensibly than I do. The painful and humiliating memory will haunt me to my dying day. Still, in looking back, calmly, on the events of my life, I feel that the slave woman ought not to be judged by the same standard as others.

The months passed on. I had many unhappy hours. I secretly mourned over the sorrow I was bringing on my grandmother, who had so tried to shield me from harm. I knew that I was the greatest comfort of her old age, and that it was a source of pride to her that I had not degraded myself, like most of the slaves. I wanted to confess to her that I was no longer worthy of her love; but I could not utter the dreaded words.

As for Dr. Flint, I had a feeling of satisfaction and triumph in the thought of telling *him*. From time to time he told me of his intended arrangements, and I was silent. At last, he came and told me the cottage was completed, and ordered me to go to it. I told him I would never enter it. He said, "I have heard enough of such talk as that. You shall go, if you are carried by force; and you shall remain there."

I replied, "I will never go there. In a few months I shall be a mother."

He stood and looked at me in dumb amazement, and left the house without a word. I thought I should be happy in my triumph over him. But now that the truth was out, and my relatives would hear of it, I felt wretched. Humble as were their circumstances, they had pride in my good character. Now, how could I look them in the face? My self-respect was gone! I had resolved that I would be virtuous, though I was a slave. I had said, "Let the storm beat! I will brave it till I die." And now, how humiliated I felt!

I went to my grandmother. My lips moved to make confession, but the words stuck in my throat. I sat down in the shade of a tree at her door and began to sew. I think she saw something unusual was the matter with me. The mother of slaves is very watchful. She knows there is no security for her children. After they have entered their teens she lives in daily expectation of trouble. This leads to many questions. If the girl is of a sensitive nature, timidity keeps her from answering truthfully, and this well-meant course has a tendency to drive her from maternal counsels. Presently, in came my mistress, like a mad woman, and accused me concerning her husband. My grandmother, whose suspicions had been previously awakened, believed what she said. She exclaimed, "O Linda! has it come to this? I had rather see you dead than to see you as you now are. You are a disgrace to your dead mother." She tore from my fingers my mother's wedding ring and her silver thimble. "Go away!" she exclaimed, "and never come to my house, again." Her reproaches fell so hot and heavy, that they left me no chance to answer. Bitter tears, such as the eyes never shed but once, were my only answer. I rose from my seat, but fell back again, sobbing. She did not speak to me; but the tears were running down her furrowed cheeks, and they scorched me like fire. She had always been so kind to me! *So* kind! How I longed to throw myself at her feet, and tell her all the truth! But she had ordered me to go, and never to come there again. After a few minutes, I mustered strength, and started to obey her. With what feelings did I now close that little gate, which I used to open with such an eager hand in my childhood! It closed upon me with a sound I never heard before.

Where could I go? I was afraid to return to my master's. I walked on reckless-ly, not caring where I went, or what would become of me. When I had gone four or five miles, fatigue compelled me to stop. I sat down on the stump of an old tree. The stars were shining through the boughs above me. How they mocked me, with their bright, calm light! The hours passed by, and as I sat there alone a chilliness and deadly sickness came over me. I sank on the ground. My mind was full of horrid thoughts. I prayed to die; but the prayer was not answered. At last, with great effort I roused myself, and walked some distance further, to the house of a woman who had been a friend of my mother. When I told her why I was there, she spoke sooth-ingly to me; but I could not be comforted. I thought I could bear my shame if I could only be reconciled to my grandmother. I longed to open my heart to her. I thought if she could know the real state of the case, and all I had been bearing for years, she would perhaps judge me less harshly. My friend advised me to send for her. I did so; but days of agonizing suspense passed before she came. Had she utterly forsak-en me? No. She came at last. I knelt before her, and told her the things that had poi-soned my life; how long I had been persecuted; that I saw no way of escape; and in an hour of extremity I had become desperate. She listened in silence. I told her I would bear any thing and do any thing, if in time I had hopes of obtaining her for-giveness. I begged of her to pity me, for my dead mother's sake. And she did pity me. She did not say, "I forgive you;" but she looked at me lovingly, with her eyes full of tears. She laid her old hand gently on my head, and murmured, "Poor child! Poor child!"

XIII. The Church and Slavery.

AFTER the alarm caused by Nat Turner's insurrection had subsided, the slavehold-ers came to the conclusion that it would be well to give the slaves enough of reli-gious instruction to keep them from murdering their masters. The Episcopal clergyman offered to hold a separate service on Sundays for their benefit. His col-ored members were very few, and also very respectable—a fact which I presume had some weight with him. The difficulty was to decide on a suitable place for them to worship. The Methodist and Baptist churches admitted them in the afternoon; but their carpets and cushions were not so costly as those at the Episcopal church. It was at last decided that they should meet at the house of a free colored man, who was a member.

I was invited to attend, because I could read. Sunday evening came, and, trust-ing to the cover of night, I ventured out. I rarely ventured out by daylight, for I always went with fear, expecting at every turn to encounter Dr. Flint, who was sure to turn me back, or order me to his office to inquire where I got my bonnet, or some other article of dress. When the Rev. Mr. Pike came, there were some twenty persons present. The reverend gentleman knelt in prayer, then seated himself, and requested all present, who could read, to open their books, while he gave out the portions he wished them to repeat or respond to.

His text was, "Servants, be obedient to them that are your masters according to the flesh, with fear and trembling, in singleness of your heart, as unto Christ."

Pious Mr. Pike brushed up his hair till it stood upright, and, in deep, solemn tones, began: "Hearken, ye servants! Give strict heed unto my words. You are rebellious sinners. Your hearts are filled with all manner of evil. 'Tis the devil who tempts you. God is angry with you, and will surely punish you, if you don't forsake your wicked ways. You that live in town are eye-servants behind your master's back. Instead of serving your masters faithfully, which is pleasing in the sight of your heavenly Master, you are idle, and shirk your work. God sees you. You tell lies. God hears you. Instead of being engaged in worshipping him, you are hidden away somewhere, feasting on your master's substance; tossing coffee-grounds with some wicked fortuneteller, or cutting cards with another old hag. Your masters may not find you out, but God sees you, and will punish you. O, the depravity of your hearts! When your master's work is done, are you quietly together, thinking of the goodness of God to such sinful creatures? No; you are quarrelling, and tying up little bags of roots to bury under the door-steps to poison each other with. God sees you. You men steal away to every grog shop to sell your master's corn, that you may buy rum to drink. God sees you. You sneak into the back streets, or among the bushes, to pitch coppers. Although your masters may not find you out, God sees you; and he will punish you. You must forsake your sinful ways, and be faithful servants. Obey your old master and your young master—your old mistress and your young mistress. If you disobey your earthly master, you offend your heavenly Master. You must obey God's commandments. When you go from here, don't stop at the corners of the streets to talk, but go directly home, and let your master and mistress see that you have come."

The benediction was pronounced. We went home, highly amused at brother Pike's gospel teaching, and we determined to hear him again. I went the next Sabbath evening, and heard pretty much a repetition of the last discourse. At the close of the meeting, Mr. Pike informed us that he found it very inconvenient to meet at the friend's house, and he should be glad to see us, every Sunday evening, at his own kitchen.

I went home with the feeling that I had heard the Reverend Mr. Pike for the last time. Some of his members repaired to his house, and found that the kitchen sported two tallow candles; the first time, I am sure, since its present occupant owned it, for the servants never had any thing but pine knots. It was so long before the reverend gentleman descended from his comfortable parlor that the slaves left, and went to enjoy a Methodist shout. They never seem so happy as when shouting and singing at religious meetings. Many of them are sincere, and nearer to the gate of heaven than sanctimonious Mr. Pike, and other long-faced Christians, who see wounded Samaritans, and pass by on the other side. . . .

I well remember one occasion when I attended a Methodist class meeting. I went with a burdened spirit, and happened to sit next a poor, bereaved mother, whose heart was still heavier than mine. The class leader was the town constable— a man who bought and sold slaves, who whipped his brethren and sisters of the church at the public whipping post, in jail or out of jail. He was ready to perform that Christian office any where for fifty cents. This white-faced, black-hearted brother came near us, and said to the stricken woman, "Sister, can't you tell us how the Lord deals with your soul? Do you love him as you did formerly?"

She rose to her feet, and said, in piteous tones, "My Lord and Master, help me! My load is more than I can bear. God has hid himself from me, and I am left in darkness and misery." Then, striking her breast, she continued, "I can't tell you what is in here! They've got all my children. Last week they took the last one. God only knows where they've sold her. They let me have her sixteen years, and then—O! O! Pray for her brothers and sisters! I've got nothing to live for now. God make my time short!"

She sat down, quivering in every limb. I saw that constable class leader become crimson in the face with suppressed laughter, while he held up his handkerchief, that those who were weeping for the poor woman's calamity might not see his merriment. Then, with assumed gravity, he said to the bereaved mother, "Sister, pray to the Lord that every dispensation of his divine will may be sanctified to the good of your poor needy soul!" . . .

The Episcopal clergyman, who, ever since my earliest recollection, had been a sort of god among the slaveholders, concluded, as his family was large, that he must go where money was more abundant. A very different clergyman took his place. The change was very agreeable to the colored people, who said, "God has sent us a good man this time." They loved him, and their children followed him for a smile or a kind word. Even the slaveholders felt his influence. He brought to the rectory five slaves. His wife taught them to read and write, and to be useful to her and themselves. As soon as he was settled, he turned his attention to the needy slaves around him. He urged upon his parishioners the duty of having a meeting expressly for them every Sunday, with a sermon adapted to their comprehension. After much argument and importunity, it was finally agreed that they might occupy the gallery of the church on Sunday evenings. Many colored people, hitherto unaccustomed to attend church, now gladly went to hear the gospel preached. The sermons were simple, and they understood them. Moreover, it was the first time they had ever been addressed as human beings. It was not long before his white parishioners began to be dissatisfied. He was accused of preaching better sermons to the negroes than he did to them. He honestly confessed that he bestowed more pains upon those sermons than upon any others; for the slaves were reared in such ignorance that it was a difficult task to adapt himself to their comprehension. Dissensions arose in the parish. Some wanted he should preach to them in the evening, and to the slaves in the afternoon. In the midst of these disputings his wife died, after a very short illness. Her slaves gathered round her dying bed in great sorrow. She said, "I have tried to do you good and promote your happiness; and if I have failed, it has not been for want of interest in your welfare. Do not weep for me; but prepare for the new duties that lie before you. I leave you all free. May we meet in a better world." Her liberated slaves were sent away, with funds to establish them comfortably. The colored people will long bless the memory of that truly Christian woman. Soon after her death her husband preached his farewell sermon, and many tears were shed at his departure.

Several years after, he passed through our town and preached to his former congregation. In his afternoon sermon he addressed the colored people. "My friends," said he, "it affords me great happiness to have an opportunity of speaking to you again. For two years I have been striving to do something for the colored people of my own parish; but nothing is yet accomplished. I have not even preached a sermon to them. Try to live according to the word of God, my friends. Your skin is darker than mine; but God judges men by their hearts, not by the color of their skins." This was strange doctrine from a southern pulpit. It was very offensive to slaveholders. They said he and his wife had made fools of their slaves, and that he preached like a fool to the negroes.

I knew an old black man, whose piety and childlike trust in God were beautiful to witness. At fifty-three years old he joined the Baptist church. He had a most earnest desire to learn to read. He thought he should know how to serve God better if he could only read the Bible. He came to me, and begged me to teach him. He said he could not pay me, for he had no money; but he would bring me nice fruit when the season for it came. I asked him if he didn't know it was contrary to law; and that slaves were whipped and imprisoned for teaching each other to read. This brought the tears into his eyes. "Don't be troubled, uncle Fred," said I. "I have no thoughts of refusing to teach you. I only told you of the law, that you might know the danger, and be on your guard." He thought he could plan to come three times a week without its being suspected. I selected a quiet nook, where no intruder was likely to penetrate, and there I taught him his A, B, C. Considering his age, his progress was astonishing. As soon as he could spell in two syllables he wanted to spell out words in the Bible. The happy smile that illuminated his face put joy into my heart. After spelling out a few words, he paused, and said, "Honey, it 'pears when

I can read dis good book I shall be nearer to God. White man is got all de sense. He can larn easy. It ain't easy for ole black man like me. I only wants to read dis book, dat I may know how to live; den I hab no fear 'bout dying."

I tried to encourage him by speaking of the rapid progress he had made. "Hab patience, child," he replied. "I larns slow."

I had no need of patience. His gratitude, and the happiness I imparted, were more than a recompense for all my trouble.

At the end of six months he had read through the New Testament, and could find any text in it. One day, when he had recited unusually well, I said, "Uncle Fred, how do you manage to get your lessons so well?"

"Lord bress you, chile," he replied. "You nebber gibs me a lesson dat I don't pray to God to help me to understan' what I spells and what I reads. And he *does* help me, chile. Bress his holy name!"

There are thousands, who, like good uncle Fred, are thirsting for the water of life; but the law forbids it, and the churches withhold it. They send the Bible to heathen abroad, and neglect the heathen at home. I am glad that missionaries go out to the dark corners of the earth; but I ask them not to overlook the dark corners at home. Talk to American slaveholders as you talk to savages in Africa. Tell *them* it is wrong to traffic in men. Tell them it is sinful to sell their own children, and atrocious to violate their own daughters. Tell them that all men are brethren, and that man has no right to shut out the light of knowledge from his brother. Tell them they are answerable to God for sealing up the Fountain of Life from souls that are thirsting for it.

There are men who would gladly undertake such missionary work as this; but, alas! their number is small. They are hated by the south, and would be driven from its soil, or dragged to prison to die, as others have been before them. The field is ripe for the harvest, and awaits the reapers. Perhaps the great grandchildren of uncle Fred may have freely imparted to them the divine treasures, which he sought by stealth, at the risk of the prison and the scourge.

Are doctors of divinity blind, or are they hypocrites? I suppose some are the one, and some the other; but I think if they felt the interest in the poor and the lowly, that they ought to feel, they would not be so *easily* blinded. A clergyman who goes to the south, for the first time, has usually some feeling, however vague, that slavery is wrong. The slaveholder suspects this, and plays his game accordingly. He makes himself as agreeable as possible; talks on theology, and other kindred topics. The reverend gentleman is asked to invoke a blessing on a table loaded with luxuries. After dinner he walks round the premises, and sees the beautiful groves and flowering vines, and the comfortable huts of favored household slaves. The southerner invites him to talk with these slaves. He asks them if they want to be free, and they say, "O, no, massa." This is sufficient to satisfy him. He comes home to publish a "South-Side View of Slavery," and to complain of the exaggerations of abolitionists. He assures people that he has been to the south, and seen slavery for himself; that it is a beautiful "patriarchal institution;" that the slaves don't want their freedom; that they have hallelujah meetings, and other religious privileges.

What does *he* know of the half-starved wretches toiling from dawn till dark on the plantations? of mothers shrieking for their children, torn from their arms by slave traders? of young girls dragged down into moral filth? of pools of blood around the whipping post? of hounds trained to tear human flesh? of men screwed into cotton gins to die? The slaveholder showed him none of these things, and the slaves dared not tell of them if he had asked them.

There is a great difference between Christianity and religion at the south. If a man goes to the communion table, and pays money into the treasury of the church, no matter if it be the price of blood, he is called religious. If a pastor has offspring by a woman not his wife, the church dismiss him, if she is a white woman; but if she is colored, it does not hinder his continuing to be their good shepherd.

When I was told that Dr. Flint had joined the Episcopal church, I was much surprised. I supposed that religion had a purifying effect on the character of men; but the worst persecutions I endured from him were after he was a communicant. The conversation of the doctor, the day after he had been confirmed, certainly gave *me* no indication that he had "renounced the devil and all his works." In answer to some of his usual talk, I reminded him that he had just joined the church. "Yes, Linda," said he. "It was proper for me to do so. I am getting in years, and my position in society requires it, and it puts an end to all the damned slang. You would do well to join the church, too, Linda."

"There are sinners enough in it already," rejoined I. "If I could be allowed to live like a Christian, I should be glad."

"You can do what I require; and if you are faithful to me, you will be as virtuous as my wife," he replied.

I answered that the Bible didn't say so.

His voice became hoarse with rage. "How dare you preach to me about your infernal Bible!" he exclaimed. "What right have you, who are my negro, to talk to me about what you would like, and what you wouldn't like? I am your master, and you shall obey me."

No wonder the slave sing,—

"Ole Satan's church is here below;
Up to God's free church I hope to go."

XIV. Another Link To Life.

I HAD not returned to my master's house since the birth of my child. The old man raved to have me thus removed from his immediate power; but his wife vowed, by all that was good and great, she would kill me if I came back; and he did not doubt her word. Sometimes he would stay away for a season. Then he would come and renew the old threadbare discourse about his forbearance and my ingratitude. He labored, most unnecessarily, to convince me that I had lowered myself. The venomous old reprobate had no need of descanting on that theme. I felt humiliated enough. My unconscious babe was the ever-present witness of my shame. I listened with silent contempt when he talked about my having forfeited *his* good opinion; but I shed bitter tears that I was no longer worthy of being respected by the good and pure. Alas! slavery still held me in its poisonous grasp. There was no chance for me to be respectable. There was no prospect of being able to lead a better life.

Sometimes, when my master found that I still refused to accept what he called his kind offers, he would threaten to sell my child. "Perhaps that will humble you," said he.

Humble *me!* Was I not already in the dust? But his threat lacerated my heart. I knew the law gave him power to fulfil it; for slaveholders have been cunning enough to enact that "the child shall follow the condition of the *mother*," not of the *father*; thus taking care that licentiousness shall not interfere with avarice. This reflection made me clasp my innocent babe all the more firmly to my heart. Horrid visions passed through my mind when I thought of his liability to fall into the slave trader's hands. I wept over him, and said, "O my child! perhaps they will leave you in some cold cabin to die, and then throw you into a hole, as if you were a dog."

When Dr. Flint learned that I was again to be a mother, he was exasperated beyond measure. He rushed from the house, and returned with a pair of shears. I had a fine head of hair; and he often railed about my pride of arranging it nicely. He cut every hair close to my head, storming and swearing all the time. I replied to some of his abuse, and he struck me. Some months before, he had pitched me down stairs in a fit of passion; and the injury I received was so serious that I was unable to turn myself in bed for many days. He then said, "Linda, I swear by God I will never raise my hand against you again;" but I knew that he would forget his promise.

After he discovered my situation, he was like a restless spirit from the pit. He came every day; and I was subjected to such insults as no pen can describe. I would not describe them if I could; they were too low, too revolting. I tried to keep them from my grandmother's knowledge as much as I could. I knew she had enough to sadden her life, without having my troubles to bear. When she saw the doctor treat me with violence, and heard him utter oaths terrible enough to palsy a man's tongue, she could not always hold her peace. It was natural and motherlike that she should try to defend me; but it only made matters worse.

When they told me my new-born babe was a girl, my heart was heavier than it had ever been before. Slavery is terrible for men; but it is far more terrible for women. Superadded to the burden common to all, *they* have wrongs, and sufferings, and mortifications peculiarly their own.

Dr. Flint had sworn that he would make me suffer, to my last day, for this new crime against *him*, as he called it; and as long as he had me in his power he kept his word. On the fourth day after the birth of my babe, he entered my room suddenly, and commanded me to rise and bring my baby to him. The nurse who took care of me had gone out of the room to prepare some nourishment, and I was alone. There was no alternative. I rose, took up my babe, and crossed the room to where he sat. "Now stand there," said he, "till I tell you to go back!" My child bore a strong resemblance to her father, and to the deceased Mrs. Sands, her grandmother. He noticed this; and while I stood before him, trembling with weakness, he heaped upon me and my little one every vile epithet he could think of. Even the grandmother in her grave did not escape his curses. In the midst of his vituperations I fainted at his feet. This recalled him to his senses. He took the baby from my arms, laid it on the bed, dashed cold water in my face, took me up, and shook me violently, to restore my consciousness before any one entered the room. Just then my grandmother came in, and he hurried out of the house. I suffered in consequence of this treatment; but I begged my friends to let me die, rather than send for the doctor. There was nothing I dreaded so much as his presence. My life was spared; and I was glad for the sake of my little ones. Had it not been for these ties to life, I should have been glad to be released by death, though I had lived only nineteen years.

Always it gave me a pang that my children had no lawful claim to a name. Their father offered his; but, if I had wished to accept the offer, I dared not while my master lived. Moreover, I knew it would not be accepted at their baptism. A Christian name they were at least entitled to; and we resolved to call my boy for our dear good Benjamin, who had gone far away from us.

My grandmother belonged to the church; and she was very desirous of having the children christened. I knew Dr. Flint would forbid it, and I did not venture to attempt it. But chance favored me. He was called to visit a patient out of town, and was obliged to be absent during Sunday. "Now is the time," said my grandmother; "we will take the children to church, and have them christened."

When I entered the church, recollections of my mother came over me, and I felt subdued in spirit. There she had presented me for baptism, without any reason to feel ashamed. She had been married, and had such legal rights as slavery allows to a slave. The vows had at least been sacred to *her*, and she had never violated them. I was glad she was not alive, to know under what different circumstances her grandchildren were presented for baptism. Why had my lot been so different from my mother's? *Her* master had died when she was a child; and she remained with her mistress till she married. She was never in the power of any master; and thus she escaped one class of the evils that generally fall upon slaves.

When my baby was about to be christened, the former mistress of my father stepped up to me, and proposed to give it her Christian name. To this I added the surname of my father, who had himself no legal right to it; for my grandfather on the paternal side was a white gentleman. What tangled skeins are the genealogies of slavery! I loved my father; but it mortified me to be obliged to bestow his name on my children.

When we left the church, my father's old mistress invited me to go home with her. She clasped a gold chain round my baby's neck. I thanked her for this kindness; but I did not like the emblem. I wanted no chain to be fastened on my daughter, not even if its links were of gold. How earnestly I prayed that she might never feel the weight of slavery's chain, whose iron entereth into the soul!

XV. Continued Persecutions.

MY children grew finely; and Dr. Flint would often say to me, with an exulting smile, "These brats will bring me a handsome sum of money one of these days."

I thought to myself that, God being my helper, they should never pass into his hands. It seemed to me I would rather see them killed than have them given up to his power. The money for the freedom of myself and my children could be obtained; but I derived no advantage from that circumstance. Dr. Flint loved money, but he loved power more. After much discussion, my friends resolved on making another trial. There was a slaveholder about to leave for Texas, and he was commissioned to buy me. He was to begin with nine hundred dollars, and go up to twelve. My master refused his offers. "Sir," said he, "she don't belong to me. She is my daughter's property, and I have no right to sell her. I mistrust that you come from her paramour. If so, you may tell him that he cannot buy her for any money; neither can he buy her children."

The doctor came to see me the next day, and my heart beat quicker as he entered. I never had seen the old man tread with so majestic a step. He seated himself and looked at me with withering scorn. My children had learned to be afraid of him. The little one would shut her eyes and hide her face on my shoulder whenever she saw him; and Benny, who was now nearly five years old, often inquired, "What makes that bad man come here so many times? Does he want to hurt us?" I would clasp the dear boy in my arms, trusting that he would be free before he was old enough to solve the problem. And now, as the doctor sat there so grim and silent, the child left his play and came and nestled up by me. At last my tormentor spoke. "So you are left in disgust, are you?" said he. "It is no more than I expected. You remember I told you years ago that you would be treated so. So he is tired of you? Ha! ha! ha! The virtuous madam don't like to hear about it, does she? Ha! ha! ha!" There was a sting in his calling me virtuous madam. I no longer had the power of answering him as I had formerly done. He continued: "So it seems you are trying to get up another intrigue. Your new paramour came to me, and offered to buy you; but you may be assured you will not succeed. You are mine; and you shall be mine for life. There lives no human being that can take you out of slavery. I would have done it; but you rejected my kind offer."

I told him I did not wish to get up any intrigue; that I had never seen the man who offered to buy me.

"Do you tell me I lie?" exclaimed he, dragging me from my chair. "Will you say again that you never saw that man?"

I answered, "I do say so."

He clinched my arm with a volley of oaths. Ben began to scream, I told him to go to his grandmother.

"Don't you stir a step, you little wretch!" said he. The child drew nearer to me, and put his arms round me, as if he wanted to protect me. This was too much for my enraged master. He caught him up and hurled him across the room. I thought he was dead, and rushed towards him to take him up.

"Not yet!" exclaimed the doctor. "Let him lie there till he comes to."

"Let me go! Let me go!" I screamed, "or I will raise the whole house." I struggled and got away; but he clinched me again. Somebody opened the door, and he released me. I picked up my insensible child, and when I turned my tormentor was gone. Anxiously I bent over the little form, so pale and still; and when the brown eyes at last opened, I don't know whether I was very happy.

All the doctor's former persecutions were renewed. He came morning, noon, and night. No jealous lover ever watched a rival more closely than he watched me and the unknown slaveholder, with whom he accused me of wishing to get up an intrigue. When my grandmother was out of the way he searched every room to find him.

In one of his visits, he happened to find a young girl, whom he had sold to a trader a few days previous. His statement was, that he sold her because she had been too familiar with the overseer. She had had a bitter life with him, and was glad to be sold. She had no mother, and no near ties. She had been torn from all her family years before. A few friends had entered into bonds for her safety, if the trader would allow her to spend with them the time that intervened between her sale and the gathering up of his human stock. Such a favor was rarely granted. It saved the trader the expense of board and jail fees, and though the amount was small, it was a weighty consideration in a slave-trader's mind.

Dr. Flint always had an aversion to meeting slaves after he had sold them. He ordered Rose out of the house; but he was no longer her master, and she took no notice of him. For once the crushed Rose was the conqueror. His gray eyes flashed angrily upon her; but that was the extent of his power. "How came this girl here?" he exclaimed. "What right had you to allow it, when you knew I had sold her?"

I answered "This is my grandmother's house, and Rose came to see her. I have no right to turn any body out of doors, that comes here for honest purposes."

He gave me the blow that would have fallen upon Rose if she had still been his slave. My grandmother's attention had been attracted by loud voices, and she entered in time to see a second blow dealt. She was not a woman to let such an outrage, in her own house, go unrebuked. The doctor undertook to explain that I had been insolent. Her indignant feelings rose higher and higher, and finally boiled over in words. "Get out of my house!" she exclaimed. "Go home, and take care of your wife and children, and you will have enough to do, without watching my family."

He threw the birth of my children in her face, and accused her of sanctioning the life I was leading. She told him I was living with her by compulsion of his wife; that he needn't accuse her, for he was the one to blame; he was the one who had caused all the trouble. She grew more and more excited as she went on. "I tell you what, Dr. Flint," said she, "you ain't got many more years to live, and you'd better be saying your prayers. It will take 'em all, and more too, to wash the dirt off your soul."

"Do you know whom you are talking to?" he exclaimed.

She replied, "Yes, I know very well who I am talking to."

He left the house in a great rage. I looked at my grandmother. Our eyes met. Their angry expression had passed away, but she looked sorrowful and weary—weary of incessant strife. I wondered that it did not lessen her love for me; but if it did she never showed it. She was always kind, always ready to sympathize with my troubles. There might have been peace and contentment in that humble home if it had not been for the demon Slavery.

The winter passed undisturbed by the doctor. The beautiful spring came; and when Nature resumes her loveliness, the human soul is apt to revive also. My drooping hopes came to life again with the flowers. I was dreaming of freedom again; more for my children's sake than my own. I planned and I planned. Obstacles hit against plans. There seemed no way of overcoming them; and yet I hoped.

Back came the wily doctor. I was not at home when he called. A friend had invited me to a small party, and to gratify her I went. To my great consternation, a messenger came in haste to say that Dr. Flint was at my grandmother's, and insisted on seeing me. They did not tell him where I was, or he would have come and raised a disturbance in my friend's house. They sent me a dark wrapper; I threw it on and hurried home. My speed did not save me; the doctor had gone away in anger. I dreaded the morning, but I could not delay it; it came, warm and bright. At an early hour the doctor came and asked me where I had been last night. I told him. He did not believe me, and sent to my friend's house to ascertain the facts. He came in the afternoon to assure me he was satisfied that I had spoken the truth. He seemed to be in a facetious mood, and I expected some jeers were coming. "I suppose you need some recreation," said he, "but I am surprised at your being there, among those negroes. It was not the place for *you*. Are you *allowed* to visit such people?"

I understood this covert fling at the white gentleman who was my friend; but I merely replied, "I went to visit my friends, and any company they keep is good enough for me."

He went on to say, "I have seen very little of you of late, but my interest in you is unchanged. When I said I would have no more mercy on you I was rash. I recall my words. Linda, you desire freedom for yourself and your children, and you can obtain it only through me. If you agree to what I am about to propose, you and they shall be free. There must be no communication of any kind between you and their father. I will procure a cottage, where you and the children can live together. Your labor shall be light, such as sewing for my family. Think what is offered you, Linda—a home and freedom! Let the past be forgotten. If I have been harsh with you at times, your wilfulness drove me to it. You know I exact obedience from my own children, and I consider you as yet a child."

He paused for an answer, but I remained silent.

"Why don't you speak?" said he. "What more do you wait for?"

"Nothing, sir."

"Then you accept my offer?"

"No, sir."

His anger was ready to break loose; but he succeeded in curbing it, and replied, "You have answered without thought. But I must let you know there are two sides to my proposition; if you reject the bright side, you will be obliged to take the dark one. You must either accept my offer, or you and your children shall be sent to your young master's plantation, there to remain till your young mistress is married; and your children shall fare like the rest of the negro children. I give you a week to consider of it."

He was shrewd; but I knew he was not to be trusted. I told him I was ready to give my answer now.

"I will not receive it now," he replied. "You act too much from impulse. Remember that you and your children can be free a week from to-day if you choose."

On what a monstrous chance hung the destiny of my children! I knew that my master's offer was a snare, and that if I entered it escape would be impossible. As for his promise, I knew him so well that I was sure if he gave me free papers, they would be so managed as to have no legal value. The alternative was inevitable. I resolved to go to the plantation. But then I thought how completely I should be in his power, and the prospect was appalling. Even if I should kneel before him, and implore him to spare me, for the sake of my children, I knew he would spurn me with his foot, and my weakness would be his triumph.

Before the week expired, I heard that young Mr. Flint was about to be married to a lady of his own stamp. I foresaw the position I should occupy in his establishment. I had once been sent to the plantation for punishment, and fear of the son had induced the father to recall me very soon. My mind was made up; I was resolved that I would foil my master and save my children, or I would perish in the attempt. I kept my plans to myself; I knew that friends would try to dissuade me from them, and I would not wound their feelings by rejecting their advice.

On the decisive day the doctor came, and said he hoped I had made a wise choice.

"I am ready to go to the plantation, sir," I replied.

"Have you thought how important your decision is to your children?" said he.

I told him I had.

"Very well. Go to the plantation, and my curse go with you," he replied. "Your boy shall be put to work, and he shall soon be sold; and your girl shall be raised for the purpose of selling well. Go your own ways!" He left the room with curses, not to be repeated.

As I stood rooted to the spot, my grandmother came and said, "Linda, child, what did you tell him?"

I answered that I was going to the plantation.

"*Must* you go?" said she. "Can't something be done to stop it?"

I told her it was useless to try; but she begged me not to give up. She said she would go to the doctor, and remind him how long and how faithfully she had served in the family, and how she had taken her own baby from her breast to nourish his wife. She would tell him I had been out of the family so long they would not miss me; that she would pay them for my time, and the money would procure a woman who had more strength for the situation than I had. I begged her not to go; but she persisted in saying, "He will listen to *me*, Linda." She went, and was treated as I expected. He coolly listened to what she said, but denied her request. He told her that what he did was for my good, that my feelings were entirely above my situation, and that on the plantation I would receive treatment that was suitable to my behavior.

My grandmother was much cast down. I had my secret hopes; but I must fight my battle alone. I had a woman's pride, and a mother's love for my children; and I resolved that out of the darkness of this hour a brighter dawn should rise for them. My master had power and law on his side; I had a determined will. There is might in each.

XVII. The Flight.

MR. FLINT was hard pushed for house servants, and rather than lose me he had restrained his malice. I did my work faithfully, though not, of course, with a willing mind. They were evidently afraid I should leave them. Mr. Flint wished that I should sleep in the great house instead of the servants' quarters. His wife agreed to the proposition, but said I mustn't bring my bed into the house, because it would scatter feathers on her carpet. I knew when I went there that they would never think of such a thing as furnishing a bed of any kind for me and my little one. I therefore carried my own bed, and now I was forbidden to use it. I did as I was ordered. But now that I was certain my children were to be put in their power, in order to give them a stronger hold on me, I resolved to leave them that night. I remembered the grief this step would bring upon my dear old grandmother; and nothing less than the freedom of my children would have induced me to disregard her advice. I went about my evening work with trembling steps. Mr. Flint twice called from his chamber door to inquire why the house was not locked up. I replied that I had not done my work. "You have had time enough to do it," said he. "Take care how you answer me!"

I shut all the windows, locked all the doors, and went up to the third story, to wait till midnight. How long those hours seemed, and how fervently I prayed that God would not forsake me in this hour of utmost need! I was about to risk every thing on the throw of a die; and if I failed, O what would become of me and my poor children? They would be made to suffer for my fault.

At half past twelve I stole softly down stairs. I stopped on the second floor, thinking I heard a noise. I felt my way down into the parlor, and looked out of the window. The night was so intensely dark that I could see nothing. I raised the window very softly and jumped out. Large drops of rain were falling, and the darkness bewildered me. I dropped on my knees, and breathed a short prayer to God for guidance and protection. I groped my way to the road, and rushed towards the town with almost lightning speed. I arrived at my grandmother's house, but dared not see her. She would say, "Linda, you are killing me;" and I knew that would unnerve me. I tapped softly at the window of a room, occupied by a woman, who had lived in the house several years. I knew she was a faithful friend, and could be trusted with my secret. I tapped several times before she heard me. At last she raised the window, and I whispered, "Sally, I have run away. Let me in, quick." She opened the door softly, and said in low tones, "For God's sake, don't. Your grandmother is trying to buy you and de chillern. Mr. Sands was here last week. He tole her he was going away on business, but he wanted her to go ahead about buying you and de chillern, and he would help her all he could. Don't run away, Linda. Your grandmother is all bowed down wid trouble now."

I replied, "Sally, they are going to carry my children to the plantation to-morrow; and they will never sell them to any body so long as they have me in their power. Now, would you advise me to go back?"

"No, chile, no," answered she. "When dey finds you is gone, dey won't want de plague ob de chillern; but where is you going to hide? Dey knows ebery inch ob dis house."

I told her I had a hiding-place, and that was all it was best for her to know. I asked her to go into my room as soon as it was light, and take all my clothes out of my trunk, and pack them in hers; for I knew Mr. Flint and the constable would be there early to search my room. I feared the sight of my children would be too much for my full heart; but I could not go out into the uncertain future without one last look. I bent over the bed where lay my little Benny and baby Ellen. Poor little ones! fatherless and motherless! Memories of their father came over me. He wanted to be kind to them; but they were not all to him, as they were to my womanly heart. I knelt and prayed for the innocent little sleepers. I kissed them lightly, and turned away.

As I was about to open the street door, Sally laid her hand on my shoulder, and said, "Linda, is you gwine all alone? Let me call your uncle."

"No Sally," I replied, "I want no one to be brought into trouble on my account."

I went forth into the darkness and rain. I ran on till I came to the house of the friend who was to conceal me.

Early the next morning Mr. Flint was at my grandmother's inquiring for me. She told him she had not seen me, and supposed I was at the plantation. He watched her face narrowly, and said, "Don't you know any thing about her running off?" She assured him that she did not. He went on to say, "Last night she ran off without the least provocation. We had treated her very kindly. My wife liked her. She will soon be found and brought back. Are her children with you?" When told that they were, he said, "I am very glad to hear that. If they are here, she cannot be far off. If I find out that any of my niggers have had any thing to do with this damned business, I'll give 'em five hundred lashes." As he started to go to his father's, he turned round and added, persuasively, "Let her be brought back, and she shall have her children to live with her."

The tidings made the old doctor rave and storm at a furious rate. It was a busy day for them. My grandmother's house was searched from top to bottom. As my trunk was empty, they concluded I had taken my clothes with me. Before ten o'clock every vessel northward bound was thoroughly examined, and the law against harboring fugitives was read to all on board. At night a watch was set over the town. Knowing how distressed my grandmother would be, I wanted to send her a message; but it could not be done. Every one who went in or out of her house was closely watched. The doctor said he would take my children, unless she became responsible for them; which of course she willingly did. The next day was spent in searching. Before night, the following advertisement was posted at every corner, and in every public place for miles round:—

> "$300 REWARD! Ran away from the subscriber, an intelligent, bright, mulatto girl, named Linda, 21 years of age. Five feet four inches high. Dark eyes, and black hair inclined to curl; but it can be made straight. Has a decayed spot on a front tooth. She can read and write, and in all probability will try to get to the Free States. All persons are forbidden, under penalty of the law, to harbor or employ said slave. $150 will be given to whoever takes her in the state, and $300 if taken out of the state and delivered to me, or lodged in jail.

DR. FLINT."

XXI. The Loophole of Retreat.

A SMALL shed had been added to my grandmother's house years ago. Some boards were laid across the joists at the top, and between these boards and the roof was a very small garret, never occupied by any thing but rats and mice. It was a pent roof, covered with nothing but shingles, according to the southern custom for such buildings. The garret was only nine feet long and seven wide. The highest part was three feet high, and sloped down abruptly to the loose board floor. There was no admission for either light or air. My uncle Philip, who was a carpenter, had very skilfully made a concealed trap-door, which communicated with the storeroom. He had been doing this while I was waiting in the swamp. The storeroom opened upon a piazza. To this hole I was conveyed as soon as I entered the house. The air was stifling; the darkness total. A bed had been spread on the floor. I could sleep quite comfortably on one side; but the slope was so sudden that I could not turn on the other without hitting the roof. The rats and mice ran over my bed; but I was weary, and I slept such sleep as the wretched may, when a tempest has passed over them. Morning came. I knew it only by the noises I heard; for in my small den day and night were all the same. I suffered for air even more than for light. But I was not comfortless. I heard the voices of my children. There was joy and there was sadness in the sound. It made my tears flow. How I longed to speak to them! I was eager to look on their faces; but there was no hole, no crack, through which I could peep.

This continued darkness was oppressive. It seemed horrible to sit or lie in a cramped position day after day, without one gleam of light. Yet I would have chosen this, rather than my lot as a slave, though white people considered it an easy one; and it was so compared with the fate of others. I was never cruelly over-worked; I was never lacerated with the whip from head to foot; I was never so beaten and bruised that I could not turn from one side to the other; I never had my heel-strings cut to prevent my running away; I was never chained to a log and forced to drag it about, while I toiled in the fields from morning till night; I was never branded with hot iron, or torn by bloodhounds. On the contrary, I had always been kindly treated, and tenderly cared for, until I came into the hands of Dr. Flint. I had never wished for freedom till then. But though my life in slavery was comparatively devoid of hardships, God pity the woman who is compelled to lead such a life!

My food was passed up to me through the trap-door my uncle had contrived; and my grandmother, my uncle Phillip, and aunt Nancy would seize such opportunities as they could, to mount up there and chat with me at the opening. But of course this was not safe in the daytime. It must all be done in darkness. It was impossible for me to move in an erect position, but I crawled about my den for exercise. One day I hit my head against something, and found it was a gimlet. My uncle had left it sticking there when he made the trap-door. I was as rejoiced as Robinson Crusoe could have been at finding such a treasure. It put a lucky thought into my head. I said to myself, "Now I will have some light. Now I will see my children." I did not dare to begin my work during the daytime, for fear of attracting attention. But I groped round; and having found the side next the street, where I could frequently see my children, I stuck the gimlet in and waited for evening. I bored three rows of holes, one above another; then I bored out the interstices between. I thus succeeded in making one hole about an inch long and an inch broad. I sat by it till late into the night, to enjoy the little whiff of air that floated in. In the morning I watched for my children. The first person I saw in the street was Dr. Flint. I had a shuddering, superstitious feeling that it was a bad omen. Several familiar faces passed by. At last I heard the merry laugh of children, and presently two sweet little faces were looking up at me, as though they knew I was there, and were conscious of the joy they imparted. How I longed to *tell* them I was there!

My condition was now a little improved. But for weeks I was tormented by hundreds of little red insects, fine as a needle's point, that pierced through my skin, and produced an intolerable burning. The good grandmother gave me herb teas and cooling medicines, and finally I got rid of them. The heat of my den was intense, for nothing but thin shingles protected me from the scorching summer's sun. But I had my consolations. Through my peeping-hole I could watch the children, and when they were near enough, I could hear their talk. Aunt Nancy brought me all the news she could hear at Dr. Flint's. From her I learned that the doctor had writ-

ten to New York to a colored woman, who had been born and raised in our neighborhood, and had breathed his contaminating atmosphere. He offered her a reward
if she could find out any thing about me. I know not what was the nature of her
reply; but he soon after started for New York in haste, saying to his family that he
had business of importance to transact. I peeped at him as he passed on his way to
the steamboat. It was a satisfaction to have miles of land and water between us, even
for a little while; and it was a still greater satisfaction to know that he believed me
to be in the Free States. My little den seemed less dreary than it had done. He
returned, as he did from his former journey to New York, without obtaining any satisfactory information. When he passed our house next morning, Benny was standing at the gate. He had heard them say that he had gone to find me, and he called
out, "Dr. Flint, did you bring my mother home? I want to see her." The doctor
stamped his foot at him in a rage, and exclaimed, "Get out of the way, you little
damned rascal! If you don't, I'll cut off your head."

Benny ran terrified into the house, saying, "You can't put me in jail again. I don't
belong to you now." It was well that the wind carried the words away from the doctor's ear. I told my grandmother of it, when we had our next conference at the trap-
door; and begged of her not to allow the children to be impertinent to the irascible
old man.

Autumn came, with a pleasant abatement of heat. My eyes had become accustomed to the dim light, and by holding my book or work in a certain position near
the aperture I contrived to read and sew. That was a great relief to the tedious
monotony of my life. But when winter came, the cold penetrated through the thin
shingle roof, and I was dreadfully chilled. The winters there are not so long, or so
severe, as in northern latitudes; but the houses are not built to shelter from cold, and
my little den was peculiarly comfortless. The kind grandmother brought me bed-
clothes and warm drinks. Often I was obliged to lie in bed all day to keep comfortable; but with all my precautions, my shoulders and feet were frostbitten. O, those
long, gloomy days, with no object for my eye to rest upon, and no thoughts to occupy my mind, except the dreary past and the uncertain future! I was thankful when
there came a day sufficiently mild for me to wrap myself up and sit at the loophole
to watch the passers by. Southerners have the habit of stopping and talking in the
streets, and I heard many conversations not intended to meet my ears. I heard slave-
hunters planning how to catch some poor fugitive. Several times I heard allusions
to Dr. Flint, myself, and the history of my children, who, perhaps, were playing near
the gate. One would say, "I wouldn't move my little finger to catch her, as old Flint's
property." Another would say, "I'll catch *any* nigger for the reward. A man ought
to have what belongs to him, if he *is* a damned brute." The opinion was often
expressed that I was in the Free States. Very rarely did any one suggest that I
might be in the vicinity. Had the least suspicion rested on my grandmother's house,

it would have been burned to the ground. But it was the last place they thought of. Yet there was no place, where slavery existed, that could have afforded me so good a place of concealment.

Dr. Flint and his family repeatedly tried to coax and bribe my children to tell something they had heard said about me. One day the doctor took them into a shop, and offered them some bright little silver pieces and gay handkerchiefs if they would tell where their mother was. Ellen shrank away from him, and would not speak; but Benny spoke up, and said, "Dr. Flint, I don't know where my mother is. I guess she's in New York; and when you go there again, I wish you'd ask her to come home, for I want to see her; but if you put her in jail, or tell her you'll cut her head off, I'll tell her to go right back."

XXIX. Preparations For Escape.

I HARDLY expect that the reader will credit me, when I affirm that I lived in that little dismal hole, almost deprived of light and air, and with no space to move my limbs, for nearly seven years. But it is a fact; and to me a sad one, even now; for my body still suffers from the effects of that long imprisonment, to say nothing of my soul. Members of my family, now living in New York and Boston, can testify to the truth of what I say.

Countless were the nights that I sat late at the little loophole scarcely large enough to give me a glimpse of one twinkling star. There, I heard the patrols and slave-hunters conferring together about the capture of runaways, well knowing how rejoiced they would be to catch me.

Season after season, year after year, I peeped at my children's faces, and heard their sweet voices, with a heart yearning all the while to say, "Your mother is here." Sometimes it appeared to me as if ages had rolled away since I entered upon that gloomy, monotonous existence. At times, I was stupefied and listless; at other times I became very impatient to know when these dark years would end, and I should again be allowed to feel the sunshine, and breathe the pure air.

After Ellen left us, this feeling increased. Mr. Sands had agreed that Benny might go to the north whenever his uncle Phillip could go with him; and I was anxious to be there also, to watch over my children, and protect them so far as I was able. Moreover, I was likely to be drowned out of my den, if I remained much longer; for the slight roof was getting badly out of repair, and uncle Phillip was afraid to remove the shingles, lest some one should get a glimpse of me. When storms occurred in the night, they spread mats and bits of carpet, which in the morning appeared to have been laid out to dry; but to cover the roof in the daytime might have attracted attention. Consequently, my clothes and bedding were often drenched; a process by which the pains and aches in my cramped and stiffened limbs were greatly increased. I revolved various plans of escape in my mind, which I sometimes imparted to my grandmother, when she came to whisper with me at the trapdoor. The kind-hearted old woman had an intense sympathy for runaways. She had known too much of the cruelties inflicted on those who were captured. Her memory always flew back at once to the sufferings of her bright and handsome son, Benjamin, the youngest and dearest of her flock. So, whenever I alluded to the subject, she would groan out, "O, don't think of it, child. You'll break my heart." I had no good old aunt Nancy now to encourage me; but my brother William and my children were continually beckoning me to the north.

And now I must go back a few months in my story. I have stated that the first of January was the time for selling slaves, or leasing them out to new masters. If time were counted by heart-throbs, the poor slaves might reckon years of suffering during that festival so joyous to the free. On the New Year's day preceding my aunt's death, one of my friends, named Fanny, was to be sold at auction, to pay her master's debts. My thoughts were with her during all the day, and at night I anxiously inquired what had been her fate. I was told that she had been sold to one master, and her four little girls to another master, far distant; that she had escaped from her purchaser, and was not to be found. Her mother was the old Aggie I have spoken of. She lived in a small tenement belonging to my grandmother, and built on the same lot with her own house. Her dwelling was searched and watched, and that brought the patrols so near me that I was obliged to keep very close in my den. The hunters were somehow eluded; and not long afterwards Benny accidentally caught sight of Fanny in her mother's hut. He told his grandmother, who charged him never to speak of it, explaining to him the frightful consequences; and he never betrayed the trust. Aggie little dreamed that my grandmother knew where her daughter was concealed, and that the stooping form of her old neighbor was bending under a similar burden of anxiety and fear; but these dangerous secrets deepened the sympathy between the two old persecuted mothers.

My friend Fanny and I remained many weeks hidden within call of each other; but she was unconscious of the fact. I longed to have her share my den, which seemed a more secure retreat than her own; but I had brought so much trouble on my grandmother, that it seemed wrong to ask her to incur greater risks. My restlessness increased. I had lived too long in bodily pain and anguish of spirit. Always I was in dread that by some accident, or some contrivance, slavery would succeed in snatching my children from me. This thought drove me nearly frantic, and I determined to steer for the North Star at all hazards. At this crisis, Providence opened an unexpected way for me to escape. My friend Peter came one evening, and asked to speak with me. "Your day has come, Linda," said he. "I have found a chance for you to go to the Free States. You have a fortnight to decide." The news seemed too good to be true; but Peter explained his arrangements, and told me all that was necessary was for me to say I would go. I was going to answer him with a joyful yes, when the thought of Benny came to my mind. I told him the temptation was exceedingly strong, but I was terribly afraid of Dr. Flint's alleged power over my child, and that I could not go and leave him behind. Peter remonstrated earnestly. He said such a good chance might never occur again; that Benny was free, and could be sent to me; and that for the sake of my children's welfare I ought not to hesitate a moment. I told him I would consult with uncle Phillip. My uncle rejoiced in the plan, and bade me to go by all means. He promised, if his life was spared, that he would either bring or send my son to me as soon as I reached a place of safety. I resolved to go, but thought nothing had better be said to my grandmother till very near the time of departure. But my uncle thought she would feel it more keenly if I left her so suddenly. "I will reason with her," said he, "and convince her how necessary it is, not only for your sake, but for hers also. You cannot be blind to the fact that she is sinking under her burdens." I was not blind to it. I knew that my concealment was an ever-present source of anxiety, and that the older she grew the more nervously fearful she was of discovery. My uncle talked with her, and finally succeeded in persuading her that it was absolutely necessary for me to seize the chance so unexpectedly offered.

The anticipation of being a free woman proved almost too much for my weak frame. The excitement stimulated me, and at the same time bewildered me. I made busy preparations for my journey, and for my son to follow me. I resolved to have an interview with him before I went, that I might give him cautions and advice, and tell him how anxiously I should be waiting for him at the north. Grandmother stole up to me as often as possible to whisper words of counsel. She insisted upon my writing to Dr. Flint, as soon as I arrived in the Free States, and asking him to sell me to her. She said she would sacrifice her house, and all she had in the world, for the sake of having me safe with my children in any part of the world. If she could only live to know *that* she could die in peace. I promised the dear old faithful friend that I would write to her as soon as I arrived, and put the letter in a safe way to reach her; but in my own mind I resolved that not another cent of her hard earnings should be spent to pay rapacious slaveholders for what they called their property. And even if I had not been unwilling to buy what I had already a right to possess, common humanity would have prevented me from accepting the generous offer, at the expense of turning my aged relative out of house and home, when she was trembling on the brink of the grave.

I was to escape in a vessel; but I forbear to mention any further particulars. I was in readiness, but the vessel was unexpectedly detained several days. Meantime, news came to town of a most horrible murder committed on a fugitive slave, named James. Charity, the mother of this unfortunate young man, had been an old acquaintance of ours. I have told the shocking particulars of his death, in my description of some of the neighboring slaveholders. My grandmother, always nervously sensitive about runaways, was terribly frightened. She felt sure that a similar fate awaited me, if I did not desist from my enterprise. She sobbed, and groaned, and entreated me not to go. Her excessive fear was somewhat contagious, and my heart was not proof against her extreme agony. I was grievously disappointed, but I promised to relinquish my project.

When my friend Peter was apprised of this, he was both disappointed and vexed. He said, that judging from our past experience, it would be a long time before I had such another chance to throw away. I told him it need not be thrown away; that I had a friend concealed near by, who would be glad enough to take the place that had been provided for me. I told him about poor Fanny, and the kind-hearted, noble fellow, who never turned his back upon any body in distress, white or black, expressed his readiness to help her. Aggie was much surprised when she found that we knew her secret. She was rejoiced to hear of such a chance for Fanny, and arrangements were made for her to go on board the vessel the next night. They both supposed that I had long been at the north, therefore my name was not mentioned in the transaction. Fanny was carried on board at the appointed time, and stowed away in a very small cabin. This accommodation had been purchased at a price that would pay for a voyage to England. But when one proposes to go to fine old England, they stop to calculate whether they can afford the cost of the pleasure; while in making a bargain to escape from slavery, the trembling victim is ready to say, "Take all I have, only don't betray me!"

The next morning I peeped through my loophole, and saw that it was dark and cloudy. At night I received news that the wind was ahead, and the vessel had not sailed. I was exceedingly anxious about Fanny, and Peter too, who was running a tremendous risk at my instigation. Next day the wind and weather remained the same. Poor Fanny had been half dead with fright when they carried her on board, and I could readily imagine how she must be suffering now. Grandmother came often to my den, to say how thankful she was I did not go. On the third morning she rapped for me to come down to the storeroom. The poor old sufferer was breaking down under her weight of trouble. She was easily flurried now. I found her in a nervous, excited state, but I was not aware that she had forgotten to lock the door behind her, as usual. She was exceedingly worried about the detention of the vessel. She was afraid all would be discovered, and then Fanny, and Peter, and I, would all be tortured to death, and Phillip would be utterly ruined, and her house would be torn down. Poor Peter! If he should die such a horrible death as the poor slave James had lately done, and all for his kindness in trying to help me, how dreadful it would be for us all! Alas, the thought was familiar to me, and had sent many a sharp pang through my heart. I tried to suppress my own anxiety, and speak sooth-ingly to her. She brought in some allusion to aunt Nancy, the dear daughter she had recently buried, and then she lost all control of herself. As she stood there, trembling and sobbing, a voice from the piazza called out, "Whar is you, aunt Marthy?" Grandmother was startled, and in her agitation opened the door, without thinking of me. In stepped Jenny, the mischievous housemaid, who had tried to enter my room, when I was concealed in the house of my white benefactress. "I's bin huntin ebery whar for you, aunt Marthy," said she. "My missis wants you to send her some crackers." I had slunk down behind a barrel, which entirely screened me, but I imagined that Jenny was looking directly at the spot, and my heart beat violently. My grandmother immediately thought what she had done, and went out quickly with Jenny to count the crackers locking the door after her. She returned to me, in a few minutes, the perfect picture of despair. "Poor child!" she exclaimed, "my carelessness has ruined you. The boat ain't gone yet. Get ready immediately, and go with Fanny. I ain't got another word to say against it now; for there's no telling what may happen this day."

Uncle Phillip was sent for, and he agreed with his mother in thinking that Jenny would inform Dr. Flint in less than twenty-four hours. He advised getting me on board the boat, if possible; if not, I had better keep very still in my den, where they could not find me without tearing the house down. He said it would not do for him to move in the matter, because suspicion would be immediately excited; but he promised to communicate with Peter. I felt reluctant to apply to him again, having implicated him too much already; but there seemed to be no alternative. Vexed as Peter had been by my indecision, he was true to his generous nature, and said at once that he would do his best to help me, trusting I should show myself a stronger woman this time.

He immediately proceeded to the wharf, and found that the wind had shifted, and the vessel was slowly beating down stream. On some pretext of urgent necessity, he offered two boatmen a dollar apiece to catch up with her. He was of lighter complexion than the boatmen he hired, and when the captain saw them coming so rapidly, he thought officers were pursuing his vessel in search of the runaway slave he had on board. They hoisted sails, but the boat gained upon them, and the indefatigable Peter sprang on board.

The captain at once recognized him. Peter asked him to go below, to speak about a bad bill he had given him. When he told his errand, the captain replied, "Why, the woman's here already; and I've put her where you or the devil would have a tough job to find her."

"But it is another woman I want to bring," said Peter. "*She* is in great distress, too, and you shall be paid any thing within reason, if you'll stop and take her."

"What's her name?" inquired the captain.

"Linda," he replied.

"That's the the name of the woman already here," rejoined the captain. "By George! I believe you mean to betray me."

"O!" exclaimed Peter, "God knows I wouldn't harm a hair of your head. I am too grateful to you. But there really *is* another woman in great danger. Do have the humanity to stop and take her!"

After a while they came to an understanding. Fanny, not dreaming I was any where about in that region, had assumed my name, though she called herself Johnson. "Linda is a common name," said Peter, "and the woman I want to bring is Linda Brent."

The captain agreed to wait at a certain place till evening, being handsomely paid for his detention.

Of course, the day was an anxious one for us all. But we concluded that if Jenny had seen me, she would be too wise to let her mistress know of it; and that she probably would not get a chance to see Dr. Flint's family till evening, for I knew very well what were the rules in that household. I afterwards believed that she did not see me; for nothing ever came of it, and she was one of those base characters that would have jumped to betray a suffering fellow being for the sake of thirty pieces of silver.

I made all my arrangements to go on board as soon as it was dusk. The intervening time I resolved to spend with my son. I had not spoken to him for seven years, though I had been under the same roof, and seen him every day, when I was well enough to sit at the loophole. I did not dare to venture beyond the storeroom; so they brought him there, and locked us up together, in a place concealed from the piazza door. It was an agitating interview for both of us. After we had talked and wept together for a little while, he said, "Mother, I'm glad you're going away. I wish I could go with you. I knew you was here; and I have been *so* afraid they would come and catch you!"

I was greatly surprised, and asked him how he had found it out.

He replied, "I was standing under the eaves, one day, before Ellen went away, and I heard somebody cough up over the wood shed. I don't know what made me think it was you, but I did think so. I missed Ellen, the night before she went away; and grandmother brought her back into the room in the night; and I thought maybe she'd been to see *you*, before she went, for I heard grandmother whisper to her, 'Now go to sleep; and remember never to tell.'"

I asked him if he ever mentioned his suspicions to his sister. He said he never did; but after he heard the cough, if he saw her playing with other children on that side of the house, he always tried to coax her round to the other side, for fear they would hear me cough, too. He said he had kept a close lookout for Dr. Flint, and if he saw him speak to a constable, or a patrol, he always told grandmother. I now recollected that I had seen him manifest uneasiness, when people were on that side of the house, and I had at the time been puzzled to conjecture a motive for his actions. Such prudence may seem extraordinary in a boy of twelve years, but slaves, being surrounded by mysteries, deceptions, and dangers, early learn to be suspicious and watchful, and prematurely cautious and cunning. He had never asked a question of grandmother, or uncle Phillip, and I had often heard him chime in with other children, when they spoke of my being at the north.

I told him I was now really going to the Free States, and if he was a good, honest boy, and a loving child to his dear old grandmother, the Lord would bless him, and bring him to me, and we and Ellen would live together. He began to tell me that grandmother had not eaten any thing all day. While he was speaking, the door was unlocked, and she came in with a small bag of money, which she wanted me to take. I begged her to keep a part of it, at least, to pay for Benny's being sent to the north; but she insisted, while her tears were falling fast, that I should take the whole. "You may be sick among strangers," she said, "and they would send you to the poorhouse to die." Ah, that good grandmother!

For the last time I went up to my nook. Its desolate appearance no longer chilled me, for the light of hope had risen in my soul. Yet, even with the blessed prospect of freedom before me, I felt very sad at leaving forever that old homestead, where I had been sheltered so long by the dear old grandmother; where I had dreamed my first young dream of love; and where, after that had faded away, my children came to twine themselves so closely round my desolate heart. As the hour approached for me to leave, I again descended to the storeroom. My grandmother and Benny were there. She took me by the hand, and said, "Linda, let us pray." We knelt down together, with my child pressed to my heart, and my other arm round the faithful, loving old friend I was about to leave forever. On no other occasion has it ever been my lot to listen to so fervent a supplication for mercy and protection. It thrilled through my heart, and inspired me with trust in God.

Peter was waiting for me in the street. I was soon by his side, faint in body, but strong of purpose. I did not look back upon the old place, though I felt that I should never see it again.

XXX. Northward Bound.

I NEVER could tell how we reached the wharf. My brain was all of a whirl, and my limbs tottered under me. At an appointed place we met my uncle Phillip, who had started before us on a different route, that he might reach the wharf first, and give us timely warning if there was any danger. A row-boat was in readiness. As I was about to step in, I felt something pull me gently, and turning round I saw Benny, looking pale and anxious. He whispered in my ear, "I've been peeping into the doctor's window, and he's at home. Good by, mother. Don't cry; I'll come." He hastened away. I clasped the hand of my good uncle, to whom I owed so much, and of Peter, the brave, generous friend who had volunteered to run such terrible risks to secure my safety. To this day I remember how his bright face beamed with joy, when he told me he had discovered a safe method for me to escape. Yet that intelligent, enterprising, noble-hearted man was a chattel! liable, by the laws of a country that calls itself civilized, to be sold with horses and pigs! We parted in silence. Our hearts were all too full for words!

Swiftly the boat glided over the water. After a while, one of the sailors said, "Don't be down-hearted, madam. We will take you safely to your husband, in_____." At first I could not imagine what he meant; but I had presence of mind to think that it probably referred to something the captain had told him; so I thanked him, and said I hoped we should have pleasant weather.

When I entered the vessel the captain came forward to meet me. He was an elderly man, with a pleasant countenance. He showed me to a little box of a cabin, where sat my friend Fanny. She started as if she had seen a spectre. She gazed on me in utter astonishment, and exclaimed, "Linda, can this be *you*? or is it your ghost?" When we were locked in each other's arms, my overwrought feelings could no longer be restrained. My sobs reached the ears of the captain, who came and very kindly reminded us, that for his safety, as well as our own, it would be prudent for us not to attract any attention. He said that when there was a sail in sight he wished us to keep below; but at other times, he had no objection to our being on deck. He assured us that he would keep a good lookout, and if we acted prudently, he thought we should be in no danger. He had represented us as women going to meet our husbands in_____. We thanked him, and promised to observe carefully all the directions he gave us.

Fanny and I now talked by ourselves, low and quietly, in our little cabin. She told me of the sufferings she had gone through in making her escape, and of her terrors while she was concealed in her mother's house. Above all, she dwelt on the agony of separation from all her children on that dreadful auction day. She could scarcely credit me, when I told her of the place where I had passed nearly seven years. "We have the same sorrows," said I. "No," replied she, "you are going to see your children soon, and there is no hope that I shall ever even hear from mine."

The vessel was soon under way, but we made slow progress. The wind was against us. I should not have cared for this, if we had been out of sight of the town; but until there were miles of water between us and our enemies, we were filled with constant apprehensions that the constables would come on board. Neither could I feel quite at ease with the captain and his men. I was an entire stranger to that class of people, and I had heard that sailors were rough, and sometimes cruel. We were so completely in their power, that if they were bad men, our situation would be dreadful. Now that the captain was paid for our passage, might he not be tempted to make more money by giving us up to those who claimed us as property? I was naturally of a confiding disposition, but slavery had made me suspicious of every body. Fanny did not share my distrust of the captain or his men. She said she was afraid at first, but she had been on board three days while the vessel lay in the dock, and nobody had betrayed her, or treated her otherwise than kindly.

The captain soon came to advise us to go on deck for fresh air. His friendly and respectful manner, combined with Fanny's testimony, reassured me, and we went with him. He placed us in a comfortable seat, and occasionally entered into conversation. He told us he was a Southerner by birth, and had spent the greater part of his life in the Slave States, and that he had recently lost a brother who traded in slaves. "But," said he, "it is a pitiable and degrading business, and I always felt ashamed to acknowledge my brother in connection with it." As we passed Snaky Swamp, he pointed to it, and said, "There is a slave territory that defies all the laws." I thought of the terrible days I had spent there, and though it was not called Dismal Swamp, it made me feel very dismal as I looked at it.

I shall never forget that night. The balmy air of spring was so refreshing! And how shall I describe my sensations when we were fairly sailing on Chesapeake Bay? O, the beautiful sunshine! the exhilarating breeze! and I could enjoy them without fear or restraint. I had never realized what grand things air and sunlight are till I had been deprived of them.

Ten days after we left land we were approaching Philadelphia. The captain said we should arrive there in the night, but he thought we had better wait till morning, and go on shore in broad daylight, as the best way to avoid suspicion.

I replied, "You know best. But will you stay on board and protect us?"

He saw that I was suspicious, and he said he was sorry, now that he had brought us to the end of our voyage, to find I had so little confidence in him. Ah, if he had ever been a slave he would have known how difficult it was to trust a white man. He assured us that we might sleep through the night without fear; that he would take care we were not left unprotected. Be it said to the honor of this captain, Southerner as he was, that if Fanny and I had been white ladies, and our passage lawfully engaged, he could not have treated us more respectfully. My intelligent friend, Peter, had rightly estimated the character of the man to whose honor he had intrusted us.

The next morning I was on deck as soon as the day dawned. I called Fanny to see the sun rise, for the first time in our lives, on free soil; for such I *then* believed it to be. We watched the reddening sky, and saw the great orb come up slowly out of the water, as it seemed. Soon the waves began to sparkle, and every thing caught the beautiful glow. Before us lay the city of strangers. We looked at each other, and the eyes of both were moistened with tears. We had escaped from slavery, and we supposed ourselves to be safe from the hunters. But we were alone in the world, and we had left dear ties behind us; ties cruelly sundered by the demon Slavery.

XXXII. The Meeting Of Mother And Daughter.

WHEN we arrived in New York, I was half crazed by the crowd of coachmen calling out, "Carriage, ma'am?" We bargained with one to take us to Sullivan Street for twelve shillings. A burly Irishman stepped up and said, "I'll tak' ye for sax shillings." The reduction of half the price was an object to us, and we asked if he could take us right away. "Troth an I will, ladies," he replied. I noticed that the hackmen smiled at each other, and I inquired whether his conveyance was decent. "Yes, it's dacent it is, marm. Devil a bit would I be after takin' ladies in a cab that was not dacent." We gave him our checks. He went for the baggage, and soon reappeared, saying, "This way, if you plase, ladies." We followed, and found our trunks on a truck, and we were invited to take our seats on them. We told him that was not what we bargained for, and he must take the trunks off. He swore they should not be touched till we had paid him six shillings. In our situation it was not prudent to attract attention, and I was about to pay him what he required, when a man near by shook his head for me not to do it. After a great ado we got rid of the Irishman, and had our trunks fastened on a hack. We had been recommended to a boarding-house in Sullivan Street, and thither we drove. There Fanny and I separated. The Anti-Slavery Society provided a home for her, and I afterwards heard of her in prosperous circumstances. I sent for an old friend from my part of the country, who had for some time been doing business in New York. He came immediately. I told him I wanted to go to my daughter, and asked him to aid me in procuring an interview.

I cautioned him not to let it be known to the family that I had just arrived from the south, because they supposed I had been at the north seven years. He told me there was a colored woman in Brooklyn who came from the same town I did, and I had better go to her house, and have my daughter meet me there. I accepted the proposition thankfully, and he agreed to escort me to Brooklyn. We crossed Fulton ferry, went up Myrtle Avenue, and stopped at the house he designated. I was just about to enter, when two girls passed. My friend called my attention to them. I turned, and recognized in the eldest, Sarah, the daughter of a woman who used to live with my grandmother, but who had left the south years ago. Surprised and rejoiced at this unexpected meeting, I threw my arms round her, and inquired concerning her mother.

"You take no notice of the other girl," said my friend. I turned, and there stood my Ellen! I pressed her to my heart, then held her away from me to take a look at her. She had changed a good deal in the two years since I parted from her. Signs of neglect could be discerned by eyes less observing than a mother's. My friend invited us all to go into the house; but Ellen said she had been sent on an errand, which she would do as quickly as possible, and go home and ask Mrs. Hobbs to let her come and see me. It was agreed that I should send for her the next day. Her companion, Sarah, hastened to tell her mother of my arrival. When I entered the house, I found the mistress of it absent, and I waited for her return. Before I saw her, I heard her saying, "Where is Linda Brent? I used to know her father and mother." Soon Sarah came with her mother. So there was quite a company of us, all from my grandmother's neighborhood. These friends gathered round me and questioned me eagerly. They laughed, they cried, and they shouted. They thanked God that I had got away from my persecutors and was safe on Long Island. It was a day of great excitement. How different from the silent days I had passed in my dreary den!

The next morning was Sunday. My first waking thoughts were occupied with the note that I was to send to Mrs. Hobbs, the lady with whom Ellen lived. That I had recently come into that vicinity was evident; otherwise I should have sooner inquired for my daughter. It would not do to let them know I had just arrived from the south, for that would involve the suspicion of my having been harbored there, and might bring trouble, if not ruin, on several people.

I like a straightforward course, and am always reluctant to resort to subterfuges. So far as my ways have been crooked, I charge them all upon slavery. It was that system of violence and wrong which now left me no alternative but to enact a falsehood. I began my note by stating that I had recently arrived from Canada, and was very desirous to have my daughter come to see me. She came and brought a message from Mrs. Hobbs, inviting me to her house, and assuring me that I need not have any fears. The conversation I had with my child did not leave my mind at ease. When I asked if she was well treated, she answered yes; but there was no heartiness in the tone, and it seemed to me that she said it from an unwillingness to have me troubled on her account. Before she left me, she asked very earnestly, "Mother, when will you take me to live with you?" It made me sad to think that I could not give her a home till I went to work and earned the means; and that might take me a long time. When she was placed with Mrs. Hobbs, the agreement was that she should be sent to school. She had been there two years, and was now nine years old, and she scarcely knew her letters. There was no excuse for this, for there were good public schools in Brooklyn, to which she could have been sent without expense.

She staid with me till dark, and I went home with her. I was received in a friendly manner by the family, and all agreed in saying that Ellen was a useful, good girl. Mrs. Hobbs looked me coolly in the face, and said, "I suppose you know that my cousin, Mr. Sands, has *given* her to my eldest daughter. She will make a nice waiting-maid for her when she grows up." I did not answer a word. How *could* she, who knew by experience the strength of a mother's love, and who was perfectly aware of the relation Mr. Sands bore to my children,—how *could* she look me in the face, while she thrust such a dagger into my heart?. . .

XXXIII. A Home Found.

MY greatest anxiety now was to obtain employment. My health was greatly improved, though my limbs continued to trouble me with swelling whenever I walked much. The greatest difficulty in my way was, that those who employed strangers required a recommendation; and in my peculiar position, I could, of course, obtain no certificates from the families I had so faithfully served.

One day an acquaintance told me of a lady who wanted a nurse for her babe, and I immediately applied for the situation. The lady told me she preferred to have one who had been a mother, and accustomed to the care of infants. I told her I had nursed two babes of my own. She asked me many questions, but, to my great relief, did not require a recommendation from my former employers. She told me she was an English woman, and that was a pleasant circumstance to me, because I had heard they had less prejudice against color than Americans entertained. It was agreed that we should try each other for a week. The trial proved satisfactory to both parties, and I was engaged for a month.

The heavenly Father had been most merciful to me in leading me to this place. Mrs. Bruce was a kind and gentle lady, and proved a true and sympathizing friend. Before the stipulated month expired, the necessity of passing up and down stairs frequently, caused my limbs to swell so painfully, that I became unable to perform my duties. Many ladies would have thoughtlessly discharged me; but Mrs. Bruce made arrangements to save me steps, and employed a physician to attend upon me. I had not yet told her that I was a fugitive slave. She noticed that I was often sad, and kindly inquired the cause. I spoke of being separated from my children, and from relatives who were dear to me; but I did not mention the constant feeling of insecurity which oppressed my spirits. I longed for some one to confide in; but I had been so deceived by white people, that I had lost all confidence in them. If they spoke kind words to me, I thought it was for some selfish purpose. I had entered this family with the distrustful feelings I had brought with me out of slavery; but ere six months had passed, I found that the gentle deportment of Mrs. Bruce and the smiles of her lovely babe were thawing my chilled heart. My narrow mind also began to expand under the influences of her intelligent conversation, and the opportunities for reading, which were gladly allowed me whenever I had leisure from my duties. I gradually became more energetic and more cheerful.

The old feeling of insecurity, especially with regard to my children, often threw its dark shadow across my sunshine. Mrs. Bruce offered me a home for Ellen; but pleasant as it would have been, I did not dare to accept it, for fear of offending the Hobbs family. Their knowledge of my precarious situation placed me in their power; and I felt that it was important for me to keep on the right side of them, till, by dint of labor and economy, I could make a home for my children. I was far from feeling satisfied with Ellen's situation. She was not well cared for. She sometimes came to New York to visit me; but she generally brought a request from Mrs. Hobbs that I would buy her a pair of shoes, or some article of clothing. This was accompanied by a promise of payment when Mr. Hobb's salary at the Custom House became due; but some how or other the pay-day never came. Thus many dollars of my earnings were expended to keep my child comfortably clothed. That, however, was a slight trouble, compared with the fear that their pecuniary embarrassments might induce them to sell my precious young daughter. I knew they were in constant communication with Southerners, and had frequent opportunities to do it. I have stated that when Dr. Flint put Ellen in jail, at two years old, she had an inflammation of the eyes, occasioned by measles. This disease still troubled her; and kind Mrs. Bruce proposed that she should come to New York for a while, to be under the care of Dr. Elliott, a well known oculist. It did not occur to me that there was any thing improper in a mother's making such a request; but Mrs. Hobbs was very angry, and refused to let her go. Situated as I was, it was not politic to insist upon it. I made no complaint, but I longed to be entirely free to act a mother's part towards my children. The next time I went over to Brooklyn, Mrs. Hobbs, as if to apologize for her anger, told me she had employed her own physician to attend to Ellen's eyes, and that she had refused my request because she did not consider it safe to trust her in New York. I accepted the explanation in silence; but she had told me that my child *belonged* to her daughter, and I suspected that her real motive was a fear of my conveying her property away from her. Perhaps I did her injustice; but my knowledge of Southerners made it difficult for me to feel otherwise.

Sweet and bitter were mixed in the cup of my life, and I was thankful that it had ceased to be entirely bitter. I loved Mrs. Bruce's babe. When it laughed and crowed in my face, and twined its little tender arms confidingly about my neck, it made me think of the time when Benny and Ellen were babies, and my wounded heart was soothed. One bright morning, as I stood at the window, tossing baby in my arms, my attention was attracted by a young man in sailor's dress, who was closely observing every house as he passed. I looked at him earnestly. Could it be my brother William? It *must* be he—and yet, how changed! I placed the baby safely, flew down stairs, opened the front door, beckoned to the sailor, and in less than a minute I was clasped in my brother's arms. How much we had to tell each other! How we laughed, and how we cried, over each other's adventures! I took him to Brooklyn, and again saw him with Ellen, the dear child whom he had loved and tended so carefully, while I was shut up in my miserable den. He staid in New York a week. His old feelings of affection for me and Ellen were as lively as ever. There are no bonds so strong as those which are formed by suffering together.

XXXVI. The Hairbreadth Escape.

AFTER we returned to New York, I took the earliest opportunity to go and see Ellen. I asked to have her called down stairs; for I supposed Mrs. Hobbs's southern brother might still be there, and I was desirous to avoid seeing him, if possible. But Mrs. Hobbs came to the kitchen, and insisted on my going up stairs. "My brother wants to see you," said she, "and he is sorry you seem to shun him. He knows you are living in New York. He told me to say to you that he owes thanks to good old aunt Martha for too many little acts of kindness for him to be base enough to betray her grandchild."

This Mr. Thorne had become poor and reckless long before he left the south, and such persons had much rather go to one of the faithful old slaves to borrow a dollar, or get a good dinner, than to go to one whom they consider an equal. It was such acts of kindness as these for which he professed to feel grateful to my grandmother. I wished he had kept at a distance, but as he was here, and knew where I was, I concluded there was nothing to be gained by trying to avoid him; on the contrary, it might be the means of exciting his ill will. I followed his sister up stairs. He met me in a very friendly manner, congratulated me on my escape from slavery, and hoped I had a good place, where I felt happy.

I continued to visit Ellen as often as I could. She, good thoughtful child, never forgot my hazardous situation, but always kept a vigilant lookout for my safety. She never made any complaint about her own inconveniences and troubles; but a mother's observing eye easily perceived that she was not happy. On the occasion of one of my visits I found her unusually serious. When I asked her what was the matter, she said nothing was the matter. But I insisted upon knowing what made her look so very grave. Finally, I ascertained that she felt troubled about the dissipation that was continually going on in the house. She was sent to the store very often for rum and brandy, and she felt ashamed to ask for it so often; and Mr. Hobbs and Mr. Thorne drank a great deal, and their hands trembled so that they had to call her to pour out the liquor for them. "But for all that," said she, "Mr. Hobbs is good to me, and I can't help liking him. I feel sorry for him." I tried to comfort her, by telling her that I had laid up a hundred dollars, and that before long I hoped to be able to give her and Benjamin a home, and send them to school. She was always desirous not to add to my troubles more than she could help, and I did not discover till years afterwards that Mr. Thorne's intemperance was not the only annoyance she suffered from him. Though he professed too much gratitude to my grandmother to injure any of her descendants, he had poured vile language into the ears of her innocent great-grandchild.

I usually went to Brooklyn to spend Sunday afternoon. One Sunday, I found Ellen anxiously waiting for me near the house. "O, mother," said she, "I've been wait-ing for you this long time. I'm afraid Mr. Thorne has written to tell Dr. Flint where you are. Make haste and come in. Mrs. Hobbs will tell you all about it!"

The story was soon told. While the children were playing in the grape-vine arbor, the day before, Mr. Thorne came out with a letter in his hand, which he tore up and scattered about. Ellen was sweeping the yard at the time, and having her mind full of suspicions of him, she picked up the pieces and carried them to the chil-dren, saying, "I wonder who Mr. Thorne has been writing to."

"I'm sure I don't know, and don't care," replied the oldest of the children; "and I don't see how it concerns you."

"But it does concern me," replied Ellen; "for I'm afraid he's been writing to the south about my mother."

They laughed at her, and called her a silly thing, but good-naturedly put the fragments of writing together, in order to read them to her. They were no sooner arranged, than the little girl exclaimed, "I declare, Ellen, I believe you are right."

The contents of Mr. Thorne's letter, as nearly as I can remember, were as fol-lows: "I have seen your slave, Linda, and conversed with her. She can be taken very easily, if you manage prudently. There are enough of us here to swear to her iden-tity as your property. I am a patriot, a lover of my country, and I do this as an act of justice to the laws." He concluded by informing the doctor of the street and num-ber where I lived. The children carried the pieces to Mrs. Hobbs, who immediate-ly went to her brother's room for an explanation. He was not to be found. The servants said they saw him go out with a letter in his hand, and they supposed he had gone to the post office. The natural inference was, that he had sent to Dr. Flint a copy of those fragments. When he returned, his sister accused him of it, and he did not deny the charge. He went immediately to his room, and the next morning he was missing. He had gone over to New York, before any of the family were astir.

It was evident that I had no time to lose; and I hastened back to the city with a heavy heart. Again I was to be torn from a comfortable home, and all my plans for the welfare of my children were to be frustrated by that demon Slavery! I now regretted that I never told Mrs. Bruce my story. I had not concealed it merely on account of being a fugitive; that would have made her anxious, but it would have excited sympathy in her kind heart. I valued her good opinion, and I was afraid of losing it, if I told her all the particulars of my sad story. But now I felt that it was necessary for her to know how I was situated. I had once left her abruptly, without explaining the reason, and it would not be proper to do it again. I went home resolved to tell her in the morning. But the sadness of my face attracted her attention, and, in answer to her kind inquiries, I poured out my full heart to her, before bed time. She listened with true womanly sympathy, and told me she would do all she could to protect me. How my heart blessed her!

Early the next morning, Judge Vanderpool and Lawyer Hopper were consulted. They said I had better leave the city at once, as the risk would be great if the case came to trial. Mrs. Bruce took me in a carriage to the house of one of her friends, where she assured me I should be safe until my brother could arrive, which would be in a few days. In the interval my thoughts were much occupied with Ellen. She was mine by birth, and she was also mine by Southern law, since my grandmother held the bill of sale that made her so. I did not feel that she was safe unless I had her with me. Mrs. Hobbs, who felt badly about her brother's treachery, yielded to my entreaties, on condition that she should return in ten days. I avoided making any promise. She came to me clad in very thin garments, all outgrown, and with a school satchel on her arm, containing a few articles. It was late in October, and I knew the child must suffer; and not daring to go out in the streets to purchase any thing, I took off my own flannel skirt and converted it into one for her. Kind Mrs. Bruce came to bid me good by, and when she saw that I had taken off my clothing for my child, the tears came to her eyes. She said, "Wait for me, Linda," and went out. She soon returned with a nice warm shawl and hood for Ellen. Truly, of such souls as hers are the kingdom of heaven.

My brother reached New York on Wednesday. Lawyer Hopper advised us to go to Boston by the Stonington route, as there was less Southern travel in that direction. Mrs. Bruce directed her servants to tell all inquirers that I formerly lived there, but had gone from the city.

We reached the steamboat Rhode Island in safety. That boat employed colored hands, but I knew that colored passengers were not admitted to the cabin. I was very desirous for the seclusion of the cabin, not only on account of exposure to the night air, but also to avoid observation. Lawyer Hopper was waiting on board for us. He spoke to the stewardess, and asked, as a particular favor, that she would treat us well. He said to me, "Go and speak to the captain yourself by and by. Take your little girl with you, and I am sure that he will not let her sleep on deck." With these kind words and a shake of the hand he departed.

The boat was soon on her way, bearing me rapidly from the friendly home where I had hoped to find security and rest. My brother had left me to purchase the tickets, thinking that I might have better success than he would. When the stewardess came to me, I paid what she asked, and she gave me three tickets with clipped corners. In the most unsophisticated manner I said, "You have made a mistake; I asked you for cabin tickets. I cannot possibly consent to sleep on deck with my little daughter." She assured me there was no mistake. She said on some of the routes colored people were allowed to sleep in the cabin, but not on this route, which was much travelled by the wealthy. I asked her to show me to the captain's office, and she said she would after tea. When the time came, I took Ellen by the hand and went to the captain, politely requesting him to change our tickets, as we should be very uncomfortable on deck. He said it was contrary to their custom, but he would see that we had berths below; he would also try to obtain comfortable seats for us in the cars; of that he was not certain, but he would speak to the conductor about it, when the boat arrived. I thanked him, and returned to the ladies' cabin. He came afterwards and told me that the conductor of the cars was on board, that he had spoken to him, and he had promised to take care of us. I was very much surprised at receiving so much kindness. I don't know whether the pleasing face of my little girl had won his heart, or whether the stewardess inferred from Lawyer Hopper's manner that I was a fugitive, and had pleaded with him in my behalf.

When the boat arrived at Stonington, the conductor kept his promise, and showed us to seats in the first car, nearest the engine. He asked us to take seats next the door, but as he passed through, we ventured to move on toward the other end of the car. No incivility was offered us, and we reached Boston in safety.

The day after my arrival was one of the happiest of my life. I felt as if I was beyond the reach of the bloodhounds; and, for the first time during many years, I had both my children together with me. They greatly enjoyed their reunion, and laughed and chatted merrily. I watched them with a swelling heart. Their every motion delighted me.

I could not feel safe in New York, and I accepted the offer of a friend, that we should share expenses and keep house together. I represented to Mrs. Hobbs that Ellen must have some schooling, and must remain with me for that purpose. She felt ashamed of being unable to read or spell at her age, so instead of sending her to school with Benny, I instructed her myself till she was fitted to enter an intermediate school. The winter passed pleasantly, while I was busy with my needle, and my children with their books.

XXXIX. The Confession.

FOR two years my daughter and I supported ourselves comfortably in Boston. At the end of that time, my brother William offered to send Ellen to a boarding school. It required a great effort for me to consent to part with her, for I had few near ties, and it was her presence that made my two little rooms seem home-like. But my judgment prevailed over my selfish feelings. I made preparations for her departure. During the two years we had lived together I had often resolved to tell her something about her father; but I had never been able to muster sufficient courage. I had a shrinking dread of diminishing my child's love. I knew she must have curiosity on the subject, but she had never asked a question. She was always very careful not to say any thing to remind me of my troubles. Now that she was going from me, I thought if I should die before she returned, she might hear my story from some one who did not understand the palliating circumstances; and that if she were entirely ignorant on the subject, her sensitive nature might receive a rude shock.

When we retired for the night, she said, "Mother, it is very hard to leave you alone. I am almost sorry I am going, though I do want to improve myself. But you will write to me often; won't you, mother?"

I did not throw my arms round her. I did not anwer her. But in a calm, solemn way, for it cost me great effort, I said, "Listen to me, Ellen; I have something to tell you!" I recounted my early sufferings in slavery, and told her how nearly they had crushed me. I began to tell her how they had driven me into a great sin, when she clasped me in her arms, and exclaimed, "O, don't, mother! Please don't tell me any more."

I said, "But, my child, I want you to know about your father."

"I know all about it, mother," she replied; "I am nothing to my father, and he is nothing to me. All my love is for you. I was with him five months in Washington, and he never cared for me. He never spoke to me as he did to his little Fanny. I knew all the time he was my father, for Fanny's nurse told me so; but she said I must never tell any body, and I never did. I used to wish he would take me in his arms and kiss me, as he did Fanny; or that he would sometimes smile at me, as he did at her. I thought if he was my own father, he ought to love me. I was a little girl then, and didn't know any better. But now I never think any thing about my father. All my love is for you." She hugged me closer as she spoke, and I thanked God that the knowledge I had so much dreaded to impart had not diminished the affection of my child. I had not the slightest idea she knew that portion of my history. If I had, I should have spoken to her long before; for my pent-up feelings had often longed to pour themselves out to some one I could trust. But I loved the dear girl better for the delicacy she had manifested towards her unfortunate mother.

The next morning, she and her uncle started on their journey to the village in New York, where she was to be placed at school. It seemed as if all the sunshine had gone away. My little room was dreadfully lonely. I was thankful when a message came from a lady, accustomed to employ me, requesting me to come and sew in her family for several weeks. On my return, I found a letter from brother William. He thought of opening an anti-slavery reading room in Rochester, and combining with it the sale of some books and stationery; and he wanted me to unite with him. We tried it, but it was not successful. We found warm anti-slavery friends there, but the feeling was not general enough to support such an establishment. I passed nearly a year in the family of Isaac and Amy Post, practical believers in the Christian doctrine of human brotherhood. They measured a man's worth by his character, not by his complexion. The memory of those beloved and honored friends will remain with me to my latest hour.

XLI. Free At Last.

MRS. BRUCE, and every member of her family, were exceedingly kind to me. I was thankful for the blessings of my lot, yet I could not always wear a cheerful countenance. I was doing harm to no one; on the contrary, I was doing all the good I could in my small way; yet I could never go out to breathe God's free air without trepidation at my heart. This seemed hard; and I could not think it was a right state of things in any civilized country.

From time to time I received news from my good old grandmother. She could not write; but she employed others to write for her. The following is an extract from one of her last letters:—

"Dear Daughter: I cannot hope to see you again on earth; but I pray to God to unite us above, where pain will no more rack this feeble body of mine; where sorrow and parting from my children will be no more. God has promised these things if we are faithful unto the end. My age and feeble health deprive me of going to church now; but God is with me here at home. Thank your brother for his kindness. Give much love to him, and tell him to remember the Creator in the days of his youth, and strive to meet me in the Father's kingdom. Love to Ellen and Benjamin. Don't neglect him. Tell him for me, to be a good boy. Strive, my child, to train them for God's children. May he protect and provide for you, is the prayer of your loving old mother."

These letters both cheered and saddened me. I was always glad to have tidings from the kind, faithful old friend of my unhappy youth; but her messages of love made my heart yearn to see her before she died, and I mourned over the fact that it was impossible. Some months after I returned from my flight to New England, I received a letter from her, in which she wrote, "Dr. Flint is dead. He has left a distressed family. Poor old man! I hope he made his peace with God."

I remembered how he had defrauded my grandmother of the hard earnings she had loaned; how he had tried to cheat her out of the freedom her mistress had promised her, and how he had persecuted her children; and I thought to myself that she was a better Christian than I was, if she could entirely forgive him. I cannot say, with truth, that the news of my old master's death softened my feelings towards him. There are wrongs which even the grave does not bury. The man was odious to me while he lived, and his memory is odious now.

His departure from this world did not diminish my danger. He had threatened my grandmother that his heirs should hold me in slavery after he was gone; that I never should be free so long as a child of his survived. As for Mrs. Flint, I had seen her in deeper afflictions than I supposed the loss of her husband would be, for she had buried several children; yet I never saw any signs of softening in her heart. The doctor had died in embarrassed circumstances, and had little to will to his heirs, except such property as he was unable to grasp. I was well aware what I had to expect from the family of Flints; and my fears were confirmed by a letter from the south, warning me to be on my guard, because Mrs. Flint openly declared that her daughter could not afford to lose so valuable a slave as I was.

I kept close watch of the newspapers for arrivals; but one Saturday night, being much occupied, I forgot to examine the Evening Express as usual. I went down into the parlor for it, early in the morning, and found the boy about to kindle a fire with it. I took it from him and examined the list of arrivals. Reader, if you have never been a slave, you cannot imagine the acute sensation of suffering at my heart, when I read the names of Mr. and Mrs. Dodge, at a hotel in Courtland Street. It was a third-rate hotel, and that circumstance convinced me of the truth of what I had heard, that they were short of funds and had need of my value, as *they* valued me; and that was by dollars and cents. I hastened with the paper to Mrs. Bruce. Her heart and hand were always open to every one in distress, and she always warmly sympathized with mine. It was impossible to tell how near the enemy was. He might have passed and repassed the house while we were sleeping. He might at that moment be waiting to pounce upon me if I ventured out of doors. I had never seen the husband of my young mistress, and therefore I could not distinguish him from any other stranger. A carriage was hastily ordered; and, closely veiled, I followed Mrs. Bruce, taking the baby again with me into exile. After various turnings and crossings and returnings, the carriage stopped at the house of one of Mrs. Bruce's friends, where I was kindly received. Mrs. Bruce returned immediately, to instruct the domestics what to say if any one came to inquire for me.

It was lucky for me that the evening paper was not burned up before I had a chance to examine the list of arrivals. It was not long after Mrs. Bruce's return to her house, before several people came to inquire for me. One inquired for me, another asked for my daughter Ellen, and another said he had a letter from my grandmother, which he was requested to deliver in person.

They were told, "She *has* lived here, but she has left."

"How long ago?"

"I don't know, sir."

"Do you know where she went?"

"I do not, sir." And the door was closed.

This Mr. Dodge, who claimed me as his property, was originally a Yankee pedler in the south; then he became a merchant, and finally a slaveholder. He managed to get introduced into what was called the first society, and married Miss Emily Flint. A quarrel arose between him and her brother, and the brother cowhided him. This led to a family feud, and he proposed to remove to Virginia. Dr. Flint left him no property, and his own means had become circumscribed, while a wife and children depended upon him for support. Under these circumstances, it was very natural that he should make an effort to put me into his pocket.

I had a colored friend, a man from my native place, in whom I had the most implicit confidence. I sent for him, and told him that Mr. and Mrs. Dodge had arrived in New York. I proposed that he should call upon them to make inquiries about his friends at the south, with whom Dr. Flint's family were well acquainted. He thought there was no impropriety in his doing so, and he consented. He went to the hotel, and knocked at the door of Mr. Dodge's room, which was opened by the gentleman himself, who gruffly inquired, "What brought you here? How came you to know I was in the city?"

"Your arrival was published in the evening papers, sir; and I called to ask Mrs. Dodge about my friends at home. I didn't suppose it would give any offence."

"Where's that negro girl, that belongs to my wife?"

"What girl, sir?"

"You know well enough. I mean Linda, that ran away from Dr. Flint's plantation, some years ago. I dare say you've seen her, and know where she is."

"Yes, sir, I've seen her, and know where she is. She is out of your reach, sir."

"Tell me where she is, or bring her to me, and I will give her a chance to buy her freedom."

"I don't think it would be of any use, sir. I have heard her say she would go to the ends of the earth, rather than pay any man or woman for her freedom, because she thinks she has a right to it. Besides, she couldn't do it, if she would, for she has spent her earnings to educate her children."

This made Mr. Dodge very angry, and some high words passed between them. My friend was afraid to come where I was; but in the course of the day I received a note from him. I supposed they had not come from the south, in the winter, for a pleasure excursion; and now the nature of their business was very plain.

Mrs. Bruce came to me and entreated me to leave the city the next morning. She said her house was watched, and it was possible that some clew to me might be obtained. I refused to take her advice. She pleaded with an earnest tenderness, that ought to have moved me; but I was in a bitter, disheartened mood. I was weary of flying from pillar to post. I had been chased during half my life, and it seemed as if the chase was never to end. There I sat, in that great city, guiltless of crime, yet not daring to worship God in any of the churches. I heard the bells ringing for afternoon service, and, with contemptuous sarcasm, I said, "Will the preachers take for their text, 'Proclaim liberty to the captive, and the opening of prison doors to them that are bound'? or will they preach from the text, 'Do unto others as ye would they should do unto you'?" Oppressed Poles and Hungarians could find a safe refuge in that city; John Mitchell was free to proclaim in the City Hall his desire for "a plantation well stocked with slaves;" but there I sat, an oppressed American, not daring to show my face. God forgive the black and bitter thoughts I indulged on that Sabbath day! The Scripture says, "Oppression makes even a wise man mad;" and I was not wise.

I had been told that Mr. Dodge said his wife had never signed away her right to my children, and if he could not get me, he would take them. This it was, more than any thing else, that roused such a tempest in my soul. Benjamin was with his uncle William in California, but my innocent young daughter had come to spend a vacation with me. I thought of what I had suffered in slavery at her age, and my heart was like a tiger's when a hunter tries to seize her young.

Dear Mrs. Bruce! I seem to see the expression of her face, as she turned away discouraged by my obstinate mood. Finding her expostulations unavailing, she sent Ellen to entreat me. When ten o'clock in the evening arrived and Ellen had not returned, this watchful and unwearied friend became anxious. She came to us in a carriage, bringing a well-filled trunk for my journey—trusting that by this time I would listen to reason. I yielded to her, as I ought to have done before.

The next day, baby and I set out in a heavy snow storm, bound for New England again. I received letters from the City of Iniquity, addressed to me under an assumed name. In a few days one came from Mrs. Bruce, informing me that my new master was still searching for me, and that she intended to put an end to this persecution by buying my freedom. I felt grateful for the kindness that prompted this offer, but the idea was not so pleasant to me as might have been expected. The more my mind had become enlightened, the more difficult it was for me to consider myself an article of property; and to pay money to those who had so grievously oppressed me seemed like taking from my sufferings the glory of triumph. I wrote to Mrs. Bruce, thanking her, but saying that being sold from one owner to another seemed too much like slavery; that such a great obligation could not be easily cancelled; and that I preferred to go to my brother in California.

Without my knowledge, Mrs. Bruce employed a gentleman in New York to enter into negotiations with Mr. Dodge. He proposed to pay three hundred dollars down, if Mr. Dodge would sell me, and enter into obligations to relinquish all claim to me or my children forever after. He who called himself my master said he scorned so small an offer for such a valuable servant. The gentleman replied, "You can do as you choose, sir. If you reject this offer you will never get any thing; for the woman has friends who will convey her and her children out of the country."

Mr. Dodge concluded that "half a loaf was better than no bread," and he agreed to the proffered terms. By the next mail I received this brief letter from Mrs.

Bruce: "I am rejoiced to tell you that the money for your freedom has been paid to Mr. Dodge. Come home to-morrow. I long to see you and my sweet babe."

My brain reeled as I read these lines. A gentleman near me said, "It's true; I have seen the bill of sale." "The bill of sale!" Those words struck me like a blow. So I was *sold* at last! A human being *sold* in the free city of New York! The bill of sale is on record, and future generations will learn from it that women were articles of traffic in New York, late in the nineteenth century of the Christian religion. It may hereafter prove a useful document to antiquaries, who are seeking to measure the progress of civilization in the United States. I well know the value of that bit of paper; but much as I love freedom, I do not like to look upon it. I am deeply grateful to the generous friend who procured it, but I despise the miscreant who demanded payment for what never rightfully belonged to him or his.

I had objected to having my freedom bought, yet I must confess that when it was done I felt as if a heavy load had been lifted from my weary shoulders. When I rode home in the cars I was no longer afraid to unveil my face and look at people as they passed. I should have been glad to have met Daniel Dodge himself; to have had him seen me and known me, that he might have mourned over the untoward circumstances which compelled him to sell me for three hundred dollars.

When I reached home, the arms of my benefactress were thrown round me, and our tears mingled. As soon as she could speak, she said, "O Linda, I'm so glad it's all over! You wrote to me as if you thought you were going to be transferred from one owner to another. But I did not buy you for your services. I should have done just the same, if you had been going to sail for California to-morrow. I should, at least, have the satisfaction of knowing that you left me a free woman."

My heart was exceedingly full. I remembered how my poor father had tried to buy me, when I was a small child, and how he had been disappointed. I hoped his spirit was rejoicing over me now. I remembered how my good old grandmother had laid up her earnings to purchase me in later years, and how often her plans had been frustrated. How that faithful, loving old heart would leap for joy, if she could look on me and my children now that we were free! My relatives had been foiled in all their efforts, but God had raised me up a friend among strangers, who had bestowed on me the precious, long-desired boon. Friend! It is a common word, often lightly used. Like other good and beautiful things, it may be tarnished by careless handling; but when I speak of Mrs. Bruce as my friend, the word is sacred.

My grandmother lived to rejoice in my freedom; but not long after, a letter came with a black seal. She had gone "where the wicked cease from troubling, and the weary are at rest."

Time passed on, and a paper came to me from the south, containing an obituary notice of my uncle Phillip. It was the only case I ever knew of such an honor conferred upon a colored person. It was written by one of his friends, and contained these words: "Now that death has laid him low, they call him a good man and a useful citizen; but what are eulogies to the black man, when the world has faded from his vision? It does not require man's praise to obtain rest in God's kingdom." So they called a colored man a *citizen*! Strange words to be uttered in that region!

Reader, my story ends with freedom; not in the usual way, with marriage. I and my children are now free! We are as free from the power of slaveholders as are the white people of the north; and though that, according to my ideas, is not saying a great deal, it is a vast improvement in *my* condition. The dream of my life is not yet realized. I do not sit with my children in a home of my own. I still long for a hearthstone of my own, however humble. I wish it for my children's sake far more than for my own. But God so orders circumstances as to keep me with my friend Mrs. Bruce. Love, duty, gratitude, also bind me to her side. It is a privilege to serve her who pities my oppressed people, and who has bestowed the inestimable boon of freedom on me and my children.

It has been painful to me, in many ways, to recall the dreary years I passed in bondage. I would gladly forget them if I could. Yet the retrospection is not altogether without solace; for with those gloomy recollections come tender memories of my good old grandmother, like light, fleecy clouds floating over a dark and troubled sea.

Further Readings

Garfield, Deborah M. and Rafia Zafar, eds. *Harriet Jacobs and Incidents in the Life of a Slave Girl: New Critical Essays.* Cambridge, England: Cambridge University Press, 1996.

Randle, Gloria T. "Between the Rock and the Hard Place: Mediating Spaces in Harriet Jacobs's *Incidents in the Life of a Slave Girl.*" *African American Review* 33 (Spring 1999):43–56.

From: *Behind the Scenes*

by Elizabeth Keckley, Formerly a Slave,
but More Recently Modiste,
and Friend to Mrs. Abraham Lincoln,

—OR—

Thirty Years a Slave,
and Four Years in the White House

1868 | SHORT POSTBELLUM SLAVE NARRATIVE

New York: *G. W. Carleton & Co.,*
Publishers. M DCCC LXVIII.

Preface.

I HAVE often been asked to write my life, as those who know me know that it has been an eventful one. At last I have acceded to the importunities of my friends, and have hastily sketched some of the striking incidents that go to make up my history. My life, so full of romance, may sound like a dream to the matter-of-fact reader, nevertheless everything I have written is strictly true; much has been omitted, but nothing has been exaggerated. In writing as I have done, I am well aware that I have invited criticism; but before the critic judges harshly, let my explanation be carefully read and weighed. If I have portrayed the dark side of slavery, I also have painted the bright side. The good that I have said of human servitude should be thrown into the scales with the evil that I have said of it. I have kind, true-hearted friends in the South as well as in the North, and I would not wound those Southern friends by sweeping condemnation, simply because I was once a slave. They were not so much responsible for the curse under which I was born, as the God of nature and the fathers who framed the Constitution for the United States. The law descended to them, and it was but natural that they should recognize it, since it manifestly was their interest to do so. And yet a wrong was inflicted upon me; a cruel custom deprived me of my liberty, and since I was robbed of my dearest right, I would not have been human had I not rebelled against the robbery. God rules the Universe. I was a feeble instrument in His hands, and through me and the enslaved millions of my race, one of the problems was solved that belongs to the great problem of human destiny; and the solution was developed so gradually that there was no great convulsion of the harmonies of natural laws. A solemn truth was thrown to the surface, and what is better still, it was recognized *as a truth* by those who give force to moral laws. An act may be wrong, but unless the ruling power recognizes the wrong, it is useless to hope for a correction of it. Principles may be right, but they are not established within an hour. The masses are slow to reason, and each principle, to acquire moral force, must come to us from the fire of the crucible; the fire may inflict unjust punishment, but then it purifies and renders stronger the principle, not in itself, but in the eyes of those who arrogate judgment to themselves. When the war of the Revolution established the independence of the American colonies, an evil was perpetuated, slavery was more firmly established; and since the evil had been planted, it must pass through certain stages before it could be eradicated. In fact, we give but little thought to the plant of evil until it grows to such monstrous proportions that it overshadows important interests; then the efforts to destroy it become earnest. As one of the victims of slavery I drank of the bitter water; but then, since destiny willed it so, and since I aided in bringing a solemn truth to the surface *as a truth*, perhaps I have no right to complain. Here, as in all things pertaining to life, I can afford to be charitable.

It may be charged that I have written too freely on some questions, especially in regard to Mrs. Lincoln. I do not think so; at least I have been prompted by the purest motive. Mrs. Lincoln, by her own acts, forced herself into notoriety. She stepped beyond the formal lines which hedge about a private life, and invited public criticism. The people have judged her harshly, and no woman was ever more traduced in the public prints of the country. The people knew nothing of the secret history of her transactions, therefore they judged her by what was thrown to the surface. For an act may be wrong judged purely by itself, but when the motive that prompted the act is understood, it is construed differently. I lay it down as an axiom, that only that is criminal in the sight of God where crime is meditated. Mrs. Lincoln may have been imprudent, but since her intentions were good, she should be judged more kindly than she has been. But the world do not know what her intentions were; they have only been made acquainted with her acts without knowing what feeling guided her actions. If the world are to judge her as I have judged her, they must be introduced to the secret history of her transactions. The veil of mystery must be drawn aside; the origin of a fact must be brought to light with the naked fact itself. If I have betrayed confidence in anything I have published, it has been to place Mrs. Lincoln in a better light before the world. A breach of trust—if breach it can be called—of this kind is always excusable. My own character, as well as the character of Mrs. Lincoln, is at stake, since I have been intimately associated with that lady in the most eventful periods of her life. I have been her confidante, and if evil charges are laid at her door, they also must be laid at mine, since I have been a party to all her movements. To defend myself I must defend the lady that I have served. The world have judged Mrs. Lincoln by the facts which float upon the surface, and through her have partially judged me, and the only way to convince them that wrong was not meditated is to explain the motives that actuated us. I have written nothing that can place Mrs. Lincoln in a worse light before the world than the light in which she now stands, therefore the secret history that I publish can do her no harm. I have excluded everything of a personal character from her letters; the extracts introduced only refer to public men, and are such as to throw light upon her unfortunate adventure in New York. These letters were not written for publication, for which reason they are all the more valuable; they are the frank overflowings of the heart, the outcropping of impulse, the key to genuine motives. They prove the motive to have been pure, and if they shall help to stifle the voice of calumny, I am content. I do not forget, before the public journals vilified Mrs. Lincoln, that ladies who moved in the Washington circle in which she moved, freely canvassed her character among themselves. They gloated over many a tale of scandal that grew out of gossip in their own circle. If these ladies could say everything bad of the wife of the President, why should I not be permitted to lay her secret history bare, especially when that history plainly shows that her life, like all lives, has its good side as well as its bad side? None of us are perfect, for which reason we should heed the voice of charity when it whispers in our ears, "Do not magnify the imperfections of others." Had Mrs. Lincoln's acts never become public property, I should not have published to the world the secret chapters of her life. I am not the special champion of the widow of our lamented President; the reader of the pages which follow will discover that I have written with the utmost frankness in regard to her—have exposed her faults as well as given her credit for honest motives. I wish the world to judge her as she is, free from the exaggerations of praise or scandal, since I have been associated with her in so many things that have provoked hostile criticism; and the judgment that the world may pass upon her, I flatter myself, will present my own actions in a better light.

Elizabeth Keckley.
14 Carroll Place, New York, March 14, 1868.

Behind the Scenes.
Chapter I. Where I Was Born.

MY life has been an eventful one. I was born a slave—was the child of slave parents—therefore I came upon the earth free in God-like thought, but fettered in action. My birthplace was Dinwiddie Court-House, in Virginia. My recollections of childhood are distinct, perhaps for the reason that many stirring incidents are associated with that period. I am now on the shady side of forty, and as I sit alone in my room the brain is busy, and a rapidly moving panorama brings scene after scene before me, some pleasant and others sad; and when I thus greet old familiar faces, I often find myself wondering if I am not living the past over again. The visions are so terribly distinct that I almost imagine them to be real. Hour after hour I sit while the scenes are being shifted; and as I gaze upon the panorama of the past, I realize how crowded with incidents my life has been. Every day seems like a romance within itself, and the years grow into ponderous volumes. As I cannot condense, I must omit many strange passages in my history. From such a wilderness of events it is difficult to make a selection, but as I am not writing altogether the history of myself, I will confine my story to the most important incidents which I believe influenced the moulding of my character. As I glance over the crowded sea of the past, these incidents stand forth prominently, the guide-posts of memory. I presume that I must have been four years old when I first began to remember; at least, I cannot now recall anything occurring previous to this period. My master, Col. A. Burwell, was somewhat unsettled in his business affairs, and while I was yet an infant he made several removals. While living at Hampton Sidney College, Prince Edward County, Va., Mrs. Burwell gave birth to a daughter, a sweet, black-eyed baby, my earliest and fondest pet. To take care of this baby was my first duty. True, I was but a child myself—only four years old—but then I had been raised in a hardy school—had been taught to rely upon myself, and to prepare myself to render assistance to others. The lesson was not a bitter one, for I was too young to indulge in philosophy, and the precepts that I then treasured and practised I believe developed those principles of character which have enabled me to triumph over so many difficulties. Notwithstanding all the wrongs that slavery heaped upon me, I can bless it for one thing—youth's important lesson of self-reliance. The baby was named Elizabeth, and it was pleasant to me to be assigned a duty in connection with it, for the discharge of that duty transferred me from the rude cabin to the household of my master. My simple attire was a short dress and a little white apron. My old mistress encouraged me in rocking the cradle, by telling me that if I would watch over the baby well, keep the flies out of its face, and not let it cry, I should be its little maid. This was a golden promise, and I required no better inducement for the faithful performance of my task. I began to rock the cradle most industriously, when lo! out pitched little pet on the floor. I instantly cried out, "Oh! the baby is on the floor," and, not knowing what to do, I seized the fire-shovel in my perplexity, and was trying to shovel up my tender charge, when my mistress called to me to let the child alone, and then ordered that I be taken out and lashed for my carelessness. The blows were not administered with a light hand, I assure you, and doubtless the severity of the lashing has made me remember the incident so well. This was the first time I was punished in this cruel way, but not the last. The black-eyed baby that I called my pet grew into a self-willed girl, and in after years was the cause of much trouble to me. I grew strong and healthy, and, notwithstanding I knit socks and attended to various kinds of work, I was repeatedly told, when even fourteen years old, that I would never be worth my salt. When I was eight, Mr. Burwell's family consisted of six sons and four daughters, with a large family of servants. My mother was kind and forbearing; Mrs. Burwell a hard task-master; and as mother had so much work to do in making clothes, etc., for the family, besides the slaves, I determined to render her all the assistance in my power, and in rendering her such assistance my young energies were taxed to the utmost. I was my mother's only child, which made her love for me all the stronger. I did not know much of my father, for he was the slave of another man, and when Mr. Burwell moved from Dinwiddie he was separated from us, and only allowed to visit my mother twice a year—during the Easter holidays and Christmas. At last Mr. Burwell determined to reward my mother, by making an arrangement with the owner of my father, by which the separation of my parents could be brought to an end. It was a bright day, indeed, for my mother when it was announced that my father was coming to live with us. The old weary look faded from her face, and she worked as if her heart was in every task. But the golden days did not last long. The radiant dream faded all too soon.

In the morning my father called me to him and kissed me, then held me out at arms' length as if he were regarding his child with pride. "She is growing into a large fine girl," he remarked to my mother. "I dun no which I like best, you or Lizzie, as both are so dear to me." My mother's name was Agnes, and my father delighted to call me his "Little Lizzie." While yet my father and mother were speaking hopefully, joyfully of the future, Mr. Burwell came to the cabin, with a letter in his hand. He was a kind master in some things, and as gently as possible informed my parents that they must part; for in two hours my father must join his master at Dinwiddie, and go with him to the West, where he had determined to make his future home. The announcement fell upon the little circle in that rude-log cabin like a thunderbolt. I can remember the scene as if it were but yesterday;—how my father cried out against the cruel separation; his last kiss; his wild straining of my mother to his bosom; the solemn prayer to Heaven; the tears and sobs—the fearful anguish of broken hearts. The last kiss, the last good-by; and he, my father, was gone,

gone forever. The shadow eclipsed the sunshine, and love brought despair. The parting was eternal. The cloud had no silver lining, but I trust that it will be all silver in heaven. We who are crushed to earth with heavy chains, who travel a weary, rugged, thorny road, groping through midnight darkness on earth, earn our right to enjoy the sunshine in the great hereafter. At the grave, at least, we should be permitted to lay our burdens down, that a new world, a world of brightness, may open to us. The light that is denied us here should grow into a flood of effulgence beyond the dark, mysterious shadows of death. Deep as was the distress of my mother in parting with my father, her sorrow did not screen her from insult. My old mistress said to her: "Stop your nonsense; there is no necessity for you putting on airs. Your husband is not the only slave that has been sold from his family, and you are not the only one that has had to part. There are plenty more men about here, and if you want a husband so badly, stop your crying and go and find another." To these unfeeling words my mother made no reply. She turned away in stoical silence, with a curl of that loathing scorn upon her lips which swelled in her heart.

My father and mother never met again in this world. They kept up a regular correspondence for years, and the most precious mementoes of my existence are the faded old letters that he wrote, full of love, and always hoping that the future would bring brighter days. In nearly every letter is a message for me. "Tell my darling little Lizzie," he writes, "to be a good girl, and to learn her book. Kiss her for me, and tell her that I will come to see her some day." Thus he wrote time and again, but he never came. He lived in hope, but died without ever seeing his wife and child.

I note a few extracts from one of my father's letters to my mother, following copy literally:

"SHELBYVILE, Sept. 6, 1833.

"MRS. AGNES HOBBS.

"Dear Wife: My dear biloved wife I am more than glad to meet with opportunty writee thes few lines to you by my Mistress who ar now about starterng to virginia, and sevl others of my old friends are with her; in compeney Mrs. Ann Rus the wife of master Thos Rus and Dan Woodiard and his family and I am very sorry that I havn the chance to go with them as I feele Determid to see you If life last again. I am now here and out at this pleace so I am not abble to get of at this time. I am write well and hearty and all the rest of masters family. I heard this eveng by Mistress that ar just from theree all sends love to you and all my old frends. I am a living in a town called Shelbyville and I have wrote a greate many letters since Ive beene here and almost been reeady to my selfe that its out of the question to write any more at tall: my dear wife I dont feeld no whys like giving out writing to you as yet and I hope when you get this letter that you be Inncougege to write me a letter. I am well satisfied at my living at this place I am a making money for my own benifit and I hope that its to yours also If I live to see Nexct year I shall heve my own time from master by giving him 100 and twenty Dollars a year and I thinke I shall be doing good bisness at that and heve something more thean all that. I hope with gods helpe that I may be abble to rejoys with you on the earth and In heaven lets meet when will I am detemnid to nuver stope praying, not in this earth and I hope to praise god In glory there weel meet to part no more forever. So my dear wife I hope to meet you In paradase to prase god forever * * * * * I want Elizabeth to be a good girl and not to thinke that becasue I am bound so fare that gods not abble to open the way * * * *

"GEORGE PLEASANT,

"Hobbs a servant of Grum."

The last letter that my mother received from my father was dated Shelbyville, Tennessee, March 20, 1839. He writes in a cheerful strain, and hopes to see her soon. Alas! he looked forward to a meeting in vain. Year after year the one great hope swelled in his heart, but the hope was only realized beyond the dark portals of the grave.

When I was about seven years old I witnessed, for the first time, the sale of a human being. We were living at Prince Edward, in Virginia, and master had just purchased his hogs for the winter, for which he was unable to pay in full. To escape from his embarrassment it was necessary to sell one of the slaves. Little Joe, the son of the cook, was selected as the victim. His mother was ordered to dress him up in his Sunday clothes, and send him to the house. He came in with a bright face, was placed in the scales, and was sold, like the hogs, at so much per pound. His mother was kept in ignorance of the transaction, but her suspicions were aroused. When her son started for Petersburgh in the wagon, the truth began to dawn upon her mind, and she pleaded piteously that her boy should not be taken from her; but master quieted her by telling her that he was simply going to town with the wagon, and would be back in the morning. Morning came, but little Joe did not return to his mother. Morning after morning passed, and the mother went down to the grave without ever seeing her child again. One day she was whipped for grieving for her lost boy. Colonel Burwell never liked to see one of his slaves wear a sorrowful face, and those who offended in this particular way were always punished. Alas! the sunny face of the slave is not always an indication of sunshine in the heart. Colonel Burwell at one time owned about seventy slaves, all of which were sold, and in a majority of instances wives were separated from husbands and children from their parents. Slavery in the Border States forty years ago was different from what it was twenty years ago. Time seemed to soften the hearts of master and mistress, and to insure kinder and more humane treatment to bondsmen and bondswomen. When I was quite a child, an incident occurred which my mother afterward impressed more strongly on my mind. One of my uncles, a slave of Colonel Burwell, lost a pair of ploughlines, and when the loss was made known the master gave him a new pair, and told him that if he did not take care of them he would punish him severely. In a few weeks the second pair of lines was stolen, and my uncle hung himself rather than meet the displeasure of his master. My mother went to the spring in the morning for a pail of water, and on looking up into the willow tree which shaded the bubbling crystal stream, she discovered the lifeless form of her brother suspended beneath one of the strong branches. Rather than be punished the way Colonel Burwell punished his servants, he took his own life. Slavery had its dark side as well as its bright side.

Chapter II. Girlhood And Its Sorrows.

I MUST pass rapidly over the stirring events of my early life. When I was about fourteen years old I went to live with my master's eldest son, a Presbyterian minister. His salary was small, and he was burdened with a helpless wife, a girl that he had married in the humble walks of life. She was morbidly sensitive, and imagined that I regarded her with contemptuous feelings because she was of poor parentage. I was their only servant, and a gracious loan at that. They were not able to buy me, so my old master sought to render them assistance by allowing them the benefit of my services. From the very first I did the work of three servants, and yet I was scolded and regarded with distrust. The years passed slowly, and I continued to serve them, and at the same time grew into strong, healthy womanhood. I was nearly eighteen when we removed from Virginia to Hillsboro', North Carolina, where young Mr. Burwell took charge of a church. The salary was small, and we still had to practise the closest economy. Mr. Bingham, a hard, cruel man, the village schoolmaster, was a member of my young master's church, and he was a frequent visitor to the parsonage. She whom I called mistress seemed to be desirous to wreak vengeance on me for something, and Bingham became her ready tool. During this time my master was unusually kind to me; he was naturally a good-hearted man, but was influenced by his wife. It was Saturday evening, and while I was bending over the bed, watching the baby that I had just hushed into slumber, Mr. Bingham came to the door and asked me to go with him to his study. Wondering what he meant by his strange request, I followed him, and when we had entered the study he closed the door, and in his blunt way remarked: "Lizzie, I am going to flog you." I was thunderstruck, and tried to think if I had been remiss in anything. I could not recollect of doing anything to deserve punishment, and with surprise exclaimed: "Whip me, Mr. Bingham! what for?"

"No matter," he replied, "I am going to whip you, so take down your dress this instant."

Recollect, I was eighteen years of age, was a woman fully developed, and yet this man coolly bade me take down my dress. I drew myself up proudly, firmly, and said: "No, Mr. Bingham, I shall not take down my dress before you. Moreover, you shall not whip me unless you prove the stronger. Nobody has a right to whip me but my own master, and nobody shall do so if I can prevent it."

My words seemed to exasperate him. He seized a rope, caught me roughly, and tried to tie me. I resisted with all my strength, but he was the stronger of the two, and after a hard struggle succeeded in binding my hands and tearing my dress from my back. Then he picked up a rawhide, and began to ply it freely over my shoulders. With steady hand and practised eye he would raise the instrument of torture, nerve himself for a blow, and with fearful force the rawhide descended upon the quivering flesh. It cut the skin, raised great welts, and the warm blood trickled down my back. Oh God! I can feel the torture now—the terrible, excruciating agony of those moments. I did not scream; I was too proud to let my tormentor know what I was suffering. I closed my lips firmly, that not even a groan might escape from them, and I stood like a statue while the keen lash cut deep into my flesh. As soon as I was released, stunned with pain, bruised and bleeding, I went home and rushed into the presence of the pastor and his wife, wildly exclaiming: "Master Robert, why did you let Mr. Bingham flog me? What have I done that I should be so punished?"

"Go away," he gruffly answered, "do not bother me."

I would not be put off thus. "What *have* I done? I *will* know why I have been flogged."

I saw his cheeks flush with anger, but I did not move. He rose to his feet, and on my refusing to go without an explanation, seized a chair, struck me, and felled me to the floor. I rose, bewildered, almost dead with pain, crept to my room, dressed my bruised arms and back as best I could, and then lay down, but not to sleep. No, I could not sleep, for I was suffering mental as well as bodily torture. My spirit rebelled against the unjustness that had been inflicted upon me, and though I tried to smother my anger and to forgive those who had been so cruel to me, it was impossible. The next morning I was more calm, and I believe that I could then have forgiven everything for the sake of one kind word. But the kind word was not proffered, and it may be possible that I grew somewhat wayward and sullen. Though I had faults, I know now, as I felt then, harshness was the poorest inducement for the correction of them. It seems that Mr. Bingham had pledged himself to Mrs. Burwell to subdue what he called my "stubborn pride." On Friday following the Saturday on which I was so savagely beaten, Mr. Bingham again directed me to come to his study. I went, but with the determination to offer resistance should he attempt to flog me again. On entering the room I found him prepared with a new rope and a new cowhide. I told him that I was ready to die, but that he could not conquer me. In struggling with him I bit his finger severely, when he seized a heavy stick and beat me with it in a shameful manner. Again I went home sore and bleeding, but with pride as strong and defiant as ever. The following Thursday Mr. Bingham again tried to conquer me, but in vain. We struggled, and he struck me many savage blows. As I stood bleeding before him, nearly exhausted with his efforts, he burst into tears, and declared that it would be a sin to beat me any more. My suffering at last subdued his hard heart; he asked my forgiveness, and afterwards was an altered man. He was never known to strike one of his servants from that day forward. Mr. Burwell, he who preached the love of Heaven, who glorified the precepts and examples of Christ, who expounded the Holy Scriptures Sabbath after Sabbath from the pulpit, when Mr. Bingham refused to whip me any more, was urged by his wife to punish me himself. One morning he went to the wood-pile, took an oak broom, cut the handle off, and with this heavy handle attempted to conquer me. I fought him, but he proved the strongest. At the sight of my bleeding form, his wife fell upon her knees and begged him to desist. My distress even touched her cold, jealous heart. I was so badly bruised that I was unable to leave my bed for five days. I will not dwell upon the bitter anguish of these hours, for even the thought of them now makes me shudder. The Rev. Mr. Burwell was not yet satisfied. He resolved to make another attempt to subdue my proud, rebellious spirit—made the attempt and again failed, when he told me, with an air of penitence, that he should never strike me another blow; and faithfully he kept his word. These revolting scenes created a great sensation at the time, were the talk of the town and neighborhood, and I flatter myself that the actions of those who had conspired against me were not viewed in a light to reflect much credit upon them.

The savage efforts to subdue my pride were not the only things that brought me suffering and deep mortification during my residence at Hillsboro'. I was regarded as fair-looking for one of my race, and for four years a white man—I spare the world his name—had base designs upon me. I do not care to dwell upon this subject, for it is one that is fraught with pain. Suffice it to say, that he persecuted me for four years, and I—I—became a mother. The child of which he was the father was the only child that I ever brought into the world. If my poor boy ever suffered any humiliating pangs on account of birth, he could not blame his mother, for God knows that she did not wish to give him life; he must blame the edicts of that society which deemed it no crime to undermine the virtue of girls in my then position.

Among the old letters preserved by my mother I find the following, written by myself while at Hillsboro'. In this connection I desire to state that Rev. Robert Burwell is now living* at Charlotte, North Carolina:—

* March, 1868.

"HILLSBORO', April 10, 1838.

"MY DEAR MOTHER:—I have been intending to write to you for a long time, but numerous things have prevented, and for that reason you must excuse me.

"I thought very hard of you for not writing to me, but hope that you will answer this letter as soon as you receive it, and tell me how you like Marsfield, and if you have seen any of my old acquaintances, or if you yet know any of the brick-house people who I think so much of. I want to hear of the family at home very much, indeed. I really believe you and all the family have forgotten me, if not I certainly should have heard from some of you since you left Boyton, if it was only a line; nevertheless I love you all very dearly, and shall, although I may never see you again, nor do I ever expect to. Miss Anna is going to Petersburgh next winter, but she says that she does not intend to take me; what reason she has for leaving me I cannot tell. I have often wished that I lived where I knew I never could see you, for then I would not have my hopes raised, and to be disappointed in this manner; however, it is said that a bad beginning makes a good ending, but I hardly expect to see that happy day at this place. Give my love to all the family, both white and black. I was very much obliged to you for the presents you sent me last summer, though it is quite late in the day to be thanking for them. Tell Aunt Bella that I was very much obliged to her for her present; I have been so particular with it that I have only worn it once.

"There have been six weddings since October; the most respectable one was about a fortnight ago; I was asked to be the first attendant, but, as usual with all my expectations, I was disappointed, for on the wedding-day I felt more like being locked up in a three-cornered box than attending a wedding. About a week before Christmas I was bridesmaid for Ann Nash; when the night came I was in quite a trouble; I did not know whether my frock was clean or dirty; I only had a week's notice, and the body and sleeves to make, and only one hour every night to work on it, so you can see with these troubles to overcome my chance was rather slim. I must now close, although I could fill ten pages with my griefs and misfortunes; no tongue could express them as I feel; don't forget me though; and answer my letters soon. I will write you again, and would write more now, but Miss Anna says it is time I had finished. Tell Miss Elizabeth that I wish she would make haste and get married, for mistress says that I belong to her when she gets married.

"I wish you would send me a pretty frock this summer; if you will send it to Mrs. Robertson's Miss Bet will send it to me.

"Farewell, darling mother.

"Your affectionate daughter,

"ELIZABETH HOBBS."

Chapter III. How I Gained My Freedom.

THE years passed and brought many changes to me, but on these I will not dwell, as I wish to hasten to the most interesting part of my story. My troubles in North Carolina were brought to an end by my unexpected return to Virginia, where I lived with Mr. Garland, who had married Miss Ann Burwell, one of my old master's daughters. His life was not a prosperous one, and after struggling with the world for several years he left his native State, a disappointed man. He moved to St. Louis, hoping to improve his fortune in the West; but ill luck followed him there, and he seemed to be unable to escape from the influence of the evil star of his destiny. When his family, myself included, joined him in his new home on the banks of the Mississippi, we found him so poor that he was unable to pay the dues on a letter advertised as in the post-office for him. The necessities of the family were so great, that it was proposed to place my mother out at service. The idea was shocking to me. Every gray hair in her old head was dear to me, and I could not bear the thought of her going to work for strangers. She had been raised in the family, had watched the growth of each child from infancy to maturity; they had been the objects of her kindest care, and she was wound round about them as the vine winds itself about the rugged oak. They had been the central figures in her dream of life—a dream beautiful to her, since she had basked in the sunshine of no other. And now they proposed to destroy each tendril of affection, to cloud the sunshine of her existence when the day was drawing to a close, when the shadows of solemn night were rapidly approaching. My mother, my poor aged mother, go among strangers to toil for a living! No, a thousand times no! I would rather work my fingers to the bone, bend over my sewing till the film of blindness gathered in my eyes; nay, even beg from street to street. I told Mr. Garland so, and he gave me permission to see what I could do. I was fortunate in obtaining work, and in a short time I had acquired something of a reputation as a seamstress and dress-maker. The best ladies in St. Louis were my patrons, and when my reputation was once established I never lacked for orders. With my needle I kept bread in the mouths of seventeen persons for two years and five months. While I was working so hard that others might live in comparative comfort, and move in those circles of society to which their birth gave them entrance, the thought often occurred to me whether I was really worth my salt or not; and then perhaps the lips curled with a bitter sneer. It may seem strange that I should place so much emphasis upon words thoughtlessly, idly spoken; but then we do many strange things in life, and cannot always explain the motives that actuate us. The heavy task was too much for me, and my health began to give way. About this time Mr. Keckley, whom I had met in Virginia, and learned to regard with more than friendship, came to St. Louis. He sought my hand in marriage, and for a long time I refused to consider his proposal; for I could not bear the thought of bringing children into slavery—of adding one single recruit to the millions bound to hopeless servitude, fettered and shackled with chains stronger and heavier than manacles of iron. I made a proposition to buy myself and son; the proposition was bluntly declined, and I was commanded never to broach the subject again. I would not be put off thus, for hope pointed to a freer, brighter life in the future. Why should my son be held in slavery? I often asked myself. He came into the world through no will of mine, and yet, God only knows how I loved him. The Anglo-Saxon blood as well as the African flowed in his veins; the two currents commingled—one singing of freedom, the other silent and sullen with generations of despair. Why should not the Anglo-Saxon triumph—why should it be weighed down with the rich blood typical of the tropics? Must the life-current of one race bind the other race in chains as strong and enduring as if there had been no Anglo-Saxon taint? By the laws of God and nature, as interpreted by man, one-half of my boy was free, and why should not this fair birthright of freedom remove the curse from the other half—raise it into the bright, joyous sunshine of liberty? I could not answer these questions of my heart that almost maddened me, and I learned to regard human philosophy with distrust. Much as I respected the authority of my master, I could not remain silent on a subject that so nearly concerned me. One day, when I insisted on knowing whether he would permit me to purchase myself, and what price I must pay for myself, he turned to me in a petulant manner, thrust his hand into his pocket, drew forth a bright silver quarter of a dollar, and proffering it to me, said:

"Lizzie, I have told you often not to trouble me with such a question. If you really wish to leave me, take this: it will pay the passage of yourself and boy on the ferryboat, and when you are on the other side of the river you will be free. It is the cheapest way that I know of to accomplish what you desire."

I looked at him in astonishment, and earnestly replied: "No, master, I do not wish to be free in such a manner. If such had been my wish, I should never have troubled you about obtaining your consent to my purchasing myself. I can cross the river any day, as you well know, and have frequently done so, but will never leave you in such a manner. By the laws of the land I am your slave—you are my master, and I will only be free by such means as the laws of the country provide." He expected this answer, and I knew that he was pleased. Some time afterwards he told me that he had reconsidered the question; that I had served his family faithfully; that I deserved my freedom, and that he would take $1200 for myself and boy.

This was joyful intelligence for me, and the reflection of hope gave a silver lining to the dark cloud of my life—faint, it is true, but still a silver lining.

Taking a prospective glance at liberty, I consented to marry. The wedding was a great event in the family. The ceremony took place in the parlor, in the presence of the family and a number of guests. Mr. Garland gave me away, and the pastor, Bishop Hawks, performed the ceremony, who had solemnized the bridals of Mr.

G.'s own children. The day was a happy one, but it faded all too soon. Mr. Keckley—let me speak kindly of his faults—proved dissipated, and a burden instead of a help-mate. More than all, I learned that he was a slave instead of a free man, as he represented himself to be. With the simple explanation that I lived with him eight years, let charity draw around him the mantle of silence.

I went to work in earnest to purchase my freedom, but the years passed, and I was still a slave. Mr. Garland's family claimed so much of my attention—in fact, I supported them—that I was not able to accumulate anything. In the mean time Mr. Garland died, and Mr. Burwell, a Mississippi planter, came to St. Louis to settle up the estate. He was a kind-hearted man, and said I should be free, and would afford me every facility to raise the necessary amount to pay the price of my liberty. Several schemes were urged upon me by my friends. At last I formed a resolution to go to New York, state my case, and appeal to the benevolence of the people. The plan seemed feasible, and I made preparations to carry it out. When I was almost ready to turn my face northward, Mrs. Garland told me that she would require the names of six gentlemen who would vouch for my return, and become responsible for the amount at which I was valued. I had many friends in St. Louis, and as I believed that they had confidence in me, I felt that I could readily obtain the names desired. I started out, stated my case, and obtained five signatures to the paper, and my heart throbbed with pleasure, for I did not believe that the sixth would refuse me. I called, he listened patiently, then remarked:

"Yes, yes, Lizzie; the scheme is a fair one, and you shall have my name. But I shall bid you good-by when you start."

"Good-by for a short time," I ventured to add.

"No, good-by for all time," and he looked at me as if he would read my very soul with his eyes.

I was startled. "What do you mean, Mr. Farrow? Surely you do not think that I do not mean to come back?"

"No."

"No, what then?"

"Simply this: you *mean* to come back, that is, you *mean* so *now*, but you never will. When you reach New York the abolitionists will tell you what savages we are, and they will prevail on you to stay there; and we shall never see you again."

"But I assure you, Mr. Farrow, you are mistaken. I not only *mean* to come back, but *will* come back, and pay every cent of the twelve hundred dollars for myself and child."

I was beginning to feel sick at heart, for I could not accept the signature of this man when he had no faith in my pledges. No; slavery, eternal slavery rather than be regarded with distrust by those whose respect I esteemed.

"But—I am not mistaken," he persisted. "Time will show. When you start for the North I shall bid you good-by."

The heart grew heavy. Every ray of sunshine was eclipsed. With humbled pride, weary step, tearful face, and a dull, aching pain, I left the house. I walked along the street mechanically. The cloud had no silver lining now. The rosebuds of hope had withered and died without lifting up their heads to receive the dew kiss of morning. There was no morning for me—all was night, dark night.

I reached my own home, and weeping threw myself upon the bed. My trunk was packed, my luncheon was prepared by mother, the cars were ready to bear me where I would not hear the clank of chains, where I would breathe the free, invigorating breezes of the glorious North. I had dreamed such a happy dream, in imagination had drunk of the water, the pure, sweet crystal water of life, but now—now—the flowers had withered before my eyes; darkness had settled down upon me like a pall, and I was left alone with cruel mocking shadows.

The first paroxysm of grief was scarcely over, when a carriage stopped in front of the house; Mrs. Le Bourgois, one of my kind patrons, got out of it and entered the door. She seemed to bring sunshine with her handsome cheery face. She came to where I was, and in her sweet way said:—

"Lizzie, I hear that you are going to New York to beg for money to buy your freedom. I have been thinking over the matter, and told Ma it would be a shame to allow you to go North to *beg* for what we should *give* you. You have many friends in St. Louis, and I am going to raise the twelve hundred dollars required among them. I have two hundred dollars put away for a present; am indebted to you one hundred dollars; mother owes you fifty dollars, and will add another fifty to it; and as I do not want the present, I will make the money a present to you. Don't start for New York now until I see what I can do among your friends."

Like a ray of sunshine she came, and like a ray of sunshine she went away. The flowers no longer were withered, drooping. Again they seemed to bud and grow in fragrance and beauty. Mrs. Le Bourgois, God bless her dear good heart, was more than successful. The twelve hundred dollars were raised, and at last my son and myself were free. Free, free! what a glorious ring to the word. Free! the bitter heart-struggle was over. Free! the soul could go out to heaven and to God with no chains to clog its flight or pull it down. Free! the earth wore a brighter look, and the very stars seemed to sing with joy. Yes, free! free by the laws of man and the smile of God—and Heaven bless them who made me so!

The following, copied from the original papers, contain, in brief, the history of my emancipation:—

"I promise to give Lizzie and her son George their freedom, on the payment of $1200.

"ANNE P. GARLAND.

"June 27, 1855."

"LIZZY:—I send you this note to sign for the sum of $75, and when I give you the whole amount you will then sign the other note for $100.

"ELLEN M. DOAN.

"In the paper you will find $25; see it is all right before the girl leaves."

"I have received of Lizzy Keckley $950, which I have deposited with Darby & Barksdale for her—$600 on the 21st July, $300 on the 27th and 28th of July, and $50 on 13th August, 1855.

"I have and shall make use of said money for Lizzy's benefit, and hereby guarantee to her one per cent. per month—as much more as can be made she shall have. The one per cent., as it may be checked out, I will be responsible for myself, as well as for the whole amount, when it shall be needed by her.

"WILLIS L. WILLIAMS.

"ST. LOUIS, 13th August, 1855."

"Know all men by these presents, that for and in consideration of the love and affection we bear towards our sister, Anne P. Garland, of St. Louis, Missouri, and for the further consideration of $5 in hand paid, we hereby sell and convey unto her, the said Anne P. Garland, a negro woman named Lizzie, and a negro boy, her son, named George; said Lizzie now resides at St. Louis, and is a seamstress, known there as Lizzie Garland, the wife of a yellow man named James, and called James Keckley; said George is a bright mulatto boy, and is known in St. Louis as Garland's George. We warrant these two slaves to be slaves for life, but make no representations as to age or health.

"Witness our hands and seals, this 10th day of August, 1855.

"JAS. R. PUTNAM, [L.S.]
"E. M. PUTNAM, [L.S.]
"A. BURWELL, [L.S.]"

"The State of Mississippi, Warren ⎱ ss.
County, City of Vicksburg. ⎰

"Be it remembered, that on the tenth day of August, in the year of our Lord one thousand eight hundred and fifty-five, before me, Francis N. Steele, a Commissioner, resident in the city of Vicksburg, duly commissioned and qualified by the executive authority, and under the laws of the State of Missouri, to take the acknowledgment of deeds, etc., to be used or recorded therein, personally appeared James R. Putnam and E. M. Putnam, his wife, and Armistead Burwell, to me known to be the individuals named in, and who executed the foregoing conveyance, and acknowledged that they executed the same for the purposes therein mentioned; and the E. M. Putnam being by me examined apart from her husband, and being fully acquainted with the contents of the foregoing conveyance, acknowledged that she executed the same freely, and relinquished her dower, and any other claim she might have in and to the property therein mentioned, freely, and without fear, compulsion, or undue influence of her said husband.

"In witness whereof I have hereunto set my hand and affixed my official seal, this 10th day of August, A.D. 1855.

"F. N. STEELE,
"Commissioner for Missouri."
[L.S.]

"Know all men that I, Anne P. Garland, of the County and City of St. Louis, State of Missouri, for and in consideration of the sum of $1200, to me in hand paid this day in cash, hereby emancipate my negro woman Lizzie, and her son George; the said Lizzie is known in St. Louis as the wife of James, who is called James Keckley; is of light complexion, about 37 years of age, by trade a dress-maker, and called by those who know her Garland's Lizzie. The said boy, George, is the only child of Lizzie, is about 16 years of age, and is almost white, and called by those who know him Garland's George.

"Witness my hand and seal, this 13th day of November, 1855.

"ANNE P. GARLAND, [L.S.]
"Witness:—JOHN WICKHAM,
"WILLIS L. WILLIAMS."

In St. Louis Circuit Court, October Term, 1855. November 15, 1855.

"State of Missouri, } *ss.*
County of St. Louis. }

"Be it remembered, that on this fifteenth day of November, eighteen hundred and fifty-five, in open court came John Wickham and Willis L. Williams, these two subscribing witnesses, examined under oath to that effect, proved the execution and acknowledgment of said deed by Anne P. Garland to Lizzie and her son George, which said proof of acknowledgment is entered on the record of the court of that day.

"In testimony whereof I hereto set my hand and affix the seal of said court, at office in the City of St. Louis, the day and year last aforesaid.

WM. J. HAMMOND, *Clerk.*"
[L. S.]

"State of Missouri, } *ss.*
County of St. Louis. }

"I, Wm. J. Hammond, Clerk of the Circuit Court within and for the county aforesaid, certify the foregoing to be a true copy of a deed of emancipation from Anne P. Garland to Lizzie and her son George, as fully as the same remain in my office.

"In testimony whereof I hereto set my hand and affix the seal of said court, at office in the City of St. Louis, this fifteenth day of November, 1855.

"WM. J. HAMMOND, *Clerk.*

"By WM. A. PENNINGTON, D. C."

"State of Missouri, $\Big\}$ *ss.*
County of St. Louis.

"I, the undersigned Recorder of said county, certify that the foregoing instrument of writing was filed for record in my office on the 14th day of November, 1855; it is truly recorded in Book No. 169, page 288.

"Witness my hand and official seal, date last aforesaid.

"C. KEEMLE, *Recorder.*"

[L.S.]

Chapter V. My Introduction To Mrs. Lincoln.

EVER since arriving in Washington I had a great desire to work for the ladies of the White House, and to accomplish this end I was ready to make almost any sacrifice consistent with propriety. Work came in slowly, and I was beginning to feel very much embarrassed, for I did not know how I was to meet the bills staring me in the face. It is true, the bills were small, but then they were formidable to me, who had little or nothing to pay them with. While in this situation I called at the Ringolds, where I met Mrs. Captain Lee. Mrs. L. was in a state bordering on excitement, as the great event of the season, the dinner-party given in honor of the Prince of Wales, was soon to come off, and she must have a dress suitable for the occasion. The silk had been purchased, but a dress-maker had not yet been found. Miss Ringold recommended me, and I received the order to make the dress. When I called on Mrs. Lee the next day, her husband was in the room, and handing me a roll of bank bills, amounting to one hundred dollars, he requested me to purchase the trimmings, and to spare no expense in making a selection. With the money in my pocket I went out in the street, entered the store of Harper & Mitchell, and asked to look at their laces. Mr. Harper waited on me himself, and was polite and kind. When I asked permission to carry the laces to Mrs. Lee, in order to learn whether she could approve my selection or not, he gave a ready assent. When I reminded him that I was a stranger, and that the goods were valuable, he remarked that he was not afraid to trust me—that he believed my face was the index to an honest heart. It was pleasant to be spoken to thus, and I shall never forget the kind words of Mr. Harper. I often recall them, for they are associated with the dawn of a brighter period in my dark life. I purchased the trimmings, and Mr. Harper allowed me a commission of twenty-five dollars on the purchase. The dress was done in time, and it gave complete satisfaction. Mrs. Lee attracted great attention at the dinner-party, and her elegant dress proved a good card for me. I received numerous orders, and was relieved from all pecuniary embarrassments. One of my patrons was Mrs. Gen. McClean, a daughter of Gen. Sumner. One day when I was very busy, Mrs. McC. drove up to my apartments, came in where I was engaged with my needle, and in her emphatic way said:

"Lizzie, I am invited to dine at Willard's on next Sunday, and positively I have not a dress fit to wear on the occasion. I have just purchased material, and you must commence work on it right away."

"But Mrs. McClean," I replied, "I have more work now promised than I can do. It is impossible for me to make a dress for you to wear on Sunday next."

"Pshaw! Nothing is impossible. I must have the dress made by Sunday;" and she spoke with some impatience.

"I am sorry," I began, but she interrupted me.

"Now don't say no again. I tell you that you must make the dress. I have often heard you say that you would like to work for the ladies of the White House. Well, I have it in my power to obtain you this privilege. I know Mrs. Lincoln well, and you shall make a dress for her provided you finish mine in time to wear at dinner on Sunday."

The inducement was the best that could have been offered. I would undertake the dress if I should have to sit up all night—every night, to make my pledge good. I sent out and employed assistants, and, after much worry and trouble, the dress was completed to the satisfaction of Mrs. McClean. It appears that Mrs. Lincoln had upset a cup of coffee on the dress she designed wearing on the evening of the reception after the inauguration of Abraham Lincoln as President of the United States, which rendered it necessary that she should have a new one for the occasion. On asking Mrs. McClean who her dress-maker was, that lady promptly informed her,

"Lizzie Keckley."

"Lizzie Keckley? The name is familiar to me. She used to work for some of my lady friends in St. Louis, and they spoke well of her. Can you recommend her to me?"

"With confidence. Shall I send her to you?"

"If you please. I shall feel under many obligations for your kindness."

The next Sunday Mrs. McClean sent me a message to call at her house at four o'clock P.M., that day. As she did not state why I was to call, I determined to wait till Monday morning. Monday morning came, and nine o'clock found me at Mrs.

McC.'s house. The streets of the capital were thronged with people, for this was Inauguration day. A new President, a man of the people from the broad prairies of the West, was to accept the solemn oath of office, was to assume the responsibilities attached to the high position of Chief Magistrate of the United States. Never was such deep interest felt in the inauguration proceedings as was felt to-day; for threats of assassination had been made, and every breeze from the South came heavily laden with the rumors of war. Around Willard's hotel swayed an excited crowd, and it was with the utmost difficulty that I worked my way to the house on the opposite side of the street, occupied by the McCleans. Mrs. McClean was out, but presently an aide on General McClean's staff called, and informed me that I was wanted at Willard's. I crossed the street, and on entering the hotel was met by Mrs. McClean, who greeted me:

"Lizzie, why did you not come yesterday, as I requested? Mrs. Lincoln wanted to see you, but I fear that now you are too late."

"I am sorry, Mrs. McClean. You did not say what you wanted with me yesterday, so I judged that this morning would do as well."

"You should have come yesterday," she insisted. "Go up to Mrs. Lincoln's room"—giving me the number—"she may find use for you yet."

With a nervous step I passed on, and knocked at Mrs. Lincoln's door. A cheery voice bade me come in, and a lady, inclined to stoutness, about forty years of age, stood before me.

"You are Lizzie Keckley, I believe."

I bowed assent.

"The dress-maker that Mrs. McClean recommended?"

"Yes, madam."

"Very well; I have not time to talk to you now, but would like to have you call at the White House, at eight o'clock to-morrow morning, where I shall then be."

I bowed myself out of the room, and returned to my apartments. The day passed slowly, for I could not help but speculate in relation to the appointed interview for the morrow. My long-cherished hope was about to be realized, and I could not rest.

Tuesday morning, at eight o'clock, I crossed the threshold of the White House for the first time. I was shown into a waiting-room, and informed that Mrs. Lincoln was at breakfast. In the waiting-room I found no less than three mantua-makers waiting for an interview with the wife of the new President. It seems that Mrs. Lincoln had told several of her lady friends that she had urgent need for a dress-maker, and that each of these friends had sent her mantua-maker to the White House. Hope fell at once. With so many rivals for the position sought after, I regarded my chances for success as extremely doubtful. I was the last one summoned to Mrs. Lincoln's presence. All the others had a hearing, and were dismissed. I went up-stairs timidly, and entering the room with nervous step, discovered the wife of the President standing by a window, looking out, and engaged in lively conversation with a lady, Mrs. Grimsly, as I afterwards learned. Mrs. L. came forward, and greeted me warmly.

"You have come at last. Mrs. Keckley, who have you worked for in the city?"

"Among others, Mrs. Senator Davis has been one of my best patrons," was my reply.

"Mrs. Davis! So you have worked for her, have you? Of course you gave satisfaction; so far, good. Can you do my work?"

"Yes, Mrs. Lincoln. Will you have much work for me to do?"

"That, Mrs. Keckley, will depend altogether upon your prices. I trust that your terms are reasonable. I cannot afford to be extravagant. We are just from the West, and are poor. If you do not charge too much, I shall be able to give you all my work."

"I do not think there will be any difficulty about charges, Mrs. Lincoln; my terms are reasonable."

"Well, if you will work cheap, you shall have plenty to do. I can't afford to pay big prices, so I frankly tell you so in the beginning."

The terms were satisfactorily arranged, and I measured Mrs. Lincoln, took the dress with me, a bright rose-colored moire-antique, and returned the next day to fit it on her. A number of ladies were in the room, all making preparations for the levee to come off on Friday night. These ladies, I learned, were relatives of Mrs. L.'s,—Mrs. Edwards and Mrs. Kellogg, her own sisters, and Elizabeth Edwards and Julia Baker, her nieces. Mrs. Lincoln this morning was dressed in a cashmere wrapper, quilted down the front; and she wore a simple head-dress. The other ladies wore morning robes.

I was hard at work on the dress, when I was informed that the levee had been postponed from Friday night till Tuesday night. This, of course, gave me more time to complete my task. Mrs. Lincoln sent for me, and suggested some alteration in style, which was made. She also requested that I make a waist of blue watered silk for Mrs. Grimsly, as work on the dress would not require all my time.

Tuesday evening came, and I had taken the last stitches on the dress. I folded it and carried it to the White House, with the waist for Mrs. Grimsly. When I went up-stairs, I found the ladies in a terrible state of excitement. Mrs. Lincoln was protesting that she could not go down, for the reason that she had nothing to wear.

"Mrs. Keckley, you have disappointed me—deceived me. Why do you bring my dress at this late hour?"

"Because I have just finished it, and I thought I should be in time."

"But you are not in time, Mrs. Keckley; you have bitterly disappointed me. I have no time now to dress, and, what is more, I will not dress, and go down-stairs."

"I am sorry if I have disappointed you, Mrs. Lincoln, for I intended to be in time. Will you let me dress you? I can have you ready in a few minutes."

"No, I won't be dressed. I will stay in my room. Mr. Lincoln can go down with the other ladies."

"But there is plenty of time for you to dress, Mary," joined in Mrs. Grimsly and Mrs. Edwards. "Let Mrs. Keckley assist you, and she will soon have you ready."

Thus urged, she consented. I dressed her hair, and arranged the dress on her. It fitted nicely, and she was pleased. Mr. Lincoln came in, threw himself on the sofa, laughed with Willie and little Tad, and then commenced pulling on his gloves, quoting poetry all the while.

"You seem to be in a poetical mood to-night," said his wife.

"Yes, mother, these are poetical times," was his pleasant reply. "I declare, you look charming in that dress. Mrs. Keckley has met with great success." And then he proceeded to compliment the other ladies.

Mrs. Lincoln looked elegant in her rose-colored moire-antique. She wore a pearl necklace, pearl ear-rings, pearl bracelets, and red roses in her hair. Mrs. Baker was dressed in lemon-colored silk; Mrs. Kellogg in a drab silk, ashes of rose; Mrs. Edwards in a brown and black silk; Miss Edwards in crimson, and Mrs. Grimsly in blue watered silk. Just before starting down-stairs, Mrs. Lincoln's lace handkerchief was the object of search. It had been displaced by Tad, who was mischievous, and hard to restrain. The handkerchief found, all became serene. Mrs. Lincoln took the President's arm, and with smiling face led the train below. I was surprised at her grace and composure. I had heard so much, in current and malicious report, of her low life, of her ignorance and vulgarity, that I expected to see her embarrassed on this occasion. Report, I soon saw, was wrong. No queen, accustomed to the usages of royalty all her life, could have comported herself with more calmness and dignity than did the wife of the President. She was confident and self-possessed, and confidence always gives grace.

This levee was a brilliant one, and the only one of the season. I became the regular modiste of Mrs. Lincoln. I made fifteen or sixteen dresses for her during the spring and early part of the summer, when she left Washington; spending the hot weather at Saratoga, Long Branch, and other places. In the mean time I was employed by Mrs. Senator Douglas, one of the loveliest ladies that I ever met, Mrs. Secretary Wells, Mrs. Secretary Stanton, and others. Mrs. Douglas always dressed in deep mourning, with excellent taste, and several of the leading ladies of Washington society were extremely jealous of her superior attractions.

Chapter VI. Willie Lincoln's Death-Bed.

MRS. LINCOLN returned to Washington in November, and again duty called me to the White House. The war was now in progress, and every day brought stirring news from the front—the front, where the Gray opposed the Blue, where flashed the bright sabre in the sunshine, where were heard the angry notes of battle, the deep roar of cannon, and the fearful rattle of musketry; where new graves were being made every day, where brother forgot a mother's early blessing and sought the life-blood of brother, and friend raised the deadly knife against friend.

Oh, the front, with its stirring battle-scenes! Oh, the front, with its ghastly heaps of dead! The life of the nation was at stake; and when the land was full of sorrow, there could not be much gayety at the capital. The days passed quietly with me. I soon learned that some people had an intense desire to penetrate the inner circle of the White House. No President and his family, heretofore occupying this mansion, ever excited so much curiosity as the present incumbents. Mr. Lincoln had grown up in the wilds of the West, and evil report had said much of him and his wife. The polite world was shocked, and the tendency to exaggerate intensified curiosity. As soon as it was known that I was the modiste of Mrs. Lincoln, parties crowded around and affected friendship for me, hoping to induce me to betray the secrets of the domestic circle. One day a woman, I will not call her a lady, drove up to my rooms, gave me an order to make a dress, and insisted on partly paying me in advance. She called on me every day, and was exceedingly kind. When she came to take her dress away, she cautiously remarked:

"Mrs. Keckley, you know Mrs. Lincoln?"

"Yes."

"You are her modiste; are you not?"

"Yes."

"You know her very well; do you not?"

"I am with her every day or two."

"Don't you think you would have some influence with her?"

"I cannot say. Mrs. Lincoln, I presume, would listen to anything I should suggest, but whether she would be influenced by a suggestion of mine is another question."

"I am sure that you could influence her, Mrs. Keckley. Now listen; I have a proposition to make. I have a great desire to become an inmate of the White House. I have heard so much of Mr. Lincoln's goodness that I should like to be near him; and if I can enter the White House no other way, I am willing to go as a menial. My dear Mrs. Keckley, will you not recommend me to Mrs. Lincoln as a friend of yours out of employment, and ask her to take me as a chambermaid? If you will do this you shall be well rewarded. It may be worth several thousand dollars to you in time."

I looked at the woman in amazement. A bribe, and to betray the confidence of my employer! Turning to her with a glance of scorn, I said:

"Madam, you are mistaken in regard to my character. Sooner than betray the trust of a friend, I would throw myself into the Potomac river. I am not so base as that. Pardon me, but there is the door, and I trust that you will never enter my room again."

She sprang to her feet in deep confusion, and passed through the door, murmuring: "Very well; you will live to regret your action today."

"Never, never!" I exclaimed, and closed the door after her with a bang. I afterwards learned that this woman was an actress, and that her object was to enter the White House as a servant, learn its secrets, and then publish a scandal to the world. I do not give her name, for such publicity would wound the sensitive feelings of friends, who would have to share her disgrace, without being responsible for her faults. I simply record the incident to show how I often was approached by unprincipled parties. It is unnecessary to say that I indignantly refused every bribe offered.

The first public appearance of Mrs. Lincoln that winter was at the reception on New Year's Day. This reception was shortly followed by a brilliant levee. The day after the levee I went to the White House, and while fitting a dress to Mrs. Lincoln, she said:

"Lizabeth"—she had learned to drop the E—"Lizabeth, I have an idea. These are war times, and we must be as economical as possible. You know the President is expected to give a series of state dinners every winter, and these dinners are very costly; Now I want to avoid this expense; and my idea is, that if I give three large receptions, the state dinners can be scratched from the programme. What do you think, Lizabeth?"

"I think that you are right, Mrs. Lincoln."

"I am glad to hear you say so. If I can make Mr. Lincoln take the same view of the case, I shall not fail to put the idea into practice."

Before I left her room that day, Mr. Lincoln came in. She at once stated the case to him. He pondered the question a few moments before answering.

"Mother, I am afraid your plan will not work."

"But it *will* work, if you will only determine that it *shall* work."

"It is breaking in on the regular custom," he mildly replied.

"But you forget, father, these are war times, and old customs can be done away with for the once. The idea is economical, you must admit."

"Yes, mother, but we must think of something besides economy."

"I do think of something else. Public receptions are more democratic than stupid state dinners—are more in keeping with the spirit of the institutions of our country, as you would say if called upon to make a stump speech. There are a great many strangers in the city, foreigners and others, whom we can entertain at our receptions, but whom we cannot invite to our dinners."

"I believe you are right, mother. You argue the point well. I think that we shall have to decide on the receptions."

So the day was carried. The question was decided, and arrangements were made for the first reception. It now was January, and cards were issued for February.

The children, Tad and Willie, were constantly receiving presents. Willie was so delighted with a little pony, that he insisted on riding it every day. The weather was changeable, and exposure resulted in a severe cold, which deepened into fever. He was very sick, and I was summoned to his bedside. It was sad to see the poor boy suffer. Always of a delicate constitution, he could not resist the strong inroads of disease. The days dragged wearily by, and he grew weaker and more shadow-like. He was his mother's favorite child, and she doted on him. It grieved her heart sorely to see him suffer. When able to be about, he was almost constantly by her side. When I would go in her room, almost always I found blue-eyed Willie there, reading from an open book, or curled up in a chair with pencil and paper in hand. He had decidedly a literary taste, and was a studious boy. . . .

Finding that Willie continued to grow worse, Mrs. Lincoln determined to withdraw her cards of invitation and postpone the reception. Mr. Lincoln thought that the cards had better not be withdrawn. At least he advised that the doctor be consulted before any steps were taken. Accordingly Dr. Stone was called in. He pronounced Willie better, and said that there was every reason for an early recovery. He thought, since the invitations had been issued, it would be best to go on with the reception. Willie, he insisted, was in no immediate danger. Mrs. Lincoln was guided by these counsels, and no postponement was announced. On the evening of the reception Willie was suddenly taken worse. His mother sat by his bedside a long while, holding his feverish hand in her own, and watching his labored breathing. The doctor claimed there was no cause for alarm. I arranged Mrs. Lincoln's hair, then assisted her to dress. Her dress was white satin, trimmed with black lace. The trail was very long, and as she swept through the room, Mr. Lincoln was standing with his back to the fire, his hands behind him, and his eyes on the carpet. His face wore a thoughtful, solemn look. The rustling of the satin dress attracted his attention. He looked at it a few moments; then, in his quaint, quiet way remarked—

"Whew! our cat has a long tail to-night."

Mrs. Lincoln did not reply. The President added:

"Mother, it is my opinion, if some of that tail was nearer the head, it would be in better style;" and he glanced at her bare arms and neck. She had a beautiful neck and arm, and low dresses were becoming to her. She turned away with a look of offended dignity, and presently took the President's arm, and both went down-stairs to their guests, leaving me alone with the sick boy.

The reception was a large and brilliant one, and the rich notes of the Marine Band in the apartments below came to the sick-room in soft, subdued murmurs, like the wild, faint sobbing of far-off spirits. Some of the young people had suggested dancing, but Mr. Lincoln met the suggestion with an emphatic veto. The brilliance of the scene could not dispel the sadness that rested upon the face of Mrs. Lincoln. During the evening she came up-stairs several times, and stood by the bedside of the suffering boy. She loved him with a mother's heart, and her anxiety was great. The night passed slowly; morning came, and Willie was worse. He lingered a few days, and died. God called the beautiful spirit home, and the house of joy was turned into the house of mourning. I was worn out with watching, and was not in the room when Willie died, but was immediately sent for. I assisted in washing him and dressing him, and then laid him on the bed, when Mr. Lincoln came in. I never saw a man so bowed down with grief. He came to the bed, lifted the cover from the face of his child, gazed at it long and earnestly, murmuring, "My poor boy, he was too good for this earth. God has called him home. I know that he is much better off in heaven, but then we loved him so. It is hard, hard to have him die!"

Great sobs choked his utterance. He buried his head in his hands, and his tall frame was convulsed with emotion. I stood at the foot of the bed, my eyes full of tears, looking at the man in silent, awe-stricken wonder. His grief unnerved him, and made him a weak, passive child. I did not dream that his rugged nature could be so moved. I shall never forget those solemn moments—genius and greatness weeping over love's idol lost. There is a grandeur as well as a simplicity about the picture that will never fade. With me it is immortal—I really believe that I shall carry it with me across the dark, mysterious river of death.

Mrs. Lincoln's grief was inconsolable. The pale face of her dead boy threw her into convulsions. Around him love's tendrils had been twined, and now that he was dressed for the tomb, it was like tearing the tendrils out of the heart by their roots. Willie, she often said, if spared by Providence, would be the hope and stay of her old age. But Providence had not spared him. The light faded from his eyes, and the death-dew had gathered on his brow.

In one of her paroxysms of grief the President kindly bent over his wife, took her by the arm, and gently led her to the window. With a stately, solemn gesture, he pointed to the lunatic asylum.

"Mother, do you see that large white building on the hill yonder? Try and control your grief, or it will drive you mad, and we may have to send you there."

Mrs. Lincoln was so completely overwhelmed with sorrow that she did not attend the funeral. Willie was laid to rest in the cemetery, and the White House was draped in mourning. Black crape everywhere met the eye, contrasting strangely with the gay and brilliant colors of a few days before. Party dresses were laid aside, and every one who crossed the threshold of the Presidential mansion spoke in subdued tones when they thought of the sweet boy at rest—"Under the sod and the dew."

Previous to this I had lost my son. Leaving Wilberforce, he went to the battle-field with the three months troops, and was killed in Missouri—found his grave on the battle-field where the gallant General Lyon fell. It was a sad blow to me, and the kind womanly letter that Mrs. Lincoln wrote to me when she heard of my bereavement was full of golden words of comfort.

Nathaniel Parker Willis, the genial poet, now sleeping in his grave, wrote this beautiful sketch of Willie Lincoln, after the sad death of the bright-eyed boy:

"This little fellow had his acquaintances among his father's friends, and I chanced to be one of them. He never failed to seek me out in the crowd, shake hands, and make some pleasant remark; and this, in a boy of ten years of age, was, to say the least, endearing to a stranger. But he had more than mere affectionateness. His self-possession—*aplomb*, as the French call it—was extraordinary. I was one day passing the White House, when he was outside with a play-fellow on the side-walk. Mr. Seward drove in, with Prince Napoleon and two of his *suite* in the carriage; and, in a mock-heroic way—terms of intimacy evidently existing between the boy and the Secretary—the official gentleman took off his hat, and the Napoleon did the same, all making the young Prince President a ceremonious salute. Not a bit staggered with the homage, Willie drew himself up to his full height, took off his little cap with graceful self-possession, and bowed down formally to the ground, like a little ambassador. They drove past, and he went on unconcernedly with his play: the impromptu readiness and good judgment being clearly a part of his nature. His genial and open expression of countenance was none the less ingenuous and fearless for a certain tincture of fun; and it was in this mingling of qualities that he so faithfully resembled his father.

"With all the splendor that was around this little fellow in his new home, he was so bravely and beautifully *himself*—and that only. A wild flower transplanted from the prairie to the hothouse, he retained his prairie habits, unalterably pure and simple, till he died. His leading trait seemed to be a fearless and kindly frankness, willing that everything should be as different as it pleased, but resting unmoved in his own conscious single-heartedness. I found I was studying him irresistibly, as one of the sweet problems of childhood that the world is blessed with in rare places; and the news of his death (I was absent from Washington, on a visit to my own children, at the time) came to me like a knell heard unexpectedly at a merry-making.

"On the day of the funeral I went before the hour, to take a near farewell look at the dear boy; for they had embalmed him to send home to the West—to sleep under the sod of his own valley—and the coffin-lid was to be closed before the service. The family had just taken their leave of him, and the servants and nurses were seeing him for the last time—and with tears and sobs wholly unrestrained, for he was loved like an idol by every one of them. He lay with eyes closed—his brown hair parted as we had known it—pale in the slumber of death; but otherwise unchanged, for he was dressed as if for the evening, and held in one of his hands, crossed upon his breast, a bunch of exquisite flowers—a message coming from his mother, while we were looking upon him, that those flowers might be preserved for her. She was lying sick in her bed, worn out with grief and overwatching.

"The funeral was very touching. Of the entertainments in the East Room the boy had been—for those who now assembled more especially—a most life-giving variation. With his bright face, and his apt greetings and replies, he was remembered in every part of that crimson-curtained hall, built only for pleasure—of all the crowds, each night, certainly the one least likely to be death's first mark. He was his father's favorite. They were intimates—often seen hand in hand. And there sat the man, with a burden on his brain at which the world marvels—bent now with the load at both heart and brain—staggering under a blow like the taking from him of his child! His men of power sat around him—McClellan, with a moist eye when he bowed to the prayer, as I could see from where I stood; and Chase and Seward, with their austere features at work; and senators, and ambassadors, and soldiers, all struggling with their tears—great hearts sorrowing with the President as a stricken man and a brother. That God may give him strength for all his burdens is, I am sure, at present the prayer of a nation." . . .

Further Reading

Sorisio, Carolyn. "Unmasking the Genteel Performer: Elizabeth Keckley's *Behind The Scenes* and the Politics of Public Wrath." *African American Review* 34 (Spring 2000):19–38.

The Two Offers

1859 | SHORT STORY

"The Two Offers." *The Anglo-African Magazine*. 1 (September-October, 1859): 288–291, 311–313. BY FRANCES ELLEN WATKINS [HARPER]

"What is the matter with you, Laura, this morning? I have been watching you this hour, and in that time you have commenced a half dozen letters and torn them all up. What matter of such grave moment is puzzling your dear little head, that you do not know how to decide?"

"Well, it is an important matter: I have two offers for marriage, and I do not know which to choose."

"I should accept neither, or to say the least, not at present."

"Why not?"

"Because I think a woman who is undecided between two offers, has not love enough for either to make a choice; and in that very hesitation, indecision, she has a reason to pause and seriously reflect, lest her marriage, instead of being an affinity of souls or a union of hearts, should only be a mere matter of bargain and sale, or an affair of convenience and selfish interest."

"But I consider them both very good offers, just such as many a girl would gladly receive. But to tell you the truth, I do not think that I regard either as a woman should the man she chooses for her husband. But then if I refuse, there is the risk of being an old maid, and that is not to be thought of."

"Well, suppose there is, is that the most dreadful fate that can befall a woman? Is there not more intense wretchedness in an ill-assorted marriage—more utter loneliness in a loveless home, than in the lot of the old maid who accepts her earthly mission as a gift from God, and strives to walk the path of life with earnest and unfaltering steps?"

"Oh! What a little preacher you are. I really believe that you were cut out for an old maid; and when nature formed you, she put in a double portion of intellect to make up for a deficiency of love; and yet you are kind and affectionate. But I do not think that you know anything of the grand, over-mastering passion, or the deep necessity of woman's heart for loving."

"Do you think so?" resumed the first speaker; and bending over her work she quietly applied herself to the knitting that had lain neglected by her side, during this brief conversation; but as she did so, a shadow flitted over her pale and intellectual brow, a mist gathered in her eyes, and a slight quivering of the lips, revealed a depth of feeling to which her companion was a stranger.

But before I proceed with my story, let me give you a slight history of the speakers. They were cousins, who had met life under different auspices. Laura Lagrange, was the only daughter of rich and indulgent parents, who had spared no pains to make her an accomplished lady. Her cousin, Janette Alston, was the child of parents, rich only in goodness and affection. Her father had been unfortunate in business, and dying before he could retrieve his fortunes, left his business in an embarrassed state. His widow was unacquainted with his business affairs, and when the estate was settled, hungry creditors had brought their claims and the lawyers had received their fees, she found herself homeless and almost penniless, and she who had been sheltered in the warm clasp of loving arms, found them too powerless to shield her from the pitiless pelting storms of adversity. Year after year she struggled with poverty and wrestled with want, till her toil-worn hands became too feeble to hold the shattered chords of existence, and her tear-dimmed eyes grew heavy with the slumber of death. Her daughter had watched over her with untiring devotion, had closed her eyes in death, and gone out into the busy, restless world, missing a precious tone from the voices of earth, a beloved step from the paths of life. Too self reliant to depend on the charity of relations, she endeavored to support herself by her own exertions, and she had succeeded. Her path for a while was marked with struggle and trial, but instead of uselessly repining, she met them bravely, and her life became not a thing of ease and indulgence, but of conquest, victory, and accomplishments. At the time when this conversation took place, the deep trials of her life had passed away. The achievements of her genius had won her a position in the literary world, where she shone as one of its bright particular stars. And with her fame came a competence of worldly means, which gave her leisure for improvement, and the riper development of her rare talents. And she, that pale intellectual woman, whose genius gave life and vivacity to the social circle, and whose presence threw a halo of beauty and grace around the charmed atmosphere in which she moved, had at one period of her life, known the mystic and solemn strength of an all-absorbing love. Years faded from the misty past, had seen the kindling of her eye, the quick flushing of her cheek, and the wild throbbing of her heart, at tones of a voice long since hushed to the stillness of death. Deeply, wildly, passionately, she had loved. Her whole life seemed like the pouring out of rich, warm and gushing affections. This love quickened her talents, inspired her genius, and threw over her life a tender and spiritual earnestness. And then came a fearful shock, a mournful waking from that "dream of beauty and delight." A shadow fell upon her path; it came between her eye and the object of her heart's worship; first a few cold words, estrangement, and then a painful separation; the old story of woman's pride—digging the sepulchre of her happiness, and then a new-made grave, and her path over it to the spirit world; and thus faded out from that young heart her bright, brief and saddened dream of life. Faint and spirit-broken, she turned from the scenes associated with the memory of the loved and lost. She tried to break the chain of sad associations that bound her to the mournful past ; and so, pressing back the bitter sobs from her almost breaking heart, like the dying dolphin, whose beauty is born of its death anguish, her genius gathered strength from suffering and wonderous power and brilliancy from the agony she hid within the desolate chambers of her soul. Men hailed her as one of earth's strangely gifted children, and wreathed the garlands of fame for her brow, when it was throbbing with a wild and fearful unrest. They breathed her name with applause, when through the lonely halls of her stricken spirit, was an earnest cry for peace, a sleep yearning for sympathy and heart-support.

But life, with its stern realities, met her; its solemn responsibilities confronted her, and turning, with an earnest and shattered spirit, to life's duties and trials, she found a calmness and strength that she had only imagined in her dreams of poetry and song. We will now pass over a period of ten years, and the cousins have met again. In that calm and lovely woman, in whose eyes is a depth of tenderness, tempering the flashes of her genius, whose looks and tones are full of sympathy and love, we recognize the once smitten and stricken Janette Alston. The bloom of her girlhood had given way to a higher type of spiritual beauty, as if some unseen hand had been polishing and refining the temple in which her lovely spirit found its habitation; and this had been the fact. Her inner life had grown beautiful, and it was this that was constantly developing the outer. Never, in the early flush of womanhood, when an absorbing love had lit up her eyes and glowed in her life, had she appeared so interesting as when, with a countenance which seemed overshadowed with a spiritual light, she bent over the deathbed of a young woman, just lingering at the shadowy gates of the unseen land.

"Has he come?" faintly but eagerly exclaimed the dying woman. "Oh! how I have longed for his coming, and even in death he forgets me."

"Oh, do not say so, dear Laura, some accident may have detained him," said Janette to her cousin; for on that bed, from whence she will never rise, lies the once-beautiful and light-hearted Laura Lagrange, the brightness of whose eyes has long since been dimmed with tears, and whose voice had become like a harp whose every chord is tuned to sadness—whose faintest thrill and loudest vibrations are but the variations of agony. A heavy hand was laid upon her once warm and bounding heart, and a voice came whispering through her soul, that she must die. But, to her, the tidings was a message of deliverance—a voice, hushing her wild sorrows to the calmness of resignation and hope. Life had grown so weary upon her head—the future looked so hopeless—she had no wish to tread again the track where thorns had pierced her feet, and clouds overcast her sky; and she hailed the coming of death's angel as the footsteps of a welcome friend. And yet, earth had one object so very dear to her weary heart. It was her absent and recreant husband; for, since that conversation, she had accepted one of his offers, and become a wife. But, before she married, she learned that great lesson of human experience and woman's life, to love the man who bowed at her shrine, a willing worshipper. He had a pleasing address, raven hair, flashing eyes, a voice of thrilling sweetness, and lips of persuasive eloquence; and being well versed in the ways of the world, he won his way to her heart, and she became his bride, and he was proud of his prize. Vain and superficial in his character, he looked upon marriage not as a divine sacrament for the soul's development and human progression, but as the title-deed that gave him possession of the woman he thought he loved. But alas for her, the laxity of his principles had rendered him unworthy of the deep and undying devotion of a pure-hearted woman; but, for awhile, he hid from her his true character, and she blindly loved him, and for a short period was happy in the consciousness of being beloved; though sometimes a vague unrest would fill her soul, when, overflowing with a sense of the good, the beautiful, and the true, she would turn to him, but find no response to the deep yearnings of her soul—no appreciation of life's highest realities—its solemn grandeur and significant importance. Their souls never met, and soon she found a void in her bosom, that his earth-born love could not fill. He did not satisfy the wants of her mental and moral nature—between him and her there was no affinity of minds, no intercommunication of souls.

Talk as you will of woman's deep capacity for loving, of the strength of her affectional nature. I do not deny it; but will the mere possession of any human love, fully satisfy all the demands of her whole being? You may paint her in poetry or fiction, as a frail vine, clinging to her brother man for support, and dying when deprived of it; and all this may sound well enough to please the imaginations of school girls, or lovelorn maidens. But woman—the true woman—if you would render her happy, it needs more than the mere development of her affectional nature. Her conscience should be enlightened, her faith in the true and right established, and scope given to her Heaven-endowed and God-given faculties. The true aim of female education should be, not a development of one or two, but all the faculties of the human soul, because no perfect womanhood is developed by imperfect culture. Intense love is often akin to intense suffering, and to trust the whole wealth of a woman's nature on the frail bark of human love, may often be like trusting a cargo of gold and precious gems, to a bark that has never battled with the storm, or buffetted the waves. Is it any wonder, then, that so many life-barks go down, paving the ocean of time with precious hearts and wasted hopes? that so many float around us, shattered and dismasted wrecks, that so many are stranded on the shoals of existence, mournful beacons and solemn warnings for the thoughtless, to whom marriage is a careless and hasty rushing together of the affections? Alas that an institution so fraught with good for humanity should be so perverted, and that state of life, which should be filled with happiness, become so replete with misery. And this was the fate of Laura Lagrange. For a brief period after her marriage her life seemed like a bright and beautiful dream, full of hope and radiant with joy. And then there came a change—he found other attractions that lay beyond the pale of home influences. The gambling saloon had power to win him from her side, he had lived in an element of unhealthy and unhallowed excitements, and the society of a loving wife, the pleasures of a well-regulated home, were enjoyments too tame for one who had vitiated his tastes by the pleasures of sin. There were charmed houses of vice, built upon dead men's loves, where, amid a flow of song, laughter, wine, and careless mirth, he would spend hour after hour, forgetting the cheek that was paling through his neglect, heedless of the tear-dimmed eyes, peering anxiously into the darkness, waiting, or watching his return.

The influence of old associations was upon him. In early life, home had been to him a place of ceilings and walls, not a true home, built upon goodness, love and truth. It was a place where velvet carpets hushed his tread, where images of loveliness and beauty invoked into being painter's art and sculptor's skill, pleased the eye and gratified the taste, where magnificence surrounded his way and costly clothing adorned his person; but it was not the place for the true culture and right development of the soul. His father had been too much engrossed in making money, and his mother in spending it, in striving to maintain a fashionable position in society, and shining in the eyes of the world, to give the proper direction to the character of their wayward and impulsive son. His mother put beautiful robes upon his body, but left ugly scars upon his soul; she pampered his appetite, but starved his spirit. Every mother should be a true artist, who knows how to weave into her child's life images of grace and beauty, the true poet capable of writing on the soul of childhood the harmony of love and truth, and teaching it how to produce the grandest of all poems—the poetry of a true and noble life. But in his home, a love for good, the true and right, had been sacrificed at the shrine of frivolity and fashion. That parental authority which should have been preserved as a string of precious pearls, unbroken and unscattered, was simply the administration of chance. At one time obedience was enforced by authority, at another by flattery and promises, and just so often it was not enforced at all. His early associations were formed as chance directed, and from his want of home-training, his character received a bias, his life a shade, which ran through every avenue of his existence, and darkened all his future hours. Oh, if we could only trace the history of all the crimes that have o'ershad-owed this sin-shrouded and sorrow-darkened world of ours, how many might be seen arising from the wrong home influences, or the weakening of the home ties. Home should always be the best school for the affections, the birthplace of high motives, and the altar upon which lofty aspirations are kindled, from whence the soul may go forth strengthened, to act its part aright in the great drama of life, with conscience enlightened, affections cultivated, and reason and judgment dominant. But alas for the young wife. Her husband had not been blessed with a home. When he entered the arena of life, the voices from home did not linger around his path as angels of guidance about his steps; they were not like so many messages to invite him to deeds of high and holy worth. The memory of no sainted mother arose between him and deeds of darkness; the earnest prayers of no father arrested him in his downward course; and before a year of his married life had waned, his young wife had learned to wait and mourn his frequent and uncalled-for absence. More than once had she seen him come home from his midnight haunts, the bright intel-ligence of his eye displaced by the drunkard's stare; and his manly gait changed to the inebriate's stagger; and she was beginning to know the bitter agony that is com-pressed in the mournful words, a drunkard's wife. And then there came a bright but brief episode in her experience; the angel of life gave to her existence a deeper mean-ing and loftier significance; she sheltered in the warm clasp of her loving arms, a dear babe, a precious child, whose love filled every chamber of her heart, and felt the fount of maternal love gushing so new within her soul. The child was hers. How overshadowing was the love with which she bent over its helplessness, how much it helped to fill the void and chasms in her soul. How many lonely hours were beguiled by its winsome ways, its answering smiles and fond caresses. How exquis-ite and solemn was the feeling that thrilled her heart when she clasped the tiny hands together and taught her dear child to call God "Our Father."

What a blessing was that child. The father paused in his headlong career, awed by the strange beauty and precocious intellect of his child; and the mother's life had a better expression through her ministrations of love. And then there came hours of bitter anguish, shading the sunlight of her home and hushing the music of her heart. The angel of death bent over the couch of her child and beaconed it away. Closer and closer the mother strained her child to her wildly heaving heart, and struggled with the heavy hand that lay upon its heart. Love and agony contended with death, and the language of the mother's heart was,

"Oh, Death, away! that innocent is mine;
I cannot spare him from my arms
To lay him, Death, in thine.
I am a mother, Death; I gave that darling birth
I could not bear his lifeless limbs
Should moulder in the earth."

But death was stronger than love and mightier than agony and won the child for the land of crystal founts and deathless flowers, and the poor, stricken mother sat down beneath the shadow of her mighty grief, feeling as if a great light had gone out from her soul, and that the sunshine had suddenly faded around her path. She turned in her deep anguish to the father of her child, the loved and cherished dead. For awhile his words were kind and tender, his heart seemed subdued, and his tenderness fell upon her worn and weary heart like rain on perishing flowers, or cooling waters to lips all parched with thirst and scorched with fever; but the change was evanescent, the influence of unhallowed associations and evil habits had vitiated and poisoned the springs of his existence. They had bound him in their meshes, and he lacked the moral strength to break his fetters, and stand erect in all the strength and dignity of a true manhood, making life's highest excellence his ideal, and striving to gain it.

And yet moments of deep contrition would sweep over him, when he would resolve to abandon the wine cup forever, when he was ready to forswear the handling of another card, and he would try to break away from the associations that he felt were working his ruin; but when the hour of temptation came his strength was weakness, his earnest purposes were cobwebs, his well-meant resolutions ropes of sand, and thus passed year after year of the married life of Laura Lagrange. She tried to hide her agony from the public gaze, to smile when her heart was almost breaking. But year after year her voice grew fainter and sadder, her once light and bounding step grew slower and faltering. Year after year she wrestled with agony, and strove with despair, till the quick eyes of her brother read, in the paling of her cheek and the dimming eye, the secret anguish of her worn and weary spirit. On that wan, sad face, he saw the death-tokens, and he knew the dark wing of the mystic angel swept coldly around her path. "Laura," said her brother to her one day, "you are not well, and I think you need your mother's tender care and nursing. You are daily losing strength, and if you will go I will accompany you." At first, she hesitated, she shrank almost instinctively from presenting that pale sad face to the loved ones at home. That face was such a tell-tale; it told of heartsickness, of hope deferred, and the mournful story of unrequited love. But then a deep yearning for home sympathy woke within her a passionate longing for love's kind words, for tenderness and heart support, and she resolved to seek the home of her childhood, and lay her weary head upon her mother's bosom, to be folded again in her loving arms, to lay that poor, bruised and aching heart where it might beat and throb closely to the loved ones at home. A kind welcome awaited her. All that love and tenderness could devise was done to bring the bloom to her cheek and the light to her eye; but it was all in vain; her's was a disease that no medicine could cure, no earthly balm could heal. It was a slow wasting of the vital forces, the sickness of the soul. The unkindness and neglect of her husband lay like a leaden weight upon her heart, and slowly oozed away its life-drops. And where was he that had won her love, and then cast it aside as a useless thing, who rifled her heart of its wealth and spread bitter ashes upon its broken altars? He was lingering away from her when the death-damps were gathering on her brow, when his name was trembling on her lips! lingering away! when she was watching his coming, though the death films were gathering before her eyes, and earthly things were fading from her vision. "I think I hear him now," said the dying woman, "surely that is his step;" but the sound died away in the distance. Again she started from an uneasy slumber, "That is his voice! I am so glad he has come." Tears gathered in the eyes of the sad watchers by that dying bed, for they knew that she was deceived. He had not returned. For her sake they wished his coming. Slowly the hours waned away, and then came the sad, soul-sickening thought that she was forgotten, forgotten in the last hour of human need, forgotten when the spirit, about to be dissolved, paused for the last time on the threshold of existence, a weary watcher at the gates of death. "He has forgotten me," again she faintly murmured, and the last tears she would ever shed on earth sprung to her mournful eyes, and clasping her hands together in silent anguish, a few broken sentences issued from her pale and quivering lips. They were prayers for strength and earnest pleading for him who had desolated her young life, by running its sunshine to shadows, its smiles to tears. "He has forgotten me," she murmured again, "but I can bear it, the bitterness of death is passed, and soon I hope to exchange the shadows of death for the brightness of eternity, the rugged paths of life for the golden streets of glory, and the care and turmoils of earth for the peace and rest of heaven." Her voice grew fainter and fainter, they saw the shadows that never deceive flit over her faded face, and knew that the death angel waited to soothe their weary one to rest, to calm the throbbing of her bosom and cool the fever of her brain. And amid the silent hush of their grief the freed spirit, refined through suffering, and brought into divine harmony through the spirit of the living Christ, passed over the dark waters of death as on a bridge of light, over whose radiant arches hovering angels bent. They parted the dark locks from her marble brow, closed the waxen lips over the once bright and laughing eye, and left her to the dreamless slumber of the grave. Her cousin turned from the deathbed a sadder and wiser woman. She resolved more earnestly than ever to make the world better by her example, gladder by her presence, and to kindle the fires of her genius on the altars of universal love and truth. She had a higher and better object in all her writings than the mere acquisition of gold, acquirement of fame. She felt that she had a high and holy mission on the battle-field of existence, that life was not given her to be frittered away in nonsense, or wasted away in trifling pursuits. She would willingly espouse an unpopular cause but not an unrighteous one. In her the downtrodden slave found an earnest advocate; the flying fugitive remembered her kindness as he stepped cautiously through our Republic, to gain his freedom in a monarchial land, having broken the chains on which the rust of centuries had gathered. Little children learned to name her with affection, the poor called her blessed, as she broke her bread to the pale lips of hunger. Her life was like a beautiful story, only it was clothed with the dignity of reality and invested with the sublimity of truth. True, she was an old maid, no husband brightened her life with his love, or shaded it with his neglect. No children nestling lovingly in her arms called her mother. No one appended Mrs. to her name; she was indeed an old maid, not vainly striving to keep up an appearance of girlishness, when departed was written on her youth. Not vainly pining at her loneliness and isolation: the world was full of warm, loving hearts, and her own beat in unison with them. Neither was she always sentimentally sighing for something to love, objects of affection were all around her, and the world was not so wealthy in love that it had no use for her's; in blessing others she made a life and benediction, and as old age descended peacefully and gently upon her, she had learned one of life's most precious lessons, that true happiness consists not so much in the fruition of our wishes as in the regulation of desires and the full development and right culture of our whole natures.

Further Reading

Foster, Frances Smith, ed. *A Brighter Coming Day: A Frances Ellen Watkins Harper Reader*. New York: Feminist Press, 1990.

"Life on the Sea Islands"

MAY AND JUNE, 1864 | SHORT ESSAY

[To THE EDITOR OF THE "ATLANTIC MONTHLY."—The following grace-
ful and picturesque description of the new condition of things on the Sea Islands of
South Carolina, originally written for private perusal, seems to me worthy of a place
in the "Atlantic." Its young author—herself akin to the long-suffering race whose
Exodus she so pleasantly describes—is still engaged in her labor of love on St. Helena
Island. —J.G.W.]

Part I.

It was on the afternoon of a warm, murky day late in October that our steamer, the
United States, touched the landing at Hilton Head. A motley assemblage had collected on the wharf,—officers, soldiers, and "contrabands" of every size and hue:
black was, however, the prevailing color. The first view of Hilton Head is desolate
enough,—a long, low, sandy point, stretching out into the sea, with no visible
dwellings upon it, except the rows of small white-roofed houses which have lately been built for the freed people.

After signing a paper wherein we declared ourselves loyal to the Government,
and wherein, also, were set forth fearful penalties, should we ever be found guilty
of treason, we were allowed to land, and immediately took General Saxton's boat,
the Flora, for Beaufort. The General was on board, and we were presented to him.

He is handsome, courteous, and affable, and looks—as he is—the gentleman and the soldier.

From Hilton Head to Beaufort the same long, low line of sandy coast, bordered by trees; formidable gunboats in the distance, and the gray ruins of an old fort, said to have been built by the Huguenots more than two hundred years ago. Arrived at Beaufort, we found that we had not yet reached our journey's end. While waiting for the boat which was to take us to our island of St. Helena, we had a little time to observe the ancient town. The houses in the main street, which fronts the "Bay," are large and handsome, built of wood, in the usual Southern style, with spacious piazzas, and surrounded by fine trees. We noticed in one yard a magnolia, as high as some of our largest shade-maples, with rich, dark, shining foliage. A large building which was once the Public Library is now a shelter for freed people from Fernandina. Did the Rebels know it, they would doubtless upturn their aristocratic noses, and exclaim in disgust, "To what base uses," etc. We confess that it was highly satisfactory to us to see how the tables are turned, now that "the whirligig of time has brought about its revenges." We saw the market-place, in which slaves were sometimes sold; but we were told that the buying and selling at auction were usually done in Charleston. The arsenal, a large stone structure, was guarded by cannon and sentinels. The houses in the smaller streets had, mostly, a dismantled, desolate look. We saw no one in the streets but soldiers and freed people. There were indications that already Northern improvements had reached this Southern town. Among them was a wharf, a convenience that one wonders how the Southerners could so long have existed without. The more we know of their mode of life, the more are we inclined to marvel at its utter shiftlessness.

Little colored children of every hue were playing about the streets, looking as merry and happy as children ought to look,—now that the evil shadow of Slavery no longer hangs over them. Some of the officers we met did not impress us favorably. They talked flippantly, and sneeringly of the negroes, whom they found we had come down to teach, using an epithet more offensive than gentlemanly. They assured us that there was great danger of Rebel attacks, that the yellow fever prevailed to an alarming extent, and that, indeed, the manufacture of coffins was the only business that was at all flourishing at present. Although by no means daunted by these alarming stories, we were glad when the announcement of our boat relieved us from their edifying conversation.

We rowed across to Ladies Island, which adjoins St. Helena, through the splendors of a grand Southern sunset. The gorgeous clouds of crimson and gold were reflected as in a mirror in the smooth, clear waters below. As we glided along, the rich tones of the negro boatmen broke upon the evening stillness,—sweet, strange, and solemn:—

"Jesus make de blind to see,
Jesus make de cripple walk,
Jesus make de deaf to hear.
Walk in, kind Jesus!
No man can hender me."

It was nearly dark when we reached the island, and then we had a three-miles' drive through the lonely roads to the house of the superintendent. We thought how easy it would be for a band of guerrillas, had they chanced that way, to seize and hang us; but we were in that excited, jubilant state of mind which makes fear impossible, and sang "John Brown" with a will, as we drove through the pines and palmettos. Oh, it was good to sing that song in the very heart of Rebeldom! Harry, our driver, amused us much. He was surprised to find that we had not heard of him before. "Why, I thought eberybody at de Nort had heard o' me!" he said, very innocently. We learned afterward that Mrs. F., who made the tour of the islands last summer, had publicly mentioned Harry. Some one had told him of it, and he of course imagined that he had become quite famous. Notwithstanding this little touch of vanity, Harry is one of the best and smartest men on the island.

Gates occurred, it seemed to us, at every few yards' distance, made in the oddest fashion,—opening in the middle, like folding-doors, for the accommodation of horsemen. The little boy who accompanied us as gate-opener answered to the name of Cupid. Arrived at the headquarters of the general superintendent, Mr. S., we were kindly received by him and the ladies, and shown into a large parlor, where a cheerful wood-fire glowed in the grate. It had a home-like look; but still there was a sense of unreality about everything, and I felt that nothing less than a vigorous "shaking-up," such as Grandfather Smallweed daily experienced, would arouse me thoroughly to the fact that I was in South Carolina.

The next morning L. and I were awakened by the cheerful voices of men and women, children and chickens, in the yard below. We ran to the window, and looked out. Women in bright-colored handkerchiefs, some carrying pails on their heads, were crossing the yard, busy with their morning work; children were playing and tumbling around them. On every face there was a look of serenity and cheerfulness. My heart gave a great throb of happiness as I looked at them, and thought, "They are free! so long down-trodden, so long crushed to the earth, but now in their old homes, forever free!" And I thanked God that I had lived to see this day.

After breakfast Miss T. drove us to Oaklands, our future home. The road leading to the house was nearly choked with weeds. The house itself was in a dilapidated condition, and the yard and garden had a sadly neglected look. But there were roses in bloom; we plucked handfuls of feathery, fragrant acacia-blossoms; ivy crept along the ground and under the house. The freed people on the place seemed glad to see us. After talking with them, and giving some directions for cleaning the house, we drove to the school, in which I was to teach. It is kept in the Baptist Church—a brick building, beautifully situated in a grove of live-oaks. These trees are the first objects that attract one's attention here: not that they are finer than our Northern oaks, but because of the singular gray moss with which every branch is heavily draped. This hanging moss grows on nearly all the trees, but on none so luxuriant-ly as on the live-oak. The pendants are often four or five feet long, very graceful and beautiful, but giving the trees a solemn, almost funereal look. The school was opened in September. Many of the children had, however, received instruction during the summer. It was evident that they had made very rapid improvement, and we noticed with pleasure how bright and eager to learn many of them seemed. They sang in rich, sweet tones, and with a peculiar swaying motion of the body, which made their singing the more effective. They sang "Marching Along," with great spir-it, and then one of their own hymns, the air of which is beautiful and touching:—

"My sister, you want to git religion,
Go down in de Lonesome Valley,
My brudder, you want to git religion,
Go down in de Lonesome Valley.
CHORUS.
"Go down in de Lonesome Valley,
Go down in de Lonesome Valley, my Lord,
Go down in de Lonesome Valley,
To meet my Jesus dere!
"Oh, feed on milk and honey,
Oh, feed on milk and honey, my Lord,
Oh, feed on milk and honey,
Meet my Jesus dere!
Oh, John he brought a letter,
Oh, John he brought a letter, my Lord,
Oh, Mary and Marta read 'em,
Meet my Jesus dere!
CHORUS.
"Go down in de Lonesome Valley," etc.

They repeat their hymns several times, and while singing keep perfect time with their hands and feet.

On our way homeward we noticed that a few of the trees were beginning to turn, but we looked in vain for the glowing autumnal hues of our Northern forests. Some brilliant scarlet berries—the cassena—were growing along the roadside, and on every hand we saw the live-oak with its moss-drapery. The palmettos disappoint-ed me; stiff and ungraceful, they have a bristling, defiant look, suggestive of Rebels starting up and defying everybody. The land is low and level,—not the slightest approach to a hill, not a rock, nor even a stone to be seen. It would have a desolate look, were it not for the trees, and the hanging moss and numberless vines which festoon them. These vines overrun the hedges, form graceful arches between the trees, encircle their trunks, and sometimes climb to the topmost branches. In February they begin to bloom, and then throughout the spring and summer we have a succession of beautiful flowers. First comes the yellow jessamine, with its perfect, gold-colored, and deliciously fragrant blossoms. It lights up the hedges, and com-pletely canopies some of the trees. Of all the wild-flowers this seems to me the most beautiful and fragrant. Then we have the snow-white, but scentless Cherokee rose, with its lovely, shining leaves. Later in the season come the brilliant trumpet-flower, the passion-flower, and innumerable others.

The Sunday after our arrival we attended service at the Baptist Church. The people came in slowly; for they have no way of knowing the hour, except by the sun. By eleven they had all assembled, and the church was well filled. They were neat-ly dressed in their Sunday-attire, the women, mostly wearing clean, dark frocks, with white aprons and bright-colored head-handkerchiefs. Some had attained to the dig-nity of straw hats with gay feathers, but these were not nearly as becoming nor as picturesque as the handkerchiefs. The day was warm, and the windows were thrown open as if it were summer, although it was the second day of November. It was very pleasant to listen to the beautiful hymns, and look from the crowd of dark, earnest faces within, upon the grove of noble oaks without. The people sang, "Roll, Jordan, roll," the grandest of all their hymns. There is a great, rolling wave of sound through it all.

"Mr. Fuller settin' on de Tree ob Life,
Fur to hear de ven Jordan roll.
Oh, roll, Jordan! roll, Jordan! roll, Jordan roll!

CHORUS.

"Oh, roll, Jordan, roll! oh, roll, Jordan, roll!
My soul arise in heab'n, Lord,
Fur to hear de ven Jordan roll!
"Little chil'en, learn to fear de Lord,
And let your days be long.
Oh, roll, Jordan! roll, Jordan! roll, Jordan,
roll!

CHORUS.

"Oh, march, de angel, march! oh, march, de
angel, march!
My soul arise in heab'n, Lord,
Fur to hear de ven Jordan roll!"

The "Mr. Fuller" referred to was their former minister, to whom they seem to have been much attached. He is a Southerner, but loyal, and is now, I believe, living in Baltimore. After the sermon the minister called upon one of the elders, a gray-headed old man, to pray. His manner was very fervent and impressive, but his language was so broken that to our unaccustomed ears it was quite unintelligible. After the services the people gathered in groups outside, talking among themselves, and exchanging kindly greetings with the superintendents and teachers. In their bright handkerchiefs and white aprons they made a striking picture under the gray-mossed trees. We drove afterward a mile farther, to the Episcopal Church, in which the aristocracy of the island used to worship. It is a small white building, situated in a fine grove of live-oaks, at the junction of several roads. On one of the tombstones in the yard is the touching inscription in memory of two children,— "Blessed little lambs, and *art thou* gathered into the fold of the only true shepherd? Sweet *lilies* of the valley, and *art thou* removed to a more congenial soil?" The floor of the church is of stone, the pews of polished oak. It has an organ, which is not so entirely out of tune as are the pianos on the island. One of the ladies played, while the gentlemen sang,—old-fashioned New-England church-music, which it was pleasant to hear, but it did not thrill us as the singing of the people had done.

During the week we moved to Oaklands, our future home. The house was of one story, with a low-roofed piazza running the whole length. The interior had been thoroughly scrubbed and whitewashed; the exterior was guiltless of whitewash or paint. There were five rooms, all quite small, and several dark little entries, in one of which we found shelves lined with old medicine-bottles. These were a part of the possessions of the former owner, a Rebel physician, Dr. Sams by name. Some of them were still filled with his nostrums. Our furniture consisted of a bedstead, two bureaus, three small pine tables, and two chairs, one of which had a broken back. These were lent to us by the people. The masters, in their hasty flight from the islands, left nearly all their furniture; but much of it was destroyed or taken by the soldiers who came first, and what they left was removed by the people to their own houses. Certainly, they have the best right to it. We had made up our minds to dispense with all luxuries and even many conveniences; but it was rather distressing to have no fire, and nothing to eat. Mr. H. had already appropriated a room for the store which he was going to open for the benefit of the freed people, and was superintending the removal of his goods. So L. and I were left to our own resources. But Cupid the elder came to the rescue,—Cupid, who, we were told, was to be our right-hand man, and who very graciously informed us that he would take care of us; which he at once proceeded to do by bringing in some wood, and busying himself in making a fire in the open fireplace. While he is thus engaged, I will try to describe him. A small, wiry figure, stockingless, shoeless, out at the knees and elbows, and wearing the remnant of an old straw hat, which looked as if it might have done good service in scaring the crows from a cornfield. The face nearly black, very ugly, but with the shrewdest expression I ever saw, and the brightest, most humorous twinkle in the eyes. One glance at Cupid's face showed that he was not a person to be imposed upon, and that he was abundantly able to take care of himself, as well as of us. The chimney obstinately refused to draw, in spite of the original and very uncomplimentary epithets which Cupid heaped upon it,—while we stood by, listening to him in amusement, although nearly suffocated by the smoke. At last, perseverance conquered, and the fire began to burn cheerily. Then Amaretta, our cook,—a neat-looking black woman, adorned with the gayest of head-handkerchiefs,—made her appearance with some eggs and hominy, after partaking of which we proceeded to arrange our scanty furniture, which was soon done. In a few days we began to look civilized, having made a table-cover of some red and yellow handkerchiefs which we found among the store-goods,—a carpet of red and black woollen plaid, originally intended for frocks and shirts,—a cushion, stuffed with corn-husks and covered with calico, for a lounge, which Ben, the carpenter, had made for us of pine boards,—and lastly some corn-husk beds, which were an unspeakable luxury, after having endured agonies for several nights, sleeping on the slats of a bedstead. It is true, the said slats were covered with blankets, but these might as well have been sheets of paper for all the good they did us. What a resting-place it was! Compared to it, the gridiron of St. Lawrence—fire excepted—was as a bed of roses.

The first day at school was rather trying. Most of my children were very small, and consequently restless. Some were too young to learn the alphabet. These little ones were brought to school because the older children—in whose care their parents leave them while at work—could not come without them. We were therefore willing to have them come, although they seemed to have discovered the secret of perpetual motion, and tried one's patience sadly. But after some days of positive, though not severe treatment, order was brought out of chaos, and I found but little difficulty in managing and quieting the tiniest and most restless spirits. I never before saw children so eager to learn, although I had had several years' experience in New-England schools. Coming to school is a constant delight and recreation to them. They come here as other children go to play. The older ones, during the summer, work in the fields from early morning until eleven or twelve o'clock, and then come into school, after their hard toil in the hot sun, as bright and as anxious to learn as ever.

Of course there are some stupid ones, but these are the minority. The majority learn with wonderful rapidity. Many of the grown people are desirous of learning to read. It is wonderful how a people who have been so long crushed to the earth, so imbruted as these have been,—and they are said to be among the most degraded negroes of the South,—can have so great a desire for knowledge, and such a capability for attaining it. One cannot believe that the haughty Anglo-Saxon race, after centuries of such an experience as these people have had, would be very much superior to them. And one's indignation increases against those who, North as well as South, taunt the colored race with inferiority while they themselves use every means in their power to crush and degrade them, denying them every right and privilege, closing against them every avenue of elevation and improvement. Were they, under such circumstances, intellectual and refined, they would certainly be vastly superior to any other race that ever existed.

After the lessons, we used to talk freely to the children, often giving them slight sketches of some of the great and good men. Before teaching them the "John Brown" song, which they learned to sing with great spirit, Miss T. told them the story of the brave old man who had died for them. I told them about Toussaint, thinking it well they should know what one of their own color had done for his race. They listened attentively, and seemed to understand. We found it rather hard to keep their attention in school. It is not strange, as they have been so entirely unused to intellectual concentration. It is necessary to interest them every moment, in order to keep their thoughts from wandering. Teaching here is consequently far more fatiguing than at the North. In the church, we had of course but one room in which to hear all the children; and to make one's self heard, when there were often as many as a hundred and forty reciting at once, it was necessary to tax the lungs very severely.

My walk to school, of about a mile, was part of the way through a road lined with trees,—on one side stately pines, on the other noble live-oaks, hung with moss and canopied with vines. The ground was carpeted with brown, fragrant pine-leaves; and as I passed through in the morning, the woods were enlivened by the delicious songs of mocking-birds, which abound here, making one realize the truthful felicity of the description in "Evangeline,"—

"The mocking-bird, wildest of singers,
Shook from his little throat such floods of delirious music.
That the whole air and the woods and the waves seemed silent to listen."

The hedges were all aglow with the brilliant scarlet berries of the cassena, and on some of the oaks we observed the mistletoe, laden with its pure white, pearl-like berries. Out of the woods the roads are generally bad, and we found it hard work plodding through the deep sand.

Mr. H.'s store was usually crowded, and Cupid was his most valuable assistant. Gay handkerchiefs for turbans, pots and kettles, and molasses, were principally in demand, especially the last. It was necessary to keep the molasses-barrel in the yard, where Cupid presided over it, and harangued and scolded the eager, noisy crowd, collected around, to his heart's content; while up the road leading to the house came constantly processions of men, women, and children, carrying on their heads cans, jugs, pitchers, and even bottles,—anything, indeed, that was capable of containing molasses. It is wonderful with what ease they carry all sorts of things on their heads,—heavy bundles of wood, hoes and rakes, everything, heavy or light, that can be carried in the hands; and I have seen a woman, with a bucketful of water on her head, stoop down and take up another in her hand, without spilling a drop from either.

We noticed that the people had much better taste in selecting materials for dresses than we had supposed. They do not generally like gaudy colors, but prefer neat, quiet patterns. They are, however, very fond of all kinds of jewelry. I once asked the children in school what their ears were for. "To put ring in," promptly replied one of the little girls.

These people are exceedingly polite in their manner towards each other, each new arrival bowing, scraping his feet, and shaking hands with the others, while there are constant greetings, such as, "Huddy? How's yer lady?" ("How d' ye do? How's your wife?") The hand-shaking is performed with the greatest possible solemnity. There is never the faintest shadow of a smile on anybody's face during this performance. The children, too, are taught to be very polite to their elders, and it is the rarest thing to hear a disrespectful word from a child to his parent, or to any grown person. They have really what the New-Englanders call "beautiful manners."

We made daily visits to the "quarters," which were a few rods from the house. The negro-houses, on this as on most of the other plantations, were miserable little huts, with nothing comfortable or home-like about them, consisting generally of but two very small rooms,—the only way of lighting them, no matter what the state of the weather, being to leave the doors and windows open. The windows, of course, have no glass in them. In such a place, a father and mother with a large family of children are often obliged to live. It is almost impossible to teach them habits of neatness and order, when they are so crowded. We look forward anxiously to the day when better houses shall increase their comfort and pride of appearance.

Oaklands is a very small plantation. There were not more than eight or nine families living on it. Some of the people interested us much. Celia, one of the best, is a cripple. Her master, she told us, was too mean to give his slaves clothes enough to protect them, and her feet and legs were so badly frozen that they required amputation. She has a lovely face,—well-featured and singularly gentle. In every household where there was illness or trouble, Celia's kind, sympathizing face was the first to be seen, and her services were always the most acceptable.

Harry, the foreman on the plantation, a man of a good deal of natural intelligence, was most desirous of learning to read. He came in at night to be taught, and learned very rapidly. I never saw any one more determined to learn. We enjoyed hearing him talk about the "gun-shoot,"—so the people call the capture of Bay Point and Hilton Head. They never weary of telling you "how Massa run when he hear de fust gun."

"Why didn't you go with him, Harry?" I asked.

"Oh, Miss, 't wasn't 'cause Massa didn't try to 'suade me. He tell we dat de Yankees would shoot we, or would sell we to Cuba, an' do all de wust tings to we, when dey come. 'Bery well, Sar,' says I. 'If I go wid you, I be good as dead. If I stay here, I can't be no wust; so if I got to dead, I might's well dead here as anywhere. So I'll stay here an' wait for de "dam Yankees." 'Lor', Miss, I knowed he wasn't tellin' de truth all de time."

"But why didn't you believe him, Harry?"

"Dunno, Miss; somehow we hear de Yankees was our friends, an' dat we'd be free when dey come, an' 'pears like we believe *dat*."

I found this to be true of nearly all the people I talked with, and I thought it strange they should have had so much faith in the Northerners. Truly, for years past, they had had but little cause to think them very friendly. Cupid told us that his master was so daring as to come back, after he had fled from the island, at the risk of being taken prisoner by our soldiers; and that he ordered the people to get all the furniture together and take it to a plantation on the opposite side of the creek, and to stay on that side themselves. "So," said Cupid, "dey could jus' sweep us all up in a heap, an' put us in de boat. An' he telled me to take Patience—dat's my wife—an' de chil'en down to a certain pint, an' den I could come back, if I choose. Jus' as if I was gwine to be sich a goat!" added he, with a look and gesture of ineffable contempt. He and the rest of the people, instead of obeying their master, left the place and hid themselves in the woods; and when he came to look for them, not one of all his "faithful servants" was to be found. A few, principally house-servants, had previously been carried away.

In the evenings, the children frequently came in to sing and shout for us. These "shouts" are very strange,—in truth, almost indescribable. It is necessary to hear and see in order to have any clear idea of them. The children form a ring, and move around in a kind of shuffling dance, singing all the time. Four or five stand apart, and sing very energetically, clapping their hands, stamping their feet, and rocking their bodies to and fro. These are the musicians, to whose performance the shouters keep perfect time. The grown people on this plantation did not shout, but they do on some of the other plantations. It is very comical to see little children, not more than three or four years old, entering into the performance with all their might. But the shouting of the grown people is rather solemn and impressive than otherwise. We cannot determine whether it has a religious character or not. Some of the people tell us that it has, others that it has not. But as the shouts of the grown people are always in connection with their religious meetings, it is probable that they are the barbarous expression of religion, handed down to them from their African ancestors, and destined to pass away under the influence of Christian teachings. The people on this island have no songs. They sing only hymns, and most of these are sad. Prince, a large black boy from a neighboring plantation, was the principal shouter among the children. It seemed impossible for him to keep still for a moment. His performances were most amusing specimens of Ethiopian gymnastics. Amaretta the younger, a cunning, kittenish little creature of only six years old, had a remarkably sweet voice. Her favorite hymn, which we used to hear her singing to herself as she walked through the yard, is one of the oddest we have heard:—

"What makes old Satan follow me so?
Satan got nuttin' 't all fur to do wid me.

CHORUS.

"Tiddy Rosa, hold your light!
Brudder Tony, hold your light!
All de member, hold bright light
On Canaan's shore!"

This is one of the most spirited shouting-tunes. "Tiddy" is their word for sister.

A very queer-looking old man came into the store one day. He was dressed in a complete suit of brilliant Brussels carpeting. Probably it had been taken from his master's house after the "gun-shoot"; but he looked so very dignified that we did not like to question him about it. The people called him Doctor Crofts,—which was, I believe, his master's name, his own being Scipio. He was very jubilant over the new state of things, and said to Mr. H.,—"Don't hab me feelins hurt now. Used to hab me feelins hurt all de time. But don't hab 'em hurt now no more." Poor old soul! We rejoiced with him that he and his brethren no longer have their "feelins" hurt, as in the old time.

On the Sunday before Thanksgiving, General Saxton's noble Proclamation was read at church. We could not listen to it without emotion. The people listened with the deepest attention, and seemed to understand and appreciate it. Whittier has said of it and its writer,—"It is the most beautiful and touching official document I ever read. God bless him! 'The bravest are the tenderest.'"

General Saxton is truly worthy of the gratitude and admiration with which the people regard him. His unfailing kindness and consideration for them—so different from the treatment they have sometimes received at the hands of other officers—have caused them to have unbounded confidence in General "*Saxby*," as they call him.

After the service, there were six couples married. Some of the dresses were unique. One was particularly fine,—doubtless a cast-off dress of the bride's former mistress. The silk and lace, ribbons, feathers and flowers, were in a rather faded and decayed condition. But, comical as the costumes were, we were not disposed to laugh at them. We were too glad to see the poor creatures trying to lead right and virtuous lives. The legal ceremony, which was formerly scarcely known among them, is now everywhere consecrated. The constant and earnest advice of the minister and teachers has not been given in vain; nearly every Sunday there are several couples married in church. Some of them are people who have grown old together.

Thanksgiving-Day was observed as a general holiday. According to General Saxton's orders, an ox had been killed on each plantation, that the people might that day have fresh meat, which was a great luxury to them, and, indeed, to all of us. In the morning, a large number—superintendents, teachers, and freed people—assembled in the Baptist Church. It was a sight not soon to be forgotten,—that crowd of eager, happy black faces, from which the shadow of Slavery had forever passed. "Forever free! forever free!" those magical words of the Proclamation were constantly singing themselves in my soul. After an appropriate prayer and sermon by Mr. P., and singing by the people, General Saxton made a short, but spirited speech, urging the young men to enlist in the regiment then forming under Colonel Higginson. Mrs. Gage told the people how the slaves in Santa Cruz had secured their liberty. It was something entirely new and strange to them to hear a woman speak in public; but they listened with great attention, and seemed much interested. Before dispersing, they sang "Marching Along," which is an especial favorite with them. It was a very happy Thanksgiving-Day for all of us. The weather was delightful; oranges and figs were hanging on the trees; roses, oleanders, and japonicas were blooming out-of-doors; the sun was warm and bright; and over all shone gloriously the blessed light of Freedom,—Freedom forevermore!

One night, L. and I were roused from our slumbers by what seemed to us loud and most distressing shrieks, proceeding from the direction of the negro-houses. Having heard of one or two attempts which the Rebels had recently made to land on the island, our first thought was, naturally, that they had forced a landing, and were trying to carry off some of the people. Every moment we expected to hear them at our doors; and knowing that they had sworn vengeance against all the superintendents and teachers, we prepared ourselves for the worst. After a little reflection, we persuaded ourselves that it could not be the Rebels; for the people had always assured us, that, in case of a Rebel attack, they would come to us at once,—evidently thinking that we should be able to protect them. But what could the shrieks mean? They ceased; then, a few moments afterwards, began again, louder, more fearful than before; then again they ceased, and all was silent. I am ashamed to confess that we had not the courage to go out and inquire into the cause of the alarm. Mr. H.'s room was in another part of the house, too far for him to give us any aid. We hailed the dawn of day gladly enough, and eagerly sought Cupid,—who was sure to know everything,—to obtain from him a solution of the mystery. "Why, you wasn't scared at *dat*?" he exclaimed, in great amusement; "'twasn't nuttin' but de black sogers dat comed up to see der folks on t' oder side ob de creek. Dar wasn't no boat fur 'em on dis side, so dey jus' blowed de whistle dey hab, so de folks might bring one ober fur 'em. Dat was all 't was." And Cupid laughed so heartily that we felt not a little ashamed of our fears. Nevertheless, we both maintained that *we* had never seen a whistle from which could be produced sounds so startling, so distressing, so perfectly like the shrieks of a human being.

Another night, while staying at a house some miles distant from ours, I was awakened by hearing, as I thought, some one trying to open the door from without. The door was locked; I lay perfectly still, and listened intently. A few moments elapsed, and the sound was repeated; whereupon I rose, and woke Miss W., who slept in the adjoining room. We lighted a candle, took our revolvers, and seated ourselves on the bed, keeping our weapons, so formidable in practised male hands, steadily pointed towards the door, and uttering dire threats against the intruders,— presumed to be Rebels, of course. Having maintained this tragical position for some time, and hearing no further noise; we began to grow sleepy, and extinguished our candle, returned to bed, and slept soundly till morning. But that mystery remained unexplained. I was sure that the door had been tried,—there could be no mistaking it. There was not the least probability that any of the people had entered the house, burglars are unknown on these islands, and there is nobody to be feared but the Rebels.

The last and greatest alarm we had was after we had removed from Oaklands to another plantation. I woke about two o'clock in the morning, hearing the tramp of many feet in the yard below,—the steady tramp of soldiers' feet. "The Rebels! they have come at last! all is over with us now!" I thought at once, with a desperate kind of resignation. And I lay still, waiting and listening. Soon I heard footsteps on the piazza; then the hall-door was opened, and steps were heard distinctly in the hall beneath; finally, I heard some one coming up the stairs. Then I grasped my revolver, rose, and woke the other ladies.

"There are soldiers in the yard! Somebody has opened the hall-door, and is coming up-stairs!"

Poor L., but half awakened, stared at me in speechless terror. The same thought filled our minds. But Mrs. B., after listening for a moment, exclaimed,—

"Why, that is my husband! I know his footsteps. He is coming up-stairs to call me."

And so it proved. Her husband, who was a lieutenant in Colonel Montgomery's regiment, had come up from camp with some of his men to look after deserters. The door had been unfastened by a servant who on that night happened to sleep in the house. I shall never forget the delightful sensation of relief that came over me when the whole matter was explained. It was almost overpowering; for, although I had made up my mind to bear the worst, and bear it bravely, the thought of falling into the hands of the Rebels was horrible in the extreme. A year of intense mental suffering seemed to have been compressed into those few moments.

Part II

A few days before Christmas, we were delighted at receiving a beautiful Christmas Hymn from Whittier, written by request, especially for our children. They learned it very easily, and enjoyed singing it. We showed them the writer's picture, and told them he was a very good friend of theirs, who felt the deepest interest in them, and had written this hymn expressly for them to sing,—which made them very proud and happy. Early Christmas morning, we were wakened by the people knocking at the doors and windows, and shouting, "Merry Christmas!" After distributing some little presents among them, we went to church, which had been decorated with holly, pine, cassena, mistletoe, and the hanging moss, and had a very Christmas-like look. The children of our school assembled there, and we gave them the nice, comfortable clothing, and the picture-books, which had been kindly sent by some Philadelphia ladies. There were at least a hundred and fifty children present. It was very pleasant to see their happy, expectant little faces. To them, it was a wonderful Christmas Day,—such as they had never dreamed of before. There was cheerful sunshine without, lighting up the beautiful moss-drapery of the oaks, and looking in joyously through the open windows; and there were bright faces and glad hearts within. The long, dark night of the Past, with all its sorrows and fears, was forgotten; and for the Future,—the eyes of these freed children see no clouds in it. It is full of sunlight, they think, and they trust in it, perfectly.

After the distribution of the gifts, the children were addressed by some of the gentlemen present. They then sang Whittier's Hymn, the "John Brown" song, and several of their own hymns, among them a very singular one, commencing,—

"I wonder where my mudder gone;
Sing, O graveyard!
Graveyard ought to know me;
Ring, Jerusalem!
Grass grow in the graveyard;
Sing, O graveyard!
Graveyard ought to know me;
Ring, Jerusalem!"

They improvise many more words as they sing. It is one of the strangest, most mournful things I ever heard. It is impossible to give any idea of the deep pathos of the refrain,—

"Sing, O graveyard!"

In this, and many other hymns, the words seem to have but little meaning; but the tones,—a whole lifetime of despairing sadness is concentrated in them. They sing, also, "Jehovyah, Hallelujah," which we like particularly:—

"De foxes hab holes,
An' de birdies hab nes',
But the Son of Man he hab not where
To lay de weary head.
CHORUS
"Jehovyah, Hallelujah! De Lord He will
provide!
"Jehovyah, Hallelujah! De Lord He will
provide!"

They repeat the words many times. "De foxes hab holes," and the succeeding lines, are sung in the most touching, mournful tones; and then the chorus—"Jehovyah, Hallelujah"—swells forth triumphantly, in glad contrast.

Christmas night, the children came in and had several grand shouts. They were too happy to keep still.

"Oh, Miss, all I want to do is sing and shout!" said our little pet, Amaretta. And sing and shout she did, to her little heart's content.

She read nicely, and was very fond of books. The tiniest children are delighted to get a book in their hands. Many of them already know their letters. The parents are eager to have them learn. They sometimes said to me,—

"Do, Miss, let de chil'en learn eberyting dey can. We nebber hab no chancee to learn nuttin', but we wants de chil'en to learn."

They are willing to make many sacrifices that their children may attend school. One old woman, who had a large family of children and grandchildren, came regularly to school in the winter, and took her seat among the little ones. She was at least sixty years old. A woman—who had one of the best faces I ever saw—came daily, and brought her baby in her arms. It happened to be one of the best babies in the world, a perfect little "model of deportment," and allowed its mother to pursue her studies without interruption.

While taking charge of the store, one day, one of the men who came in told me a story which interested me much. He was a carpenter, living on this island, and just before the capture of Port Royal had been taken by his master to the mainland,—"the Main," as the people call it,—to assist in building some houses which were to shelter the families of the Rebels in case the "Yankees" should come. The master afterward sent him back to the island, providing him with a pass, to bring away a boat and some of the people. On his arrival he found that the Union troops were in possession, and determined to remain here with his family instead of returning to his master. Some of his fellow servants, who had been left on "the Main," hearing that the Federal troops had come, resolved to make their escape to the islands. They found a boat of their master's, out of which a piece six feet square had been cut. In the night they went to the boat, which had been sunk in a creek near the house, measured the hole, and after several nights' work in the woods, made a piece large enough to fit in. They then mended and sank it again, as they had found it. The next night five of them embarked. They had a perilous journey, often passing quite near the enemy's boats. They travelled at night, and in the day ran close up to the shore out of sight. Sometimes they could hear the hounds, which had been sent in pursuit of them, baying in the woods. Their provisions gave out, and they were nearly exhausted. At last they succeeded in passing all the enemy's boats, and reached one of our gun boats in safety. They were taken on board and kindly cared for, and then sent to this island, where their families, who had no hope of ever seeing them again, welcomed them with great rejoicing.

We were also told the story of two girls, one about ten, the other fifteen, who, having been taken by their master up into the country, on the mainland, at the time of the capture of the islands, determined to try to escape to their parents, who had been left on this island. They stole away at night, and traveled through woods and swamps for two days, without eating. Sometimes their strength gave out, and they would sink down, thinking they could go no farther; but they had brave little hearts, and got up again and struggled on, till at last they reached Port Royal Ferry, in a state of utter exhaustion. They were seen there by a boat-load of people who were also making their escape. The boat was too full to take them in; but the people, on reaching the island, told the children's father of their whereabouts, and he immediately took a boat, and hastened to the ferry. The poor little creatures were about wild with joy when they saw him. When they were brought to their mother, she fell down "jes' as if she was dead,"—so our informant expressed it,—overpowered with joy on beholding the "lost who were found."

New-Year's-Day—Emancipation Day—was a glorious one to us. The morning was quite cold, the coldest we had experienced; but we were determined to go to the celebration at Camp Saxton,—the camp of the First Regiment South-Carolina Volunteers,—whither the General and Colonel Higginson had bidden us, on this, "the greatest day in the nation's history." We enjoyed perfectly the exciting scene on board the Flora. There was an eager, wondering crowd of freed people in their holiday-attire, with the gayest of head-handkerchiefs, the whitest of aprons, and the happiest of faces. The band was playing, the flags streaming, everybody talking merrily and feeling strangely happy. The sun shone brightly, the very waves seemed to partake of the universal gayety, and danced and sparkled more joyously than ever before. Long before we reached Camp Saxton we could see the beautiful grove, and the ruins of the old Huguenot fort near it. Some companies of the First Regiment were drawn up in line under the trees, near the landing, to receive us. A fine, soldierly-looking set of men; their brilliant dress against the trees (they were then wearing red pantaloons) invested them with a semi-barbaric splendor. It was my good fortune to find among the officers an old friend,—and what it was to meet a friend from the North, in our isolated Southern life, no one can imagine who has not experienced the pleasure. Letters were an unspeakable luxury,—we hungered for them, we could never get enough; but to meet old friends,—that was "too much, too much," as the people here say, when they are very much in earnest. Our friend took us over the camp, and showed us all the arrangements. Everything looked clean and comfortable, much neater, we were told, than in most of the white camps. An officer told us that he had never seen a regiment in which the men were so honest. "In many other camps," said he, "the colonel and the rest of us would find it necessary to place a guard before our tents. We never do here. They are left entirely unguarded. Yet nothing has ever been touched." We were glad to know that. It is a remarkable fact, when we consider that these men have all their lives been *slaves;* and we know what the teachings of Slavery are.

The celebration took place in the beautiful grove of live oaks adjoining the camp. It was the largest grove we had seen. I wish it were possible to describe fitly the scene which met our eyes as we sat upon the stand, and looked down on the crowd before us. There were the black soldiers in their blue coats and scarlet pantaloons, the officers of this and other regiments in their handsome uniforms, and crowds of lookers-on,—men, women, and children, of every complexion, grouped in various attitudes under the moss-hung trees. The faces of all wore a happy, interested look. The exercises commenced with a prayer by the chaplain of the regiment. An ode, written for the occasion by Professor Zachos, was read by him, and then sung. Colonel Higginson then introduced Dr. Brisbane, who read the President's Proclamation, which was enthusiastically cheered. Rev. Mr. French presented to the Colonel two very elegant flags, a gift to the regiment from the Church of the Puritans, accompanying them by an appropriate and enthusiastic speech. At its conclusion, before Colonel Higginson could reply, and while he still stood holding the flags in his hand, some of the colored people, of their own accord, commenced singing, "My Country, 't is of thee." It was a touching and beautiful incident, and sent a thrill through all our hearts. The Colonel was deeply moved by it. He said that that reply was far more effective than any speech he could make. But he did make one of those stirring speeches which are "half battles." All hearts swelled with emotion as we listened to his glorious words,—"stirring the soul like the sound of a trumpet."

His soldiers are warmly attached to him, and he evidently feels towards them all as if they were his children. The people speak of him as "the officer who never leaves his regiment for pleasure," but devotes himself, with all his rich gifts of mind and heart, to their interests. It is not strange that his judicious kindness, ready sympathy, and rare fascination of manner should attach them to him strongly. He is one's ideal of an officer. There is in him much of the grand, knightly spirit of the olden time,—scorn of all that is mean ignoble, pity for the weak, chilvarous devotion to the cause of the oppressed.

General Saxton spoke also, and was received with great enthusiasm. Throughout the morning, repeated cheers were given for him by the regiment, and joined in heartily by all the people. They knew him to be one of the best and noblest men in the world. His Proclamation for Emancipation Day we thought, if possible, even more beautiful than the Thanksgiving Proclamation.

At the close of Colonel Higginson's speech he presented the flags to the color-bearers, Sergeant Rivers and Sergeant Sutton, with an earnest charge, to which they made appropriate replies. We were particularly pleased with Robert Sutton, who is a man of great natural intelligence, and whose remarks were simple, eloquent, and forcible.

Mrs. Gage also uttered some earnest words; and then the regiment sang "John Brown" with much spirit. After the meeting we saw the dress-parade, a brilliant and beautiful sight. An officer told us that the men went through the drill remarkably well,—that the ease and rapidity with which they learned the movements were wonderful. To us it seemed as a miracle,—this black regiment, the first mustered into the service of the United States, doing itself honor in the sight of the officers of other regiments, many of whom, doubtless, "came to scoff." The men afterwards had a great feast, ten oxen having been roasted whole for their especial benefit.

We went to the landing, intending to take the next boat for Beaufort; but finding it very much crowded, waited for another. It was the softest, loveliest moonlight; we seated ourselves on the ruined wall of the old fort; and when the boat had got a short distance from the shore the band in it commenced playing "Sweet Home." The moonlight on the water, the perfect stillness around, the wildness and solitude of the ruins, all seemed to give new pathos to that ever dear and beautiful old song. It came very near to all of us,—strangers in that strange Southern land. After a while we retired to one of the tents,—for the night-air, as usual, grew dangerously damp,—and, sitting around the bright wood fire, enjoyed the brilliant and entertaining conversation. Very unwilling were we to go home; for, besides the attractive society, we knew that the soldiers were to have grand shouts and a general jubilee that night. But the Flora was coming, and we were obliged to say a reluctant farewell to Camp Saxton and the hospitable dwellers therein, and hasten to the landing. We promenaded the deck of the steamer, sang patriotic songs, and agreed that moonlight and water had never looked so beautiful as on that night. At Beaufort we took the row-boat for St. Helena; and the boatmen, as they rowed, sang some of their sweetest, wildest hymns. It was a fitting close to such a day. Our hearts were filled with an exceeding great gladness; for, although the Government had left much undone, we knew that Freedom was surely born in our land that day. It seemed too glorious a good to realize,—this beginning of the great work we so longed and prayed for.

L. and I had one day an interesting visit to a plantation about six miles from ours. The house is beautifully situated in the midst of noble pine-trees, on the banks of a large creek. The place was owned by a very wealthy Rebel family, and is one of the pleasantest and healthiest on the island. The vicinity of the pines makes it quite healthy. There were a hundred and fifty people on it,—one hundred of whom had come from Edisto Island at the time of its evacuation by our troops. There were not houses enough to accommodate them, and they had to take shelter in barns, out-houses, or any other place they could find. They afterwards built rude dwellings for themselves, which did not, however, afford them much protection in bad weather. The superintendent told us that they were well-behaved and industrious. One old woman interested us greatly. Her name was Daphne; she was probably more than a hundred years old; had had fifty grandchildren, sixty-five great grandchildren, and three great-great-grandchildren. Entirely blind, she yet seemed very cheerful and happy. She told us that she was brought with her parents from Africa at the time of the Revolution. A bright, happy old face was hers, and she retained her faculties remarkably well. Fifteen of the people had escaped from the mainland in the previous spring. They were pursued, and one of them was overtaken by his master in the swamps. A fierce grapple ensued,—the master on horseback, the man on feet. The former drew a pistol and shot his slave through the arm, shattering it dreadfully. Still, the heroic man fought desperately, and at least succeeded in unhorsing his master, and beating him until he was senseless. He then made his escape, and joined the rest of the party.

One of the most interesting sights we saw was a baptism among the people. On one Sunday there were a hundred and fifty baptized in the creek near the church. They looked very picturesque in their white aprons and bright frocks and handker-chiefs. As they marched in procession down to river's edge, and during the ceremo-ny, the spectators, with whom the banks were crowded, sang glad, triumphant songs. The freed people on the island are all Baptists.

We were much disappointed in the Southern climate. We found it much cold-er than we had expected,—quite cold enough for as thick winter clothing as one would wear at the North. The houses, heated only by open fires, were never com-fortably warm. In the floor of out sitting-room there was a large crack through which we could see the ground beneath; and through this and the crevices of the numer-ous doors and windows the wind came chillingly. The church in which we taught school was particularly damp and cold. There was no chimney, and we could have no fire at all. Near the close of the winter a stove came for us, but it could not be made to draw; we were nearly suffocated with smoke, and gave it up in despair. We got so thoroughly chilled and benumbed within, that for several days we had school out-of-doors, where it was much warmer. Our school-room was a pleasant one,—for ceiling the blue sky above, for walls the grand old oaks with their beautiful moss-drapery,—but the dampness of the ground made it unsafe for us to continue the experiment.

At a later period, during a few days' visit to some friends living on the Milne Plantation, then the head-quarters of the First South-Carolina, which was on picket-duty at Port-Royal Ferry, we had an opportunity of seeing something of the Port-Royal Island. We had pleasant rides through the pine barrens. Indeed, riding on horseback was our chief recreation at the South, and we enjoyed it thoroughly. The "Secesh" horses, though small, poor, and mean-looking, when compared with ours, are generally excellent for the saddle, well-trained and very easy. I remember particularly one ride that we had while on Port-Royal Island. We visited the Barnwell Plantation, one of the finest places on the island. It is situated on the Broad River. The grounds are extensive, and are filled with magnificent live-oaks, mag-nolias, and other trees. We saw one noble old oak, said to be the largest on these islands. Some of the branches have been cut off, but the remaining ones cover an area more than a hundred feet in circumference. We rode to a point where the Rebels on the opposite side of the river are sometimes to be seen. But they were not visi-ble that day; and we were disappointed in our long-cherished hope of seeing a "real live Rebel." On leaving the plantation, we rode through a long avenue of oaks,—the moss-hung branches forming a perfect arch over our heads,—and then for miles through the pine barrens. There was an Italian softness in the April air. Only a low, faint murmur—hardly "the slow song of the sea"—could be heard among the pines. The ground was thickly carpeted with ferns of a vivid green. We found large violets, purple and white, and azaleas of a deeper pink and heavier fragrance than ours. It was leaving Paradise, to emerge from the beautiful woods upon the public road,— the shell-road which runs from Beaufort to the Ferry. Then we entered a by-way leading to the plantation, where we found Cherokee rose in all its glory. The hedges were white with it; it canopied the trees, and hung from their branches its long sprays of snowy blossoms and dark, shiny leaves, forming perfect arches, and bowers which seemed fitting places for fairies to dwell in. How it gladdened our eyes and hearts! It was as if all the dark shadows that have so long hung over this Southern land had flitted away, and, in this garment of purest white, it shone forth transfigured, beautiful, forevermore.

On returning to the house, we were met by the exciting news that the Rebels were bringing up pontoon-bridges, and were expected to attempt crossing over near the Ferry, which was only two or three miles from us. Couriers came in every few moments with various reports. A superintendent whose plantation was very near the Ferry had been watching through his glass the movements on the opposite side, and reported that the Rebels were gathering in large force, and evidently preparing for some kind of demonstration. A messenger was dispatched to Beaufort for reinforcements, and for some time we were in a state of expectancy, not entirely without excitement, but entirely without fear. The officers evidently enjoyed the prospect of a fight. One of them assured me that I should have the pleasure of seeing a Rebel shell during the afternoon. It was proposed that the women should be sent into Beaufort in an ambulance; against which ignoble treatment we indignantly protested, and declared our intention of remaining at our post, if the Colonel would consent; and finally, to our great joy, the best of colonels did consent that we should remain, as he considered it quite safe for us to do so. Soon a light battery arrived, and during the evening a brisk firing was kept up. We could hear the explosion of the shells. It was quite like being in the war; and as the firing was principally on our side, and the enemy was getting the worst of it, we rather enjoyed it. For a little while the Colonel read to us, in his spirited way, some of the stirring "Lays of the Old Cavaliers." It was just the time to appreciate them thoroughly, and he was of all men the fittest person to read them. But soon came a courier, "in hot haste," to make a report of the doings without, and the reading was at an end. In the midst of the firing, Mrs. D. and I went to bed, and slept soundly until morning. We learned afterward that the Rebels had not intended to cross over, but were attempting to take the guns off one of their boats, which they had sunk a few days previous. The timely arrival of the battery from Beaufort prevented them from accomplishing their purpose.

In April we left Oaklands, which had always been considered a particularly unhealthy place during the summer, and came to "Seaside," a plantation on another healthier part of the island. The place contains nearly a hundred people. The house is large and comparatively comfortable. Notwithstanding the name, we have not even a distant glimpse of the sea, although we can sometimes hear its roar. At low tide there is not a drop of water to be seen,—only dreary stretches of marsh-land, reminding us of the sad outlook of Mariana in the Moated Grange,—

"The level waste and rounding gray."

But at night we have generally a good sea-breeze, and during the hottest weather the air is purer and more invigorating than in many parts of the island.

On this, as in several other larger plantations, there is a "Praise-House," which is the special property of the people. Even in the old days of Slavery, they were allowed to hold meetings here; and they still keep up the custom. They assemble on several nights of the week, and on Sunday afternoons. First, they hold what is called the "Praise-Meeting," which consists of singing, praying, and preaching. We have heard some of the old negro preachers make prayers that were beautiful and touching. In these meetings they sing only the church-hymns which the Northern ministers have taught them, and which are far less suited to their voices than their own. At the close of the Praise-Meeting they all shake hands with each other in the most solemn manner. Afterward, as a kind of appendix, they have a grand "shout," during which they sing their own hymns. Maurice, an old blind man, leads the singing. He has a remarkable voice, and sings with the greatest enthusiasm. The first shout that we witnessed in the Praise-House impressed us very much. The large, gloomy room, with its blackened walls,—the wild, whirling dance of the shouters,—the crowd of dark faces gathered around,—the figure of the old blind man, whose excitement could hardly be controlled, and whose attitudes and gestures while singing were very fine,—and over all, the red glare of the burning pine-knot, which shed a circle of light around it, but only seemed to deepen and darken the shadows in the other parts of the room,—these all formed a wild, strange, and deepening impressive picture, not soon to be forgotten.

Maurice's favorite is one of the grandest hymns that we have yet heard:—

"De tallest tree in Paradise
De Christian calls de Tree of Life,
An' I hope dat trumpet blow me home
To my New Jerusalem
Chorus
"Blow, Gabriel! Trumpet, blow louder, louder!
An' I hope dat trumpet blow me home

To my new Jerusalem
"Paul and Silas jail-bound
Sing God's praise both night and day,
An' I hope dat trumpet blow me home
To my New Jerusalem.
Chorus
"Blow, Gabriel! Trumpet, blow louder, louder!
An' I hope dat trumpet blow me home
To my New Jerusalem!"

The chorus has a glad, triumphal sound, and in singing it the voice of old Maurice rings out in wonderfully clear, trumpet-like tones. His blindness was caused by a blow on the head from a loaded whip. He was struck by his master in a fit of anger. "I feel great distress when I become blind," said Maurice; "but den I went to seek de Lord; and eber since I know I see in de next world, I always hab great satisfaction." We are told that the master was not a "hard man" except when in a passion, and then he seems to have been very cruel.

One of the women on the place, Old Bess, bears on her limbs many marks of the whip. Some of the scars are three and four inches long. She was used principally as a house-servant. She says, "Ebery time I lay de table I put cowskin on one end, an' I git beatin' and thumpin' all de time. Hab all kinds o' work to do, and sich a gang (of children) to look after! One person could n't git along wid so much work, so it go wrong, and den I git beatin'."

But the cruelty of Bess's master sinks into insignificance, when compared with the far-famed wickedness of another slaveholder, known all over the island as "Old Joe Eddings." There seems to have been no bounds to his cruelty and licentiousness; and the people tell tales of him which make one shudder. We were once asking some questions about him of an old, half-witted woman, a former slave of his. The look of horror and loathing which overspread her face was perfectly indescribable, as, with upraised hands, she exclaimed, "What! Old Joe Eddings? Lord, Missus, he second to none in de world but de Debil!" She had, indeed, good cause to detest him; for some years before, her daughter, a young black girl, maddened by his persecutions, had thrown herself into the creek and been drowned, after having been severely beaten for refusing to degrade herself. Outraged, despised, and black, she yet preferred death to dishonor. But these are things too heart-sickening to dwell upon. God alone knows how many hundreds of plantations, all over the South, might furnish a similar record.

Early in June, before the summer heat had become unendurable, we made a pleasant excursion to Edisto Island. We left St. Helena village in the morning, dined on one of the gun-boats stationed near our island, and in the afternoon proceeded to Edisto in two row-boats. There were six of us, besides an officer and the boats' crews, who were armed with guns and cutlasses. There was no actual danger; but as we were going into the enemy's country, we thought it wisest to guard against surprises. After a delightful row, we reached the island near sunset, landing at a place called Eddingsville, which was a favorite summer resort with the aristocracy of Edisto. It has a fine beach several miles in length. Along the beach there is a row of houses, which must once have been very desirable dwellings, but have now a desolate, dismantled look. The sailors explored the beach for some distance, and returned, reporting "all quiet, and nobody to be seen"; so we walked on, feeling quite safe, stopping here and there to gather the beautiful tiny shells which were buried deep in the sands.

We took supper in a room of one of the deserted houses, using for seats some old bureau-drawers turned edgewise. Afterward we sat on the piazza, watching the lightning playing from a low, black cloud over a sky flushed with sunset, and listening to the merry songs of the sailors who occupied the next house. They had built a large fire, the cheerful glow of which shone through the windows, and we could see them dancing, evidently in great glee. Later, we had another walk on the beach, in the lovely moonlight. It was very quiet then. The deep stillness was broken only by the low, musical murmur of the waves. The moon shone bright and clear over the deserted houses and gardens, and gave them a still wilder and more desolate look.

We went within-doors for the night but unwillingly. Having, of course, no beds, we made ourselves as comfortable as we could on the floor, with boat-cushions, blankets, and shawls. No fear of Rebels disturbed us. There was but one road by which they could get to us, and on that a watch was kept, and in case of their approach, we knew we should have ample time to get to the boats and make our escape. So, despite the mosquitoes, we had a sound night's sleep.

The next morning we took the boats again, and followed the course of the most winding of little creeks. In and out, in and out, the boats went. Sometimes it seemed as if we were going into the very heart of the woods; and through the deep silence we half expected the sound of a Rebel rifle. The banks were overhung with a thick tangle of shrubs and bushes, which threatened to catch our boats, as we passed close beneath their branches. In some places the stream was so narrow that we ran aground, and then the men had to get out, drag and pull with all their might before we could be got clear again. After a row full of excitement and pleasure, we reached our place of destination,—Eddings Plantation, whither some of the freedmen had proceeded us in their search for corn. It must once have been a beautiful place. The grounds were laid out with great taste, and filled with fine trees, among which we noticed particularly the oleander, laden with deep rose-hued and deliciously fragrant flowers, and the magnolia, with its wonderful, large blossoms, which shone dazzlingly white among the dark leaves. We explored the house,—after it had first been examined by our guard, to see that no foes lurked there,—but found nothing but heaps of rubbish, an old bedstead, and a bathing-tub, of which we afterward made good use. When we returned to the shore, we found that the tide had gone out, and between us and the boats lay a tract of marsh-land, which it would have been impossible to cross without a wetting. The gentlemen determined on wading. But what were we to do? In this dilemma somebody suggested the bathing-tub, a suggestion which was eagerly seized upon. We were placed in it, one at a time, borne aloft in triumph on the shoulders of four stout sailors, and safely deposited in the boat. But, through a mistake, the tub was not sent back for two of the ladies, and they were brought over on the crossed hands of two of the sailors, in the "carry-a-lady-to-London" style. Again we rowed though the windings of the creek, then out into the open sea, among the white, exhilarating breakers,—reached the gun-boat, dined again with the hospitable officers, and then returned to our island, which we reached after nightfall, feeling thoroughly tired, but well pleased with our excursion.

From what we saw at Edisto, however, we did not like it better than our own island,—except, of course, the beach; but we are told that farther in the interior it is much more beautiful. The freed people, who left it at the time of its evacuation, think it is the loveliest place in the world, and long to return. When we were going to Miss T.—the much-loved and untiring friend and physician of the people—asked some whom we met if we should give their love to Edisto. "Oh, yes, Miss!" they said. "Ah, Edisto a beautiful city!" And when we came back, they inquired, eagerly,— "How you like Edisto: How Edisto stan'?" Only the fear of falling into the hands of the "Secesh" prevents them from returning to their much-loved home.

As the summer advanced, the heat became intense. We found it almost over-powering, driving to school near middle of the day, as we were obliged to do. I gave up riding, and mounted a sulky, such as a single gentleman drives in at the North. It was exceedingly high and I found it no small task to mount up into it. Its already very comical appearance was enhanced by the addition of a cover of black India-rubber cloth, with which a friend kindly provided me. Thus adorned, it looked like the skeleton of some strange creature surmounted by a huge bonnet, and afforded endless amusement to the soldiers we chanced to meet, who hailed its appearance with shouts of laughter, and cries of "Here comes the Calithumpian!" The unique vehicle, with several others on our island, kindred but not quite equal to it, would create a decided sensation in the streets of Northern city.

No description of life on these islands would be complete without a word concerning the fleas. They appeared at the opening of spring and kept constantly "risin'," as the people said, until they reached a height the possibility of which we had never conceived. We had heard and read of fleas. We had never *realized* them before. Words utterly fail to describe the tortures we endured for months before those horrible little tyrants. Remembering our sufferings "through weary day and weary *night*," we warn everybody not gifted with extraordinary powers of endurance to beware of a summer on the Sea Islands.

Notwithstanding the heat, we determined to celebrate the Fourth of July as worthily as we could. The freed people and the children of the different schools assembled in the grove near the Baptist Church. The flag was hung across the road, between two magnificent live-oaks, and the children, being grouped under it, sang "The Star-Spangled Banner" with much spirit. Our good General could not come, but addresses were made by Mr. P.,—the noble-hearted founder of the movement for the benefit of the people here, and from first to last their stanch and much-loved friend,—Mr. L., a young colored minister, and others. Then the people sang some of their hymns; and the woods resounded with the grand notes of "Roll, Jordan, roll." They all afterward partook of refreshments, consisting of molasses and water,—a very great luxury to them,—and hardtack.

Among the visitors present was the noble young Colonel Shaw, whose regiment was then stationed on the island. We had met him a few nights before, when he came to our house to witness one of the people's shouts. We looked upon him with the deepest interest. There was something in his face finer, more exquisite, than one often sees in a man's face, yet it was full of courage and decision. The rare and singular charm of his manner drew all hearts to him. He was deeply interested in the singing and the appearance of the people. A few days afterwards we saw his regiment on dress parade, and admired its remarkably fine and manly appearance. After taking supper with the Colonel we sat outside the tent, while some of his men entertained us with excellent singing. Every moment we became more and more charmed with him. How full of life and hope and lofty aspirations he was that night! How eagerly he expressed his wish that they might soon be ordered to Charleston! "I do hope they will give *us* a chance," he said. It was the desire of his soul that his men should do themselves honor,—that they should prove themselves to an unbelieving world as brave soldiers as though their skins were white. And for himself, he was like the Chevalier of old, "without reproach or fear." After we had mounted our horses and rode away, we seemed still to feel the kind clasp of his hand,—to hear the pleasant, genial tones of his voice, as he bade us goodbye, and hoped that we might meet again. We never saw him afterward. In two short weeks came the terrible massacre at Fort Wagner, and the beautiful head of the young hero and martyr was laid low in the dust. Never shall we forget the heart-sickness with which we heard of his death. We could not realize it at first,—we, who had seen him so lately in all the strength and glory of his young manhood. For days we clung to a vain hope; then it fell away,—from us, and we knew that he was gone. We knew that he died gloriously, but still it seemed very hard. Our hearts bled for the mother whom he so loved,—for the young wife, left desolate. And then we said, as we say now,— "God comfort them! He only can." During a few of the sad days which followed the attack on Fort Wagner, I was in one of the hospitals in Beaufort, occupied with the wounded soldiers of the Fifty-Fourth Massachusetts. The first morning was spent in mending the bullet-holes and rents in their clothing. What a story they told! Some of the jackets of the poor fellows were literally cut in pieces. It was pleasant to see the brave, cheerful spirit among them. Some of them were severely wounded, but they uttered no complaint; and in the letters which they dictated to their absent friends there was no word of regret, but the same cheerful tone throughout. They expressed an eager desire to get well, that they might "go at it again." Their attachment to their young colonel was beautiful to see. They felt his death deeply. One and all united in the warmest and most enthusiastic praise of him. He was, indeed, exactly the person to inspire the most loyal devotion in the hearts of his men. And with everything to live for, he had given up his life for them. Heaven's best gifts had been showered upon him, but for them he had laid them all down. I think they truly appreciated the greatness of his sacrifice. May they ever prove worthy of such a leader! Already, they, and the regiments of freedmen here, as well, have shown that true manhood has no limitations of color.

Daily the long-oppressed people of these islands are demonstrating their capacity for improvement in learning and labor. What they have accomplished in one short year exceeds our utmost expectations. Still the sky is dark; but through the darkness we can discern a brighter future. We cannot but feel that the day of final and entire deliverance, so long and often so hopelessly prayed for, has at length begun to dawn upon this much-enduring race. An old freedman said to me one day, "De Lord make me suffer long time, Miss. 'Peared like we nebber was gwine to git troo. But now we's free. He bring us all out right at las'." In their darkest hours they have clung to Him, and we know He will not forsake them.

"The poor among men shall rejoice,
For the terrible one is brought to naught."

While writing these pages I am once more nearing Port Royal. The Fortunate Isles of Freedom are before me. I shall again tread the flower-skirted wood-paths of St. Helena, and the sombre pines and bearded oaks shall whisper in the sea-wind their grave welcome. I shall dwell again among "mine own people." I shall gather my scholars about me, and see smiles of greeting over their dusk faces. My heart sings a song of thanksgiving, at the thought that even I am permitted to do something for a long-abused race, and aid in promoting a higher, holier, and happier life on the Sea Islands.

Further Reading

http://users.aol.com/queenmut/Forten.html

*Womanhood a Vital Element in the Regeneration and Progress of a Race

From: *A Voice from the South*

1892 | SHORT ESSAY

THE two sources from which, perhaps, modern civilization has derived its noble and ennobling ideal of woman are Christianity and the Feudal System.

In Oriental countries woman has been uniformly devoted to a life of ignorance, infamy, and complete stagnation. The Chinese shoe of to-day does not more entirely dwarf, cramp, and destroy her physical powers, than have the customs, laws, and social instincts, which from remotest ages have governed our Sister of the East, enervated and blighted her mental and moral life.

Mahomet makes no account of woman whatever in his polity. The Koran, which, unlike our Bible, was a product and not a growth, tried to address itself to the needs of Arabian civilization as Mahomet with his circumscribed powers saw them. The Arab was a nomad. Home to him meant his present camping place. That deity who, according to our western ideals, makes and sanctifies the home, was to him a transient bauble to be toyed with so long as it gave pleasure and then to be thrown aside for a new one. As a personality, an individual soul, capable of eternal growth and unlimited development, and destined to mould and shape the civilization of the future to an incalculable extent, Mahomet did not know woman. There was no hereafter, no paradise for her. The heaven of the Mussulman is peopled and made gladsome not by the departed wife, or sister, or mother, but by *houri*—a fig-

---

*Read before the convocation of colored clergy of the Protestant Episcopal Church at Washington, D. C., 1886.

ment of Mahomet's brain, partaking of the ethereal qualities of angels, yet imbued with all the vices and inanity of Oriental women. The harem here, and—"dust to dust" hereafter, this was the hope, the inspiration, *summum bonum* of the Eastern woman's life! With what result on the life of the nation, the "Unspeakable Turk," the "sick man" of modern Europe can to-day exemplify.

Says a certain writer: "The private life of the Turk is vilest of the vile, unprogressive, unambitious, and inconceivably low." And yet Turkey is not without her great men. She has produced most brilliant minds; men skilled in all the intricacies of diplomacy and statesmanship; men whose intellects could grapple with the deep problems of empire and manipulate the subtle agencies which check-mate kings. But these minds were not the normal outgrowth of a healthy trunk. They seemed rather ephemeral excrescencies which shoot far out with all the vigor and promise, apparently, of strong branches; but soon alas fall into decay and ugliness because there is no soundness in the root, no life-giving sap, permeating, strengthening and perpetuating the whole. There is a worm at the core! The homelife is impure! and when we look for fruit, like apples of Sodom, it crumbles within our grasp into dust and ashes.

It is pleasing to turn from this effete and immobile civilization to a society still fresh and vigorous, whose seed is in itself, and whose very name is synonymous with all that is progressive, elevating and inspiring, viz., the European bud and the American flower of modern civilization.

And here let me say parenthetically that our satisfaction in American institutions rests not on the fruition we now enjoy, but springs rather from the possibilities and promise that are inherent in the system, though as yet, perhaps, far in the future.

"Happiness," says Madame de Stael, "consists not in perfections attained, but in a sense of progress, the result of our own endeavor under conspiring circumstances toward a goal which continually advances and broadens and deepens till it is swallowed up in the Infinite." Such conditions in embryo are all that we claim for the land of the West. We have not yet reached our ideal in American civilization. The pessimists even declare that we are not marching in that direction. But there can be no doubt that here in America is the arena in which the next triumph of civilization is to be won; and here too we find promise abundant and possibilities infinite.

Now let us see on what basis this hope for our country primarily and fundamentally rests. Can any one doubt that it is chiefly on the homelife and on the influence of good women in those homes? Says Macaulay: "You may judge a nation's rank in the scale of civilization from the way they treat their women." And Emerson, "I have thought that a sufficient measure of civilization is the influence of good women." Now this high regard for woman, this germ of a prolific idea which in our own day is bearing such rich and varied fruit, was ingrafted into European civilization, we have said, from two sources, the Christian Church and the Feudal System. For although the Feudal System can in no sense be said to have originated the idea, yet there can be no doubt that the habits of life and modes of thought to which Feudalism gave rise, materially fostered and developed it; for they gave us chivalry, than which no institution has more sensibly magnified and elevated woman's position in society.

Tacitus dwells on the tender regard for woman entertained by these rugged barbarians before they left their northern homes to overrun Europe. Old Norse legends too, and primitive poems, all breathe the same spirit of love of home and veneration for the pure and noble influence there presiding—the wife, the sister, the mother.

And when later on we see the settled life of the Middle Ages "oozing out," as M. Guizot expresses it, from the plundering and aging life of barbarism and crystallizing into the Feudal System, the tiger of the field is brought once more within the charmed circle of the goddesses of the castle, and his imagination weaves around them a halo whose reflection possibly has not yet altogether vanished.

It is true the spirit of Christianity had not yet put the seal of catholicity on this sentiment. Chivalry, according to Bascom, was the toning down and softening of a rough and lawless period. Those who looked out from castle windows revelled in its " amethyst tints." But God's poor, the weak, the unlovely, the commonplace were freezing and starving none the less in unpitied, unrelieved loneliness.

Respect for woman, the much lauded chivalry of the Middle Ages, meant what I fear it still means to some men in our own day—respect for the elect few among whom they expect to consort.

The idea of the radical amelioration of womankind, reverence for woman as woman regardless of rank, wealth, or culture, was to come from that rich and bounteous fountain from which flow all our liberal and universal ideas—the Gospel of Jesus Christ.

And yet the Christian Church at the time of which we have been speaking would seem to have been doing even less to protect and elevate woman than the little done by secular society. The Church as an organization committed a double offense against woman in the Middle Ages. Making of marriage a sacrament and at the same time insisting on the celibacy of the clergy and other religious orders, she gave an inferior if not an impure character to the marriage relation, especially fitted to reflect discredit on woman. Would this were all or worst! but the Church by the licentiousness of its chosen servants invaded the household and established too often as vicious connections those relations which it forbade to assume openly and in good faith. "Thus," to use the words of our authority, "the religious corps became as numerous, as searching, and as unclean as the frogs of Egypt, which penetrated into all quarters, into the ovens and kneading troughs, leaving their filthy trail wherever they went." Says Chaucer with characteristic satire, speaking to the Friars:

"Women may now go safely up and down,
In every bush, and under every tree,
Ther is non other incubus but he,
And he ne will don hem no dishonour."

Henry, Bishop of Liege, could unblushingly boast the birth of twenty-two children in fourteen years.[*]

It may help us under some of the perplexities which beset our way in "the one Catholic and Apostolic Church" to-day, to recall some of the corruptions and incongruities against which the Bride of Christ has had to struggle in her past history and in spite of which she has kept, through many vicissitudes, the faith once delivered to the saints. Individuals, organizations, whole sections of the church militant may outrage the Christ whom they profess, may ruthlessly trample under foot both the spirit and the letter of his precepts, yet not till we hear the voices audibly saying "Come let us depart hence," shall we cease to believe and cling to the promise, "*I am with you to the end of the world.*"

"Yet saints their watch are keeping,
The cry goes up 'How long!'
And soon the night of weeping
Shall be the morn of song."

However much then the facts of any particular period of history may seem to deny it, I for one do not doubt that the source of the vitalizing principle of woman's development and amelioration is the Christian Church, so far as that church is coincident with Christianity.

Christ gave ideals for formulae. The Gospel is a germ requiring millennia for its growth and ripening. It needs and at the same time helps to form around itself a soil enriched in civilization, and perfected in culture and insight without which the embryo can neither be unfolded or comprehended. With all the strides our civilization has made from the first to the nineteenth century, we can boast not an idea, not a principle of action, not a progressive social force but was already mutely foreshadowed, or directly enjoined in that simple tale of a meek and lowly life. The quiet face of the Nazarene is ever seen a little way ahead, never too far to come down to and touch the life of the lowest in days the darkest, yet after leading onward, the tottering childish feet of our strangely boastful civilization.

---

[*]Bascom

By laying down for woman the same code of morality, the same standard of purity, as for man; by refusing to countenance the shameless and equally guilty monsters who were gloating over fall,—graciously stooping in all the majesty of his own spotlessness to wipe away the filth and grime of her guilty past and bid her go in peace and sin no more; and again in the moments of his own careworn and footsore dejection, turning trustfully and lovingly, away from the heartless snubbing and sneers, away from the cruel malignity of mobs and prelates in the dusty marts of Jerusalem to the ready sympathy, loving appreciation and unfaltering friendship of that quiet home at Bethany; and even at the last, by his dying bequest to the disciple whom he loved, signifying the protection and tender regard to be extended to that sorrowing mother and ever afterward to the sex she represented;—throughout his life and in his death he has given to men a rule and guide for the estimation of woman as equal, as a helper, as a friend, and as a sacred charge to be sheltered and cared for with a brother's love and sympathy, lessons which nineteen centuries' gigantic strides in knowledge, arts, and sciences, in social and ethical principles have not been able to probe to their depth or to exhaust in practice.

It seems not too much to say then of the vitalizing, regenerating, and progressive influence of womanhood on the civilization of to-day, that, while it was foreshadowed among Germanic nations in the far away dawn of their history as a narrow, sickly and stunted growth, it yet owes its catholicity and power, the deepening of its roots and broadening of its branches to Christianity.

The union of these two forces, the Barbaric and the Christian, was not long delayed after the Fall of the Empire. The Church, which fell with Rome, finding herself in danger of being swallowed up by barbarism, with characteristic vigor and fertility of resources, addresses herself immediately to the task of conquering her conquerers. The means chosen does credit to her power of penetration and adaptability, as well as to her profound, unerring, all-compassing diplomacy; and make us even now wonder if aught human can successfully and ultimately withstand her far-seeing designs and brilliant policy, or gainsay her well-earned claim to the word *Catholic.*

She saw the barbarian, little more developed than a wild beast. She forbade to antagonize and mystify his warlike nature by a full blaze of the heartsearching and humanizing tenets of her great Head. She said little of the rule "If thy brother smite thee on one cheek, turn to him the other also;" but thought it sufficient for the needs of those times, to establish the so-called "Truce of God" under which men were bound to abstain from butchering one another for three of each week and on Church festivals. In other words, she respected their individuality: non-resistance pure and simple being for them an utter impossibility, she contented herself with less radical measures calculated to lead up finally to the full measure of the benevolence of Christ.

Next she took advantage of the barbarian's sensuous love of gaudy display and put all her magnificent garments on. She could not capture him by physical force, she would dazzle him by her gorgeous spectacles. It is said that Romanism gained more in pomp and ritual during this trying period of the Dark Ages than throughout all her former history,

The result was she carried her point. Once more Rome laid her ambitious hand on the temporal power, and allied with Charlemagne, aspired to rule the world through a civilization dominated by Christianity and permeated by the traditions and instincts of these sturdy barbarians.

Here was the confluence of the two streams we have been tracing, which, united now, stretch before us as a broad majestic river. In regard to woman it was the meeting of two noble and ennobling forces, two kindred ideas the resultant of which, we doubt not, is destined to be a potent force in the betterment of the world.

Now after our appeal to history comparing nations destitute of this force and so destitute also of the principle of progress, with other nations among whom the influence of woman is prominent coupled with a brisk, progressive, satisfying civilization,—if in addition we find this strong presumptive evidence corroborated by reason and experience, we may conclude that these two equally varying concomitants are linked as cause and effect; in other words, that the position of woman in society determines the vital elements of its regeneration and progress.

Now that this is so on *a priori* grounds all must admit. And this not because woman is better or stronger or wiser than man, but from the nature of the case, because it is she who must first form the man by directing the earliest impulses of his character.

Byron and Wordsworth were both geniuses and would have stamped themselves on the thought of their age under any circumstances; and yet we find the one a savor of life unto life, the other of death unto death. "Byron, like a rocket, shot his way upward with scorn and repulsion, flamed out in wild, explosive, brilliant excesses and disappeared in darkness made all the more palpable."[*]

Wordsworth lent of his gifts to reinforce that "power in the Universe which makes for righteousness" by taking the harp handed him from Heaven and using it to swell the strains of angelic choirs. Two locomotives equally mighty stand facing opposite tracks; the one to rush headlong to destruction with all its precious freight, the other to toil grandly and gloriously up the steep embattlements to Heaven and to God. Who—who can say what a world of consequences hung on the first placing and starting of these enormous forces!

Woman, Mother,—your responsibility is one that might make angels tremble and fear to take hold! To trifle with it, to ignore or misuse it, is to treat lightly the

---

[*]Bascom's Eng. Lit. p. 253.

most sacred and solemn trust ever confided by God to human kind. The training of children is a task on which an infinity of weal or woe depends. Who does not covet it? Yet who does not stand awe-struck before its momentous issues! It is a matter of small moment, it seems to me, whether that lovely girl in whose accomplishments you take such pride and delight, can enter the gay and crowded salon with the ease and elegance of this or that French or English gentlewoman, compared with the decision as to whether her individuality is going to reinforce the good or the evil elements of the world. The lace and the diamonds, the dance and the theater, gain a new significance when scanned in their bearings on such issues. Their influence on the individual personality, and through her on the society and civilization which she vitalizes and inspires—all this and more must be weighed in the balance before the jury can return a just and intelligent verdict as to the innocence or bane-fulness of these apparently simple amusements.

Now the fact of woman's influence on society being granted, what are its practical bearings on the work which brought together this inference of colored clergy and laymen in Washington? "We come not here to talk." Life is too busy, too pregnant with meaning and far reaching consequences to allow you to come this far for mere intellectual entertainment.

The vital agency of womanhood in the regeneration and progress of a race, as a general question, is conceded almost before it is fairly stated. I confess one of the difficulties for me in the subject assigned lay in its obviousness. The plea is taken away by the opposite attorney's granting the whole question.

"Woman's influence on social progress"—who in Christendom doubts or questions it? One may as well be called on to prove that the sun is the source of light and heat and energy to this many-sided little world.

Nor, on the other hand, could it have been intended that I should apply the position when taken and proven, to the needs and responsibilities of the women of our race in the South. For is it not written, "Cursed is he that cometh after the king?" and has not the King already preceded me in "The Black Woman of the South"?*

They have had both Moses and the Prophets in Dr. Crummell and if they hear not him, neither would they be persuaded though one came up from the South.

I would beg, however, with the Doctor's permission, to add my plea for the *Colored Girls* of the South:—that large, bright, promising fatally beautiful class that stand shivering like a delicate plantlet before the fury of tempestuous elements, so full of promise and possibilities, yet so sure of destruction; often without a father to whom they dare apply the loving term, often without a stronger brother to espouse their cause and defend their honor with his life's blood; in the midst of pitfalls and snares, waylaid by the lower classes of white men, with no shelter, no pro-

---

*Pamphlet published by Dr. Alex. Crummell.

tection nearer than the great blue vault above, which half conceals and half reveals the one Care-Taker they know so little of. Oh, save them, help them, shield, train, develop, teach, inspire them! Snatch them, in God's name, as brands from the burning! There is material in them well worth your while, the hope in germ of a staunch, helpful, regenerating womanhood on which, primarily, rests the foundation stones of our future as a race.

It is absurd to quote statistics showing the Negro's bank account and rent rolls, to point to the hundreds of newspapers edited by colored men and lists of lawyers, doctors, professors, D. D's, LL D's, etc., etc., etc., while the source from which the life-blood of the race is to flow is subject to taint and corruption in the enemy's camp.

True progress is never made by spasms. Real progress is growth. It must begin in the seed. Then, "first the blade, then the ear, after that the full corn in the ear." There is something to encourage and inspire us in the advancement of individuals since their emancipation from slavery. It at least proves that there is nothing irretrievably wrong in the shape of the black man's skull, and that under given circumstances his development, downward or upward, will be similar to that of other average human beings.

But there is no time to be wasted in mere felicitation. That the Negro has his niche in the infinite purposes of the Eternal, no one who has studied the history of the last fifty years in America will deny. That much depends on his own right comprehension of his responsibility and rising to the demands of the hour, it will be good for him to see; and how best to use his present so that the structure of the future shall be stronger and higher and brighter and nobler and holier than that of the past, is a question to be decided each day by every one of us.

The race is just twenty-one years removed from the conception and experience of a chattel, just at the age of ruddy manhood. It is well enough to pause a moment for retrospection, introspection, and prospection. We look back, not to become inflated with conceit because of the depths from which we have arisen, but that we may learn wisdom from experience. We look within that we may gather together once more our forces, and, by improved and more practical methods, address ourselves to the tasks before us. We look forward with hope and trust that the same God whose guiding hand led our fathers through and out of the gall and bitterness of oppression, will still lead and direct their children, to the honor of His name, and for their ultimate salvation.

But this survey of failures or achievements of the past, the difficulties and embarrassments of the present, and the mingled hopes and fears for the future, must not denigrate into mere dreaming nor consume the time which belongs to the practical questions of the hour; and there can be no issue more vital than this of the womanhood of the race.

Here is the vulnerable point, not in the heel, but at the heart of the young Achilles; and here must the defenses be strengthened and the watch redoubled.

We are the heirs of a past which was not our fathers' moulding. "Every man the arbiter of his own destiny" was not true for the American Negro of the past: and it is no fault of his that he finds himself to-day the inheritor of a manhood and womanhood impoverished and debased by two centuries and more of compression and degradation.

But weaknesses and malformations, which to-day are attributable to a vicious schoolmaster and a pernicious system, will a century hence be rightly regarded as proofs of innate corruptness and radical incurability.

Now the fundamental agency under God in the regeneration, the re-training of the race, as well as the ground work and starting point of its progress upward, must be the *black woman*.

With all the wrongs and neglects of her past, with all the weakness, the debasement, the moral thralldom of her present, the black woman of to-day stands mute and wondering at the Herculean task devolving upon her. But the cycles wait for her. No other hand can move the lever. She must be loosed from her bands and set to work.

Our meager and superficial results from past efforts prove their futility; and every attempt to elevate the Negro, whether undertaken by himself or through the philanthropy of others, cannot but prove abortive unless so directed as to utilize the indispensable agency of an elevated and trained womanhood.

A race cannot be purified from without. Preachers and teachers are helps, and stimulants and conditions as necessary as the gracious rain and sunshine are to plant growth. But what are rain and dew and sunshine and cloud if there be no life in the plant germ? We must go to the root and see that that is sound and healthy and vigorous; and not deceive ourselves with waxen flowers and painted leaves of mock chlorophyll.

We too often mistake individuals' honor for race development and so are ready to substitute pretty accomplishments for sound sense and earnest purpose.

A stream cannot rise higher than its source. The atmosphere of homes is no rarer and purer and sweeter than are the mothers in those homes. A race is but a total of families. The nation is the aggregate of its homes. As the whole is sum of all its parts, so the character of the parts will determine the characteristics of the whole. These are all axioms and so evident that it seems gratuitous to remark it; and yet, unless I am greatly mistaken, most of the unsatisfaction from our past results arises from just such a radical and palpable error, as much almost on our own part as on that of our benevolent white friends.

The Negro is constitutionally hopeful and proverbially irrepressible; and naturally stands in danger of being dazzled by the shimmer and tinsel of superficials.

We often mistake foliage for fruit and overestimate or wrongly estimate brilliant results.

The late Martin R. Delany, who was an unadulterated black man, used to say when honors of state fell upon him, that when he entered the council of kings the black race entered with him; meaning, I suppose, that there was no discounting his race identity and attributing his achievements to some admixture of Saxon blood. But our present record of eminent men, when placed beside the actual status of the race in America to-day, proves that no man can represent the race. Whatever the attainments of the individual may be, unless his home has moved on *pari passu*, he can never be regarded as identical with or representative of the whole.

Not by pointing to sun-bathed mountain tops do we prove that Phoebus warms the valleys. We must point to homes, average homes of the rank and file of horny handed toiling men and women of the south (where the masses are) lighted and cheered by the good, and the true,—then and not until then will the whole plateau be lifted into the sunlight.

Only the BLACK WOMAN can say "when and where I enter, in the quiet, undisputed dignity of my womanhood, without violence and without suing or special patronage, then and there the whole *Negro race enters with me.*" Is it not evident then that as individual workers for this race we must address ourselves with no half-hearted zeal to this feature of our mission. The need is felt and must be recognized by all. There is a call for workers, for missionaries, for men and women with the double consecration of a fundamental love of humanity and a desire for its melioration through the Gospel; but superadded to this we demand an intelligent and sympathetic comprehension of the interests and special needs of the Negro.

I see not why there should not be an organized effort for the protection and elevation of our girls such as the White Cross League in England. English women are strengthened and protected by more than twelve centuries of Christian influences, freedom and civilization; English girls are dispirited and crushed down by no such all-levelling prejudice as that supercilious caste spirit in America which cynically assumes "A Negro woman cannot be a lady." English womanhood is beset by no such snares and traps as betray the unprotected, untrained colored girl of the South, whose only crime and dire destruction often is her unconscious and marvelous beauty. Surely then if English indignation is aroused and English manhood thrilled under the leadership of a Bishop of the English church to build up bulwarks around their wronged sisters, Negro sentiment cannot remain callous and Negro effort nerveless in view of the imminent peril of the mothers of the next generation. "*I am my Sister's keeper!*" should be the hearty response of every man and woman of the race, and this conviction should purify and exalt the narrow, selfish and petty personal aims of life into a noble and sacred purpose.

We need men who can let their interest and gallantry extend outside the circle of their aesthetic appreciation; men who can be a father, a brother, a friend to every weak, struggling unshielded girl. We need women who are so sure of their own social footing that they need not fear leaning to lend a hand to a fallen or falling sister. We need men and women who do not exhaust their genius splitting hairs on aristocratic distinctions and thanking God they are not as others; but earnest, unselfish souls, who can go into the highways and byways, lifting up and leading, advising and encouraging with the truly catholic benevolence of the Gospel of Christ.

As Church workers we must confess our path of duty is less obvious; or rather our ability to adapt our machinery to our conception of the peculiar exigencies of this work as taught by experience and our own consciousness of the needs of the Negro, is as yet not demonstrable. Flexibility and aggressiveness are not such strong characteristics of the Church to-day as in the Dark Ages.

As a Mission field for the Church the Southern Negro is in some aspects most promising; in others, perplexing. Aliens neither in language and customs, nor in associations and sympathies, naturally of deeply rooted religious instincts and taking most readily and kindly to the worship and teachings of the Church, surely the task of proselytizing the American Negro is infinitely less formidable than that which confronted the Church in the Barbarians of Europe. Besides, this people already look to the Church as the hope of their race. Thinking colored men almost uniformly admit that the Protestant Episcopal Church with its quiet, chaste dignity and decorous solemnity, its instructive and elevating ritual, its bright chanting and joyous hymning, is eminently fitted to correct the peculiar faults of worship—the rank exuberance and often ludicrous demonstrativeness of their people. Yet, strange to say, the Church, claiming to be missionary and Catholic, urging that schism is sin and denominationalism inexcusable, has made in all these years almost no inroads upon this semi-civilized religionism.

Harvests from this over ripe field of home missions have been gathered in by Methodists, Baptists, and not least by Congregationalists, who were unknown to the Freedmen before their emancipation.

Our clergy numbers less than two dozen* priests of Negro blood and we have hardly more than one self-supporting colored congregation in the entire Southland. While the organization known as the A. M. E. Church has 14,063 ministers, itinerant and local, 4,069 self-supporting churches, 4,275 Sunday-schools, with property valued at $7,772,284, raising yearly for church purposes $1,427,000.

Stranger and more significant than all, the leading men of this race (I do not mean demagogues and politicians, but men of intellect, heart, and race devotion,

---

*The published report of '91 shows 26 priests for the entire country, including one not engaged in work and one a professor in a non-sectarian school, since made Dean of an Episcopal Annex to Howard University known as King Hall.

men to whom the elevation of their people means more than personal ambition and sordid gain—and the men of that stamp have not all died yet) the Christian workers for the race, of younger and more cultured growth, are noticeably drifting into sectarian churches, many of them declaring all the time that they acknowledge the historic claims of the Church, believe her apostolicity, and would experience greater personal comfort, spiritual and intellectual, in her revered communion. It is a fact which any one may verify for himself, that representative colored men, professing that in their heart of hearts they are Episcopalians, are actually working in Methodist and Baptist pulpits; while the ranks of the Episcopal clergy are left to be filled largely by men who certainly suggest the propriety of a *"perpetual* Diaconate"* if they cannot be said to have created the necessity for it.

Now where is the trouble? Something must be wrong. What is it?

A certain Southern Bishop of our Church reviewing the situation, whether in Godly anxiety or in "Gothic antipathy" I know not, deprecates the fact that the colored people do not seem drawn to the Episcopal Church, and comes to the sage conclusion that the Church is not adapted to the rude untutored minds of the Freedmen, and that they may be left to go to the Methodists and Baptists whither their racial proclivities undeniably tend. How the good Bishop can agree that all-foreseeing Wisdom, and Catholic Love would have framed his Church as typified in his seamless garment and unbroken body, and yet not leave it broad enough and deep enough and loving enough to seek and save and hold seven millions of God's poor, I cannot see.

But the doctors while discussing their scientifically conclusive diagnosis of the disease, will perhaps not think it presumptuous in the patient if he dares to suggest where at least the pain is. If this be allowed, a Black woman of the South would beg to point out two possible oversights in this southern work which may indicate in part both a cause and a remedy for some failure. The first is not *calculating for the Black man's personality;* not having respect, if I may so express it, to his manhood or deferring at all to conceptions of the needs of his people. When colored persons have been employed it was too often as machines or as manikins. There has been no disposition, generally, to get the black man's ideal or to let his individuality work by its own gravity, as it were. A conference of earnest Christian men have met at regular intervals for some years past to discuss the best methods of promoting the welfare and development of colored people in this country. Yet, strange as it may seem, they have never invited a colored man or even intimated that one would be welcome to take part in their deliberations. Their remedial contrivances are purely theoretical or empirical, therefore, and the whole machinery devoid of soul.

The second important oversight in my judgment is closely allied to this and probably grows out of it, and that is not developing Negro womanhood as an essential fundamental for the elevation of the race, and utilizing this agency in extending the work of the Church.

Of the first I have possibly already presumed to say too much since it does not strictly come within the province of my subject. However, Macaulay somewhere criticises the Church of England as not knowing how to use fanatics, and declares that had Ignatius Loyola been in the Anglican instead of the Roman communion, the Jesuits would have been schismatics instead of Catholics; and if the religious awakenings of the Wesleys had been in Rome, she would have shaven their heads, tied ropes around their waists, and sent them out under her own banner and blessing. Whether this be true or not, there is certainly a vast amount of force potential for Negro evangelization rendered latent, or worse, antagonistic by the halting, uncertain, I had almost said, trimming policy of the Church in the South. This may sound both presumptuous and ungrateful. It is mortifying, I know, to benevolent wisdom, after having spent itself in the execution of well conned theories for the ideal development of a particular work, to hear perhaps the weakest and humblest element of that work asking "what doest thou?"

Yet so it will be in life. The "thus far and no farther" pattern cannot be fitted to any growth in God's kingdom. The universal law of development is "onward and upward." It is God-given and inviolable. From the unfolding of the germ in the acorn to reach the sturdy oak, to the growth of a human soul into the full knowledge and likeness of its Creator, the breath and scope of the movement in each and all are too grand, too mysterious, too like God himself, to be encompassed and locked down in human molds.

After all the Southern slave owners were right; either the very alphabet of intellectual growth must be forbidden and the Negro dealt with absolutely as a chattel having neither rights nor sensibilities; or else the clamps and irons of mental and moral, as well as civil compression must be driven asunder and the truly enfranchised soul led to the entrance of that boundless vista through which it is to toil upwards to its beckoning God as the buried seed germ to meet the sun.

A perpetual colored diaconate, carefully and kindly superintended by the white clergy; congregations of shiny faced peasants with their clean white aprons and sunbonnets catechized at regular intervals and taught to recite the creed, the Lord's prayer and the ten commandments—duty towards God and duty towards neighbor, surely such well tended sheep ought to be grateful to their shepherds and content in that station of life to which it pleased God to call them. True, like the old professor lecturing to his solitary student, we make no provision here for irregularities. "Questions must be kept till after class," or dispensed with altogether. That some do ask questions and insist on answers, in class too, must be both impertinent and annoying. Let not our spiritual pastors and masters however be grieved at such self-assertion as merely signifies we have a destiny to fulfill and as men and women we must *be about our Father's business.*

It is a mistake to suppose that the Negro is prejudiced against a white ministry. Naturally there is not a more kindly and implicit follower of a white man's guidance than the average colored peasant. What would to others be an ordinary act of friendly or pastoral interest he would be more inclined to regard gratefully as condescension. And he never forgets such kindness. Could the Negro be brought near to his white priest or bishop, he, is not suspicious. He is not only willing but often longs to unburden his soul to this intelligent guide. There are no reservations when he is convinced that you are his friend. It is a saddening satire on American history and manners that it takes something to convince him.

That our people are not "drawn" to a church whose chief dignitaries they see only in the chancel, and whom they reverence as they would a painting or an angel, whose life never comes down to and touches theirs with the inspiration of an objective reality, may be "perplexing" truly (American caste and American Christianity both being facts) but it need not be surprising. There must be something of human nature in it, the same as that which brought about that "the Word was made flesh and dwelt among us" that He might "draw" us towards God.

Men are not "drawn" by abstractions. Only sympathy and love can draw, and until our Church in America realizes this and provides a clergy that can come in touch with our life and have a fellow feeling for our woes, without being imbedded and frozen up in their "Gothic antipathies," the good bishops are likely to continue "perplexed" by the sparsity of colored Episcopalians.

A colored priest of my acquaintance recently related to me, with tears in his eyes, how his reverend Father in God, the Bishop who had ordained him, had met him on the cars on his way to the diocesan convention and warned him, not unkindly, not to take a seat in the body of the convention with the white clergy. To avoid disturbance of their godly placidity he would of course please sit back and somewhat apart. I do not imagine that that clergyman had very much heart for the Christly (!) deliberations of that convention.

To return, however, it is not on this broader view of Church work, which I mentioned as a primary cause of its halting progress with the colored people, that I am to speak. My proper theme is the second oversight of which in my judgment our Christian propagandists have been guilty: or, the necessity of church training, protecting and uplifting our colored womanhood as indispensable to the evangelization of the race.

Apelles did not disdain even that criticism of his lofty art which came from an uncouth cobbler; and may I not hope that the writer's oneness with her subject both in feeling and in being may palliate undue obtrusiveness of opinions here. That the race cannot be effectually lifted up till its women are truly elevated we take as proven. It is not for us to dwell on the needs, the neglects, and the ways of succor, pertaining to the black woman of the South. The ground, has been ably discussed and an admirable and practical plan proposed by the oldest Negro priest in America, advising and urging that special organizations such as Church Sisterhoods and industrial schools be devised to meet her pressing needs in the Southland. That some such movements are vital to the life of this people and the extension of the Church among them, is not hard to see. Yet the pamphlet fell still-born from the press. So far as I am informed the Church has made no motion towards carrying out Dr. Crummell's suggestion.

The denomination which comes next our own in opposing the proverbial emotionalism of Negro worship in the South, and which in consequence like ours receives the cold shoulder from the old heads, resting as we do under charge of not "having, religion" and not believing in conversion—the Congregationalists—have quietly gone to work on the young, have established industrial and training schools, and now almost every community in the South is yearly enriched by a fresh infusion of vigorous young hearts, cultivated heads, and helpful hands that have been trained at Fisk, at Hampton, in Atlanta University, and in Tuskegee, Alabama.

These young people are missionaries actual or virtual both here and in Africa. They have learned to love the methods and doctrines of the Church which trained and educated them; and so Congregationalism surely and steadily progresses.

Need I compare these well known facts with results shown by the Church in the same field and during the same or even a longer time.

The institution of the Church in the South to which she mainly looks for the training of her colored clergy and for the help of the "Black Woman" and "Colored Girl" of the South, has graduated since the year 1868, when the school was founded, *five young women;** and while yearly numerous young men have been kept and trained for the ministry by the charities of the Church, the number of indigent females who have been supported, sheltered and trained, is phenomenally small. Indeed, to my mind, the attitude of the Church toward this feature of her work is as if the solution of the problem of Negro missions depended solely on sending a quota of deacons and priests into the field, girls being a sort of *tertium quid* whose development may be promoted if they can pay their way and fall in with the plans mapped out for the training of the other sex.

Now I could ask in all earnestness, does not this force potential deserve by education and stimulus to be made dynamic? Is it not a solemn duty incumbent on all colored churchmen to make it so? Will not the aid of the Church be given to prepare our girls in head, heart, and hand for the duties and responsibilities that await the intelligent wife, the Christian mother, the earnest, virtuous, helpful woman, at once both the lever and the fulcrum for uplifting the race.

As Negroes and churchmen we cannot be indifferent to these questions. They

---

*Five have been graduated since '86, two in '91, two in '92.

touch us most vitally on both sides. We believe in the Holy Catholic Church. We believe that however gigantic and apparently remote the consummation, the Church will go on conquering and to conquer till the kingdoms of the world, not excepting the black man and the black woman of the South, shall have become the kingdoms of the Lord and of his Christ.

That past work in this direction has been unsatisfactory we must admit. That without a change of policy results in the future will be as meager, we greatly fear. Our life as a race is at stake. The dearest interests of our hearts are in the scales. We must either break away from dear old landmarks and plunge out in any line and every line that enables us to meet the pressing need of our people, or we must ask the church to allow and help us, untrammelled by the prejudices and theories of individuals, to work aggressively under her direction as we alone can, with God's help, for the salvation of our people.

The time is ripe for action. Self-seeking and ambition must be laid on the altar. The battle is one of sacrifice and hardship, but our duty is plain. We have been recipients of missionary bounty in some sort for twenty-one years. Not even the senseless vegetable is content to be mere reservoir. Receiving without giving is an anomaly in nature. Nature's cells are all little workshops for manufacturing sunbeams, the product to be *given out* to earth's inhabitants in warmth, energy, thought, action. Inanimate creation always pays back an equivalent.

Now, *How much owest thou my Lord?* Will his account be overdrawn if he call for singleness of purpose and self-sacrificing labor for your brethren? Having passed through your drill school, will you refuse a general's commission even if it entail responsibility, risk and anxiety, with possibly some adverse criticism? Is it too much to ask you to step forward and direct the work for your race along those lines which you know to be of first and vital importance?

Will you allow these words of Ralph Waldo Emerson? "In ordinary," says he, "we have a snappish criticism which watches and contradicts the opposite party. We want the will which advances and dictates [acts]. Nature has made up her mind and what cannot defend itself, shall not be defended. Complaining never so loud and with never so much reason, is of no use. What cannot stand must fall; *and the measure of our sincerity and therefore of the respect of men is the amount of health and wealth we will hazard in the defense of our right.*"

Further Reading

Alexander, Elizabeth. "'We Must Be about Our Father's Business': Anna Julia Cooper and the In-Corporation of the Nineteenth-Century African American Woman Intellectual." In *Her Own Voice: Nineteenth Century American Women Essayists.* Sherry Lee Linkon, ed. New York: Garland Publishing, 1997.

Southern Horrors

Lynch Law in All Its Phases

THE NEW YORK AGE PRINT, 1892 | SHORT ESSAY

Preface

The greater part of what is contained in these pages was published in the *New York Age*, June 25, 1892, in explanation of the editorial which the Memphis whites considered sufficiently infamous to justify the destruction of my paper, *The Free Speech*.

Since the appearance of that statement, requests have come from all parts of the country that "Exiled" (the name under which it then appeared) be issued in pamphlet form. Some donations were made, but not enough for that purpose. The noble effort of the ladies of New York and Brooklyn Oct. 5 have enabled me to comply with this request and give the world a true, unvarnished account of the causes of lynch law in the South.

This statement is not a shield for the despoiler of virtue, nor altogether a defense for the poor blind Afro-American Sampsons who suffer themselves to be betrayed by white Delilahs. It is a contribution to truth, an array of facts, the perusal of which it is hoped will stimulate this great American Republic to demand that justice be done though the heavens fall.

It is with no pleasure I have dipped my hands in the corruption here exposed. Somebody must show that the Afro-American race is more sinned against than sinning, and it seems to have fallen upon me to do so. The awful death-roll that Judge Lynch is calling every week is appalling, not only because of the lives it takes, the rank cruelty and outrage to the victims, but because of the prejudice it fosters and the stain it places against the good name of a weak race.

The Afro-American is not a bestial race. If this work can contribute in any way toward proving this, and at the same time arouse the conscience of the American people to a demand for justice to every citizen, and punishment by law for the lawless, I shall feel I have done my race a service. Other considerations are of minor importance.

IDA B. WELLS
New York City, Oct. 26, 1892

To the Afro-American women of New York and Brooklyn, whose race love, earnest zeal and unselfish effort at Lyric Hall, in the City of New York, on the night of October 5, 1892,—made possible its publication, this pamphlet is gratefully dedicated by the author.

Hon. Fred. Douglass's Letter

Dear Miss Wells:

Let me give you thanks for your faithful paper on the lynch abomination now generally practiced against colored people in the South. There has been no word equal to it in convincing power. I have spoken, but my word is feeble in comparison. You give us what you know and testify from actual knowledge. You have dealt with the facts with cool, painstaking fidelity and left those naked and uncontradicted facts to speak for themselves.

Brave woman! you have done your people and mine a service which can neither be weighed nor measured. If American conscience were only half alive, if the American church and clergy were only half christianized, if American moral sensibility were not hardened by persistent infliction of outrage and crime against colored people, a scream of horror, shame and indignation would rise to Heaven wherever your pamphlet shall be read.

But alas! even crime has power to reproduce itself and create conditions favorable to its own existence. It sometimes seems we are deserted by earth and Heaven— yet we must still think, speak and work, and trust in the power of a merciful God for final deliverance.

Very truly and gratefully yours,
FREDERICK DOUGLASS
Cedar Hill, Anacostia, D.C., Oct. 25, 1892

Chapter 1. The Offense

Wednesday evening May 24th, 1892, the city of Memphis was filled with excitement. Editorials in the daily papers of that date caused a meeting to be held in the Cotton Exchange Building; a committee was sent for the editors of the "Free Speech" an Afro-American journal published in that city, and the only reason the open threats of lynching that were made were not carried out was because they could not be found. The cause of all this commotion was the following editorial published in the "Free Speech" May 21st, 1892, the Saturday previous.

"Eight negroes lynched since last issue of the "Free Speech" one at Little Rock, Ark., last Saturday morning where the citizens broke(?) into the penitentiary and got their man; three near Anniston, Ala., one near New Orleans, and three at Clarksville, Ga., the last three for killing a white man, and five on the same old racket—the new alarm about raping white women. The same programme of hanging, then shooting bullets into the lifeless bodies was carried out to the letter.

Nobody in this section of the country believes the old threadbare lie that Negro men rape white women. If Southern white men are not careful, they will overreach themselves and public sentiment will have a reaction; a conclusion will then be reached which will be very damaging to the moral reputation of their women."

"The Daily Commercial" of Wednesday following, May 25th, contained the following leader:

"Those negroes who are attempting to make the lynching of individuals of their race a means for arousing the worst passions of their kind are playing with a dangerous sentiment. The negroes may as well understand that there is no mercy for the negro rapist and little patience with his defenders. A negro organ printed in this city, in a recent issue publishes the following atrocious paragraph: 'Nobody in this section of the country believes the old thread-bare lie that negro men rape white women. If Southern white men are not careful they will overreach themselves, and public sentiment will have a reaction; and a conclusion will be reached which will be very damaging to the moral reputation of their women.'

The fact that a black scoundrel is allowed to live and utter such loathsome and repulsive calumnies is a volume of evidence as to the wonderful patience of Southern whites. But we have had enough of it.

There are some things that the Southern white man will not tolerate, and the obscene intimations of the foregoing have brought the writer to the very outermost limit of public patience. We hope we have said enough."

The "Evening Scimitar" of same date, copied the "Commercial's" editorial with these words of comment: "Patience under such circumstances is not a virtue. If the negroes themselves do not apply the remedy without delay it will be the duty of those whom he has attacked to tie the wretch who utters these calumnies to a stake at the intersection of Main and Madison Sts., brand him in the forehead with a hot iron and perform upon him a surgical operation with a pair of tailor's shears."

Acting upon this advice, the leading citizens met in the Cotton Exchange Building the same evening, and threats of lynching were freely indulged, not by the lawless element upon which the deviltry of the South is usually saddled—but by the leading business men, in their leading business centre. Mr. Fleming, the business manager and owning a half interest the Free Speech, had to leave town to escape the mob, and was afterwards ordered not to return; letters and telegrams sent me in New York where I was spending my vacation advised me that bodily harm awaited my return. Creditors took possession of the office and sold the outfit, and the "Free Speech" was as if it had never been.

The editorial in question was prompted by the many inhuman and fiendish lynchings of Afro-Americans which have recently taken place and was meant as a warning. Eight lynched in one week and five of them charged with rape! The thinking public will not easily believe freedom and education more brutalizing than slavery, and the world knows that the crime of rape was unknown during four years of civil war, when the white women of the South were at the mercy of the race which is all at once charged with being a bestial one.

Since my business has been destroyed and I am an exile from home because of that editorial, the issue has been forced, and as the writer of it I feel that the race and the public generally should have a statement of the facts as they exist. They will serve at the same time as a defense for the Afro-Americans Sampsons who suffer themselves to be betrayed by white Delilahs.

The whites of Montgomery, Ala., knew J.C. Duke sounded the keynote of the situation—which they would gladly hide from the world, when he said in his paper, "The Herald," five years ago: "Why is it that white women attract negro men now more than in former days? There was a time when such a thing was unheard of. There is a secret to this thing, and we greatly suspect it is the growing appreciation of white Juliets for colored Romeos." Mr. Duke, like the "Free Speech" proprietors, was forced to leave the city for reflecting on the "honah" of white women and his paper suppressed; but the truth remains that Afro-American men do not always rape(?) white women without their consent.

Mr. Duke, before leaving Montgomery, signed a card disclaiming any intention of slandering Southern white women. The editor of the "Free Speech" has no disclaimer to enter, but asserts instead that there are many white women in the South who would marry colored men if such an act would not place them at once beyond the pale of society and within the clutches of the law. The miscegnation laws of the South only operate against the legitimate union of the races; they leave the white man free to seduce all the colored girls he can, but it is death to the colored man who yields to the force and advances of a similar attraction in white women. White men lynch the offending Afro-American, not because he is a despoiler of virtue, but because he succumbs to the smiles of white women.

Chapter II. The Black and White of It

The "Cleveland Gazette" of January 16, 1892, publishes a case in point. Mrs. J.S. Underwood, the wife of a minister of Elyria, Ohio, accused an Afro-American of rape. She told her husband that during his absence in 1888, stumping the State for the Prohibition Party, the man came to the kitchen door, forced his way in the house and insulted her. She tried to drive him out with a heavy poker, but he overpowered and chloroformed her, and when she revived her clothing was torn and she was in a horrible condition. She did not know the man but could identify him. She pointed out William Offett, a married man, who was arrested and, being in Ohio, was granted a trial.

The prisoner vehemently denied the charge of rape, but confessed he went to Mrs. Underwood's residence at her invitation and was criminally intimate with her at her request. This availed him nothing against the sworn testimony of a minister's wife, a lady of the highest respectability. He was found guilty, and entered the penitentiary, December 14, 1888, for fifteen years. Some time afterwards the woman's remorse led her to confess to her husband that the man was innocent.

These are her words: "I met Offett at the Post Office. It was raining. He was polite to me, and as I had several bundles in my arms he offered to carry them home for me, which he did. He had a strange fascination for me, and I invited him to call on me. He called, bringing chestnuts and candy for the children. By this means we got them to leave us alone in the room. Then I sat on his lap. He made a proposal to me and I readily consented. Why I did so, I do not know, but that I did is true. He visited me several times after that and each time I was indiscreet. I did not care after the first time. In fact I could not have resisted, and had no desire to resist."

When asked by her husband why she told him she had been outraged, she said: "I had several reasons for telling you. One was the neighbors saw the fellows here, another was, I was afraid I had contracted a loathsome disease, and still another was that I feared I might give birth to a Negro baby. I hoped to save my reputation by telling you a deliberate lie." Her husband horrified by the confession had Offett, who had already served four years, released and secured a divorce.

There are thousands of such cases throughout the South, with the difference that the Southern white men in insatiate fury wreak their vengeance without intervention of law upon the Afro-Americans who consort with their women. A few instances to substantiate the assertion that some white women love the company of the Afro-American will not be out of place. Most of these cases were reported by the daily papers of the South.

In the winter of 1885–86 the wife of a practicing physician in Memphis, in good social standing whose name has escaped me, left home, husband and children, and ran away with her black coachman. She was with him a month before her husband found and brought her home. The coachman could not be found. The doctor moved his family away from Memphis, and is living in another city under an assumed name.

In the same city last year a white girl in the dusk of evening screamed at the approach of some parties that a Negro had assaulted her on the street. He was captured, tried by a white judge and jury, that acquitted him of the charge. It is needless to add if there had been a scrap of evidence on which to convict him of so grave a charge he would have been convicted.

Sarah Clark of Memphis loved a black man and lived openly with him. When she was indicted last spring for miscegenation, she swore in court that she was *not* a white woman. This she did to escape the penitentiary and continued her illicit relation undisturbed. That she is of the lower class of whites, does not disturb the fact that she is a white woman. "The leading citizens" of Memphis are defending the "honor" of *all* white women, *demi-monde* included.

Since the manager of the "Free Speech" has been run away from Memphis by the guardians of the honor of Southern white women, a young girl living on Poplar St., who was discovered in intimate relations with a handsome mulatto young colored man, Will Morgan by name, stole her father's money to send the young fellow away from that father's wrath. She has since joined him in Chicago.

The Memphis "Ledger" for June 8th has the following: "If Lillie Bailey, a rather pretty white girl seventeen years of age, who is now at the City Hospital, would be somewhat less reserved about her disgrace there would be some very nauseating details in the story of her life. She is the mother of a little coon. The truth might reveal fearful depravity or it might reveal the evidence of a rank outrage. She will not divulge the name of the man who has left such black evidence of her disgrace, and, in fact, says it is a matter in which there can be no interest to the outside world. She came to Memphis nearly three months ago and was taken in at the Woman's Refuge in the southern part of the city. She remained there until a few weeks ago, when the child was born. The ladies in charge of the Refuge were horrified. The girl was at once sent to the City Hospital, where she has been since May 30th. She is a country girl. She came to Memphis from her father's farm, a short distance from Hernando, Miss. Just when she left there she would not say. In fact she says she came to Memphis from Arkansas, and says her home is in that State. She is rather good looking, has blue eyes, a low forehead and dark red hair. The ladies at the Woman's Refuge do not know anything about the girl further than what they learned when she was an inmate of the institution; and she would not tell much.

When the child was born an attempt was made to get the girl to reveal the name of the Negro who had disgraced her, she obstinately refused and it was impossible to elicit any information from her on the subject."

Note the wording. "The truth might reveal fearful depravity or rank outrage." If it had been a white child or Lillie Bailey had told a pitiful story of Negro outrage, it would have been a case of woman's weakness or assault and she could have remained at the Woman's Refuge. But a Negro child and to withhold its father's name and thus prevent the killing of another Negro "rapist." A case of "fearful depravity."

The very week the "leading citizens" of Memphis were making a spectacle of themselves in defense of all white women of every kind, an Afro-American, M. Stricklin, was found in a white woman's room in that city. Although she made no outcry of rape, he was jailed and would have been lynched, but the woman stated she bought curtains of him (he was a furniture dealer) and his business in her room that night was to put them up. A white woman's word was taken as absolutely in this case as when the cry of rape is made, and he was freed.

What is true of Memphis is true of the entire South. The daily papers last year reported a farmer's wife in Alabama had given birth to a Negro child. When the Negro farm hand who was plowing in the field heard it he took the mule from the plow and fled. The dispatches also told of a woman in South Carolina who gave birth to a Negro child and charged three men with being its father, *every one of whom has since disappeared.* In Tuscumbia, Ala., the colored boy who was lynched there last year for assaulting a white girl told her before his accusers that he had met her there in the woods often before.

Frank Weems of Chattanooga who was not lynched in May only because the prominent citizens became his body guard until the doors of the penitentiary closed on him, had letters in his pocket from the white woman in the case, making the appointment with him. Edward Coy who was burned alive in Texarkana, January 1, 1892, died protesting his innocence. Investigation since as given by the Bystander in the Chicago Inter Ocean, October 1, proves:

"1. The woman who was paraded as a victim of violence was of bad character; her husband was a drunkard and a gambler.
2. She was publicly reported and generally known to have been criminally intimate with Coy for more than a year previous.
3. She was compelled by threats, if not by violence, to make the charge against the victim.
4. When she came to apply the match Coy asked her if she would burn him after they had "been sweethearting" so long.
5. A large majority of the 'superior' white men prominent in the affair are the

reputed fathers of mulatto children.

These are not pleasant facts, but they are illustrative of the vital phase of the so-called 'race question,' which should properly be designated an earnest inquiry as to the best methods by which religion, science, law and political power may be employed to excuse injustice, barbarity and crime done to a people because of race and color. There can be no possible belief that these people were inspired by any consuming zeal to vindicate God's law against miscegnationists of the most practical sort. The woman was a willing partner in the victim's guilt, and being of the 'superior' race must naturally have been more guilty."

In Natchez, Miss., Mrs. Marshall, one of the *creme de la creme* of the city, created a tremendous sensation several years ago. She has a black coachman who was married, and had been in her employ several years. During this time she gave birth to a child whose color was remarked, but traced to some brunette ancestor, and one of the fashionable dames of the city was its godmother. Mrs. Marshall's social position was unquestioned, and wealth showered every dainty on this child which was idolized with its brothers and sisters by its white papa. In course of time another child appeared on the scene, but it was unmistakably dark. All were alarmed, and "rush of blood, strangulation" were the conjectures, but the doctor, when asked the cause, grimly told them it was a Negro child. There was a family conclave, the coachman heard of it and leaving his own family went West, and has never returned. As soon as Mrs. Marshall was able to travel she was sent away in deep disgrace. Her husband died within the year of a broken heart.

Ebenzer Fowler, the wealthiest colored man in Issaquena County, Miss., was shot down on the street in Mayersville, January 30, 1885, just before dark by an armed body of white men who filled his body with bullets. They charged him with writing a note to a white woman of the place, which they intercepted and which proved there was an intimacy existing between them.

Hundreds of such cases might be cited, but enough have been given to prove the assertion that there are white women in the South who love the Afro-American's company even as there are white men notorious for their preference for Afro-American women.

There is hardly a town in the South which has not an instance of the kind which is well known, and hence the assertion is reiterated that "nobody in the South believes the old thread bare lie that negro men rape white women." Hence there is a growing demand among Afro-Americans that the guilt or innocence of parties accused of rape be fully established. They know the men of the section of the country who refuse this are not so desirous of punishing rapists as they pretend. The utterances of the leading white men show that with them it is not the crime but the *class*. Bishop Fitzgerald has become apologist for lynchers of the rapists of *white* women only. Governor Tillman, of South Carolina, in the month of June, standing under the tree in Barnwell, S.C., on which eight Afro-Americans were hung last year, declared that he would lead a mob to lynch a *negro* who raped a *white* woman" [sic]. So say the pulpits, officials and newspapers of the South. But when the victim is a colored woman it is different.

Last winter in Baltimore, Md., three white ruffians assaulted a Miss Camphor, a young Afro-American girl, while out walking with a young man of her own race. They held her escort and outraged the girl. It was a deed dastardly enough to arouse Southern blood, which gives its horror of rape as excuse for lawlessness, but she was an Afro-American. The case went to the courts, an Afro-American lawyer defended the men and they were acquitted.

In Nashville, Tenn., there is a white man, Pat Hanifan, who outraged a little Afro-American girl, and, from the physical injuries received, she has been ruined for life. He was jailed for six months, discharged, and is now a detective in that city. In the same city, last May, a white man outraged an Afro-American girl in a drug store. He was arrested, and released on bail at the trial. It was rumored that five hundred Afro-Americans had organized to lynch him. Two hundred and fifty white citizens armed themselves with Winchesters and guarded him. A cannon was placed in front of his home, and the Buchanan Rifles (State Militia) ordered to the scene for his protection. The Afro-American mob did not materialize. Only two weeks before Eph. Grizzard, who had only been *charged* with rape upon a white woman, had been taken from the jail, with Governor Buchanan and the police and militia standing by, dragged through the streets in broad daylight, knives plunged into him at every step, and with every fiendish cruelty a frenzied mob could devise, he was at last swung out on the bridge with hands cut to pieces as he tried to climb up the stanchions. A naked, bloody example of the blood-thirstiness of the nineteenth-century civilization of the Athens of the South! No cannon or military was called out in his defense. He dared to visit a white woman.

At the very moment these civilized whites were announcing their determination "to protect their wives and daughters," by murdering Grizzard, a white man was in the same jail for raping eight-year-old Maggie Reese, an Afro-American girl. He was not harmed. The "honor" of grown women who were glad enough to be supported by the Grizzard boys and Ed Coy, as long as the liaison was not known, needed protection; they were white. The outrage upon helpless childhood needed no avenging in this case; she was black.

A white man in Guthrie, Oklahoma Territory, two months ago inflicted such injuries upon another Afro-American child that she died. He was not punished, but an attempt was made in the same town in the month of June to lynch an Afro-American who visited a white woman.

In Memphis, Tenn., in the month of June, Ellerton L. Dorr, who is the husband of Russell Hancock's widow, was arrested for attempted rape on Mattie Cole, a neighbor's cook; he was only prevented from accomplishing his purpose, by the appearance of Mattie's employer. Dorr's friends say he was drunk and not responsible for his actions. The grand jury refused to indict him and he was discharged.

Chapter III. The New Cry

The appeal of Southern whites to Northern sympathy and sanction, the adroit, insidious plea made by Bishop Fitzgerald for suspension of judgment because those "who condemn lynching express no sympathy for the *white* woman in the case," falls to the ground in the light of the foregoing.

From this exposition of the race issue in lynch law, the whole matter is explained by the well-known opposition growing out of slavery to the progress of the race. This is crystallized in the oft-repeated slogan: "This is a white man's country and the white man must rule." The South resented giving the Afro-American his freedom, the ballot box and the Civil Rights Law. The raids of the Ku-Klux and White Liners to subvert reconstruction government, the Hamburg and Ellerton, S.C., the Copiah County, Miss., and the Layfayette Parish, La., massacres were excused as the natural resentment of intelligence against government by ignorance.

Honest white men practically conceded the necessity of intelligence murdering ignorance to correct the mistake of the general government, and the race was left to the tender mercies of the solid South. Thoughtful Afro-Americans with the strong arm of the government withdrawn and with the hope to stop such wholesale massacres urged the race to sacrifice its political rights for sake of peace. They honestly believed the race should fit itself for government, and when that should be done, the objection to race participation in politics would be removed.

But the sacrifice did not remove the trouble, nor move the South to justice. One by one the Southern States have legally(?) disfranchised the Afro-American, and since the repeal of the Civil Rights Bill nearly every Southern State has passed separate car laws with a penalty against their infringement. The race regardless of advancement is penned into filthy, stifling partitions cut off from smoking cars. All this while, although the political cause has been removed, the butcheries of black men at Barnwell, S.C., Carrolton, Miss., Waycross, Ga., and Memphis, Tenn., have gone on; also the flaying alive of a man in Kentucky, the burning of one in Arkansas, the hanging of a fifteen-year-old girl in Louisiana, a woman in Jackson, Tenn., and one in Hollendale, Miss., until the dark and bloody record of the South shows 728 Afro-Americans lynched during the past eight years. Not fifty of these were for political causes; the rest were for all manner of accusations from that of rape of white women, to the case of the boy Will Lewis who was hanged at Tullahoma,

Tenn., last year for being drunk and "sassy" to white folks.

These statistics compiled by the Chicago "Tribune" were given the first of this year (1892). Since then, not less than one hundred and fifty have been known to have met violent death at the hands of cruel bloodthirsty mobs during the past nine months.

To palliate this record (which grows worse as the Afro-American becomes intelligent) and excuse some of the most heinous crimes that ever stained the history of a country, the South is shielding itself behind the plausible screen of defending the honor of its women. This, too, in the face of the fact that only *one-third* of the 728 victims to mobs have been *charged* with rape, to say nothing of those of that one-third who were innocent of the charge. A white correspondent of the Baltimore Sun declares that the Afro-American who was lynched in Chestertown, Md., in May for assault on a white girl was innocent; that the deed was done by a white man who had since disappeared. The girl herself maintained that her assailant was a white man. When that poor Afro-American was murdered, the whites excused their refusal of a trial on the ground that they wished to spare the white girl the mortification of having to testify in court.

This cry has had its effect. It has closed the heart, stifled the conscience, warped the judgment and hushed the voice of press and pulpit on the subject of lynch law throughout this "land of liberty." Men who stand high in the esteem of the public for Christian character, for moral and physical courage, for devotion to the principles of equal and exact justice to all, and for great sagacity, stand as cowards who fear to open their mouths before this great outrage. They do not see that by their tacit encouragement, their silent acquiescence, the black shadow of lawlessness in the form of lynch law is spreading its wings over the whole country.

Men who, like Governor Tillman, start the ball of lynch law rolling for a certain crime, are powerless to stop it when drunken or criminal white toughs feel like hanging an Afro-American on any pretext.

Even to the better class of Afro-Americans the crime of rape is so revolting they have too often taken the white man's word and given lynch law neither the investigation nor condemnation it deserved.

They forget that a concession of the right to lynch a man for a certain crime, not only concedes the right to lynch any person for any crime, but (so frequently is the cry of rape now raised) it is in a fair way to stamp us a race of rapists and desperadoes. They have gone on hoping and believing that general education and financial strength would solve the difficulty, and are devoting their energies to the accumulation of both.

The mob spirit has grown with the increasing intelligence of the Afro-American. It has left the out-of-the-way places where ignorance prevails, has thrown off the mask and with this new cry stalks in broad daylight in large cities, the centres of civilization, and is encouraged by the "leading citizens" and the press.

Chapter IV. The Malicious And Untruthful White Press

The "Daily Commercial" and "Evening Scimitar" of Memphis, Tenn., are owned by leading business men of that city, and yet, in spite of the fact that there had been no white woman in Memphis outraged by an Afro-American, and that Memphis possessed a thrifty law-abiding, property-owning class of Afro-Americans the "Commercial" of May 17th, under the head of "More Rapes, More Lynchings" gave utterance to the following:

The lynching of three Negro scoundrels reported in our dispatches from Anniston, Ala., for a brutal outrage committed upon a white woman will be a text for much comment on "Southern barbarism" by Northern newspapers; but we fancy it will hardly prove effective for campaign purposes among intelligent people. The frequency of these lynchings calls attention to the frequency of the crimes which causes lynching. The "Southern barbarism" which deserves the serious attention of all people North and South, is the barbarism which preys upon weak and defenseless women. Nothing but the most prompt, speedy and extreme punishment can hold in check the horrible and bestial propensities of the Negro race. There is a strange similarity about a number of cases of this character which have lately occurred.

In each case the crime was deliberately planned and perpetrated by several Negroes. They watched for an opportunity when the women were left without a protector. It was not a sudden yielding to a fit of passion, but the consummation of a devilish purpose which has been seeking and waiting for the opportunity. This feature of the crime not only makes it the most fiendishly brutal, but it adds to the terror of the situation in the thinly settled country communities. No man can leave his family at night without the dread that some roving Negro ruffian is watching and waiting for this opportunity. The swift punishment which invariably follows these horrible crimes doubtless acts as a deterring effect upon the Negroes in that immediate neighborhood for a short time. But the lesson is not widely learned nor long remembered. Then such crimes, equally atrocious, have happened in quick succession, one in Tennessee, one in Arkansas, and one in Alabama. The facts of the crime appear to appeal more to the Negro's lustful imagination than the facts of the punishment do to his fears. He sets aside all fear of death in any form when opportunity is found for the gratification of his bestial desires.

There is small reason to hope for any change for the better. The commission of this crime grows more frequent every year. The generation of Negroes which have grown up since the war have lost in large measure the traditional and wholesome awe of the white race which kept the Negroes in subjection, even when their masters were in the army, and their families left unprotected except by the slaves themselves. There is no longer a restraint upon the brute passion of the Negro.

What is to be done? The crime of rape is always horrible, but the Southern man there is nothing which so fills the soul with horror, loathing and fury as the outraging of a white woman by a Negro. It is the race question in the ugliest, vilest, most dangerous aspect. The Negro as a political factor can be controlled. But neither laws nor lynchings can subdue his lusts. Sooner or later it will force a crisis. We do not know in what form it will come.

In its issue of June 4th, the Memphis "Evening Scimitar" gives the following excuse for lynch law:

"Aside from the violation of white women by Negroes, which is the outcropping of a bestial perversion of instinct, the chief cause of trouble between the races in the South is the Negro's lack of manners. In the state of slavery he learned politeness from association with white people, who took pains to teach him. Since the emancipation came and the tie of mutual interest and regard between master and servant was broken, the Negro has drifted away into a state which is neither freedom nor bondage. Lacking the proper inspiration of the one and the restraining force of the other he has taken up the idea that boorish insolence is independence, and the exercise of a decent degree of breeding toward white people is identical with servile submission. In consequence of the prevalence of this notion there are many Negroes who use every opportunity to make themselves offensive, particularly when they think it can be done with impunity.

We have had too many instances right here in Memphis to doubt this, and our experience is not exceptional. *The white people won't stand this sort of thing, and whether they be insulted as individuals are as a race, the response will be prompt and effectual.* The bloody riot of 1866, in which so many Negroes perished, was brought on principally by the outrageous conduct of the blacks toward the whites on the streets. It is also a remarkable and discouraging fact that the majority of such scoundrels are Negroes who have received educational advantages at the hands of the white taxpayers. They have got just enough of learning to make them realize how hopelessly their race is behind the other in everything that makes a great people, and they attempt to "get even" by insolence, which is ever the resentment of inferiors. There are well-bred Negroes among us, and it is truly unfortunate that they should have to pay, even in part, the penalty of the offenses committed by the baser sort, but this is the way of the world. The innocent must suffer for the guilty. If the Negroes as a people possessed a hundredth part of the self-respect which is evidenced by the courteous bearing of some that the "Scimitar" could name, the friction between the races would be reduced to a minimum. It will not do to beg the question by pleading that many white men are also stirring up strife. The Caucasian blackguard simply obeys the promptings of a depraved disposition, and he is seldom deliberately rough or offensive toward strangers or unprotected women.

The Negro tough, on the contrary, is given to just that kind of offending, and he almost invariably singles out white people as his victims."

On March 9th, 1892, there were lynched in this same city three of the best specimens of young since-the-war Afro-American manhood. They were peaceful, law-abiding citizens and energetic business men.

They believed the problem was to be solved by eschewing politics and putting money in the purse. They owned a flourishing grocery business in a thickly populated suburb of Memphis, and a white man named Barrett had one on the opposite corner. After a personal difficulty which Barrett sought by going into the "People's Grocery" drawing a pistol and was thrashed by Calvin McDowell, he (Barrett) threatened to "clean them out." These men were a mile beyond the city limits and police protection; hearing that Barrett's crowd was coming to attack them Saturday night, they mustered forces, and prepared to defend themselves against the attack.

When Barrett came he led a *posse* of officers, twelve in number, who afterward claimed to be hunting a man for whom they had a warrant. That twelve men in citizen's clothes should think it necessary to go in the night to hunt one man who had never before been arrested, or made any record as a criminal has never been explained. When they entered the back door the young men thought the threatened attack was on, and fired into them. Three of the officers were wounded, and when the *defending* party found it was officers of the law upon whom they had fired, they ceased and got away.

Thirty-one men were arrested and thrown in jail as "conspirators," although they all declared more than once they did not know they were firing on officers. Excitement was at fever beat until the morning papers, two days after, announced that the wounded deputy sheriffs were out of danger. This hindered rather than helped the plans of the whites. There was no law on the statute books which would execute an Afro-American for wounding a white man, but the "unwritten law" did. Three of these men, the president, the manager and clerk of the grocery—"the leaders of the conspiracy"—were secretly taken from jail and lynched in a shockingly brutal manner. "The Negroes are getting too independent," they say, "we must teach them a lesson."

"What lesson? The lesson of subordination. "Kill the leaders and it will cow the Negro who dares to shoot a white man, even in self-defense."

Although the race was wild over the outrage, the mockery of law and justice which disarmed men and locked them up in jails where they could be easily and safely reached by the mob—- the Afro-American ministers, newspapers and leaders counselled obedience to the law which did not protect them.

Their counsel was heeded and not a hand was uplifted to resent the outrage; following the advice of the "Free Speech," people left the city in great numbers.

The dailies and associated press reports heralded these men to the country as "toughs," and "Negro desperadoes who kept a low dive." This same press service printed that the Negro who was lynched at Indianola, Miss., in May, had outraged the sheriff's eight-year-old daughter. The girl was more than eighteen years old, and was found by her father in this man's room, who was a servant on the place.

Not content with misrepresenting the race, the mob spirit was not to be satisfied until the paper which was doing all it could to counteract this impression was silenced. The colored people were resenting their bad treatment in a way to make itself felt, yet gave the mob no excuse for further murder, until the appearance of the editorial which is construed as a reflection on the "honor" of the Southern white women. It is not half so libelous as that of the "Commercial" which appeared four days before, and which has been given in these pages. They would have lynched the manager of the "Free Speech" for exercising the right of free speech if they had found him as quickly as they would have hung a rapist, and glad of the excuse to do so. The owners were ordered not to return, the "Free Speech" was suspended with as little compunction as the business of the "People's Grocery" broken up and the proprietors murdered.

Chapter V. The South's Position

Henry W. Grady in his well-remembered speeches in New England and New York pictured the Afro-American as incapable of self-government. Through him and other leading men the cry of the South to the country has been "Hands off! Leave us to solve our problem." To the Afro-American the South says, "the white man must and will rule." There is little difference between the Antebellum South and the New South.

Her white citizens are wedded to any method however revolting, any measure however extreme, for the subjugation of the young manhood of the race. They have cheated him out of his ballot, deprived him of civil rights or redress therefore in the civil courts, robbed him of the fruits of his labor, and are still murdering, burning and lynching him.

The result is a growing disregard of human life. Lynch law has spread its insidious influence till men in New York State, Pennsylvania and on the free Western plains feel they can take the law in their own hands with impunity, especially where an Afro-American is concerned. The South is brutalized to a degree not realized by its own inhabitants, and the very foundation of government, law and order, are imperiled.

Public sentiment has had a slight "reaction" though not sufficient to stop the crusade of lawlessness and lynching. The spirit of christianity of the great M.E. Church was aroused to the frequent and revolting crimes against a weak people, enough to pass strong condemnatory resolutions at its General Conference in Omaha last May. The spirit of justice of the grand old party asserted itself sufficiently to secure a denunciation of the wrongs, and a feeble declaration of the belief in human rights in the Republican platform at Minneapolis, June 7th. Some of the great dailies and weeklies have swung into line declaring that lynch law must go. The President of the United States issued a proclamation that it be not tolerated in the territories over which he has jurisdiction. Governor Northern and Chief Justice Bleckley of Georgia have proclaimed against it. The citizens of Chattanooga, Tenn., have set a worthy example in that they not only condemn lynch law, but her public men demanded a trial for Weems, the accused rapist, and guarded him while the trial was in progress. The trial only lasted ten minutes, and Weems chose to plead guilty and accept twenty-one years sentence, than invite the certain death which awaited him outside that cordon of police if he had told the truth and shown the letters he had from the white woman in the case.

Col. A.S. Colyar, of Nashville, Tenn., is so overcome with the horrible state of affairs that he addressed the following earnest letter to the Nashville "American." "Nothing since I have been a reading man has so impressed me with the decay of manhood among the people of Tennessee as the dastardly submission to the mob reign. We have reached the unprecedented low level; the awful criminal depravity of substituting the mob for the court and jury, of giving up the jail keys to the mob whenever they are demanded. We do it in the largest cities and in the country towns; we do it in midday; we do it after full, not to say formal, notice, and so thoroughly and generally is it acquiesced in that the murderers have discarded the formula of masks. They go into the town where everybody knows them, sometimes under the gaze of the governor, in the presence of the courts, in the presence of the sheriff and his deputies, in the presence of the entire police force, take out the prisoner, take his life, often with fiendish glee, and often with acts of cruelty and barbarism which impress the reader with a degeneracy rapidly approaching savage life. That the State is disgraced but faintly expresses the humiliation which has settled upon the once proud people of Tennessee. The State, in its majesty, through its organized life, for which the people pay liberally, makes but one record, but one note, and that a criminal falsehood, 'was hung by persons to the jury unknown.' The murder at Shelbyville is only a verification of what every intelligent man knew would come, because with a mob a rumor is as good as a proof."

These efforts brought forth apologies and a short halt, but the lynching mania was raged again through the past three months with unabated fury.

The strong arm of the law must be brought to bear upon lynchers in severe punishment, but this cannot and will not be done unless a healthy public sentiment demands and sustains such action.

The men and women in the South who disapprove of lynching and remain silent on the perpetration of such outrages, are particeps criminis, accomplices, accessories before and after the fact, equally guilty with the actual lawbreakers who would not persist if they did not know that neither the law nor militia would be employed against them.

Chapter VI. Self-Help

In the creation of this healthier public sentiment, the Afro-American can do for himself what no one else can do for him. The world looks on with wonder that we have conceded so much and remain law-abiding under such great outrage and provocation.

To Northern capital and Afro-American labor the South owes its rehabilitation. If labor is withdrawn capital will not remain. The Afro-American is thus the backbone of the South. A thorough knowledge and judicious exercise of this power in lynching localities could many times effect a bloodless revolution. The white man's dollar is his god, and to stop this will be to stop outrages in many localities.

The Afro-Americans of Memphis denounced the lynching of three of their best citizens, and urged and waited for the authorities to act in the matter and bring the lynchers to justice. No attempt was made to do so, and the black men left the city by thousands, bringing about great stagnation in every branch of business. Those who remained so injured the business of the street car company by staying off the cars, that the superintendent, manager and treasurer called personally on the editor of the "Free Speech," asked them to urge our people to give them their patronage again. Other business men became alarmed over the situation and the "Free Speech" was run away that the colored people might be more easily controlled. A meeting of white citizens in June, three months after the lynching, passed resolutions for the first time, condemning it. *But they did not punish the lynchers.* Every one of them was known by name, because they had been selected to do the dirty work, by some of the very citizens who passed these resolutions. Memphis is fast losing her black population, who proclaim as they go that there is no protection for the life and property of any Afro-American citizen in Memphis who is not a slave.

The Afro-American citizens of Kentucky, whose intellectual and financial improvement has been phenomenal, have never had a separate car law until now. Delegations and petitions poured into the Legislature against it, yet the bill passed and the Jim Crow Car of Kentucky is a legalized institution. Will the great mass of Negroes continue to patronize the railroad? A special from Covington, Ky., says:

Covington, June 13th.—The railroads of the State are beginning to feel very markedly, the effects of the separate coach bill recently passed by the Legislature. No class of people in the State have so many and so largely attended excursions as the blacks. All these have been abandoned, and regular travel is reduced to a minimum. A competent authority says the loss to the various roads will reach $1,000,000 this year.

A call to a State Conference in Lexington, Ky., last June had delegates from every county in the State. Those delegates, the ministers, teachers, heads of secret and others orders, and the head of every family should pass the word around for every member of the race in Kentucky to stay off railroads unless obliged to ride. If they did so, and their advice was followed persistently the convention would not need to petition the Legislature to repeal the law or raise money to file a suit. The railroad corporations would be so affected they would in self-defense lobby to have the separate car law repealed. On the other hand, as long as the railroads can get Afro-American excursions they will always have plenty of money to fight all the suits brought against them. They will be aided in so doing by the same partisan public sentiment which passed the law. White men passed the law, and white judges and juries would pass upon the suits against the law, and render judgment in line with their prejudices and in deference to the greater financial power.

The appeal to the white man's pocket has ever been more effectual than all the appeals ever made to his conscience. Nothing, absolutely nothing, is to be gained by a further sacrifice of manhood and self-respect. By the right exercise of his power as the industrial factor of the South, the Afro-American can demand and secure his rights, the punishment of lynchers, and a fair trial for accused rapists.

Of the many inhuman outrages of this present year, the only case where the proposed lynching did *not* occur, was where the men armed themselves in Jacksonville, Fla., and Paducah, Ky., and prevented it. The only times an Afro-American who was assaulted got away has been when he had a gun and used it in self-defense.

The lesson this teaches and which every Afro-American should ponder well, is that a Winchester rifle should have a place of honor in every black home, and it should be used for that protection which the law refuses to give. When the white man who is always the aggressor knows he runs at great risk of biting the dust every time his Afro-American victim does, he will have greater respect for Afro-American life. The more the Afro-American yields and cringes and begs, the more he has to do so, the more he is insulted, outraged and lynched.

The assertion has been substantiated throughout these pages that the press contains unreliable and doctored reports of lynchings, and one of the most necessary things for the race to do is to get these facts before the public. The people must know before they can act, and there is no educator to compare with the press.

The Afro-American papers are the only ones which will print the truth, and they lack means to employ agents and detectives to get at the facts. The race must rally a mighty host to the support of their journals, and thus enable them to do much in the way of investigation.

A lynching occurred at Port Jarvis, N.Y., the first week in June. A white and colored man were implicated in the assault upon a white girl. It was charged that the white man paid the colored boy to make the assault, which he did on the public highway in broad day time, and was lynched. This, too was done by "parties unknown." The white man in the case still lives. He was imprisoned and promises to fight the case on trial. At the preliminary examination, it developed that he had been a suitor of the girl's. She had repulsed and refused him, yet had given him money, and he had sent threatening letters demanding more.

The day before this examination she was so wrought up, she left home and wandered miles away. When found she said she did so because she was afraid of the man's testimony. Why should she be afraid of the prisoner? Why should she yield to his demands for money if not to prevent him exposing something he knew? It seems explainable only on the hypothesis that a *liaison* existed between the colored boy and the girl, and the white man knew of it. The press is singularly silent. Has it a motive? We owe it to ourselves to find out.

The story comes from Larned, Kansas, Oct. 1st, that a young white lady held at bay until daylight, without alarming any one in the house, "a burly Negro" who entered her room and bed. The "burly Negro" was promptly lynched without investigation or examination of inconsistent stories.

A house was found burned down near Montgomery, Ala., in Monroe County, Oct. 13th, a few weeks ago; also the burned bodies of the owners and melted piles of gold and silver.

These discoveries led to the conclusion that the awful crime was not prompted by motives of robbery. The suggestion of the whites was that "brutal lust was the incentive, and as there are nearly 200 Negroes living within a radius of five miles of the place the conclusion was inevitable that some of them were the perpetrators."

Upon this "suggestion" probably made by the real criminal, the mob acted upon the "conclusion" and arrested ten Afro-Americans, four of whom, they tell the world, confessed to the deed of murdering Richard L. Johnson and outraging his daughter, Jeanette. These four men, Berrell Jones, Moses Johnson, Jim and John Packer, none of them 25 years of age, upon this conclusion, were taken from jail, hanged, shot, and burned while yet alive the night of Oct. 12th. The same report says Mr. Johnson was on the best of terms with his Negro tenants.

The race thus outraged must find out the facts of this awful hurling of men into eternity on supposition, and give them to the indifferent and apathetic country. We feel this to be a garbled report, but how can we prove it?

Near Vicksburg, Miss., a murder was committed by a gang of burglars. Of course it must have been done by Negroes, and Negroes were arrested for it. It is believed that 2 men, Smith Tooley and John Adams belonged to a gang controlled by white men and, fearing exposure, on the night of July 4th, they were hanged in the Court House yard by those interested in silencing them. Robberies since committed in the same vicinity have been known to be by white men who had their faces blackened. We strongly believe in the innocence of these murdered men, but we have no proof. No other news goes out to the world save that which stamps us as a race of cutthroats, robbers and lustful wild beasts. So great is Southern hate and prejudice, they legally(?) hung poor little thirteen-year-old Mildrey Brown at Columbia, S.C., Oct. 7th, on the circumstantial evidence that she poisoned a white infant. If her guilt had been proven unmistakably, had she been white, Mildrey Brown would never have been hung.

The country would have been aroused and South Carolina disgraced forever for such a crime. The Afro-American himself did not know as he should have known as his journals should be in a position to have him know and act.

Nothing is more definitely settled than he must act for himself. I have shown how he may employ the boycott, emigration and the press, and I feel that by a combination of all these agencies can be effectually stamped out lynch law, that last relic of barbarism and slavery. "The gods help those who help themselves."

Further Reading

Decosta-Willis, Miriam, ed. *The Memphis Diary of Ida B. Wells: An Intimate Portrait of the Activist as a Young Woman*. Boston, MA: Beacon Press, 1995.

Rachel

A Play in Three Acts

1920 | SHORT PLAY

Characters

MRS MARY LOVING, *a widow.*
RACHEL LOVING, *her daughter.*
THOMAS LOVING, *her son.*
JIMMY MASON, *a small boy.*
JOHN STRONG, *a friend of the family.*
MRS. LANE, *a caller.*
ETHEL LANE, *her daughter.*
MARY,
NANCY,
EDITH,
JENNY,
LOUISE,
MARTHA,
little friends of Rachel.
TIME: The first decade of the Twentieth Century.
ACT I. October 16th.
ACT II. October 16th, four years later.
ACT III. One week later.

PLACE: A northern city. The living room in the small apartment of Mrs. Loving.

All of the characters are colored.

Rachel

Act I.

The scene is a room scrupulously neat and clean and plainly furnished. The walls are painted green, the woodwork, white. In the rear at the left an open doorway leads into a hall. Its bare, green wall and white baseboard are all that can be seen of it. It leads into the other rooms of the flat. In the centre of the rear wall of the room is a window. It is shut. The white sash curtains are pushed to right and left as far as they will go. The green shade is rolled up to the top. Through the window can be seen the red bricks of a house wall, and the tops of a couple of trees moving now and then in the wind. Within the window, and just below the sill, is a shelf upon which are a few potted plants. Between the window and the door is a bookcase full of books and above it, hanging on the wall, a simply framed, inexpensive copy of Millet's "The Reapers." There is a run extending from the right center to just below the right upper entrance. It is the vestibule of the flat. Its open doorway faces the left wall. In the right wall near the front is another window. Here the sash curtains are drawn together and the green shade is partly lowered. The window is up from the bottom. Through it street noises can be heard. In front of this window is an open, threaded sewing-machine. Some frail, white fabric is lying upon it. There is a chair in front of the machine and at the machine's left a small table covered with a green cloth. In the rear of the left wall and directly opposite to the entrance to the flat is the doorway leading into the kitchenette, dishes on shelves can be seen behind glass doors.

In the center of the left wall is a fireplace with a grate in it for coals; over this is a wooden mantel painted white. In the center is a small clock. A pair of vases, green and white in coloring, one at each end, complete the ornaments. Over the mantel is a narrow mirror; and over this, hanging on the wall, Burne-Jones' "Golden Stairs," simply framed. Against the front end of the left wall is an upright piano with a stool in front of it. On top is music neatly piled. Hanging over the piano is Raphael's "Sistine Madonna." In the center of the floor is a green rug, and in the center of this, a rectangular dining-room table, the long side facing front. It is covered with a green table-cloth. Three dining-room chairs are at the table, one at either end and one at the rear facing front. Above the table is a chandelier with four gas jets enclosed by glass globes. At the right front center is a rather shabby arm-chair upholstered in green.

Left and right from the spectator's point of view.

Before the sewing-machine, Mrs. Loving is seated. She looks worried. She is sewing swiftly and deftly by hand upon a waist in her lap. It is a white, beautiful thing and she sews upon it delicately. It is about half-past four in the afternoon; and the light is failing. Mrs. Loving pauses in her sewing, rises and lets the window-shade near her go up to the top. She pushes the sash-curtains to either side, the corner of a red brick house wall being thus brought into view. She shivers slightly, then pushes the window down at the bottom and lowers it a trifle from the top. The street noises become less distinct. She takes off her thimble, rubs her hands gently, puts the thimble on again, and looks at the clock on the mantel. She then reseats herself, with her chair as close to the window as possible and begins to sew. Presently a key is heard, and the door opens and shuts noisily. Rachel comes in from the vestibule. In her left arm she carries four or five books strapped together; under her right, a roll of music. Her hat is twisted over her left ear and her hair is falling in tendrils about her face. She brings into the room with her the spirit of abounding life, health, joy, youth. Mrs. Loving pauses, needle in hand, as soon as she hears the turning key and the banging door. There is a smile on her face. For a second, mother and daughter smile at each other. Then Rachel throws her books upon the dining-room table, places the music there also, but with care, and rushing to her mother, gives her a bear hug and a kiss.

RACHEL:	Ma dear! dear, old Ma dear!
MRS. LOVING:	Look out for the needle, Rachel! The waist! Oh, Rachel!
RACHEL	(*On her knees and shaking her finger directly under her mother's nose.*): You old, old fraud! You know you adore being hugged. I've a good mind . . .
MRS. LOVING:	Now, Rachel, please! Besides, I know your tricks. You think you can make me forget you are late. What time is it?
RACHEL	(*Looking at the clock and expressing surprise*): Jiminy Xmas! (*Whistles*) Why, it's five o'clock!
MRS. LOVING	(*Severely*): Well!
RACHEL	(*Plaintively*): Now, Ma dear, you're going to be horrid and cross.
MRS. LOVING	(*Laughing*): Really, Rachel, that expression is not particularly affecting, when your hat is over your ear, and you look, with your hair over your eyes, exactly like some one's pet poodle. I wonder if you are ever going to grow up and be ladylike.
RACHEL:	Oh! Ma dear, I hope not, not for the longest time, two long, long years at least. I just want to be silly

and irresponsible, and have you to love and torment, and, of course, Tom, too.

MRS. LOVING   (*Smiling down at Rachel*): You'll not make me forget, young lady. Why are you late, Rachel?

RACHEL: Well, Ma dear, I'm your pet poodle, and my hat is over my ear, and I'm late, for the loveliest reason.

MRS. LOVING: Don't be silly, Rachel.

RACHEL: That may sound silly, but it isn't. And please don't "Rachel" me so much. It was honestly one whole hour ago when I opened the front door down stairs. I know it was, because I heard the postman telling some one it was four o'clock. Well, I climbed the first flight, and was just starting up the second, when a little shrill voice said, "'Lo!" I raised my eyes, and there, half-way up the stairs, sitting in the middle of a step, was just the dearest, cutest, darlingest little brown baby boy you ever saw. "'Lo! yourself," I said. "What are you doing, and who are you anyway?" I'm Jimmy; and I'm widing to New York on the choo-choo tars." As he looked entirely too young to be going such a distance by himself, I asked him if I might go too. For a minute or two he considered the question and me very seriously, and then he said, "'Es," and made room for me on the step beside him. We've been everywhere: New York, Chicago, Boston, London, Paris and Oshkosh. I wish you could have heard him say that last place. I suggested going there just to hear him. Now, Ma dear, is it any wonder I am late? See all the places we have been in just one "teeny, weeny" hour? We would have been traveling yet, but his horrid, little mother came out and called him in. They're in the flat below, the new people. But before he went, Ma dear, he said the "cunningest" thing. He said, "Will you tum out an' p'ay wif me aden in two minutes?" I nearly hugged him to death, and it's a wonder my hat is on my head at all. Hats are such unimportant nuisances anyway!

MRS. LOVING: Unimportant nuisances! What ridiculous language you do use, Rachel! Well, I'm no prophet, but I see

	very distinctly what is going to happen. This little brown baby will be living here night and day. You're not happy unless some child is trailing along in your rear.
RACHEL	(*Mischievously*): Now, Ma dear, whose a hypocrite? What? I suppose you don't like children! I can tell you one thing, though, it won't be my fault if he isn't here night and day. Oh, I wish he were all mine, every bit of him! Ma dear, do you suppose that "she woman" he calls mother would let him come up here until it is time for him to go to bed? I'm going down there this minute. (*Rises impetuously*).
MRS. LOVING :	Rachel, for Heaven's sake! No! I am entirely too busy and tired today without being bothered with a child romping around in here.
RACHEL	(*Reluctantly and a trifle petulantly*): Very well, then. (*For several moments she watches her mother, who has begun to sew again. The displeasure vanishes from her face*). Ma dear!
MRS. LOVING:	Well.
RACHEL:	Is there anything wrong today?
MRS. LOVING:	I'm just tired, chickabiddy, that's all.
RACHEL	(*Moves over to the table. Mechanically takes off her hat and coat and carries them out into the entryway of the flat. She returns and goes to the looking glass over the fireplace and tucks in the tendrils of her hair in rather a preoccupied manner. The electric doorbell rings. She returns to the speaking tube in the vestibule. Her voice is heard answering*): Yes!—Yes!—No, I'm not Mrs. Loving. She's here, yes! What? Oh! come right up! (*Appearing in the doorway*). Ma dear, it's some man, who is coming for Mrs. Strong's waist.
MRS. LOVING	(*Pausing and looking at Rachel*): It is probably her son. She said she would send for it this afternoon. (*Rachel disappears. A door is heard opening and closing. There is the sound of a man's voice. Rachel ushers in Mr. John Strong.*)
STRONG	(*Bowing pleasantly to Mrs. Loving*): Mrs. Loving? (*Mrs. Loving bows, puts down her sewing, rises and*

goes toward Strong). My name is Strong. My mother asked me to come by and get her waist this afternoon. She hoped it would be finished.

MRS. LOVING: Yes, Mr. Strong, it is all ready. If you'll sit down a minute, I'll wrap it up for you. (*She goes into hallway leading to other rooms in flat*).

RACHEL (*Manifestly ill at ease at being left alone with a stranger; attempting, however, to be the polite hostess*): Do sit down, Mr. Strong. (*They both sit*).

RACHEL (*Nervously after a pause*): It's a very pleasant day, isn't it, Mr. Strong?

STRONG: Yes, very. (*He leans back composedly, his hat on his knee, the faintest expression of amusement in his eyes*).

RACHEL (*After a pause*): It's quite a climb up to our flat, don't you think?

STRONG: Why, no! It didn't strike me so. I'm not old enough yet to mind stairs.

RACHEL (*Nervously*): Oh! I didn't mean that you are old! Anyone can see you are quite young, that is, of course, not too young, but,—(*Strong laughs quietly*). There! I don't blame you for laughing. I'm always clumsy just like that.

MRS. LOVING (*Calling from the other room*): Rachel, bring me a needle and the sixty cotton, please.

RACHEL: All right, Ma dear! (*Rummages for the cotton in the machine drawer, and upsets several spools upon the floor. To Strong*): You see! I can't even get a spool of cotton without spilling things all over the floor. (*Strong smiles, Rachel picks up the spools and finally gets the cotton and needle*). Excuse me! (*Goes out door leading to other rooms. Strong left to himself, looks around casually. The "Golden Stairs" interests him and the "Sistine Madonna."*)

RACHEL (*Reenters, evidently continuing her function of hostess*): We were talking about the climb to our flat, weren't we? You see, when you're poor, you have to live in a top flat. There is always a compensation, though; we have bully—I mean nice air, better light, a lovely view, and nobody "thud-thudding" up and down over our heads night and day. The people below have our "thud-thudding," and it must be something *awful*, especially when Tom and I play "Ivanhoe" and have a tournament up here. We're entirely too old, but we still play. Ma dear rather dreads the climb up three flights, so Tom and I do all the errands. We don't mind climbing the stairs, particularly when we go up two or three at a time,—that is—Tom still does. I can't, Ma dear stopped me. (*Sighs*). I've got to grow up it seems.

STRONG (*Evidently amused*): It is rather hard being a girl, isn't it?

RACHEL: Oh, no! It's not hard at all. That's the trouble; they won't let me be a girl. I'd love to be.

MRS. LOVING (*Reentering with parcel. She smiles*): My chatterbox, I see, is entertaining you, Mr. Strong. I'm sorry to have kept you waiting, but I forgot, I found, to sew the ruching in the neck. I hope everything is satisfactory. If it isn't, I'll be glad to make any changes.

STRONG (*Who has risen upon her entrance*): Thank you, Mrs. Loving, I'm sure everything is all right. (*He takes the package and bows to her and Rachel. He moves towards the vestibule, Mrs. Loving following him. She passes through the doorway first. Before leaving, Strong turns for a second and looks back quietly at Rachel. He goes out too. Rachel returns to the mirror, looks at her face for a second, and then begins to touch and pat her hair lightly and delicately here and there. Mrs. Loving returns*).

RACHEL (*Still at the glass*): He was rather nice, wasn't he, Ma dear?—for a man? (*Laughs*). I guess my reason's a vain one,—he let me do all the talking. (*Pauses*). Strong? Strong? Ma dear, is his mother the little woman with the sad, black eyes?

MRS. LOVING (*Resuming her sewing sitting before the machine*). Yes. I was rather curious, I confess, to see this son of hers. The whole time I'm fitting her she talks of nothing else. She worships him. (*Pauses*). It's rather a sad case, I believe. She is a widow. Her husband was a doctor and left her a little money. She came up from the South to educate this boy. Both of them worked hard and the boy got through college. Three months he hunted for work that a college man might expect to get. You see he had the tremendous handicap of being colored. As the two of them had to live, one day, without her knowing it, he hired himself out as a waiter. He has been one now for two years. He is evidently goodness itself to his mother.

RACHEL

(*Slowly and thoughtfully*): Just because he is colored! (*Pauses*). We sing a song at school, I believe, about "The land of the free and the home of the brave." What an amusing nation it is.

MRS. LOVING

(*Watching Rachel anxiously*): Come, Rachel, you haven't time for "amusing nations." Remember, you haven't practised any this afternoon. And put your books away; don't leave them on the table. You didn't practise any this morning either, did you?

RACHEL:

No, Ma dear,—didn't wake up in time. (*Goes to the table and in an abstracted manner puts books on the bookcase; returns to the table; picks up the roll of sheet music she has brought home with her; brightens; impulsively*). Ma dear, just listen to this lullaby. It's the sweetest thing. I was so "daffy" over it, one of the girls at school lent it to me. (*She rushes to the piano with the music and plays the accompaniment through softly and then sings, still softly and with great expression, Jessie Gaynor's "Slumber Boat"*)—

Baby's boat's the silver moon;
 Sailing in the sky,
Sailing o'er the sea of sleep,
 While the clouds float by.

Sail, baby, sail,
 Out upon that sea,
Only don't forget to sail
 Back again to me.

Baby's fishing for a dream,
 Fishing near and far,
His line a silver moonbeam is,

His bait a silver star.

Sail, baby, sail, etc.

Listen, Ma dear, right here. Isn't it lovely? (*Plays and sings very softly and slowly*):

"Only don't forget to sail
Back again to me."

(*Pauses; in hushed tones*) Ma dear, it's so beautiful—it—it hurts.

MRS. LOVING	(*Quietly*): Yes, dear, it is pretty.
RACHEL	(*For several minutes watches her mother's profile from the piano stool. Her expression is rather wistful*): Ma dear!
MRS. LOVING:	Yes, Rachel.
RACHEL:	What's the matter?
MRS. LOVING	(*Without turning*): Matter! What do you mean?
RACHEL:	I don't know. I just feel something is not quite right with you.
MRS. LOVING:	I'm only tired—that's all.
RACHEL:	Perhaps. But—(*Watches her mother a moment or two longer; shakes her head; turns back to the piano. She is thoughtful; looks at her hands in her lap*). Ma dear, wouldn't it be nice if we could keep all the babies in the world—always little babies? Then they'd be always little, and cunning, and lovable; and they could never grow up, then, and—and—be bad. I'm so sorry for mothers, whose little babies—grow up—and—and—are bad.
MRS. LOVING	(*Startled; controlling herself, looks at Rachel anxiously, perplexedly. Rachel's eyes are still on her hands. Attempting a light tone*): Come, Rachel, what experience have you had with mothers whose babies have grown up to be bad? You—you talk like an old, old woman.
RACHEL	(*Without raising her eyes, quietly*): I know I'm not old; but, just the same I know that is true. (*Softly*) And I'm so sorry for the mothers.

MRS. LOVING   (*With a forced laugh*): Well, Miss Methuselah, how do you happen to know all this? Mothers whose babies grow up to be bad don't, as a rule, parade their faults before the world.

RACHEL: That's just it—that's how you know. They don't talk at all.

MRS. LOVING   (*Involuntarily*): Oh! (*Ceases to sew; looks at Rachel sharply; she is plainly worried. There is a long silence. Presently Rachel raises her eyes to Raphael's "Madonna" over the piano. Her expression becomes rapt; then, very softly, her eyes still on the picture, she plays and sings Nevin's "Mighty Lak A Rose"*)—

> Sweetest li'l feller,
> > Ev'rybody knows;
> Dunno what to call him,
> > But he mighty lak' a rose!
> Lookin' at his Mammy
> > W 'id eyes so shiny blue,
> Mek' you think that heav'n
> > Is comin' clost ter you !
>
> W'en his dar a sleepin'
> > In his li'l place
> Think I see de angels
> > Lookin' thro' de lace:
> W'en de dark is fallin',
>
> > W'en de shadders creep,
> Den dey comes on tip-toe,
> > Ter kiss him in his sleep.
>
> Sweetest li'l feller, etc.

(*With head still raised, after she has finished, she closes her eyes. Half to herself and slowly*) I think the loveliest thing of all the lovely things in this world is just (*almost in a whisper*) being a mother!

MRS. LOVING   (*Turns and laughs*): Well, of all the startling children, Rachel! I am getting to feel, when you're around as though I'm shut up with dynamite. What next? (*Rachel rises, goes slowly to her mother, and kneels down beside her. She does not touch her mother*).

	Why so serious, chickabiddy?
RACHEL	(*Slowly and quietly*): It is not kind to laugh at sacred things. When you laughed, it was as though you laughed at God!
MRS. LOVING	(*Startled*): Rachel!
RACHEL	(*Still quietly*): It's true. It was the best in me that said that—it was God! (*Pauses*). And, Ma dear, if I believed that I should grow up and not be a mother, I'd pray to die now. I've thought about it a lot, Ma dear, and once I dreamed, and a voice said to me—oh! it was so real—"Rachel, you are to be a mother to little children." Wasn't that beautiful? Ever since I have known how Mary felt at the "Annunciation." (*Almost in a whisper*) God spoke to me through some one, and I believe. And it has explained so much to me. I know now why I just can't resist any child. I have to love it—it calls me—it draws me. I want to take care of it, wash it, dress it, live for it. I want the feel of its little warm body against me, its breath on my neck, its hands against my face. (*Pauses thoughtfully for a few moments*). Ma dear, here's something I don't understand: I love the little black and brown babies best of all. There is something about them that—that—clutches at my heart. Why—why—should they be—oh!—pathetic? I don't understand. It's dim. More than the other babies, I feel that I must protect them. They're in danger, but from what? I don't know. I've tried so hard to understand, but I can't. (*Her face radiant and beautiful*). Ma dear, I think their white teeth and the clear whites of their big black eyes and their dimples everywhere—are—are (*Breaks off*). And, Ma dear, because I love them best, I pray God every night to give me, when I grow up, little black and brown babies—to protect and guard. (*Wistfully*). Now, Ma dear, don't you see why you must never laugh at me again? Dear, dear, Ma dear? (*Buries her head in her mother's lap and sobs*).
MRS. LOVING	(*For a few seconds, sits as though dazed, and then instinctively begins to caress the head in her lap. To her-*

self) And I suppose my experience is every mother's. Sooner or later—of a sudden she finds her own child a stranger to her. (*To Rachel, very tenderly*) Poor little girl ! Poor little chickabiddy!

RACHEL

(*Raising her head*): Why do you say, "Poor little girl," like that? I don't understand. Why, Ma dear, I never saw tears in your eyes before. Is it—is it—because you know the things I do not understand? Oh! it is that.

MRS. LOVING

(*Simply*): Yes, Rachel, and I cannot save you.

RACHEL:

Ma dear, you frighten me. Save me from *what*?

MRS. LOVING:

Just life, my little chickabiddy!

RACHEL:

Is life so terrible? I had found it mostly beautiful. How can life be terrible, when the world is full of little children?

MRS. LOVING

(*Very sadly*): Oh, Rachel! Rachel!

RACHEL:

Ma dear, what have I said?

MRS. LOVING

(*Forcing a smile*): Why, the truth, of course, Rachel. Life is not terrible when there are little children—and you—and Tom—and a roof over our heads—and work—and food—and clothes—and sleep at night. (*Pauses*). Rachel, I am not myself today. I'm tired. Forget what I've said. Come, chickabiddy, wipe your eyes and smile. That's only an imitation smile, but it's better than none. Jump up now, and light the lamp for me, will you? Tom's late, isn't he? I shall want you to go, too, for the rolls and pie for supper.

RACHEL

(*Rises rather wearily and goes into the kitchenette. While she is out of the room Mrs. Loving does not move. She sits staring in front of her. The room for some time has been growing dark. Mrs. Loving can just be seen when Rachel reenters with the lamp. She places it on the small table near her mother, adjusts it, so the light falls on her mother's work, and then lowers the window shades at the windows. She still droops. Mrs. Loving, while Rachel is in the room, is industrious. Rachel puts on her hat and coat listlessly. She does not look in the glass*). Where is the money, Ma dear? I'm ready.

MRS. LOVING:	Before you go, Rachel, just give a look at the meat and see if it is cooking all right, will you, dearie?
RACHEL	(*Goes out into the kitchenette and presently returns*): It's all right, Ma dear.
MRS. LOVING	(*While Rachel is out of the room, she takes her pocket-book out of the machine-drawer, opens it, takes out money and gives it to Rachel upon her return*): A dozen brown rolls. Rachel. Be sure they're brown! And, I guess,—an apple pie. As you and Tom never seem to get enough apple pie, get the largest she has. And here is a quarter. Get some candy—any kind you like, Chickabiddy. Let's have a party tonight, I feel extravagant. Why, Rachel! why are you crying?
RACHEL:	Nothing, dear Ma dear. I'll be all right when I get in the air. Goodbye! (*Rushes out of the flat. Mrs. Loving sits idle. Presently the outer door of the flat opens and shuts with a bang, and Tom appears. Mrs. Loving begins to work as soon as she hears the banging door*).
TOM:	'Lo, Ma! Where's Sis,—out? The door's off the latch. (*Kisses his mother and hangs hat in entryway*).
MRS. LOVING	(*Greeting him with the same beautiful smile with which she greeted Rachel*): Rachel just went after the rolls and pie. She'll be back in a few minutes. You're late, Tommy.
TOM:	No, Ma—you forget—it's pay day. (*With decided shyness and awkwardness he hands her his wages*). Here, Ma!
MRS. LOVING	(*Proudly counting it*): But, Tommy, this is every bit of it. You'll need some.
TOM:	Not yet! (*Constrainedly*) I only wish—. Say, Ma, I hate to see you work so hard. (*Fiercely*) Some day— some day—. (*Breaks off*).
MRS. LOVING:	Son, I'm as proud as though you had given me a million dollars.
TOM	(*Emphatically*): I may some day,—you see. (*Abruptly changing the subject*): Gee! Ma, I'm hungry. What's for dinner? Smell's good.

MRS. LOVING:	Lamb and dumplings and rice.
TOM:	Gee! I'm glad I'm living—and a pie too?
MRS. LOVING:	Apple pie, Tommy.
TOM:	Say, Ma, don't wake me up. And shall " muzzer's" own little boy set the table?
MRS. LOVING:	Thank you, Son.
TOM	(*Folds the green cloth, hangs it over the back of the arm-chair, gets white table-cloth from kitchenette and sets the table. The whole time he is whistling blithely a popular air. He lights one of the gas jets over the table*): Ma!
MRS. LOVING:	Yes, Son.
TOM:	I made "squad" today, I'm—quarterback. Five other fellows tried to make it. We'll all have to buy new hats, now.
MRS. LOVING	(*With surprise*) : Buy new hats ! Why?
TOM	(*Makes a ridiculous gesture to show that his head and hers are both swelling*): Honest, Ma, I had to carry my hat in my hand tonight,—couldn't even get it to perch aloft.
MRS. LOVING	(*Smiling*): Well, I for one, Son, am not going to say anything to make you more conceited.
TOM:	You don't have to say anything. Why, Ma, ever since I told you, you can almost look down your own back your head is so high. What? (*Mrs. Loving laughs. The outer door of the flat opens and shuts. Rachel's voice is heard*).
RACHEL	(*Without*): My! that was a "drefful" climb, wasn't it? Ma, I've got something here for you. (*Appears in the doorway carrying packages and leading a little boy by the hand. The little fellow is shy but smiling*). Hello, Tommy! Here, take these things for me. This is Jimmy. Isn't he a dear? Come, Jimmy. (*Tom carries the packages into the kitchenette. Rachel leads Jimmy to Mrs. Loving*). Ma dear, this is my brown baby. I'm going to take him right down stairs again. His mother is as sweet as can be, and let me bring him up just to see you. Jimmy, this is Ma dear. (*Mrs. Loving turns expectantly to see the child. Standing before her, he raises his face to hers with an engaging*

	smile. Suddenly, without word or warning, her body stiffens; her hands grip her sewing convulsively; her eyes stare. She makes no sound).
RACHEL	(*Frightened*): Ma dear! What is the matter? Tom! Quick! (*Tom reenters and goes to them*).
MRS. LOVING	(*Controlling herself with an effort and breathing hard*): Nothing, dears, nothing. I must be—I am—nervous tonight. (*With a forced smile*) How do-you-do, Jimmy? Now, Rachel—perhaps—don't you think—you had better take him back to his mother? Goodnight, Jimmy! (*Eyes the child in a fascinated way the whole time he is in the room. Rachel, very much perturbed, takes the child out*). Tom, open that window, please! There! That's better! (*Still breathing deeply*). What a fool I am!
TOM	(*Patting his mother awkwardly on the back*): You're all pegged out, that's the trouble—working entirely too hard. Can't you stop for the night and go to bed right after supper?
MRS. LOVING:	I'll see, Tommy dear. Now, I must look after the supper.
TOM:	Huh! Well, I guess not. How old do you think Rachel and I are anyway? I see; you think we'll break some of this be-au-ti-ful Hav-i-land china, we bought at the "Five and Ten Cent Store." (*To Rachel who has just reentered wearing a puzzled and worried expression. She is without hat and coat*). Say, Rachel, do you think you're old enough?
RACHEL:	Old enough for what, Tommy?
TOM:	To dish up the supper for Ma.
RACHEL	(*With attempted sprightliness*): Ma dear thinks nothing can go on in this little flat unless she does it. Let's show her a thing or two. (*They bring in the dinner. Mrs. Loving with trembling hands tries to sew. Tom and Rachel watch her covertly. Presently she gets up.*)
MRS. LOVING:	I'll be back in a minute, children. (*Goes out the door that leads to the other rooms of the flat. Tom and Rachel look at each other*).
RACHEL	(*In a low voice keeping her eyes on the door*): Why do

	you suppose she acted so strangely about Jimmy?
TOM:	Don't know—nervous, I guess,—worn out. I wish *(Breaks off)*.
RACHEL	*(Slowly)*: It may be that; but she hasn't been herself this afternoon. I wonder—. Look out! Here she comes!
TOM	*(In a whisper)*: Liven her up. *(Rachel nods. Mrs. Loving reenters. Both rush to her and lead her to her place at the right end of the table. She smiles and tries to appear cheerful. They sit down, Tom opposite Mrs. Loving and Rachel at the side facing front. Mrs Loving asks grace. Her voice trembles. She helps the children bountifully, herself sparingly. Every once in a while she stops eating and stares blankly into her plate; then, re-membering where she is suddenly, looks around with a start and goes on eating. Tom and Rachel appear not to notice her)*.
TOM:	Ma's "some" cook, isn't she?
RACHEL:	Is she! Delmonico's isn't in it.
TOM	*(Presently)*: Say, Rachel, do you remember that Rey-nolds boy in the fourth year?
RACHEL:	Yes. You mean the one who is flat-nosed, freckled, and who squints and sneers?
TOM	*(Looking at Rachel admiringly)*: The same.
RACHEL	*(Vehemently)*: I hate him!
MRS. LOVING:	Rachel, you do use such violent language. Why hate him?
RACHEL:	I do—that's all.
TOM:	Ma, if you saw him just once, you'd understand. No one likes him. But, then, what can you expect? His father's in "quod" doing time for something, I don't know just what. One of the fellows says he has a real decent mother, though. She never mentions him in any way, shape or form, he says. Hard on her, isn't it? Bet I'd keep my head shut too;—you'd never get a yap out of me. *(Rachel looks up quickly at her mother; Mrs. Loving stiffens perceptibly, but keeps her eyes on her plate. Rachel catches Tom's eye; silently draws his attention to their mother; and shakes her head warningly at him)*.

TOM	(*Continuing hastily and clumsily*): Well, anyway, he called me "Nigger" today. If his face isn't black, his eye is.
RACHEL:	Good! Oh! Why did you let the other one go?
TOM	(*Grinning*): I knew he said things behind my back; but today he was hopping mad, because I made quarterback. He didn't!
RACHEL:	Oh, Tommy! How lovely! Ma dear, did you hear that? (*Chants*) Our Tommy's on the team! Our Tommy's on the team!
TOM	(*Trying not to appear pleased*): Ma dear, what did I say about er—er "capital" enlargements?
MRS. LOVING	(*Smiling*): You're right, Son.
TOM:	I hope you got that "capital," Rachel. How's that for Latin knowledge? Eh?
RACHEL:	I don't think much of your knowledge, Tommy dear; but (*continuing to chant*) Our Tommy's on the team! Our Tommy's on the team! Our—(*Breaks off*). I've a good mind to kiss you.
TOM	(*Threateningly*): Don't you dare.
RACHEL	(*Rising and going toward him*): I will! I will! I will!
TOM	(*Rising, too, and dodging her*): No, you don't, young lady. (*A tremendous tussle and scuffle ensues*).
MRS. LOVING	(*Laughing*): For Heaven's sake! children, do stop playing and eat your supper. (*They nod brightly at each other behind her back and return smiling to the table*).
RACHEL	(*Sticking out her tongue at Tom*): I will!
TOM	(*Mimicking her*): You won't!
MRS. LOVING:	Children! (*They eat for a time in silence*).
RACHEL:	Ma dear, have you noticed Mary Shaw doesn't come here much these days?
MRS. LOVING:	Why, that's so, she doesn't. Have you two quarreled?
RACHEL:	No, Ma dear. (*Uncomfortably*). I—think I know the reason—but I don't like to say, unless I'm certain.
TOM:	Well, I know. I've seen her lately with those two girls who have just come from the South. Twice she bowed stiffly, and the last time made believe she

	didn't see me.
RACHEL:	Then you think—? Oh! I was afraid it was that.
TOM	(*Bitterly*): Yes—we're "niggers"—that's why.
MRS. LOVING	(*Slowly and sadly*): Rachel, that's one of the things I can't save you from. I worried considerably about Mary, at first—you do take your friendships so seriously. I knew exactly how it would end. (*Pauses*). And then I saw that if Mary Shaw didn't teach you the lesson—some one else would. They don't want you, dearies, when you and they grow up. You may have everything in your favor—but they don't dare to like you.
RACHEL:	I know all that is generally true—but I had hoped that Mary—(*Breaks off*).
TOM:	Well, I guess we can still go on living even if people don't speak to us. I'll never bow to her again—that's certain.
MRS. LOVING:	But, Son, that wouldn't be polite, if she bowed to you first.
TOM:	Can't help it. I guess I can be blind, too.
MRS. LOVING	(*Wearily*): Well—perhaps you are right—I don't know. It's the way I feel about it too—but—but I wish my son always to be a gentleman.
TOM:	If being a gentleman means not being a man—I don't wish to be one.
RACHEL:	Oh! well, perhaps we're wrong about Mary—I hope we are. (*Sighs*). Anyway, let's forget it. Tommy guess what I've got. (*Rises, goes out into entryway swiftly, and returns holding up a small bag*). Ma dear treated. Guess!
TOM:	Ma, you're a thoroughbred. Well, let's see—it's—a dozen dill pickles?
RACHEL:	Oh ! stop fooling.
TOM:	I'm not. Tripe?
RACHEL:	Silly!
TOM:	Hog's jowl?
RACHEL:	Ugh! Give it up—quarter-back.
TOM:	Pig's feet?
RACHEL	(*In pretended disgust*): Oh! Ma dear—send him from the table. It's CANDY!

TOM:	Candy? Funny, I never thought of that! And I was just about to say some nice, delicious chitlings. Candy! Well! Well! (*Rachel disdainfully carries the candy to her mother, returns to her own seat with the bag and helps herself. She ignores Tom*).
TOM	(*In an aggrieved voice*): You see, Ma, how she treats me. (*In affected tones*) I have a good mind, young lady to punish you, er—er corporeally speaking. Tut! Tut! I have a mind to master thee—I mean—you. Methinks that if I should advance upon you, apply, perchance, two or three digits to your glossy locks and extract—aha!—say, a strand—you would no more defy me. (*He starts to rise*).
MRS. LOVING	(*Quickly and sharply*): Rachel! give Tom the candy and stop playing. (*Rachel obeys. They eat in silence. The old depression returns. When the candy is all gone, Rachel pushes her chair back, and is just about to rise, when her mother, who is very evidently nerving herself for something, stops her*). Just a moment, Rachel. (*Pauses, continuing slowly and very seriously*). Tom and Rachel! I have been trying to make up my mind for some time whether a certain thing is my duty or not. Today—I have decided it is. You are old enough, now,—and I see you ought to be told. Do you know what day this is? (*Both Tom and Rachel have been watching their mother intently*). It's the sixteenth of October. Does that mean anything to either of you?
TOM and RACHEL (*Wonderingly*): No.	
MRS. LOVING	(*Looking at both of them thoughtfully, half to herself*): No—I don't know why it should. (*Slowly*) Ten years ago—today—your father and your half-brother died.
TOM:	I do remember, now, that you told us it was in October.
RACHEL	(*With a sigh*): That explains—today.
MRS. LOVING:	Yes, Rachel. (*Pauses*). Do you know—how they—died?
TOM and RACHEL: Why, no.	
MRS. LOVING:	Did it ever strike you as strange—that they—

	died—the same day?
TOM:	Well, yes.
RACHEL:	We often wondered, Tom and I; but—but somehow we never quite dared to ask you. You—you—always refused to talk about them, you know, Ma dear.
MRS. LOVING:	Did you think—that—perhaps—the reason I—I—wouldn't talk about them—was—because, because—I was ashamed—of them? (*Tom and Rachel look uncomfortable*).
RACHEL:	Well, Ma dear—we—we—did—wonder.
MRS. LOVING	(*Questioningly*): And you thought?
RACHEL	(*Haltingly*): W-e-l-l
MRS. LOVING	(*Sharply*): Yes?
TOM:	Oh! come, now, Rachel, you know we haven't bothered about it at all. Why should we? We've been happy.
MRS. LOVING:	But when you have thought—you've been ashamed? (*Intensely*) Have you?
TOM:	Now, Ma, aren't you making a lot out of nothing?
MRS. LOVING	(*Slowly*): No. (*Half to herself*) You evade—both—of you. You *have* been ashamed. And I never dreamed until today you *could* take it this way. How blind—how almost criminally blind, I have been.
RACHEL	(*Tremulously*): Oh! Ma dear, don't! (*Tom and Rachel watch their mother anxiously and uncomfortably. Mrs. Loving is very evidently nerving herself for something*).
MRS. LOVING	(*Very slowly, with restrained emotion*): Tom—and Rachel!
TOM:	Ma!
RACHEL:	Ma dear! (*A tense, breathless pause*).
MRS. LOVING	(*Bracing herself*) : They—they—were lynched!!
TOM and RACHEL	(*In a whisper*): Lynched!
MRS. LOVING	(*Slowly, laboring under strong but restrained emotion*): Yes by Christian people—in a Christian land. We found out afterwards they were all church members in good standing the best people. (*A silence*). Your father was a man among men. He was a fanatic. He was a Saint!

TOM	(*Breathing with difficulty*): Ma—can you—will you—tell us—about it?
MRS. LOVING:	I believe it to be my duty. (*A silence*). When I married your father I was a widow. My little George was seven years old. From the very beginning he worshiped your father. He followed him around—just like a little dog. All children were like that with him. I myself have never seen anybody like him. "Big" seems to fit him better than any other word. He was big-bodied—big-souled. His loves were big and his hates. You can imagine, then, how the wrongs of the Negro—ate into his soul. (*Pauses*). He was utterly fearless. (*A silence*). He edited and owned, for several years, a small negro paper. In it he said a great many daring things. I used to plead with him to be more careful. I was always afraid for him. For a long time, nothing happened—he was too important to the community. And then—one night—ten years ago—a mob made up of the respectable people in the town lynched an innocent black man and what was worse—they knew him to be innocent. A white man was guilty. I never saw your father so wrought up over anything: he couldn't eat; he couldn't sleep; he brooded night and day over it. And then—realizing fully the great risk he was running, although I begged him not to—and all his friends also—he deliberately and calmly went to work and published a most terrific denunciation of that mob. The old prophets in the Bible were not more terrible than he. A day or two later, he received an anonymous letter, very evidently from an educated man, calling upon him to retract his words in the next issue. If he refused his life was threatened. The next week's issue contained an arraignment as frightful, if not more so, than the previous one. Each word was white-hot, searing. That night, some dozen masked men came to our house.
RACHEL	(*Moaning*): Oh, Ma dear ! Ma dear!
MRS. LOVING	(*Too absorbed to hear*): We were not asleep—your

father and I. They broke down the front door and made their way to our bedroom. Your father kissed me—and took up his revolver. It was always loaded. They broke down the door. (*A silence. She continues slowly and quietly*) I tried to shut my eyes—I could not. Four masked men fell—they did not move any more—after a little. (*Pauses*). Your father was finally overpowered and dragged out. In the hall—my little seventeen-year-old George tried to rescue him. Your father begged him not to interfere. He paid no attention. It ended in their dragging them both out. (*Pauses*). My little George—was—a man! (*Controls herself with an effort*). He never made an outcry. His last words to me were: "Ma, I am glad to go with Father. " I could only nod to him. (*Pauses*). While they were dragging them down the steps, I crept into the room where you were. You were both asleep. Rachel, I remember, was smiling. I knelt down by you—and covered my ears with my hands—and waited. I could not pray—I couldn't for a long time—afterwards. (*A silence*). It was very still when I finally uncovered my ears. The only sounds were the faint rustle of leaves and the "tap-tapping of the twig of a tree" against the window. I hear it still—sometimes in my dreams. It was the tree-where they were. (*A silence*). While I had knelt there waiting—I had made up my mind what to do. I dressed myself and then I woke you both up and dressed you. (*Pauses*). We set forth. It was a black, still night. Alternately dragging you along and carrying you—I walked five miles to the house of some friends. They took us in, and we remained there until I had seen my dead laid comfortably at rest. They lent me money to come North—I couldn't bring you up—in the South. (*A silence*). Always remember this: There never lived anywhere—or at any time—any two whiter or more beautiful souls. God gave me one for a husband and one for a son and I am proud. (*Brokenly*) You—must—be—proud—too. (*A long silence. Mrs. Loving bows her head in her hands. Tom controls himself with an effort. Rachel creeps softly to her mother, kneels beside her and lifts the hem of her dress to her lips. She does not dare touch her. She adores her with her eyes).*

MRS. LOVING
(*Presently raising her head and glancing at the clock*): Tom, it's time, now, for you to go to work. Rachel and I will finish up here.

TOM
(*Still laboring under great emotion goes out into the entryway and comes back and stands in the doorway with his cap. He twirls it around and around nervously*): I want you to know, Ma, before I go—how—how proud I am. Why, I didn't believe two people could be like that—and live. And then to find out that one—was your own father—and one—your own brother.—It's wonderful! I'm—not much yet, Ma, but—I've—I've just got to be something now. (*Breaks off*). (*His face becomes distorted with passion and hatred*). When I think—when I think—of those devils with white skins—living somewhere today—living and happy—I—see—red!—goodbye! (*Rushes out, the door bangs*).

MRS. LOVING
(*Half to herself*): I was afraid—of just that. I wonder—if I did the wise thing—after all.

RACHEL
(*With a gesture infinitely tender, puts her arms around her mother*): Yes, Ma dear, you did. And, hereafter, Tom and I share and share alike with you. To think, Ma dear, of ten years of this—all alone. It's wicked! (*A short silence*).

MRS. LOVING:
And, Rachel, about that dear, little boy, Jimmy.

RACHEL:
Now, Ma dear, tell me tomorrow. You've stood enough for one day.

MRS. LOVING:
No, it's better over and done with—all at once. If I had seen that dear child suddenly any other day than this—I might have borne it better. When he lifted his little face to me—and smiled—for a moment—I thought it was the end—of all things. Rachel, he is the image of my boy—my George!

RACHEL:
Ma dear!

MRS. LOVING:
And, Rachel—it will hurt—to see him again.

RACHEL:
I understand, Ma dear. (*A silence. Suddenly*) Ma

	dear, I am beginning to see—to understand—so much. (*Slowly and thoughtfully*) Ten years ago, all things being equal, Jimmy might have been—George? Isn't that so?
MRS. LOVING:	Why—yes, if I understand you.
RACHEL:	I guess that doesn't sound very clear. It's only getting clear to me, little by little. Do you mind my thinking out loud to you?
MRS. LOVING:	No, chickabiddy.
RACHEL:	If Jimmy went South now—and grew up—he might be—a George?
MRS. LOVING:	Yes.
RACHEL:	Then, the South is full of tens, hundreds, thousands of little boys, who, one day may be—and some of them with certainty—Georges?
MRS. LOVING:	Yes, Rachel.
RACHEL:	And the little babies, the dear, little, helpless babies, being born today—now—and those who will be, tomorrow, and all the tomorrows to come—have that sooner or later to look forward to? They will laugh and play and sing and be happy and grow up, perhaps, and be ambitious—just for *that*?
MRS. LOVING:	Yes, Rachel.
RACHEL:	Then, everywhere, everywhere, throughout the South, there are hundreds of dark mothers who live in fear, terrible, suffocating fear, whose rest by night is broken, and whose joy by day in their babies on their hearts is three parts—pain. Oh, I know this is true—for this is the way I should feel, if I were little Jimmy's mother. How horrible! Why—it would be more merciful—to strangle the little things at birth. And so this nation—this white Christian nation—has deliberately set its curse upon the most beautiful—the most holy thing in life—motherhood! Why—it—makes—you doubt—God!
MRS. LOVING:	Oh, hush! little girl. Hush!
RACHEL	(*Suddenly with a great cry*): Why, Ma dear, you know. You were a mother, George's mother. So,

this is what it means. Oh, Ma dear! Ma dear! (*Faints in her mother's arms*).

Act II.

TIME: *October sixteenth, four years later; seven o'clock in the morning.*
SCENE: *The same room. There have been very evident improvements made. The room is not so bare; it is cosier. On the shelf, before each window, are potted red geraniums. At the windows are green denim drapery curtains covering fresh white dotted Swiss inner curtains. At each doorway are green denim portieres. On the wall between the kitchenette and the entrance to the outer rooms of the flat, a new picture is hanging, Millet's "The Man With the Hoe." Hanging against the side of the run that faces front is Watts's "Hope." There is another easy-chair at the left front. The table in the center is covered with a white table-cloth. A small asparagus fern is in the middle of this. When the curtain rises there is the clatter of dishes in the kitchenette. Presently Rachel enters with dishes and silver in her hands. She is clad in a bungalow apron. She is noticeably all of four years older. She frowns as she sets the table. There is a set expression about the mouth. A child's voice is heard from the rooms within.*

JIMMY	(*Still unseen*): Ma Rachel!
RACHEL	(*Pauses and smiles*): What is it, Jimmy boy?
JIMMY	(*Appearing in rear doorway, half-dressed, breathless, and tremendously excited over something. Rushes toward Rachel*): Three guesses! Three guesses! Ma Rachel!
RACHEL	(*Her whole face softening*): Well, let's see—maybe there is a circus in town.
JIMMY:	No siree! (*In a sing-song*) You're not right! You're not right!
RACHEL:	Well, maybe Ma Loving's going to take you somewhere.
JIMMY:	No! (*Vigorously shaking his head*) It's—
RACHEL	(*Interrupting quickly*) You said I could have three guesses, honey. I've only had two.
JIMMY:	I thought you had three. How many are three?
RACHEL	(*Counting on her fingers*): One! Two! Three! I've only had one! two!—See? Perhaps Uncle Tom is going to give you some candy.

JIMMY	(*Dancing up and down*): No! No! No! (*Catches his breath*) I leaned over the bathtub, way over, and got hold of the chain with the button on the end, and dropped it into the little round place in the bottom. And then I runned lots and lots of water in the tub and climbed over and fell in splash! just like a big stone; (*Loudly*) and took a bath all by myself alone.
RACHEL	(*Laughing and hugging him*): All by yourself, honey? You ran the water, too, boy, not "runned" it. What I want to know is, where was Ma Loving all this time?
JIMMY:	I stole in "creepy-creep" and looked at Ma Loving and she was awful fast asleep. (*Proudly*) Ma Rachel, I'm a "nawful," big boy now, aren't I? I are almost a man, aren't I?
RACHEL:	Oh! Boy, I'm getting tired of correcting you—"I am almost a man, am I not?" Jimmy, boy, what will Ma Rachel do, if you grow up? Why, I won't have a little boy any more! Honey, you mustn't grow up, do you hear? You mustn't.
JIMMY:	Oh, yes, I must; and you'll have me just the same, Ma Rachel. I'm going to be a policeman and make lots of money for you and Ma Loving and Uncle Tom, and I'm going to buy you some trains and fire-engines, and little, cunning ponies, and some rabbits, and some great 'normous banks full of money—lots of it. And then, we are going to live in a great, big castle and eat lots of ice cream, all the time, and drink lots and lots of nice pink lemonade.
RACHEL:	What a generous Jimmy boy! (*Hugs him*). Before I give you "morning kiss," I must see how clean my boy is. (*Inspects teeth, ears and neck*). Jimmy, you're sweet and clean enough to eat. (*Kisses him; he tries to strangle her with hugs*). Now the hands. Oh! Jimmy, look at those nails! Oh! Jimmy! (*Jimmy wriggles and tries to get his hands away*). Honey, get my file off of my bureau and go to Ma Loving; she must be awake by this time. Why, honey, what's the matter with your feet?

JIMMY.	I don't know. I thought they looked kind of queer, myself. What's the matter with them?
RACHEL	(*Laughing*): You have your shoes on the wrong feet.
JIMMY	(*Bursts out laughing*): Isn't that most 'normously funny? I'm a case, aren't I—(*pauses thoughtfully*) I mean—am I not, Ma Rachel?
RACHEL:	Yes, honey, a great big case of molasses. Come, you must hurry now, and get dressed. You don't want to be late for school, you know.
JIMMY:	Ma Rachel! (*Shyly*) I—I have been making something for you all the morning—ever since I waked up. It's awful nice. It's—stoop down, Ma Rachel, please—a great, big (*puts both arms about her neck and gives her noisy kiss. Rachel kisses him in return, then pushes his head back. For a long moment they look at each other; and, then, laughing joyously, he makes believe he is a horse, and goes prancing out of the room. Rachel, with a softer, gentler expression, continues setting the table. Presently, Mrs. Loving, bent and worn-looking, appears in the doorway in the rear. She limps a trifle.*
MRS. LOVING:	Good morning, dearie. How's my little girl, this morning? (*Looks around the room*). Why, where's Tom? I was certain I heard him running the water in the tub, sometime ago. (*Limps into the room*).
RACHEL	(*Laughing*): Tom isn't up yet. Have you seen Jimmy?
MRS. LOVING:	Jimmy? No. I didn't know he was awake, even.
RACHEL	(*Going to her mother and kissing her*): Well! What do you think of that! I sent the young gentleman to you, a few minutes ago, for help with his nails. He is very much grown up this morning, so I suppose that explains why he didn't come to you. Yesterday, all day, you know, he was a puppy. No one knows what he will be by tomorrow. All of this, Ma dear, is preliminary to telling you that Jimmy boy has stolen a march on you, this morning.
MRS. LOVING:	Stolen a march! How?
RACHEL:	It appears that he took his bath all by himself and, as a result, he is so conceited, peacocks aren't in it

	with him.
MRS. LOVING:	I heard the water running and thought, of course, it was Tom. Why, the little rascal! I must go and see how he has left things. I was just about to wake him up.
RACHEL:	Rheumatism's not much better this morning, Ma dear. (*Confronting her mother*) Tell me the truth, now, did you or did you not try that liniment I bought you yesterday?
MRS. LOVING	(*Guiltily*): Well, Rachel, you see—it was this way, I was—I was so tired, last night,—I—I really forgot it.
RACHEL:	I thought as much. Shame on you!
MRS. LOVING:	As soon as I walk around a bit it will be all right. It always is. It's bad, when I first get up—that's all. I'll be spry enough in a few minutes. (*Limps to the door; pauses*) Rachel, I don't know why the thought should strike me, but how very strangely things turn out. If any one had told me four years ago that Jimmy would be living with us, I should have laughed at him. Then it hurt to see him; now it would hurt not to. (*Softly*) Rachel, sometimes—I wonder—if, perhaps, God—hasn't relented a little—and given me back my boy,—my George.
RACHEL:	The whole thing was strange, wasn't it?
MRS. LOVING:	Yes, God's ways are strange and often very beautiful; perhaps all would be beautiful—if we only understood.
RACHEL:	God's ways are certainly very mysterious. Why, of all the people in this apartment-house, should Jimmy's father and mother be the only two to take the smallpox, and the only two to die. It's queer!
MRS. LOVING:	It doesn't seem like two years ago, does it?
RACHEL:	Two years, Ma dear! Why it's three the third of January.
MRS. LOVING:	Are you sure, Rachel?
RACHEL	(*Gently*): I don't believe I could ever forget that, Ma dear.
MRS. LOVING:	No, I suppose not. That is one of the differences between youth and old age—youth attaches tre-

mendous importance to dates,—old age does not.

RACHEL (*Quickly*): Ma dear, don't talk like that. You're not old.

MRS. LOVING: Oh! yes, I am, dearie. It's sixty long years since I was born; and I am much older than that, much older.

RACHEL: Please, Ma dear, please!

MRS. LOVING (*Smiling*): Very well, dearie, I won't say it any more. (*A pause*). By the way,—how—does Tom strike you, these days?

RACHEL (*Avoiding her mother's eye*): The same old, bantering, cheerful Tom. Why?

MRS. LOVING: I know he's all that, dearie, but it isn't possible for him to be really cheerful. (*Pauses; goes on wistfully*) When you are little, we mothers can kiss away all the trouble, but when you grow up—and go out—into the world—and get hurt we are helpless. There is nothing we can do.

RACHEL: Don't worry about Tom, Ma dear, he's game. He doesn't show the white feather.

MRS. LOVING: Did you see him, when he came in, last night?

RACHEL: Yes.

MRS. LOVING: Had he had—any luck?

RACHEL: No. (*Firmly*) Ma dear, we may as well face it—it's hopeless, I'm afraid.

MRS. LOVING: I'm afraid—you are right. (*Shakes her head sadly*) Well, I'll go and see how Jimmy has left things and wake up Tom, if he isn't awake yet. It's the waking up in the mornings that's hard. (*Goes limping out rear door. Rachel frowns as she continues going back and forth between the kitchenette and the table. Presently Tom appears in the door at the rear. He watches Rachel several moments before he speaks or enters. Rachel looks grim enough*).

TOM (*Entering and smiling*): Good-morning, "Merry Sun-shine"! Have you, perhaps, been taking a—er—prolonged draught of that very delightful beverage—vinegar? (*Rachel, with a knife in her hand, looks up unsmiling. In pretended fright*) I take it all back, I'm sure. May I request, humbly, that before I press my chaste, morning salute upon your forbidding lips, that you—that you—that you—er—in some way rid yourself of that—er—knife? (*Bows as Rachel puts it down*). I thank you. (*He comes to her and tips her head back; gently*) What's the matter with my little Sis?

RACHEL (*Her face softening*): Tommy dear, don't mind me. I'm getting wicked, I guess. At present I feel just like—like curdled milk. Once upon a time, I used to have quite a nice disposition, didn't I, Tommy?

TOM (*Smiling*): Did you, indeed! I'm not going to flatter you. Well, brace yourself, old lady. Ready, One! Two! Three! Go! (*Kisses her, then puts his hands on either side of her face, and raising it, looks down into it*). You're a pretty, decent little sister, Sis, that's what T. Loving thinks about it; and he knows a thing or two. (*Abruptly looking around*) Has the paper come yet?

RACHEL: I haven't looked, it must have, though, by this time. (*Tom, hands in his pockets, goes into the vestibule. He whistles. The outer door opens and closes, and presently he saunters back, newspaper in hand. He lounges carelessly in the arm-chair and looks at Rachel*).

TOM: May T. Loving be of any service to you?

RACHEL : Service ! How?

TOM: May he run, say, any errands, set the table, cook the breakfast? Anything?

RACHEL (*Watching the lazy figure*): You look like working.

TOM (*Grinning*): It's at least—polite—to offer.

RACHEL: You can't do anything; I don't trust you to do it right. You may just sit there, and read your paper—and try to behave yourself.

TOM (*In affectedly meek tones*): Thank you, ma'am. (*Opens the paper, but does not read. Jimmy presently enters riding around the table on a cane. Rachel peeps in from the kitchenette and smiles. Tom puts down his paper*). 'Lo! Big Fellow, what's this?

JIMMY (*Disgustedly*): How can I hear? I'm miles and miles away yet. (*Prances around and around the room; presently stops near Tom, attempting a gruff voice*) Good-morning !

TOM	(*Lowering his paper again*): Bless my stars! Who's this? Well, if it isn't Mr. Mason! How-do-you-do, Mr. Mason? That's a beautiful horse you have there. He limps a trifle in his left, hind, front foot, though.
JIMMY:	He doesn't!
TOM:	He does!
JIMMY	(*Fiercely*): He doesn't!
TOM	(*As fiercely*): I say he does!
MRS. LOVING	(*Appearing in the doorway in the rear*): For Heaven's sake! What is this? Good-morning, Tommy.
TOM	(*Rising and going toward his mother, Jimmy following astride of the cane in his rear*): Good-morning, Ma. (*Kisses her; lays his head on her shoulder and makes believe he is crying; in a high falsetto*) Ma! Jimmy says his horse doesn't limp in his hind, front right leg, and I say he does.
JIMMY	(*Throws his cane aside, rolls on the floor and kicks up his heels. He roars with laughter*): I think Uncle Tom is funnier than any clown in the "Kickus."
TOM	(*Raising his head and looking down at Jimmy; Rachel stands in the kitchenette doorway*): In the *what*, Jimmy?
JIMMY:	In the "kickus," of course.
TOM:	"Kickus"! "Kickus"! Oh, Lordy! (*Tom and Rachel shriek with laughter; Mrs. Loving looks amused; Jimmy, very much affronted, gets upon his feet again. Tom leans over and swings Jimmy high in the air*). Boy, you'll be the death of me yet. Circus, son! Circus!
JIMMY	(*From on high, soberly and with injured dignity*): Well, I thinks "Kickus" and circus are very much alike. Please put me down.
RACHEL	(*From the doorway*): We laugh, honey, because we love you so much.
JIMMY	(*Somewhat mollified, to Tom*): Is that so, Uncle Tom?
TOM:	Surest thing in the world! (*Severely*) Come, get down, young man. Don't you know you'll wear my arms out? Besides, there is something in my lower vest pocket, that's just dying to come to you. Get down, I say.

JIMMY	(*Laughing*): How can I get down? (*Wriggles around*).
TOM:	How should I know? Just get down, of course. (*Very suddenly puts Jimmy down on his feet. Jimmy tries to climb up over him*).
JIMMY:	Please sit down, Uncle Tom?
TOM	(*In feigned surprise*): Sit down! What for?
JIMMY	(*Pummeling him with his little fists, loudly*): Why, you said there was something for me in your pocket.
TOM	(*Sitting down*): So I did. How forgetful I am!
JIMMY	(*Finding a bright, shiny penny, shrieks*): Oh! Oh! Oh! (*Climbs up and kisses Tom noisily*).
TOM:	Why, Jimmy! You embarrass me. My! My!
JIMMY:	What is 'barrass?
TOM:	You make me blush.
JIMMY:	What's that?
MRS. LOVING:	Come, come, children! Rachel has the breakfast on the table. (*Tom sits in Jimmy's place and Jimmy tries to drag him out*).
TOM:	What's the matter, now?
JIMMY:	You're in *my* place.
TOM:	Well, can't you sit in mine?
JIMMY	(*Wistfully*): I wants to sit by my Ma Rachel.
TOM:	Well, so do I.
RACHEL:	Tom, stop teasing Jimmy. Honey, don't you let him bother you; ask him please prettily.
JIMMY:	Please prettily, Uncle Tom.
TOM:	Oh! well then. (*Gets up and takes his own place. They sit as they did in Act I. only Jimmy sits between Tom, at the end, and Rachel*).
JIMMY	(*Loudly*): Oh, goody! goody! goody! We've got sausages.
MRS. LOVING:	Sh!
JIMMY	(*Silenced for a few moments; Rachel ties a big napkin around his neck, and prepares his breakfast. He breaks forth again suddenly and excitedly*): Uncle Tom!
TOM:	Sir?
JIMMY:	I took a bath this morning, all by myself alone, in the bath-tub, and I ranned, no (*Doubtfully*) I runned, I think—the water all in it, and got in it all

by myself; and Ma Loving thought it was you; but it was *me.*

TOM (*In feignedly severe tones*): See here, young man, this won't do. Don't you know I'm the only one who is allowed to do that here? It's a perfect waste of water—that's what it is.

JIMMY (*Undaunted*): Oh! no, you're not the only one, 'cause Ma Loving and Ma Rachel and me—alls takes baths every single morning. So, there!

TOM: You 'barrass me. (*Jimmy opens his mouth to ask a question; Tom quickly*) Young gentleman, your mouth is open. Close it, sir; close it.

MRS. LOVING: Tom, you're as big a child exactly as Jimmy.

TOM (*Bowing to right and left*): You compliment me. I thank you, I am sure. (*They finish in silence.*)

JIMMY (*Sighing with contentment*): I'm through, Ma Rachel.

MRS. LOVING: Jimmy, you're a big boy, now, aren't you? (*Jimmy nods his head vigorously and looks proud.*) I wonder if you're big enough to wash your own hands, this morning?

JIMMY (*Shrilly*): Yes, ma'am.

MRS. LOVING: Well, if they're beautifully clean, I'll give you another penny.

JIMMY (*Excitedly to Rachel*): Please untie my napkin, Ma Rachel! (*Rachel does so.*) "Excoose" me, please.

MRS. LOVING and RACHEL : Certainly. (*Jimmy climbs down and rushes out at the rear doorway.*)

MRS. LOVING (*Solemnly and slowly; breaking the silence*): Rachel, do you know what day this is?

RACHEL (*Looking at her plate; slowly*): Yes, Ma dear.

MRS. LOVING: Tom.

TOM (*Grimly and slowly*): Yes, Ma.
(*A silence.*)

MRS. LOVING (*Impressively*): We must never—as long—as we live—forget this day.

RACHEL: No, Ma dear.

TOM: No, Ma.
(*Another silence*)

TOM (*Slowly; as though thinking aloud*): I hear people talk about God's justice—and I wonder. There, are you, Ma. There isn't a sacrifice—that you haven't made. You're still working your fingers to the bone—sewing just so all of us may keep on living. Rachel is a graduate in Domestic Science; she was high in her class; most of the girls below her in rank have positions in the schools. I'm an electrical engineer—and I've tried steadily for several months—to practice my profession. It seems our educations aren't of much use to us: we aren't allowed to make good—because our skins are dark. (*Pauses*) And, in the South today, there are white men—(*Controls himself*). They have everything; they're well-dressed, well-fed, well-housed; they're prosperous in business; they're important politically; they're pillars in the church. I know all this is true—I've inquired. Their children (our ages, some of them) are growing up around them; and they are having a square deal handed out to them—college, position, wealth, and best of all, freedom, without galling restrictions, to work out their own salvations. With ability, they may become—anything; and all this will be true of their children's children after them. (*A pause*). Look at us—and look at them. We are destined to failure—they, to success. Their children shall grow up in hope; ours, in despair. Our hands are clean;—theirs are red with blood—red with the blood of a noble man—and a boy. They're nothing but low, cowardly, bestial murderers. The scum of the earth shall succeed.—God's justice, I suppose.

MRS. LOVING (*Rising and going to Tom; brokenly*): Tom, promise me—one thing.

TOM (*Rises gently*): What is it, Ma?

MRS. LOVING: That—you'll try—not to lose faith—in God. I've been where you are now—and it's black. Tom, we don't understand God's ways. My son, I know, now—He is beautiful. Tom, won't you try to believe, again?

TOM (*Slowly, but not convincingly*): I'll try, Ma.

MRS. LOVING	(*Sighs*): Each one, I suppose, has to work out his own salvation. (*After a pause*) Rachel, if you'll get Jimmy ready, I'll take him to school. I've got to go down town shopping for a customer, this morning. (*Rachel rises and goes out the rear doorway; Mrs. Loving, limping very slightly now, follows. She turns and looks back yearningly at Tom, who has seated himself again, and is staring unseeingly at his plate. She goes out. Tom sits without moving until he hears Mrs. Loving's voice within and Rachel's faintly; then he gets the paper, sits in the arm-chair and pretends to read*).
MRS. LOVING	(*From within*): A yard, you say, Rachel? You're sure that will be enough. Oh! you've measured it. Anything else?—What?—Oh! all right. I'll be back by one o'clock, anyway. Good-bye. (*Enters with Jimmy. Both are dressed for the street. Tom looks up brightly at Jimmy*).
TOM:	Hello! Big Fellow, where are you taking *my* mother, I'd like to know? This is a pretty kettle of fish.
JIMMY	(*Laughing*): Aren't you funny, Uncle Tom! Why, I'm not taking her anywhere. She's taking me. (*Importantly*) I'm going to school.
TOM:	Big Fellow, come here. (*Jimmy comes with a rush*). Now, where's that penny I gave you? No, I don't want to see it. All right. Did Ma Loving give you another? (*Vigorous noddings of the head from Jimmy*). I wish you to promise me solemnly—Now, listen! Here, don't wriggle so! not to buy—Listen! too many pints of ice-cream with my penny. Understand?
JIMMY	(*Very seriously*): Yes, Uncle Tom, cross my "tummy"! I promise.
TOM:	Well, then, you may go. I guess that will be all for the present. (*Jimmy loiters around looking up wistfully into his face*). Well?
JIMMY:	Haven't you—aren't you—isn't you—forgetting something?
TOM	(*Grabbing at his pockets*): Bless my stars! what-now?
JIMMY:	If you could kind of lean over this way. (*Tom*

leans forward). No, not that way. (*Tom leans toward the side away from Jimmy*). No, this way, this way! (*Laughs and pummels him with his little fists*). This way!

TOM   (*Leaning toward Jimmy*): Well, why didn't you say so, at first?

JIMMY   (*Puts his arms around Tom's neck and kisses him*): Good-bye, dear old Uncle Tom. (*Tom catches him and hugs him hard*). I likes to be hugged like that— I can taste—sau-sa-ges.

TOM: You 'barrass me, son. Here, Ma, take your boy. Now remember all I told you, Jimmy.

JIMMY: I 'members.

MRS. LOVING: God bless you, Tom. Good luck.

JIMMY   (*To Tom*): God bless you, Uncle Tom. Good luck!

TOM   (*Much affected, but with restraint, rising*): Thank you—Good-bye. (*Mrs. Loving and Jimmy go out through the vestibule. Tom lights a cigarette and tries to read the paper. He soon sinks into a brown study. Presently Rachel enters humming. Tom relights his cigarette; and Rachel proceeds to clear the table. In the midst of this, the bell rings three distinct times*).

RACHEL and TOM: John!

TOM: I wonder what's up—It's rather early for him.—I'll go. (*Rises leisurely and goes out into the vestibule. The outer door opens and shuts. Men's voices are heard. Tom and John Strong enter. During the ensuing conversation Rachel finishes clearing the table, takes the fern off, puts on the green table-cloth, places a doily carefully in the centre, and replaces the fern. She apparently pays no attention to the conversation between her brother and Strong. After she has finished, she goes to the kitchenette. The rattle of dishes can be heard now and then*).

RACHEL   (*Brightly*): Well, stranger, how does it happen you're out so early in the morning?

STRONG: I hadn't seen any of you for a week, and I thought I'd come by, on my way to work, and find out how things are going. There is no need of asking how you are, Rachel. And the mother and the boy?

RACHEL:	Ma dear's rheumatism still holds on.—Jimmy's fine.
STRONG :	I'm sorry to hear that your mother is not well. There isn't a remedy going that my mother doesn't know about. I'll get her advice and let you know. (*Turning to Tom*) Well, Tom, how goes it? (*Strong and Tom sit*).
TOM	(*Smiling grimly*): There's plenty of "go," but no "git there." (*There is a pause*).
STRONG:	I was hoping for better news.
TOM:	If I remember rightly, not so many years ago, you tried—and failed. Then, a colored man had hardly a ghost of a show;—now he hasn't even the ghost of a ghost. (*Rachel has finished and goes into the kitchenette*).
STRONG:	That's true enough. (*A pause*). What are you going to do?
TOM	(*Slowly*): I'll do this little "going act" of mine the rest of the week; (*pauses*) and then, I'll do anything I can get to do. If necessary, I suppose, I can be a "White-wing."
STRONG:	Tom, I came—(*Breaks off; continuing slowly*) Six years ago, I found I was up against a stone wall—your experience, you see, to the letter. I couldn't let my mother starve, so I became a waiter. (*Pauses*). I studied waiting; I made a science of it, an art. In a comparatively short time, I'm a head-waiter and I'm up against another stonewall. I've reached my limit. I'm thirty-two now, and I'll die a head-waiter. (*A pause*). College friends, so-called, and acquaintances used to come into the restaurant. One or two at first—attempted to commiserate with me. They didn't do it again. I waited upon them—I did my best. Many of them tipped me. (*Pauses and smiles grimly*). I can remember my first tip, still. They come in yet; many of them are already powers, not only in this city, but in the country. Some of them make a personal request that I wait upon them. I am an artist, now, in my proper sphere. They tip me well, extremely well—

the larger the tip, the more pleased they are with me. Because of me, in their own eyes, they're philanthropists. Amusing, isn't it? I can stand their attitude now. My philosophy—learned hard, is to make the best of everything you can, and go on. At best, life isn't so very long. You're wondering why I'm telling you all this. I wish you to see things exactly as they are. There are many disadvantages and some advantages in being a waiter. My mother can live comfortably; I am able, even, to see that she gets some of the luxuries. Tom, it's this way— I can always get you a job as a waiter; I'll teach you the art. If you care to begin the end of the week— all right. And remember this, as long as I keep my job—this offer holds good.

TOM: I—I—(*Breaks off*) Thank you. (*A pause; then smiling wryly*) I guess it's safe enough to say, you'll see me at the end of the week. John you're—(*Breaking off again. A silence interrupted presently by the sound of much vigorous rapping on the outer door of the flat. Rachel appears and crosses over to the vestibule*). Hear the racket! My kiddies gently begging for admittance. It's about twenty minutes of nine, isn't it? (*Tom nods*). I thought so. (*Goes into the entryway; presently reappears with a group of six little girls ranging in age from five to about nine. All are fighting to be close to her; and all are talking at once. There is one exception: the smallest tot is self-possessed and self-sufficient. She carries a red geranium in her hand and gives it her full attention*).

LITTLE MARY: It's my turn to get "Morning kiss" first, this morning, Miss Rachel. You kissed Louise first yesterday. You said you'd kiss us "alphebettically." (*Ending in a shriek*). *You* promised! (*Rachel kisses Mary, who subsides*).

LITTLE NANCY   (*Imperiously*): Now, me. (*Rachel kisses her, and then amid shrieks, recriminations, pulling of hair, jostling, etc., she kisses the rest. The small tot is still oblivious to everything that is going on*).

RACHEL   (*Laughing*): *You* children will pull me limb from limb; and then I'll be all dead; and you'll be sorry—see, if you aren't. (*They fall back immediately. Tom and John watch in amused silence. Rachel loses all self-consciousness, and seems to bloom in the children's midst*). Edith! come here this minute, and let me tie your hair ribbon again. Nancy, I'm ashamed of you, I saw you trying to pull it off. (*Nancy looks abashed but mischievous*). Louise, you look as sweet as sweet, this morning; and Jenny, where did you get the pretty, pretty dress?

LITTLE JENNY   (*Snuffling, but proud*): My mother made it. (*Pauses with more snuffles*). My mother says I have a very bad cold. (*There is a brief silence interrupted by the small tot with the geranium*).

LITTLE MARTHA (*In a sweet, little voice*): I—have—a—pitty—'ittle flower.

RACHEL: Honey, it's beautiful. Don't you want "Morning kiss" too?

LITTLE MARTHA: Yes, I do.

RACHEL: Come, honey. (*Rachel kisses her*). Are you going to give the pretty flower to Jenny's teacher: (*Vigorous shakings of the head in denial*). Is it for—mother? (*More shakings of the head*). Is it for—let's see—Daddy? (*More shakings of the head*). I give up. To whom are you going to give the pretty flower, honey?

LITTLE MARTHA (*Shyly*): "Oo."

RACHEL: You, darling!

LITTLE MARTHA: Muzzer and I picked it—for "oo." Here 't is. (*Puts her finger in her mouth, and gives it shyly*).

RACHEL: Well, I'm going to pay you with three big kisses. One! Two! Three!

LITTLE MARTHA: I can count, One! Two! Free! Tan't I? I am going to school soon; and I wants to put the flower in your hair.

RACHEL   (*Kneels*): All right, baby. (*Little Martha fumbles and Rachel helps her*).

LITTLE MARTHA (*Dreamily*): Miss Rachel, the 'ittle flower loves you. It told me so. It said it wanted to lie in your hair. It is going to tell you a pitty 'ittle secret. You listen

	awful hard—and you'll hear. I wish I were a fairy and had a little wand, I'd turn everything into flowers. Wouldn't that be nice, Miss Rachel?
RACHEL:	Lovely, honey!
LITTLE JENNY	(*Snuffling loudly*): If I were a fairy and had a wand, I'd turn you, Miss Rachel, into a queen—and then I'd always be near you and see that you were happy.
RACHEL:	Honey, how beautiful!
LITTLE LOUISE:	I'd make my mother happy—if I were a fairy. She cries all the time. My father can't get anything to do.
LITTLE NANCY:	If I were a fairy, I'd turn a boy in my school into a spider. I hate him.
RACHEL:	Honey, why?
LITTLE NANCY:	I'll tell you sometime—I hate him.
LITTLE EDITH:	Where's Jimmy, Miss Rachel?
RACHEL:	He went long ago; and chickies, you'll have to clear out, all of you, now, or you'll be late. Shoo! Shoo! (*She drives them out prettily before her. They laugh merrily. They all go into the vestibule*).
TOM	(*Slowly*): Does it ever strike you—how pathetic and tragic a thing—a little colored child is?
STRONG:	Yes.
TOM:	Today, we colored men and women, everywhere— are up against it. Every year, we are having a harder time of it. In the South, they make it as impossible as they can for us to get an education. We're hemmed in on all sides. Our one safeguard— the ballot—in most states, is taken away already, or is being taken away. Economically, in a few lines, we have a slight show—but at what a cost! In the North, they make a pretence of liberality: they give us the ballot and a good education, and then— snuff us out. Each year, the problem just to live, gets more difficult to solve. How about these children—if we're fools enough to have any? (**RACHEL re-enters. Her face is drawn and pale. She returns to the kitchenette**).
STRONG	(*Slowly, with emphasis*): That part—is damnable! (*A silence.*)

TOM	(*Suddenly looking at the clock*): It's later than I thought. I'll have to be pulling out of here now, if you don't mind. (*Raising his voice*) Rachel! (*Rachel still drawn and pale, appears in the doorway of the kitchenette. She is without her apron*). I've got to go now, Sis. I leave John in your hands.
STRONG:	I've got to go, myself, in a few minutes.
TOM:	Nonsense, man! Sit still. I'll begin to think, in a minute, you're afraid of the ladies.
STRONG:	I am.
TOM:	What! And not ashamed to acknowledge it?
STRONG:	No.
TOM:	You're lots wiser than I dreamed. So long! (*Gets hat out in the entry-way and returns; smiles wryly.*) "Morituri Salutamus". (*They nod at him—Rachel wistfully. He goes out. There is the sound of an opening and closing door. Rachel sits down. A rather uncomfortable silence, on the part of Rachel, ensues. Strong is imperturbable.*)
RACHEL	(*Nervously*): John!
STRONG:	Well?
RACHEL:	I—I listened.
STRONG:	Listened! To what?
RACHEL:	To you and Tom.
STRONG:	Well, what of it?
RACHEL:	I didn't think it was quite fair not to tell you. It—it seemed, well, like eavesdropping.
STRONG:	Don't worry about it. Nonsense!
RACHEL:	I'm glad—I want to thank you for what you did for Tom. He needs you, and will need you. You'll help him?
STRONG:	(*Thoughtfully*): Rachel, each one—has his own little battles. I'll do what I can. After all, an outsider doesn't help much.
RACHEL:	But friendship—just friendship—helps.
STRONG:	Yes. (*A silence*). Rachel, do you hear anything encouraging from the schools? Any hope for you yet?
RACHEL:	No, nor ever will be. I know that now. There's no more chance for me than there is for Tom,—or

than there was for you—or for any of us with dark skins. It's lucky for me that I love to keep house, and cook, and sew. I'll never get anything else. Ma dear's sewing, the little work Tom has been able to get, and the little sewing I sometimes get to do— keep us from the poorhouse. We live. According to your philosophy, I suppose, make the best of it—it might be worse.

STRONG (*Quietly*): *You* don't want to get morbid over these things, you know.

RACHEL (*Scornfully*): That's it. If you see things as they are, you're either pessimistic or morbid.

STRONG: In the long run, do you believe, that attitude of mind—will be—beneficial to you? I'm ten years older than you. I tried your way. I know. Mine is the only sane one. (*Goes over to her slowly; deliberately puts his hands on her hair, and tips her head back. He looks down into her face quietly without saying anything*).

RACHEL (*Nervous and startled*): Why, John, don't! (*He pays no attention, but continues to look down into her face*).

STRONG (*Half to himself*): Perhaps—if you had—a little more fun in your life, your point of view would be—more normal. I'll arrange it so I can take you to some theatre, one night, this week.

RACHEL (*Irritably*): *You* talk as though I were a—a jelly-fish. You'll take me, how do you know I'll go?

STRONG: You will.

RACHEL (*Sarcastically*): Indeed! (STRONG *makes no reply*). I wonder if you know how—how—maddening you are. Why, you talk as though my will counts for nothing. It's as if you're trying to master me. I think a domineering man is detestable.

STRONG (*Softly*): If he's, perhaps, *the* man?

RACHEL (*Hurriedly, as though she had not heard*): Besides, some of these theatres put you off by yourself as though you had leprosy. I'm not going.

STRONG (*Smiling at her*): *You* know I wouldn't ask you to go, under those circumstances. (*A silence*). Well, I must be going now. (*He takes her hand, and looks at it reverently. Rachel, at first resists; but he refuses to let go. When she finds it useless, she ceases to resist. He turns his head and smiles down into her face).* Rachel, I am coming back to see you, this evening.

RACHEL: I'm sure *we'll* all be very glad to see you.

STRONG (*Looking at her calmly*): I said—you. (*Very deliberately, he turns her hand palm upwards, leans over and kisses it; then he puts it back into her lap. He touches her cheek lightly*). Good-bye—little Rachel. (*Turns in the vestibule door and looks back, smiling*). Until tonight. (*He goes out. Rachel sits for some time without moving. She is lost in a beautiful daydream. Presently she sighs happily, and after looking furtively around the room, lifts the palm John has kissed to her lips. She laughs shyly and jumping up, begins to hum. She opens the window at the rear of the room and then commences to thread the sewing machine. She hums happily the whole time. A light rapping is heard at the outer door. Rachel listens. It stops, and begins again. There is something insistent, and yet hopeless in the sound. Rachel looking puzzled, goes out into the vestibule . . . The door closes. Rachel, a black woman, poorly dressed, and a little ugly, black child come in. There is the stoniness of despair in the woman's face. The child is thin, nervous, suspicious, frightened*).

MRS. LANE (*In a sharp, but toneless voice*): May I sit down? I'm tired.

RACHEL (*Puzzled, but gracious; draws up a chair for her*): Why, certainly.

MRS. LANE: No, you don't know me—never even heard of me— nor I of you. I was looking at the vacant flat on this floor—and saw your name—on your door,— "Loving!" It's a strange name to come across—in this world.—I thought, perhaps, you might give me some information. (*The child hides behind her mother and looks around at Rachel in a frightened way*).

RACHEL (*Smiling at the woman and child in a kindly manner*): I'll be glad to tell you anything, I am able Mrs.—

MRS. LANE: Lane. What I want to know is, how do they treat the colored children in the school I noticed around

	the corner? (*The child clutches at her mother's dress*).
RACHEL	(*Perplexed*): Very well—I'm sure.
MRS. LANE	(*Bluntly*): What reason have you for being sure?
RACHEL:	Why, the little boy I've adopted goes there; and he's very happy. All the children in this apartment-house go there too; and I know they're happy.
MRS. LANE:	Do you know how many colored children there are in the school?
RACHEL:	Why, I should guess around thirty.
MRS. LANE:	I see. (*Pauses*). What color is this little adopted boy of yours?
RACHEL	(*Gently*): Why—he's brown.
MRS. LANE:	Any black children there?
RACHEL	(*Nervously*): Why—yes.
MRS. LANE:	Do you mind if I send Ethel over by the piano to sit?
RACHEL:	N—no, certainly not. (*Places a chair by the piano and goes to the little girl holding out her hand. She smiles beautifully. The child gets farther behind her mother*).
MRS. LANE:	She won't go to you—she's afraid of everybody now but her father and me. Come Ethel. (*Mrs. Lane takes the little girl by the hand and leads her to the chair. In a gentler voice*) Sit down, Ethel. (*Ethel obeys. When her mother starts back again toward Rachel, she holds out her hands pitifully. She makes no sound*). I'm not going to leave you, Ethel. I'll be right over here. You can see me. (*The look of agony on the child's face, as her mother leaves her, makes Rachel shudder*). Do you mind if we sit over here by the sewing-machine? Thank you. (*They move their chairs*).
RACHEL	(*Looking at the little, pitiful figure watching its mother almost unblinkingly*): Does Ethel like apples, Mrs. Lane?
MRS. LANE:	Yes.
RACHEL:	Do you mind if I give her one?
MRS. LANE:	No. Thank you, very much.
RACHEL	(*Goes into the kitchenette and returns with a fringed napkin, a plate, and a big, red apple, cut into quarters.*

She goes to the little girl, who cowers away from her; very gently). Here, dear, little girl, is a beautiful apple for you. (*The gentle tones have no appeal for the trembling child before her*).

MRS. LANE (*Coming forward*): I'm sorry, but I'm afraid she won't take it from you. Ethel, the kind lady has given you an apple. Thank her nicely. Here! I'll spread the napkin for you, and put the plate in your lap. Thank the lady like a good little girl.

ETHEL (*Very low*): Thank you. (*They return to their seats. Ethel with difficulty holds the plate in her lap. During the rest of the interview between Rachel and her mother, she divides her attention between the apple on the plate and her mother's face. She makes no attempt to eat the apple, but holds the plate in her lap with a care that is painful to watch. Often, too, she looks over her shoulder fearfully. The conversation between Rachel and her mother is carried on in low tones*).

MRS. LANE: I've got to move—it's Ethel.

RACHEL: What is the matter with that child? It's—it's heartbreaking to see her.

MRS. LANE: I understand how you feel,—I don't feel anything, myself, any more. (*A pause*). My husband and I are poor, and we're ugly and we're black. Ethel looks like her father more than she does like me. We live in 55th Street—near the railroad. It's a poor neighborhood, but the rent's cheap. My husband is a porter in a store; and, to help out, I'm a caretaker. (*Pauses*). I don't know why I'm telling you all this. We had a nice little home—and the three of us were happy. Now we've got to move.

RACHEL: Move! Why?

MRS. LANE: It's Ethel. I put her in school this September. She stayed two weeks. (*Pointing to Ethel*) That's the result.

RACHEL (*In horror*): You mean—that just two weeks—in school—did that?

MRS. LANE: Yes. Ethel never had a sick day in her life—before. (*A brief pause*). I took her to the doctor at the end of the two weeks. He says she's a nervous wreck.

RACHEL: But what could they have done to her?

MRS. LANE (*Laughs grimly and mirthlessly*): I'll tell you what they did the first day. Ethel is naturally sensitive and backward. She's not assertive. The teacher saw that, and, after I had left, told her to sit in a seat in the rear of the class. She was alone there—in a corner. The children, immediately feeling there was something wrong with Ethel because of the teacher's attitude, turned and stared at her. When the teacher's back was turned they whispered about her, pointed their fingers at her and tittered. The teacher divided the class into two parts, divisions, I believe, they are called. She forgot all about Ethel, of course, until the last minute, and then, looking back, said sharply: "That little girl there may join this division," meaning the group of pupils standing around her. Ethel naturally moved slowly. The teacher called her sulky and told her to lose a part of her recess. When Ethel came up—the children drew away from her in every direction. She was left standing alone. The teacher then proceeded to give a lesson about kindness to animals. Funny, isn't it, *kindness* to *animals?* The children forgot Ethel in the excitement of talking about their pets. Presently, the teacher turned to Ethel and said disagreeably: "Have you a pet?" Ethel said, "Yes," very low. "Come, speak up, you sulky child, what is it?" Ethel said: "A blind puppy." They all laughed, the teacher and all. Strange, isn't it, but Ethel loves that puppy. She spoke up: "It's mean to laugh at a little blind puppy. I'm glad he's blind." This remark brought forth more laughter. "Why are you glad," the teacher asked curiously. Ethel refused to say. (*Pauses*). When I asked her why, do you know what she told me? "If he saw me, he might not love me any more." (*A pause*). Did I tell you that Ethel is only seven years old?

RACHEL (*Drawing her breath sharply*): Oh! I didn't believe any one could be as cruel as that—to a little child.

MRS. LANE: It isn't very pleasant, is it? When the teacher found out that Ethel wouldn't answer, she said severely: "Take your seat!" At recess, all the children went out. Ethel could hear them playing and laughing and shrieking. Even the teacher went too. She was made to sit there all alone—in that big room— because God made her ugly—and black. (*Pauses*). When the recess was half over the teacher came back. "You may go now," she said coldly. Ethel didn't stir. "Did you hear me?" "Yes'm." "Why don't you obey?" "I don't want to go out, please." "You don't, don't you, you stubborn child! Go immediately!" Ethel went. She stood by the school steps. No one spoke to her. The children near her moved away in every direction. They stopped playing, many of them, and watched her. They stared as only children can stare. Some began whispering about her. Presently one child came up and ran her hand roughly over Ethel's face. She looked at her hand and Ethel's face and ran screaming back to the others, "It won't come off! See!" Other children followed the first child's example. Then one boy spoke up loudly: "I know what she is, she's a nigger!" Many took up the cry. God or the devil interfered—the bell rang. The children filed in. One boy boldly called her "Nigger!" before the teacher. She said, "That isn't nice,"—but she smiled at the boy. Things went on about the same for the rest of the day. At the end of school, Ethel put on her hat and coat—the teacher made her hang them at a distance from the other pupils' wraps; and started for home. Quite a crowd escorted her. They called her "Nigger!" all the way. *I made* Ethel go the next day. I complained to the authorities. They treated me lightly. I was determined not to let them force my child out of school. At the end of two weeks—I had to take her out.

RACHEL   (*Brokenly*): Why,—I never—in all my life—heard anything—so—pitiful.

MRS. LANE: Did you ever go to school here?

RACHEL: Yes. I was made to feel my color—but I never had

an experience like that.

MRS. LANE: How many years ago were you in the graded schools?

RACHEL: Oh!—around ten.

MRS. LANE   (*Laughs grimly*): Ten years! Every year things are getting worse. Last year wasn't as bad as this. (*Pauses.*) So they treat the children all right in this school?

RACHEL: Yes! Yes! I know that.

MRS. LANE: I can't afford to take this flat here, but I'll take it. I'm going to have Ethel educated. Although, when you think of it,—it's all rather useless—this education! What are our children going to do with it, when they get it? We strive and save and sacrifice to educate them—and the whole time—down underneath, we know—they'll have no chance.

RACHEL   (*Sadly*): Yes, that's true, all right.—God seems to have forgotten us.

MRS. LANE: God! It's all a lie about God. I know.—This fall I sent Ethel to a white Sunday-school near us. She received the same treatment there she did in the day school. Her being there, nearly broke up the school. At the end, the superintendent called her to him and asked her if she didn't know of some nice colored Sunday-school. He told her she must feel out of place, and uncomfortable there. That's your Church of God!

RACHEL: Oh! how unspeakably brutal. (*Controls herself with an effort; after a pause*) Have you any other children?

MRS. LANE   (*Dryly*): Hardly! If I had another—I'd kill it. It's kinder. (*Rising presently*) Well, I must go, now. Thank you, for your information—and for listening. (*Suddenly*) You aren't married, are you?

RACHEL: No.

MRS. LANE: Don't marry—that's my advice. Come, Ethel. (*Ethel gets up and puts down the things in her lap, carefully upon her chair. She goes in a hurried, timid way to her mother and clutches her hand*). Say good-bye to the lady.

ETHEL   (*Faintly*): Good-bye.

RACHEL

(*Kneeling by the little girl—a beautiful smile on her face*) Dear little girl, won't you let me kiss you good-bye? I love little girls. (*The child hides behind her mother; continuing brokenly*) Oh!—no child—ever did—that to me—before!

MRS. LANE

(*In a gentler voice*): Perhaps, when we move in here, the first of the month, things may be better. Thank you, again. Good-morning! You don't belie your name. (*All three go into the vestibule. The outside door opens and closes. Rachel as though dazed and stricken returns. She sits in a chair, leans forward, and clasping her hands loosely between her knees, stares at the chair with the apple on it where Ethel Lane has sat. She does not move for some time. Then she gets up and goes to the window in the rear center and sits there. She breathes in the air deeply and then goes to the sewing-machine and begins to sew on something she is making. Presently her feet slow down on the pedals; she stops; and begins brooding again. After a short pause, she gets up and begins to pace up and down slowly, mechanically, her head bent forward. The sharp ringing of the electric bell breaks in upon this. Rachel starts and goes slowly into the vestibule. She is heard speaking dully through the tube*).

RACHEL:

Yes!—All right! Bring it up! (*Presently she returns with a long flower box. She opens it listlessly at the table. Within are six, beautiful crimson rosebuds with long stems. Rachel looks at the name on the card. She sinks down slowly on her knees and leans her head against the table. She sighs wearily*) Oh! John! John!—What are we to do?—I'm—I'm—afraid! Everywhere—it is the same thing. My mother! My little brother! Little, black, crushed Ethel! (*In a whisper*) Oh! God! You who I have been taught to believe are so good, so beautiful how could—You permit—these things? (*Pauses, raises her head and sees the rosebuds. Her face softens and grows beautiful, very sweetly*). Dear little rosebuds—you—make me think—of sleeping, curled up, happy babies. Dear beautiful, little rosebuds! (*Pauses; goes on thoughtful-*

ly to the rosebuds) When—I look—at you—I believe—God is beautiful. He who can make a little exquisite thing like this, and this can't be cruel. Oh! He can't mean me—to give up—love—and the hope of little children. (*There is the sound of a small hand knocking at the outer door. Rachel smiles*). My Jimmy! It must be twelve o'clock. (*Rises*). I didn't dream it was so late. (*Starts for the vestibule*). Oh! the world can't be so bad. I don't believe it. I won't. I must forget that little girl. My little Jimmy is happy—and today John—sent me beautiful rosebuds. Oh, there are lovely things, yet. (*Goes into the vestibule. A child's eager cry is heard; and Rachel carrying Jimmy in her arms comes in. He has both arms about her neck and is hugging her. With him in her arms, she sits down in the armchair at the right front*).

RACHEL: Well, honey, how was school today?

JIMMY (*Sobering a trifle*): All right, Ma Rachel. (*Suddenly sees the roses*) Oh ! look at the pretty flowers. Why, Ma Rachel, you forgot to put them in water. They'll die.

RACHEL: Well, so they will. Hop down this minute, and I'll put them in right away. (*Gathers up box and flowers and goes into the kitchenette. Jimmy climbs back into the chair. He looks thoughtful and serious. Rachel comes back with the buds in a tall, glass vase. She puts the fern on top of the piano, and places the vase in the centre of the table*). There, honey, that's better, isn't it? Aren't they lovely?

JIMMY: Yes, that's lots better. Now they won't die, will they? Rosebuds are just like little "chilyun," aren't they, Ma Rachel? If you are good to them, they'll grow up into lovely roses, won't they? And if you hurt them, they'll die. Ma Rachel do you think all peoples are kind to little rosebuds?

RACHEL (*Watching Jimmy shortly*): Why, of course. Who could hurt little children? Who would have the heart to do such a thing?

JIMMY: If you hurt them it would be lots kinder, wouldn't it, to kill them all at once, and not a little bit and a

	little bit?
RACHEL	(*Sharply*): Why, honey boy, why are you talking like this?
JIMMY:	Ma Rachel, what is a "Nigger"? (*Rachel recoils as though she had been struck*).
RACHEL:	Honey boy, why—why do you ask that?
JIMMY:	Some big boys called me that when I came out of school just now. They said: "Look at the little nigger!" And they laughed. One of them runned, no ranned, after me and threw stones; and they all kept calling "Nigger! Nigger! Nigger!" One stone struck me hard in the back, and it hurt awful bad; but I didn't cry, Ma Rachel. I wouldn't let them make me cry. The stone hurts me there, Ma Rachel; but what they called me hurts and hurts here. What is a "Nigger," Ma Rachel?
RACHEL	(*Controlling herself with a tremendous effort. At last she sweeps down upon him and hugs and kisses him*): Why, honey boy, those boys didn't mean anything. Silly, little, honey boy! They're rough, that's all. How *could* they mean anything?
JIMMY:	You're only saying that, Ma Rachel, so I won't be hurt. I know. It wouldn't ache here like it does—if they didn't mean something.
RACHEL	(*Abruptly*): Where's Mary, honey?
JIMMY:	She's in her flat. She came in just after I did.
RACHEL:	Well, honey, I'm going to give you two big cookies and two to take to Mary; and you may stay in there and play with her, till I get your lunch ready. Won't that be jolly?
JIMMY	(*Brightening a little*): Why, you never give me but one at a time. You'll give me two?—One? Two? (*Rachel gets the cookies and brings them to him. Jimmy climbs down from the chair*). Shoo! now, little honey boy. See how many laughs you can make for me, before I come after you. Hear? Have a good time, now. (*Jimmy starts for the door quickly; but he begins to slow down. His face gets long and serious again. Rachel watches him*).
RACHEL	(*Jumping at him*): Shoo! Shoo! Get out of here

quickly, little chicken. (*She follows him out. The outer door opens and shuts. Presently she returns. She looks old and worn and grey; calmly. Pauses*). First, it's little, black Ethel—and then's it's Jimmy. Tomorrow, it will be some other little child. The blight—sooner or later—strikes all. My little Jimmy, only seven years old poisoned! (*Through the open window comes the laughter of little children at play. Rachel, shuddering, covers her ears*). And once I said, centuries ago, it must have been: "How can life be so terrible, when there are little children in the world?" Terrible! Terrible! (*In a whisper, slowly*) That's the reason it is so terrible. (*The laughter reaches her again; this time she listens*). And, suddenly, some day, from out of the black, the blight shall descend, and shall still forever—the laughter on those little lips, and in those little hearts. (*Pauses thoughtfully*). And the loveliest thing—almost, that ever happened to me, that beautiful voice, in my dream, those beautiful words: "Rachel, you are to be the mother to little children. (*Pauses, then slowly and with dawning surprise*). Why, God, you were making a mock of me; you were laughing at me. I didn't believe God could laugh at our sufferings, but He can. We are accursed, accursed! We have nothing, absolutely nothing. (*Strong's rosebuds attract her attention. She goes over to them, puts her hand out as if to touch them, and then shakes her head, very sweetly*) No, little rosebuds, I may not touch you. Dear, little, baby rosebuds,—I am accursed. (*Gradually her whole form stiffens, she breathes deeply; at last slowly*). You God!—You terrible, laughing God! Listen! I swear—and may my soul be damned to all eternity if I do break this oath—I swear—that no child of mine shall ever lie upon my breast, for I will not have it rise up, in the terrible days that are to be—and call me cursed. (*A pause, very wistfully; questioningly*). Never to know the loveliest thing in all the world—the feel of a little head, the touch of little hands, the beautiful utter dependence—of a little child? (*With sudden frenzy*) You can laugh, Oh God! Well, so can I. (*Bursts into terrible, racking laughter*) But I can be kinder than You. (*Fiercely she snatches the rosebuds from the vase, grasps them roughly, tears each head from the stem, and grinds it under her feet. The vase goes over with a crash; the water drips unheeded over the table-cloth and floor*). If I kill, You Mighty God, I kill at once—I do not torture. (*Falls face downward on the floor. The laughter of the children shrills loudly through the window*).

Act III.

TIME: *Seven o'clock in the evening, one week later.*
PLACE: *The same room. There is a coal fire in the grate. The curtains are drawn. A lighted oil lamp with a dark green porcelain shade is in the center of the table. Mrs. Loving and Tom are sitting by the table, Mrs. Loving sewing, Tom reading. There is the sound of much laughter and the shrill screaming of a child from the bedrooms. Presently Jimmy clad in a flannelet sleeping suit, covering all of him but his head and hands, chases a pillow, which has come flying through the doorway at the rear. He struggles with it, finally gets it in his arms, and rushes as fast as he can through the doorway again. Rachel jumps at him with a cry. He drops the pillow and shrieks. There is a tussle for possession of it, and they disappear. The noise grows louder and merrier. Tom puts down his paper and grins. He looks at his mother.*

TOM:	Well, who's the giddy one in this family now?
MRS. LOVING	(*Shaking her head in a troubled manner*): I don't like it. It worries me. Rachel—(*Breaks off*).
TOM:	Have you found out, yet—
MRS. LOVING	(*Turning and looking toward the rear doorway, quickly interrupting him*): Sh! (*Rachel, laughing, her hair tumbling over her shoulders, comes rushing into the room. Jimmy is in close pursuit. He tries to catch her, but she dodges him. They are both breathless*).
MRS. LOVING	(*Deprecatingly*): Really, Rachel, Jimmy will be so excited he won't be able to sleep. It's after his bed-time, now. Don't you think you had better stop?
RACHEL:	All right, Ma dear. Come on, Jimmy; let's play "Old Folks" and sit by the fire. (*She begins to push the*

big armchair over to the fire. Tom jumps up, moves her aside, and pushes it himself. Jimmy renders assistance.)

TOM: Thanks, Big Fellow, you are "sure some" strong. I'll remember you when these people around here come for me to move pianos and such things around. Shake! (*They shake hands*).

JIMMY (*Proudly*): I am awful strong, am I not?

TOM: You "sure" are a Hercules. (*Hurriedly, as Jimmy's mouth and eyes open wide*). And see here! don't ask me tonight who that was. I'll tell you the first thing tomorrow morning. Hear? (*Returns to his chair and paper*).

RACHEL (*Sitting down*): Come on, honey boy, and sit in my lap.

JIMMY (*Doubtfully*): I thought we were going to play "Old Folks."

RACHEL: We are.

JIMMY: Do old folks sit in each other's laps?

RACHEL: Old folks do anything. Come on.

JIMMY (*Hesitatingly climbs into her lap, but presently snuggles down and sighs audibly from sheer content; Rachel starts to bind up her hair*): Ma Rachel, don't please! I like your hair like that. You're—you're pretty. I like to feel of it; and it smells like—like—oh!—like a barn.

RACHEL: My! how complimentary! I like that. Like a barn, indeed!

JIMMY: What's "complimentry"?

RACHEL: Oh! saying nice things about me. (*Pinching his cheek and laughing*) That my hair is like a barn, for instance.

JIMMY (*Stoutly*): Well, that is "complimentary." It smells like hay—like the hay in the barn you took me to, one day, last summer. 'Member?

RACHEL: Yes honey.

JIMMY (*After a brief pause*): Ma Rachel!

RACHEL: Well?

JIMMY: Tell me a story, please. It's "story-time," now, isn't it?

RACHEL: Well, let's see. (*They both look into the fire for a space;*

beginning softly) Once upon a time, there were two, dear, little boys, and they were all alone in the world. They lived with a cruel, old man and woman, who made them work hard, very hard—all day, and beat them when they did not move fast enough, and always, every night, before they went to bed. They slept in an attic on a rickety, narrow bed, that went screech! screech! whenever they moved. And, in summer, they nearly died with the heat up there, and in winter, with the cold. One wintry night, when they were both weeping very bitterly after a particularly hard beating, they suddenly heard a pleasant voice saying: "Why are you crying, little boys?" They looked up, and there, in the moonlight, by their bed, was the dearest, little old lady. She was dressed all in gray, from the peak of her little pointed hat to her little, buckled shoes. She held a black cane much taller than her little self. Her hair fell about her ears in tiny, grey corkscrew curls, and they bobbed about as she moved. Her eyes were black and bright as bright as—well, as that lovely, white light there. No, there! And her cheeks were as red as the apple I gave you yesterday. Do you remember?

JIMMY (*Dreamily*): Yes.

RACHEL: "Why are you crying, little boys ?" she asked again, in a lovely, low, little voice. "Because we are tired and sore and hungry and cold; and we are all alone in the world; and we don't know how to laugh any more. We should so like to laugh again." "Why, that's easy," she said, "it's just like this." And she laughed a little, joyous, musical laugh. "Try!" she commanded. They tried, but their laughing boxes were very rusty, and they made horrid sounds. "Well," she said, "I advise you to pack up, and go away, as soon as you can, to the Land of Laughter. You'll soon learn there, I can tell you." "Is there such a land?" they asked doubtfully. "To be sure there is," she answered the least bit sharply. "We never heard of it," they said. "Well, I'm sure there must be plenty of things you never heard about," she said just the "leastest" bit more sharply. "In a moment you'll be telling me flowers don't talk together, and the birds." "We never heard of such a thing," they said in surprise, their eyes like saucers. "There!" she said, bobbing her little curls. "What did I tell you? You have much to learn." "How do you get to the Land of Laughter?" they asked. "You go out of the eastern gate of the town, just as the sun is rising; and you take the highway there, and follow it; and if you go with it long enough, it will bring you to the very gates of the Land of Laughter. It's a long, long way from here; and it will take you many days." The words had scarcely left her mouth, when, lo! the little lady disappeared, and where she had stood was the white square of moonlight— nothing else. And without more ado these two little boys put their arms around each other and fell fast asleep. And in the grey, just before daybreak, they awoke and dressed; and, putting on their ragged caps and mittens, for it was a wintry day, they stole out of the house and made for the eastern gate. And just as they reached it, and passed through, the whole east leapt into fire. All day they walked, and many days thereafter, and kindly people, by the way, took them in and gave them food and drink and sometimes a bed at night. Often they slept by the roadside, but they didn't mind that for the climate was delightful—not too hot, and not too cold. They soon threw away their ragged little mittens. They walked for many days, and there was no Land of Laughter. Once they met an old man, richly dressed, with shining jewels on his fingers, and he stopped them and asked: "Where are you going so fast, little boys?" "We are going to the Land of Laughter," they said together gravely. "That," said the old man, "is a very foolish thing to do. Come with me, and I will take you to the Land of Riches. I will cover you with garments of beauty, and give you jewels and a castle to live in and servants and horses and many things besides." And they said to him: "No, we wish to learn how to laugh again; we have forgotten how, and we are going to the Land of Laughter." "You will regret not going with me. See, if you don't," he said; and he left them in quite a huff. And they walked again, many days, and again they met an old man. He was tall and imposing-looking and very dignified. And he said: "Where are you going so fast, little boys?" "We are going to the Land of Laughter," they said together very seriously. "What!" he said, "that is an extremely foolish thing to do. Come with me, and I will give you power. I will make you great men: generals, kings, emperors. Whatever you desire to accomplish will be permitted you." And they smiled politely: "Thank you very much, but we have forgotten how to laugh, and we are going there to learn how." He looked upon them haughtily, without speaking, and disappeared. And they walked and walked more days; and they met another old man. And he was clad in rags, and his face was thin, and his eyes were unhappy. And he whispered to them: "Where are you going so fast, little boys?" "We are going to the Land of Laughter," they answered, without a smile. "Laughter! Laughter! that is useless. Come with me and I will show you the beauty of life through sacrifice, suffering for others. That is the only life. I come from the Land of Sacrifice." And they thanked him kindly, but said: "We have suffered long enough. We have forgotten how to laugh. We would learn again." And they went on; and he looked after them very wistfully. They walked more days, and at last they came to the Land of Laughter. And how do you suppose they knew this? Because they could hear, over the wall, the sound of joyous laughter,—the laughter of men, women, and children. And one sat guarding the gate, and they went to her. "We have come a long, long distance; and we would enter the Land of Laughter." "Let me see you smile, first," she said gently. "I sit at the gate; and no one who does not know how to smile may enter the Land of Laughter." And they tried to smile, but could not. "Go away and practice," she said kindly, "and come back tomorrow." And they went away, and practiced all night how to smile; and in the morning they returned, and the gentle lady at the gate said: "Dear little boys, have you learned how to smile?" And they said: "We have tried. How is this?" "Better," she said, "much better. Practice some more, and come back tomorrow." And they went away obediently and practiced. And they came the third day. And she said: "Now try again." And tears of delight came into her lovely eyes. "Those were very beautiful smiles," she said. "Now, you may enter." And she unlocked the gate, and kissed them both, and they entered the Land—the beautiful Land of Laughter. Never had they seen such blue skies, such green trees and grass; never had they heard such birds songs. And people, men, women and children, laughing softly, came to meet them, and took them in, and made them at home; and soon, very soon they learned to sleep. And they grew up here, and married, and had laughing, happy children. And sometimes they thought of the Land of Riches, and said: "Ah! well!" and sometimes of the Land of Power, and sighed a little; and sometimes of the Land of Sacrifice—and their eyes were wistful. But they soon forgot, and laughed again. And they grew old, laughing. And then when they died—a laugh was on their lips. Thus are things in the beautiful Land of Laughter. (*There is a long pause*).

JIMMY: I like that story, Ma Rachel. It's nice to laugh, isn't it? Is there such a land?

RACHEL (*Softly*): What do you think, honey?

JIMMY: I thinks it would be awful nice if there was. Don't you?

RACHEL (*Wistfully*): If there only were! If there only were!

JIMMY: Ma Rachel.

RACHEL:	Well?
JIMMY:	It makes you think—kind of—doesn't it—of sunshine medicine?
RACHEL:	Yes, honey,—but it isn't medicine there. It's always ways there—just like—well—like our air here. It's *always* sunshine there.
JIMMY:	Always , sunshine? Never any dark?
RACHEL:	No honey.
JIMMY:	You'd—never—be—afraid there, then, would you? Never afraid of nothing?
RACHEL:	No, honey.
JIMMY	(*With a big sigh*): Oh!—Oh! *I wisht* it was here–not there. (*Puts his hand up to Rachel's face; suddenly sits up and looks at her*) Why, Ma Rachel dear, you're crying. Your face is all wet. Why! Don't cry! Don't cry!
RACHEL	(*Gently*): Do you remember that I told you the lady at the gate had tears of joy in her eyes, when the two, dear, little boys smiled that beautiful smile?
JIMMY:	Yes.
RACHEL:	Well, these are tears of joy, honey, that's all—tears of joy.
JIMMY:	It must be awful queer to have tears of joy, 'cause you're happy. I never did. (*With a sigh*). But, if you say they are, dear Ma Rachel, they must be. You knows everything, don't you?
RACHEL	(*Sadly*): Some things, honey. Some things. (*A silence*).
JIMMY	(*Sighing happily*): This is the beautiful-est night I ever knew. If you would do just one more thing, it would be lots more beautiful. Will you, Ma Rachel?
RACHEL:	Well, what, honey?
JIMMY:	Will you sing—at the piano, I mean, it's lots prettier that way—the little song you used to rock me to sleep by? You know, the one about the "Slumber boat"?
RACHEL:	Oh! Honey, not tonight, You're too tired. It's bedtime now.
JIMMY	(*Patting her face with his little hand; wheedlingly*): Please! Ma Rachel, please! Pretty please!

RACHEL:	Well, honey boy, this once, then. Tonight you shall have the little song—I used to sing you to sleep by (*half to herself*) perhaps, for the last time.
JIMMY:	Why, Ma Rachel, why the last time?
RACHEL	(*Shaking her head sadly goes to the piano; in a whisper*): The last time. (*She twists up her hair into a knot at the back of her head and looks at the keys for a few moments: then she plays her accompaniment of the "Slumber Boat" through softly, and, after a moment, sings. Her voice is full of pent-up longing, and heartbreak, and hopelessness. She ends in a little sob, but attempts to cover it by singing, lightly and daintily, the chorus of "The Owl and the Moon."..Then softly and with infinite tenderness, almost against her will, she plays and sings again the refrain of the "Slumber Boat"*):

> "Sail, baby, sail
>   Out from that sea,
> Only don't forget to sail
>   Back again to me."

(*Presently she rises and goes to Jimmy, who is lolling back happily in the big chair. During the singing, Tom and Mrs. Loving apparently do not listen; when she sobs, however, Tom's hand on his paper tightens; Mrs. Loving's needle poises for a moment in mid-air. Neither looks at Rachel. Jimmy evidently has not noticed the sob*).

RACHEL	(*Kneeling by Jimmy*): Well, honey, how did you like it?
JIMMY	(*Proceeding to pull down her hair from the twist*): It was lovely, Ma Rachel. (*Yawns audibly*). Now, Ma Rachel, I'm just beautifully sleepy. (*Dreamily*) I think that p'r'aps I'll go to the Land of Laughter tonight in my dreams. I'll go in the "Slumber Boat" and come back in the morning and tell you all about it. Shall I?
RACHEL:	Yes, honey. (*Whispers*)

> "Only don't forget to sail
>   Back again to me."

TOM	(*Suddenly*): Rachel! (*Rachel starts slightly*). I nearly forgot. John is coming here tonight to see how you are. He told me to tell you so.
RACHEL	(*Stiffens perceptibly, then in different tones*): Very well. Thank you. (*Suddenly with a little cry she puts her arms around Jimmy*) Jimmy! honey! don't go tonight. Don't go without Ma Rachel. Wait for me, honey. I do so wish to go, too, to the Land of Laughter. Think of it, Jimmy; nothing but birds always singing, and flowers always blooming, and skies always blue—and people, all of them, always laughing, laughing. You'll wait for Ma Rachel, won't you, honey?
JIMMY:	Is there really and truly, Ma Rachel, a Land of Laughter?
RACHEL:	Oh! Jimmy, let's hope so; let's pray so.
JIMMY	(*Frowns*): I've been thinking—(*Pauses*). You have to smile at the gate, don't you, to get in?
RACHEL:	Yes, honey.
JIMMY:	Well, I guess I couldn't smile if my Ma Rachel wasn't somewhere close to me. So I couldn't get in after all, could I? Tonight, I'll go somewhere else, and tell you all about it. And then, some day, we'll go together, won't we?
RACHEL	(*Sadly*): Yes, honey, some day—some day. (*A short silence*). Well, this isn't going to "sleepy-sleep," is it? Go, now, and say good-night to Ma Loving and Uncle Tom.
JIMMY	(*Gets down obediently, and goes first to Mrs. Loving. She leans over, and he puts his little arms around her neck. They kiss; very sweetly*): Sweet dreams! God keep you all the night!
MRS. LOVING:	The sweetest of sweet dreams to you, dear little boy! Good-night! (*Rachel watches, unwatched, the scene. Her eyes are full of yearning*).
JIMMY	(*Going to Tom, who makes believe he does not see him*): Uncle Tom!
TOM	(*Jumps as though tremendously startled; Jimmy laughs*): My! how you frightened me. You'll put my gizzard out of commission, if you do that often. Well, sir,

	what can I do for you?
JIMMY:	I came to say good-night.
TOM	(*Gathering Jimmy up in his arms and kissing him; gently and with emotion*) Good-night, dear little Big Fellow ! Good-night!
JIMMY:	Sweet dreams! God keep you all the night! (*Goes sedately to Rachel, and holds out his little hand*). I'm ready, Ma Rachel. (*Yawns*) I'm so nice and sleepy.
RACHEL	(*With Jimmy's hand in hers, she hesitates a moment, and then approaches Tom slowly. For a short time she stands looking down at him; suddenly leaning over him*): Why, Tom, what a pretty tie! Is it new?
TOM:	Well, no, not exactly. I've had it about a month. It is rather a beauty, isn't it?
RACHEL:	Why, I never remember seeing it.
TOM	(*Laughing*): I guess not. I saw to that.
RACHEL:	Stingy!
TOM:	Well, I am—where my ties are concerned. I've had experience.
RACHEL	(*Tentatively*): Tom!
TOM:	Well?
RACHEL	(*Nervously and wistfully*): Are you—will you—I mean, won't you be home this evening?
TOM:	You've got a long memory, Sis. I've that engagement, you know. Why?
RACHEL	(*Slowly*): I forgot; so you have.
TOM:	Why?
RACHEL	(*Hastily*): Oh! nothing—nothing. Come on, Jimmy boy, you can hardly keep those little peepers open, can you? Come on, honey. (*Rachel and Jimmy go out the rear doorway. There is a silence*).
MRS. LOVING	(*Slowly, as though thinking aloud*): I try to make out what could have happened; but it's no use—I can't. Those four days, she lay in bed hardly moving, scarcely speaking. Only her eyes seemed alive. I never saw such a wide, tragic look in my life. It was as though her soul had been mortally wounded. But how? how? What could have happened?
TOM	(*Quietly*): I don't know. She generally tells me everything; but she avoids me now. If we are alone

in a room—she gets out. I don't know what it means.

MRS. LOVING: She will hardly let Jimmy out of her sight. While he's at school, she's nervous and excited. She seems always to be listening, but for what? When he returns, she nearly devours him. And she always asks him in a frightened sort of way, her face as pale and tense as can be: "Well, honey boy, how was school today?" And he always answers, "Fine, Ma Rachel, fine! I learned—"; and then he goes on to tell her everything that has happened. And when he has finished, she says in an uneasy sort of way: "Is—is that all?" And when he says "Yes," she relaxes and becomes limp. After a little while she becomes feverishly happy. She plays with Jimmy and the children more than ever she did—and she played a good deal, as you know. They're here, or she's with them. Yesterday, I said in remonstrance, when she came in, her face pale and haggard and black hollows under her eyes: "Rachel, remember you're just out of a sickbed. You're not well enough to go on like this." "I know," was all she would say, "but I've got to. I can't help myself. This part of their little lives must be happy—it just must be." (*Pauses*). The last couple of nights, Jimmy has awakened and cried most pitifully. She wouldn't let me go to him; said I had enough trouble, and she could quiet him. She never will let me know why he cries; but she stays with him, and soothes him until, at last, he falls asleep again. Every time she has come out like a rag; and her face is like a dead woman's. Strange isn't it, this is the first time we have ever been able to talk it over? Tom, what could have happened?

TOM: I don't know, Ma, but I feel, as you do; something terrible and sudden has hurt her soul; and, poor little thing, she's trying bravely to readjust herself to life again. (*Pauses, looks at his watch and then rises, and goes to her. He pats her back awkwardly*). Well, Ma, I'm going now. Don't worry too much. Youth, you, know, gets over things finally. It takes them hard, that's all—. At least, that's what the older heads tell us. (*Gets his hat and stands in the vestibule doorway*). Ma, you know, I begin with John tomorrow. *(With emotion)* I don't believe we'll ever forget John. Good-night! (*Exit. Mrs. Loving continues to sew. Rachel, her hair arranged, re-enters through the rear doorway. She is humming*).

RACHEL: He's sleeping like a top. Aren't little children, Ma dear, the sweetest things, when they're all helpless and asleep? One little hand is under his cheek; and he's smiling. (*Stops suddenly, biting her lips. A pause*) Where's Tom?

MRS. LOVING: He went out a few minutes ago.

RACHEL (*Sitting in Tom's chair and picking up his paper. She is exceedingly nervous. She looks the paper over rapidly; presently trying to make her tone casual*): Ma,—you—you—aren't going anywhere tonight, are you?

MRS. LOVING: I've got to go out for a short time about half-past eight. Mrs. Jordan, you know. I'll not be gone very long, though. Why?

RACHEL: Oh! nothing particular. I just thought it would be cosy if we could sit here together the rest of the evening. Can't you—can't you go tomorrow?

MRS. LOVING: Why, I don't see how I can. I've made the engagement. It's about a new reception gown; and she's exceedingly exacting, as you know. I can't afford to lose her.

RACHEL: No, I suppose not. All right, Ma dear. (*Presently, paper in hand, she laughs, but not quite naturally*). Look! Ma dear! How is that for fashion, anyway? Isn't it the "limit"? (*Rises and shows her mother a picture in the paper. As she is in the act, the bell rings. With a startled cry*). Oh! (*Drops the paper, and grips her mother's hand*).

MRS. LOVING (*Anxiously*): Rachel, your nerves are right on edge; and your hand feels like fire. I'll have to see a doctor about you; and that's all there is to it.

RACHEL (*Laughing nervously, and moving toward the vestibule*). Nonsense, Ma dear! Just because I let out a whoop now and then, and have nice warm hands? (*Goes out, is heard talking through the tube*) Yes! (*Her voice emitting tremendous relief*). Oh! bring it right up! (*Appearing in the doorway*) Ma dear, did you buy anything at Goddard's today?

MRS. LOVING: Yes; and I've been wondering why they were so late in delivering it. I bought it early this morning. (*Rachel goes out again. A door opens and shuts. She reappears with a bundle*).

MRS. LOVING: Put it on my bed, Rachel, please. (*Exit Rachel rear doorway; presently returns empty-handed; sits down again at the table with the paper between herself and mother; sinks in a deep revery. Suddenly there is the sound of many loud knocks made by numerous small fists. Rachel drops the paper, and comes to a sitting posture, tense again. Her mother looks at her, but says nothing. Almost immediately Rachel relaxes*).

RACHEL: My kiddies! They're late, this evening. (*Goes out into the vestibule. A door opens and shuts. There is the shrill, excited sound of childish voices. Rachel comes in surrounded by the children, all trying to say something to her at once. Rachel puts her finger on her lip and points toward the doorway in the rear. They all quiet down. She sits on the floor in the front of the stage, and the children all cluster around her. Their conversation takes place in a half-whisper. As they enter they nod brightly at Mrs. Loving, who smiles in return*). Why so late, kiddies? It's long past "sleepy-time."

LITTLE NANCY: We've been playing "Hide and Seek," and having the mostest fun. We promised, all of us, that if we could play until half-past seven tonight we would-n't make any fuss about going to bed at seven o'clock the rest of the week. It's awful hard to go. I *hate* to go to bed!

LITTLE MARY, LOUISE and EDITH: So do I! So do I! So do I!

LITTLE MARTHA: I don't. I love bed. My bed, after my muzzer tucks me all in, is like a nice warm bag. I just stick my nose out. When I lifts my head up I can see the light from the dining-room come in the door. I can hear my muzzer and fazzer talking nice and low; and then, before I know it, I'm fast asleep, and I dream pretty things, and in about a minute it's morning again. I love my little bed, and I love to dream.

LITTLE MARY (*Aggressively*): Well, I guess I love to dream too. I wish I could dream, though, without going to bed.

LITTLE NANCY: When I grow up, I'm never going to bed at night! (*Darkly*) You see.

LITTLE LOUISE: "Grown-ups" just love to poke their heads out of windows and cry, "Child'run, it's time for bed now; and you'd better hurry, too, I can tell you." They "sure" are queer, for sometimes when I wake up, it must be about twelve o'clock, I can hear my big sister giggling and talking to some silly man. If it's good for me to go to bed early—I should think—

RACHEL (*Interrupting suddenly*): Why, where is my little Jenny? Excuse me, Louise dear.

LITTLE MARTHA: Her cold is awful bad. She coughs like this (*giving a distressing imitation*) and snuffles all the time. She can't talk out loud, and she can't go to sleep. Muzzer says she's fev'rish—I thinks that's what she says. Jenny says she knows she could go to sleep, if you would come and sit with her a little while.

RACHEL: I certainly will. I'll go when you do, honey.

LITTLE MARTHA (*Softly stroking Rachel's arm*): You're the very nicest "grown-up", (*loyally*) except my muzzer, of course, I ever knew. You knows all about little chil'-run and you can be one, although you're all grown up. I think you would make a lovely muzzer. (*To the rest of the children*) Don't you?

ALL (*In excited whispers*): Yes, I do

RACHEL (*Winces, then says gently*): Come, kiddies, you must go now, or your mothers will blame me for keeping you. (*Rises, as do the rest. Little Martha puts her hand into Rachel's*). Ma dear, I'm going down to sit a little while with Jenny. I'll be back before you go, though. Come, kiddies, say good-night to my mother.

ALL (*Gravely*): Good-night! Sweet dreams! God keep

	you all the night.
MRS. LOVING:	Good-night dears! Sweet dreams, all!
	(*Exeunt Rachel and the children. Mrs. Loving continues to sew. The bell presently rings three distinct times. In a few moments, Mrs. Loving gets up and goes out into the vestibule. A door opens and closes. Mrs. Loving and John Strong come in. He is a trifle pale but his imperturbable self. Mrs. Loving, somewhat nervous, takes her seat and resumes her sewing. She motions Strong to a chair. He returns to the vestibule, leaves his hat, returns, and sits down*).
STRONG:	Well, how is everything?
MRS. LOVING:	Oh! about the same, I guess. Tom's out. John, we'll never forget you—and your kindness.
STRONG:	That was nothing. And Rachel?
MRS. LOVING:	She'll be back presently. She went to sit with a sick child for a little while.
STRONG:	And how is she?
MRS. LOVING:	She's not herself yet, but I think she is better.
STRONG	(*After a short pause*): Well, what *did* happen—exactly?
MRS. LOVING:	That's just what I don't know.
STRONG:	When you came home—you couldn't get in—was that it?
MRS. LOVING:	Yes. (*Pauses*). It was just a week ago today. I was down town all the morning. It was about one o'clock when I got back. I had forgotten my key. I rapped on the door and then called. There was no answer. A window was open, and I could feel the air under the door, and I could hear it as the draught sucked it through. There was no other sound. Presently I made such a noise the people began to come out into the hall. Jimmy was in one of the flats playing with a little girl named Mary. He told me he had left Rachel here a short time before. She had given him four cookies, two for him and two for Mary, and had told him he could play with her until she came to tell him his lunch was ready. I saw he was getting frightened, so I got the little girl and her mother to keep him in their flat. Then, as no

man was at home, I sent out for help. Three men broke the door down. (*Pauses*). We found Rachel unconscious, lying on her face. For a few minutes I thought she was dead. (*Pauses*). A vase had fallen over on the table and the water had dripped through the cloth and onto the floor. There had been flowers in it. When I left, there were no flowers here. What she could have done to them, I can't say. The long stems were lying everywhere, and the flowers had been ground into the floor. I could tell that they must have been roses from the stems. After we had put her to bed and called the doctor, and she had finally regained consciousness, I very naturally asked her what had happened. All she would say was, "Ma dear, I'm too—tired—please." For four days she lay in bed scarcely moving, speaking only when spoken to. That first day, when Jimmy came in to see her, she shrank away from him. We had to take him out, and comfort him as best we could. We kept him away, almost by force, until she got up. And, then, she was utterly miserable when he was out of her sight. What happened, I don't know. She avoids Tom, and she won't tell me. (*Pauses*). Tom and I both believe her soul has been hurt. The trouble isn't with her body. You'll find her highly nervous. Sometimes she is very much depressed; again she is feverishly gay—almost reckless. What do you think about it, John?

STRONG	(*Who has listened quietly*): Had anybody been here, do you know?
MRS. LOVING:	No, I don't. I don't like to ask Rachel; and I can't ask the neighbors.
STRONG:	No, of course not. (*Pauses*). You say there were some flowers?
MRS. LOVING:	Yes.
STRONG:	And the flowers were ground into the carpet?
MRS. LOVING:	Yes.
STRONG:	Did you happen to notice the box? They must have come in a box, don't you think?
MRS. LOVING:	Yes, there was a box in the kitchenette. It was from

	"Marcy's." I saw no card.
STRONG	(*Slowly*): It is rather strange. (*A long silence, during which the outer door opens and shuts. Rachel is heard singing. She stops abruptly. In a second or two she appears in the door. There is an air of suppressed excitement about her*).
RACHEL:	Hello! John. (*Strong rises, nods at her, and brings forward for her the big arm-chair near the fire*). I thought that was your hat in the hall. It's brand new, I know—but it looks—"Johnlike." How are you? Ma! Jenny went to sleep like a little lamb. I don't like her breathing, though. (*Looks from one to the other; flippantly*) Who's dead? (*Nods her thanks to Strong for the chair and sits down*).
MRS. LOVING:	Dead, Rachel?
RACHEL:	Yes. The atmosphere here is so funereal,—it's positively "crapey."
STRONG:	I don't know why it should be—I was just asking how you are.
RACHEL:	Heavens! Does the mere inquiry into my health precipitate such an atmosphere? Your two faces were as long, as long—(*Breaks off*). Kind sir, let me assure you, I am in the very best of health. And how are you, John?
STRONG:	Oh! I'm always well. (*Sits down*).
MRS. LOVING:	Rachel, I'll have to get ready to go now. John, don't hurry. I'll be back shortly, probably in three-quarters of an hour—maybe less.
RACHEL:	And maybe more, if I remember Mrs. Jordan. However, Ma dear, I'll do the best I can—while you are away. I'll try to be a credit to your training. (*Mrs. Loving smiles and goes out the rear doorway*). Now, let's see—in the books of etiquette, I believe, the properly reared young lady, always asks the young gentleman caller—you're young enough, aren't you, to be classed still as a "young gentleman caller?" (*No answer*). Well, anyway, she always asks the young gentleman caller sweetly something about the weather. (*Primly*) This has been an exceedingly beautiful day, hasn't it, Mr. Strong?

(*No answer from Strong, who, with his head resting against the back of the chair, and his knees crossed is watching her in an amused, quizzical manner*). Well, really, every properly brought up young gentleman, I'm sure, ought to know, that it's exceedingly rude not to answer a civil question.

STRONG   (*Lazily*): Tell me what to answer, Rachel.

RACHEL: Say, "Yes, very"; and look interested and pleased when you say it.

STRONG   (*With a half-smile*): Yes, very.

RACHEL: Well, I certainly wouldn't characterize that as a particularly animated remark. Besides, when you look at me through half-closed lids like that and kind of smile—what are you thinking? (*No answer*) John Strong, are you deaf or—just plain stupid?

STRONG: Plain stupid, I guess.

RACHEL   (*In wheedling tones*): What were you thinking, John?

STRONG   (*Slowly*): I was thinking—(*Breaks off*)

RACHEL   (*Irritably*): Well?

STRONG: I've changed my mind.

RACHEL: You're not going to tell me?

STRONG: No.
                 (*Mrs. Loving dressed for the street comes in*)

MRS. LOVING: Goodbye, children. Rachel, don't quarrel so much with John. Let me see—if I have my key. (*Feels in her bag*) Yes, I have it. I'll be back shortly. Goodbye. (*Strong and Rachel rise. He bows*).

RACHEL: Good-bye, Ma dear. Hurry back as soon as you can, won't you? (*Exit Mrs. Loving through the vestibule. Strong leans back again in his chair, and watches Rachel through half-closed eyes. Rachel sits in her chair nervously*)

STRONG: Do you mind, if I smoke?

RACHEL: You know I don't.

STRONG: I am trying to behave like—Reginald—"the properly reared young gentleman caller." (*Lights a cigar; goes over to the fire, and throws his match away. Rachel goes into the kitchenette, and brings him a saucer for his ashes. She places it on the table near him*). Thank you.

(They both sit again, Strong very evidently enjoying his cigar and Rachel). Now this is what I call cosy.

RACHEL: Cosy! Why?

STRONG: A nice warm room—shut in—curtains drawn—a cheerful fire crackling at my back—a lamp, not an electric or gas one, but one of your plain, old-fashioned kerosene ones—

RACHEL *(Interrupting)*: Ma dear would like to catch you, I am sure, talking about *her* lamp like that. "Old-fashioned! plain!"—You have nerve.

STRONG *(Continuing as though he had not been interrupted)*: A comfortable chair—a good cigar—and not very far away, a little lady, who is looking charming, so near, that if I reached over, I could touch her. You there—and I here.—It's living.

RACHEL: Well! of all things! A compliment and from you! How did it slip out, pray? *(No answer).* I suppose that you realize that a conversation between two persons is absolutely impossible, if one has to do her share all alone. Soon my ingenuity for introducing interesting subjects will be exhausted; and then will follow what, I believe, the story books call, "an uncomfortable silence."

STRONG *(Slowly)*: Silence—between friends—isn't such a bad thing.

RACHEL: Thanks awfully. *(Leans back; cups her cheek in her hand, and makes no pretense at further conversation. The old look of introspection returns to her eyes. She does not move).*

STRONG *(Quietly)*: Rachel! *(Rachel starts perceptibly)* You must remember I'm here. I don't like looking into your soul—when you forget you're not alone.

RACHEL: I hadn't forgotten.

STRONG: Wouldn't it be easier for you, little girl, if you could tell—some one?

RACHEL: No. *(A silence)*

STRONG: Rachel, you're fond of flowers,—aren't you?

RACHEL: Yes.

STRONG: Rosebuds—red rosebuds—particularly?

RACHEL *(Nervously)*: Yes.

STRONG:	Did you—dislike—the giver?
RACHEL	(*More nervously; bracing herself*): No, of course not.
STRONG:	Rachel,—why—why—did you—kill the roses then?
RACHEL	(*Twisting her hands*): Oh, John! I'm so sorry, Ma dear told you that. She didn't know, you sent them.
STRONG:	So I gathered. (*Pauses and then leans forward; quietly*). Rachel, little girl, why—did you kill them?
RACHEL	(*Breathing quickly*): Don't you believe—it—a—a —kindness—sometimes—to kill?
STRONG	(*After a pause*): You—considered—it—a—kindness—to kill them?
RACHEL:	Yes. (*Another pause*)
STRONG:	Do you mean—just—the roses?
RACHEL	(*Breathing more quickly*): John!—Oh! must I say?
STRONG:	Yes, little Rachel.
RACHEL	(*In a whisper*): No. (*There is a long pause. Rachel leans back limply, and closes her eyes. Presently Strong rises, and moves his chair very close to hers. She does not stir. He puts his cigar on the saucer*).
STRONG	(*Leaning forward; very gently*): Little girl, little girl, can't you tell me why?
RACHEL	(*Wearily*): I can't.—It hurts—too much—to talk about it yet,—please.
STRONG	(*Takes her hand; looks at it a few minutes and then at her quietly*). You—don't—care, then? (*She winces*) Rachel!—Look at me, little girl! (*As if against her will, she looks at him. Her eyes are fearful, hunted. She tries to look away, to draw away her hand; but he holds her gaze and her hand steadily*). Do you?
RACHEL	(*Almost sobbing*): John! John! don't ask me. You are drawing my very soul out of my body with your eyes. You must not talk this way. You mustn't look—John, don't! (*Tries to shield her eyes*).
STRONG	(*Quietly takes both of her hands, and kisses the backs and the palms slowly. A look of horror creeps into her face. He deliberately raises his eyes and looks at her mouth. She recoils as though she expected him to strike her. He resumes slowly*) If—you—do—care, and I know now—that you do—nothing else, *nothing*

RACHEL	should count.
	(*Wrenching herself from his grasp and rising. She covers her ears; she breathes rapidly*): No! No! No!—You *must* stop. (*Laughs nervously; continues feverishly*) I'm not behaving very well as a hostess, am I? Let's see. What shall I do? I'll play you something, John. How will that do? Or I'll sing to you. You used to like to hear me sing; you said my voice, I remember, was sympathetic, didn't you? (*Moves quickly to the piano*). I'll sing you a pretty little song. I think it's beautiful. You've never heard it, I know. I've never sung it to you before. It's Nevin's "At Twilight." (*Pauses, looks down, before she begins, then turns toward him and says quietly and sweetly*) Sometimes—in the coming years—I want—you to remember—I sang you this little song.—Will you?—I think it will make it easier for me—when I—when I—(*Breaks off and begins the first chords. Strong goes slowly to the piano. He leans there watching intently. Rachel sings*):

> "The roses of yester-year
> Were all of the white and red;
> It fills my heart with silent fear
> To find all their beauty fled.
> The roses of white are sere,
> All faded the roses red,
> And one who loves me is not here
> And one that I love is dead."

	(*A long pause. Then Strong goes to her and lifts her from the piano-stool. He puts one arm around her very tenderly and pushes her head back so he can look into her eyes. She shuts them, but is passive*).
STRONG	(*Gently*): Little girl, little girl, don't you know that suggestions—suggestions—like those you are sending yourself constantly—are wicked things? You, who are so gentle, so loving, so warm—(*Breaks off and crushes her to him. He kisses her many times. She does not resist, but in the midst of his caresses she breaks suddenly into convulsive laughter. He tries to hush the terrible sound with his mouth; then brokenly*) Little

RACHEL

girl—don't laugh—like that.

(*Interrupted throughout by her laughter*): I have to.—God is laughing.—We're his puppets.—He pulls the wires,—and we're so funny to Him.—I'm laughing too—because I can hear—my little children—weeping. They come to me generally while I'm asleep,—but I can hear them now.—They've begged me—do you understand?—begged me—not to bring them here;—and I've promised them—not to.—I've promised. I can't stand the sound of their crying.—I have to laugh—Oh ! John ! laugh!—laugh too!—I can't drown their weeping. (*Strong picks her up bodily and carries her to the arm-chair*).

STRONG

(*Harshly*): Now, stop that!

RACHEL

(*In sheer surprise*): W-h-a-t?

STRONG

(*Still harshly*): Stop that!—You've lost your self-control.—Find yourself again!

(*He leaves her and goes over to the fireplace, and stands looking down into it for some little time. Rachel, little by little, becomes calmer. Strong returns and sits beside her again. She doesn't move. He smoothes her hair back gently, and kisses her forehead—and then, slowly, her mouth. She does not resist; simply sits there, with shut eyes, inert, limp*).

STRONG:

Rachel!—(*Pauses*). There is a little flat on 43rd Street. It faces south and overlooks a little park. Do you remember it?—it's on the top floor?—Once I remember your saying—you liked it. That was over a year ago. That same day—I rented it. I've never lived there. No one knows about it—not even my mother. It's completely furnished now—and waiting—do you know for whom? Every single thing in it, I've bought myself—even to the pins on the little bird's-eye maple dresser. It has been the happiest year I have ever known. I furnished it—one room at a time. It's the prettiest, the most home-like little flat I've ever seen. (*Very low*) Everything there—breathes love. Do you know for whom it is waiting? On the sitting-room floor is a beautiful,

Turkish rug—red, and blue and gold. It's soft—and rich—and do you know for whose little feet it is waiting? There are delicate curtains at the windows and a bookcase full of friendly, eager, little books.—Do you know for whom they are waiting? There are comfortable leather chairs, just the right size, and a beautiful piano—that I leave open—sometimes, and lovely pictures of Madonnas. Do you know for whom they are waiting? There is an open fireplace with logs of wood, all carefully piled on gleaming andirons—and waiting. There is a bellows and a pair of shining tongs—waiting. And in the kitchenette painted blue and white, and smelling sweet with paint is everything: bright pots and pans and kettles, and blue and white enamel-ware, and all kinds of knives and forks and spoons—and on the door—a roller-towel. Little girl, do you know for whom they are all waiting? And somewhere—there's a big, strong man—with broad shoulders. And he's willing and anxious to do anything—-everything, and he's waiting very patiently. Little girl, is it to be—yes or no?

RACHEL   (*During Strong's speech life has come flooding back to her. Her eyes are shining; her face, eager. For a moment she is beautifully happy*). Oh! you're too good to me and mine, John. I—didn't dream any one—could be—so good. (*Leans forward and puts his big hand against her cheek and kisses it shyly*).

STRONG   (*Quietly*): Is it—yes—or no, little girl?

RACHEL   (*Feverishly, gripping his hands*): Oh, yes! yes! yes! and take me quickly, John. Take me before I can think any more. You mustn't let me think, John. And you'll be good to me, won't you? Every second of every minute, of every hour, of every day, you'll have me in your thoughts, won't you? And you'll be with me every minute that you can? And, John, John!—you'll keep away the weeping of my little children. You won't let me hear it, will you? You'll make me forget everything everything—won't you?—Life is so short, John. (*Shivers and then fear-*

fully and slowly) And eternity so—long. (*Feverishly again*) And, John, after I am dead—promise me, promise me you'll love me more. (*Shivers again*). I'll need love then. Oh! I'll need it. (*Suddenly there comes to their ears the sound of a child's weeping. It is monotonous, hopeless, terribly afraid. Rachel recoils*). Oh! John!—Listen!—It's my boy, again.—I— John—I'll be back in a little while. (*Goes swiftly to the door in the rear, pauses and looks back. The weeping continues. Her eyes are tragic. Slowly she kisses her hand to him and disappears. John stands where she has left him looking down. The weeping stops. Presently Rachel appears in the doorway. She is haggard, and grey. She does not enter the room. She speaks as one dead might speak—tonelessly, slowly*).

RACHEL: Do you wish to know why Jimmy is crying?

STRONG: Yes.

RACHEL: I am twenty-two—and I'm old; you're thirty-two— and you're old; Tom's twenty-three—and he is old. Ma dear's sixty—and she said once she is much older than that. She is. We are all blighted; we are all accursed—all of us—; everywhere, we whose skins are dark—our lives blasted by the white man's prejudice. (*Pauses*) And my little Jimmy—seven years old, that's all—is blighted too. In a year or two, at best, he will be made old by suffering. (*Pauses*). One week ago, today, some white boys, older and larger than my little Jimmy, as he leaving the school—called him "Nigger"! They chased him through the streets calling him, "Nigger"! One boy threw stones at him. There is still a bruise on his back where one struck him. That will get well; but they bruised his soul—and that—will never—get well. He asked me what "Nigger" meant. I made light of the whole thing, laughed it off. He went to his little playmates, and very naturally asked them. The oldest of them is nine!—and they knew, poor little things—and they told him. (*Pauses*). For the last couple of nights he has been dreaming—about these boys. And he always awakes in the dark—

afraid—afraid—of the now—and the future—I have seen that look of deadly fear—in the eyes— of other little children. I know what it is myself.— I was twelve—when some big boys chased me and called me names.—I never left the house after- wards—without being afraid. I was afraid, in the streets—in the school—in the church, everywhere, always, afraid of being hurt. And I—was not— afraid in vain. (*The weeping begins again*). He's only a baby and he's blighted. (*To Jimmy*) Honey, I'm right here. I'm coming in just a minute. Don't cry. (*To Strong*) If it really kills me to hear my Jimmy's crying, do you think I could stand it, when my own child, flesh of my flesh, blood of my blood— learned the same reason for weeping? Do you? (*Pauses*) Ever since I fell here—a week ago—I am afraid—to go—to sleep, for every time I do—my children come—and beg me—weeping—not to— bring them here—to suffer. Tonight, they came— when I was awake. (*Pauses*). I have promised them again, now—by Jimmy's bed. (*In a whisper*) I have damned—my soul to all eternity—if I do. (*To Jimmy*) Honey, don't! I'm coming. (*To Strong*) And John,—dear John—you see—it can never be—all the beautiful, beautiful things—you have—told me about. (*Wistfully*) No—they—can never be—now. (*Strong comes toward her*) No,—John dear,—you— must not—touch me—any more. (*Pauses*). Dear, this—is—"Good-bye."

STRONG	(*Quietly*): It's not fair—to you, Rachel, to take you—at your word—tonight. You're sick; you've brooded so long, so continuously, you've lost—your perspective. Don't answer, yet. Think it over for another week and I'll come back.
RACHEL	(*Wearily*): No,—I can't think—any more.
STRONG:	You realize—fully—you're sending me—for always?
RACHEL:	Yes.
STRONG:	And you care?
RACHEL:	Yes.

STRONG: It's settled, then for all time— "Good-bye!"

RACHEL (*After a pause*): Yes.

STRONG (*Stands looking at her steadily a long time, and then moves to the door and turns, facing her; with infinite tenderness*): Good-bye, dear, little Rachel—God bless you.

RACHEL: Good-bye, John! (*Strong goes out. A door opens and shuts. There is finality in the sound. The weeping continues. Suddenly; with a great cry*) John! John! (*Runs out into the vestibule. She presently returns. She is calm again. Slowly*) No! No! John. Not for us. (*A pause; with infinite yearning*) Oh! John,—if it only—if it only—(*Breaks off, controls herself. Slowly again; thoughtfully*) No—No sunshine—no laughter—always, always—darkness. That is it. Even our little flat—(*In a whisper*) John's and mine—the little flat that calls, calls us—through darkness. It shall wait—and wait—in vain—in darkness. Oh, John! (*Pauses*). And my little children! my little children! (*The weeping ceases; pauses*). I shall never—see—you—now. Your little, brown, beautiful bodies—I shall never see.—Your dimples—everywhere—your laughter—your tears—the beautiful, lovely feel of you here. (*Puts her hands against her heart*). Never—never—to be. (*A pause, fiercely*) But you are somewhere—and wherever you are you are mine! You are mine! All of you! Every bit of you! Even God can't take you away. (*A pause; very sweetly; pathetically*) Little children!—My little children!—No more need you come to me—weeping—weeping. You may be happy now—you are safe. Little weeping, voices, hush! hush! (*The weeping begins again. To Jimmy, her whole soul in her voice*) Jimmy! My little Jimmy! Honey! I'm coming.—Ma Rachel loves you so. (*Sobs and goes blindly, unsteadily to the rear doorway; she leans her head there one second against the door; and then stumbles through and disappears. The light in the lamp flickers and goes out . . . It is black. The terrible, heart-breaking weeping continues*).

THE END

Further Reading

Brown-Guillory, Elizabeth. "Disrupted Motherlines: Mothers and Daughters in a Genderized, Sexualized, and Racialized World." *Women of Color: Mother-Daughter Relationships in 20ᵗʰ-Century Literature*. Elizabeth Brown-Guillory, ed. (Austin, TX: University of Texas Press, 1996), pp. 188–207.

AFRICAN AMERICAN LITERATURE AND CULTURE

EXPANDING AND EXPLODING THE BOUNDARIES

General Editor
Carlyle V. Thompson

The purpose of this series is to present innovative, in-depth, and provocatively critical literary and cultural investigations of critical issues in African American literature and life. We welcome critiques of fiction, poetry, drama, film, sports, and popular culture. Of particular interest are literary and cultural analyses that involve contemporary psychoanalytical criticism, new historicism, deconstructionism, critical race theory, critical legal theory, and critical gender theory.

For additional information about this series or for the submission of manuscripts, please contact:

Peter Lang Publishing, Inc.
Acquisitions Department
29 Broadway, 18th floor
New York, New York 10006

To order other books in this series, please contact our Customer Service Department:

(800) 770-LANG (within the U.S.)
(212) 647-7706 (outside the U.S.)
(212) 647-7707 FAX

Or browse online by series:

www.peterlang.com

www.ingramcontent.com/pod-product-compliance
Lightning Source LLC
Chambersburg PA
CBHW071153100726
47908CB00002B/356